THE LAW OF WAR
BETWEEN
BELLIGERENTS

THE LAW OF WAR BETWEEN BELLIGERENTS

A
HISTORY
AND
COMMENTARY

BY

PERCY BORDWELL, PH. D., LL. B.

PROFESSOR OF CONSTITUTIONAL LAW IN THE UNIVERSITY OF MISSOURI

Fred B. Rothman & Co.
Littleton, Colorado
1994

Library of Congress Cataloging-in-Publication Data

Bordwell, Percy, b. 1878.
The law of war between belligerents : a history and commentary / by Percy Bordwell.
p. cm.
Originally published: Chicago : Callaghan & Co., 1908.
Includes index.
ISBN 0-8377-1975-5
1. War (International law) I. Title.
JX4511.B7 1994
341.6--dc20 93-43371
CIP

Printed in United States of America

The paper used in this publication meets the minimum requirements of American National Standard for Information Sciences—Permanence of Paper for Printed Library Materials, ANSI Z39.48-1984.

THE LAW OF WAR BETWEEN BELLIGERENTS

A

HISTORY

AND

COMMENTARY

BY

PERCY BORDWELL, PH. D., LL. B.

PROFESSOR OF CONSTITUTIONAL LAW IN THE UNIVERSITY OF MISSOURI

CHICAGO
CALLAGHAN & CO.
1908

TO

MY MOTHER.

PREFACE.

This work is a history of and commentary on the laws of war as between belligerents. Some time in the future it is hoped to complete the treatment of the laws of war by a like work on the laws of war as affecting neutrals and eventually to supplement them by a third on amicable means of settling international disputes.

Part I is a history of war practice and of the development of a well-recognized body of law regulating it. It attempts to show how changes have come about in war practice and to show the historical position of the great Congresses and Conferences such as those of Paris, Geneva and The Hague. Especially is the Second Peace Conference the subject of careful treatment. Finally it takes up questions which have arisen in late wars such as the conduct of the Germans in France, the reconcentration measures in South Africa and the opening of hostilities in the Russo-Japanese War, and considers them in the light of International Law. The treatment of Russian subjects by the Japanese Government during the Russo-Japanese War is given in special detail in Appendix I.

Part II is intended to be a thorough commentary on war practice between belligerents. Particular emphasis is laid on the military as distinguished from the civil side of the laws of war. Comment is made on the international conventions such as those drawn up at the Second Peace Conference, and the Regulations respecting the Laws and Customs of War on Land and the Red Cross Conventions are treated in great detail. For convenience of reference it has been thought best to follow Professor Westlake in referring to the articles of the Regulations as H I, H II, etc., and to those of the Geneva Convention as G I, GII, etc. Articles of the naval Red Cross Convention are also referred to as G N I, G N II, etc. It is hoped that this part may be of use to army and navy officers as a manual.

Aside from this practical purpose, the work is intended

as a study in law and it is hoped that the first part especially will not be without interest to the general reader.

So many authorities are levied on for contributions in a book of this kind that it is hard to show proper appreciation without largely duplicating the list of authorities cited, but of living authors probably Professor Nys and Professor Westlake have been of the greatest assistance; the former, for his researches in the law of the Middle Ages, the latter for his clearheaded analysis of the modern law and especially his comments on the work of the Second Peace Conference. To Dr. Masanosuké Akiyama, of Tokio, especial thanks is due for a copy of his Traitement de Sujets Russes and permission to make extensive use of the same.

It is my further pleasure as well as duty to express my thanks here to General George B. Davis for having read the manuscript at an earlier stage; also to the friends who have assisted in the manual preparation of the work and to the Faculty in Public Law and Jurisprudence of Columbia University. To two members of that Faculty especial thanks are due. Professor Munroe Smith has put me under undying obligations by the stimulus of his lectures on Roman Law and the History of European Law and besides has kindly read a portion of the manuscript while Professor John Bassett Moore, under whom most of my work was done, has been as a lamp unto my feet and a light unto my path. If there be any value in these pages, let it be regarded as the inspiration of his unfailing kindness and profound insight.

PERCY BORDWELL.

NEW YORK, July 28, 1908.

TABLE OF CONTENTS.

PART I.

HISTORY.

CHAPTER I.

CHAPTER II.

CHAPTER III.

CHAPTER IV.

CHAPTER V.

CHAPTER XIV.

CHAPTER XV.

PART II.

COMMENTARY.

CHAPTER I.

CHAPTER II.

CHAPTER III.

CHAPTER IV.

CHAPTER V.

CHAPTER IX.

APPENDICES.

I.

II.

III.

LIST OF AUTHORITIES.

Adams, Henry, History of the United States, New York, 1889-1891.

Aegidi und Klauhold, Frei Schiff unter Feindes-Flagge, Hamburg, 1866.

Akiyama, Masanosuké, Traitement des Sujets Russes, Brussels, 1907.

American State Papers, Foreign Relations.

Annual Register, London, 1762.

Annuaire de l'Institut de Droit International, Paris.

Archives Diplomatiques.

Ariga, Nagao, La Guerre Sino-Japonaise, Paris, 1896.

Asakawa, K., The Russo-Japanese Conflict, Cambridge, U. S. A., 1904.

Azuni, The Maritime Law of Europe (translation), New York, 1806.

Beaumanoir, Philippe de, Les Coutumes du Beauvoisis, edited by Le Comte Beugnot, Paris, 1842.

Bernard, Mountague, The Growth of Laws and Usages of War, Oxford Essays, 1856, London.

Blaine, James G., Twenty Years of Congress, Norwich, Conn., 1884-1893.

Bluntschli, Le Droit International Codifié, Paris, 1881.

Bray, Joseph, Le Droit Penal Militaire Romain et l'Occupation en Temps de Guerre, Paris, 1894.

Brenet, A., La France et L'Allemagne devant le Droit International pendant les Operations Militaires de la Guerre de 1870-1871, Paris, 1902.

British and Foreign State Papers.

Brunner, Heinrich, Grundzüge der deutschen Rechtsgeschichte, Leipzig, 1901.

Burigny, de, Life of Grotius, London, 1754.

Bynkershoek, Law of War (translated by Du Ponceau), Philadelphia, 1810.

Calvo, Charles, Le Droit International, Paris, 1896.

Clarendon, Edward, Earl of, Life of, written by himself, Oxford, 1827.

Columbia Law Review.
Conférence International de la Paix, The Hague, 1899.
Corpus Juris Canonici, Lyons, 1661.
Davis, George B., The Elements of International Law, New York and London, 1903.
Despagnet, Frantz, La Guerre Sud-Africaine au Point de Vue du Droit International, Paris, 1902.
De Wet, Christian, Three Years' War, New York, 1902.
Digesta Justiniani Augusti, Th. Mommsen, Berlin, 1870.
Diodorus Siculus, Historical Library (translated by G. Booth), London, 1700.
Doyle, Sir A. Conan, The War in South Africa, New York, 1902.
Du Cange, Des Guerres Privées et du Droit de Guerre par Coutume, in the Collection des Meilleurs Dissertations—Relatifs à l'Histoire de France par C. Leber, Paris, 1838.
Glossarium Mediae et Infimae Latinitatis, etc., Paris, 1840-1850.
Dumont, Corps Universel Diplomatique du Droit des Gens, Amsterdam, 1726-1731.
Estrades, Comte d', Lettres, Memoires et Negotiations, London, 1743.
Féraud-Giraud, Recours à Raison des Dommages Causés par la Guerre.
Ferrand, Georges, Des Requisitions Militaires, Paris, 1892.
Firth, Charles, Oliver Cromwell, New York, 1900.
Fortescue, J. W., A History of the British Army, London, 1899.
Franklin, Works of Benjamin (Bigelow), New York and London, 1887-1888.
Galiani, Recht der Neutralität (translation, Cäsar), Leipzig, 1790.
Gillot, Louis, La Revision de la Convention de Genève, Paris, 1902.
Gleig, The Campaigns of the British Army at Washington and New Orleans, London, 1836.
Grotius, De Jure Belli et Pacis (with translation by W. Whewell), Cambridge, 1853.
Guelle, Jules, Précis des Lois de la Guerre, Paris, 1884.
Gurlt, Zur Geschichte der Internationalen und Freiwilligen Krankenpflege im Kriege, Leipzig, 1873.

Hall, A Treatise on International Law, Fourth Edition, Oxford, 1895; Fifth Edition, Oxford, 1904.
Halleck, International Law, revised by Sir Sherston Baker, London, 1893.
Hansard's Parliamentary Debates.
Harte, Walter, History of Gustavus Adolphus, London, 1807.
Heffter, Le Droit International Public de l'Europe (translation), Berlin and Paris, 1866.
Hershey, Amos, The International Law and Diplomacy of the Russo-Japanese War, New York, 1906.
Holland, Studies in International Law, Oxford 1898.
The Laws and Customs of War on Land, London, 1904.
Holls, Frederick W., The Peace Conference at The Hague, New York, 1900.
Holtzendorff et Rivier, Introduction au Droit des Gens, Hamburg, 1889.
Imperatoris Justinianii Institutionum, J. B. Moyle, Oxford, 1883.
Institutes of Gaius and Rules of Ulpian, Muirhead, Edinburg, 1880.
James, History of the War in America, London, 1818.
Jomini, Art of War (translation), New York, 1854.
Kennet, White, History of England, London, 1706.
Lameire, Irénée, Theorie et Pratique de la Conquete dans l'Ancien Droit, Paris, 1902.
Les Occupations Militaires en Italie pendant les Guerres de Louis XIV, Paris, 1903.
Les Occupations Militaires en Espagne pendant les Guerres de l'Ancien Droit, Paris, 1905.
Laurent, F., Histoire de l'Humanité, Brussels, 1860-70.
Lawrence, T. J., War and Neutrality in the Far East, London, 1904.
Lediard, Thomas, The Naval History of England, London, 1735.
Livy, Roman History (translated by William Gordon), Glasgow, 1805.
Lorriot, A., De la Nature de l'Occupation de Guerre, Paris, 1903.
Mably, L'Abbe de, Le Droit Public de l'Europe, Geneva, 1776.

Machiavelli, Nicolo, The Prince (translated by John Morley), London, 1889.
McPherson, Edward, History of the Rebellion, Washington, 1876.
Manuel de Droit International a l'Usage des Officers de l'Armée de Terre, Paris, 1893.
Martens, G. F. de, Summary of the Law of Nations (translation), Philadelphia, 1795.
Précis du Droit des Gens, Paris, 1858.
Martens, F., Recueil des Traites conclus par la Russie.
Mathes, Capt. J. Harvey, General Forrest, New York, 1902.
Maurice, J. F., Hostilities without Declaration of War, London, 1883.
Merighnac, A., Les Lois et Coutumes de la Guerre sur Terre, Paris, 1903.
Military Correspondent of the Times, The War in the Far East, New York, 1905.
Minutes of a Court of Inquiry upon the case of Major John Andrè, Albany, 1865.
Montesquieu, Spirit of Laws (translated by Thomas Nugent), London, 1793.
Moore, John Bassett, History and Digest of the International Arbitrations to which the United States has been a Party, Washington, 1898.
International Law Situations with Solutions and Notes—Naval War College, Washington, 1901.
Digest of International Law, Washington, 1906.
Morley, John, Oliver Cromwell, London, 1900.
Moser, J. J., Versuch des neuesten Europäischen Völker-Rechts, etc., Frankfort on Main, 1777-1780.
Moynier, Gustave, Etude sur la Convention de Genève, Paris, 1870.
La Convention de Genève pendant la Guerre Franco-Allemande, Genève, 1873.
Nys, Ernest, Le Droit de la Guerre et les Precurseurs de Grotius, Brussels and Leipzig, 1882.
Les Origines du Droit International, Brussels, 1894.
Le Droit International, Brussels and Paris, 1905 and 1906.

Oman, Charles, Art of War in the Middle Ages, Lothian prize essay, Oxford, 1885.
History of the Art of War in the Middle Ages, New York, 1898.
Ortolan, Theodore, Regles Internationales et Diplomatiques de la Mer, Paris, 1864.
Parliamentary Papers.
Phillimore, Commentaries upon International Law, Second Edition, London, 1873.
Plutarch, Morals, edited by Wm. W. Goodwin, Boston, 1871.
Pont, Ch., Les Requisitions Militaires du Temps de Guerre, Paris, 1905.
Pothier, Oeuvres de Pothier, Paris, 1821-1824.
Pradier-Fodere, Droit International Public, Paris, 1885-1906.
Pufendorf, Samuel, De Jure Naturae et Gentium, London, 1672.
Querry, A., Droit Musulman, Recueil de Lois Concernant les Musulmans Schyites, 1871-1872.
Rebellion Records.
Report of the United States Delegation to the Geneva Conference.
Revue de Droit International, Brussels.
Revue Générale de Droit International Public, Paris.
Rivier, Principes du Droit des Gens, Paris, 1896.
Roby, John Henry, Roman Private Law, Cambridge, 1902.
Ropes, John C., The Army under Pope, New York, 1881.
Rousseau, J. J., Du Contract Social, Paris, 1896.
Saxe, Marshal, Reveries or Memoirs upon the Art of War (translation), London, 1757.
Schwab, J. C., The Confederate States of America, New York, 1901.
Scott, James Brown, Cases on International Law, Boston, 1902.
Seaman, Dr. L. L., The Real Triumph of Japan, New York, 1906.
From Tokio through Manchuria with the Japanese, New York, 1905.
Sheridan, Gen. P. H., Personal Memoirs of, New York, 1888.
Sherman, Gen. Wm. T., Memoirs of, by himself, New York, 1875.

Sohm, Rudolph, The Institutes (translated by Ledlie), Oxford, 1901.

Stark, Francis R., The Abolition of Privateering and The Declaration of Paris, New York, 1897.

Stubbs, William, Select Charters and other Illustrations of English Constitutional History, Oxford, 1895.

Smith, F. E., and Sibley, N. W., International Law as interpreted during the Russo-Japanese War, Boston, 1905.

Takahashi, Sakuyé, Cases on International Law during the Chino-Japanese War, Cambridge, 1899.

International Law as applied to the Russo-Japanese War, New York, 1908.

Taylor, Hannis, International Public Law, Chicago, 1901.

The Second International Peace Conference, Washington, Government Printing Office, 1908.

Twiss, Sir Travers, Law of Nations in Time of War, Oxford, 1875.

Valin, Traité des Prises, La Rochelle, 1763.

Vattel, Law of Nations (translation), Northampton, Mass., 1805.

Walker, Thomas Alfred, History of the Law of Nations, Cambridge, 1899.

Ward, Robert Plummer, Enquiry into the Foundation and History of the Law of Nations in Europe, etc., London, 1795.

An Enquiry into the Manner in which the Different Wars in Europe have been commenced during the last two centuries, London, 1805.

Westlake, John, Chapters on the Principles of International Law, Cambridge, 1894.

International Law, Cambridge, 1904 and 1907.

Wharton, Digest of the International Law of the United States, Washington, 1886.

Wheaton, International Law, Dana's Edition, London and Boston, 1866.

Wicquefort, Abraham de, Histoire des Provinces Unies, Amsterdam, 1861.

Wyeth, John Allen, Life of General Nathan Forrest, New York, and London, 1901.

Zorn, Albert, Das Kriegsrecht zu Lande, Berlin, 1906.

PART I.

HISTORY.

THE LAW OF WAR BETWEEN BELLIGERENTS

CHAPTER I.

INTRODUCTION.

High-minded men in every age have longed for the time when wars shall be no more; and they find today in the Tribunal of The Hague the beginnings of an institution which shall realize their hopes by substituting for the appeal to force the appeal to justice and right. But apparently the time for the realization of such hopes has not yet come, and until it does the rules according to which warfare must be conducted will continue to be of vital concern. These rules are scarcely less certain and are probably less often violated than the rules of private law which are enforced by the courts; but the passions of war often cast doubt on their certainty as well as on their efficacy, so that even more than in the case of private law it becomes necessary to resort to fundamental principles to see what has guided the making of rules in the past and is likely to have a similar influence in the future.

Much of the progress in the conduct of warfare has been due to the improvement in military science, but humanity has also played its part.—In the first place, it cannot be questioned that much of what is best in the laws of war has grown up independently of any set principles. The respect with which private property on land is regarded today is largely due to the change from pillage to the system of contributions, a change that was induced mainly by the greater efficiency of the latter; and many other instances could be cited of ameliorations which have been brought about by the selfish interests of belligerents. Civilization is so complex, and so many elements have gone into its making, that it is often hard to say just what influence has been most efficient; but, alongside the selfish motives, we know that the great commanders who have wrought important changes in the conduct of warfare have also had the higher motives of humanity, and it is these which have been crystalized and applied by the great martial jurists, and especially the greatest of them all, Grotius, so as to be recognized as fundamental principles of the laws of war.

The avoidance of useless injury a fundamental principle.—Of principles that may be considered fundamental, the greatest is, that comparatively useless injury is unlawful. Grotius applied this principle exhaustively to the possible incidents of land warfare, and backed up his opinions with such an array of writers of every kind and age that the greatest men of his time, men like Gustavus Adolphus, became his ardent admirers and devoted followers. He taught with new force that a belligerent should injure his enemy not because of the mere injury to the enemy, but because of the advantage to himself, and that means not leading to such advantage must be condemned. To state such a principle is to obtain its acceptance, and it has been of vital force in making the laws of war what they are today.

The proposition that war should be a relation between governments.—It is the principle that useless injury should be avoided and that a war of revenge is absolutely condemnable that characterizes the difference between civilized and uncivilized warfare. But the attempt has been made to introduce another principle—that of confining wars to governments themselves. Under this principle the state would become in effect a corporation with limited liability, for whose debts the general property of its citizens would not be liable, and war would take on the character of an athletic contest between two schools, whose members, no matter how enthusiastic, must not participate except as members of the duly authorized teams.

The advantages to be derived therefrom.—The carrying out of either of these analogies would have many advantages. A war is undoubtedly the concern of the whole country, and it is desirable that the country as a whole should bear its burdens instead of their falling even temporarily upon individuals. A government is able to distribute the burdens over the entire country, and to shift them if necessary to future generations, and thus to make comparatively imperceptible a burden that would be crushing to the few. The assimilation of war to an athletic contest has also other considerations in its favor. One of the crying evils of war in the past has been irregular fighting. Military men and publicists are at one in decrying its inefficiency and the lawlessness and recrimination which accompany it.

Its application during the 17th and 18th centuries.—Probably the most perfect application of both of these analogies was in the period preceding the French Revolution, when Rousseau generalized the war conduct of his time in the famous statement that has served as the text ever since for those who wish to confine wars to governments themselves, a statement which followed closely a similar generalization made by Vattel four years previous.

But most wars are now contests of peoples rather than of princes.—But since Vattel and Rousseau wrote, the prevailing ideas of government have vastly changed. Wars for the most part are no longer the contests of princes in which the people have little concern, but national struggles to which the peoples themselves are parties rather than the governments which represent them. It is the opposing people then that is to be coerced into the recognition of the claim of the other belligerent; and it may well be doubted whether a principle that would altogether prevent direct pressure from being brought to bear on the people of a country might not greatly lengthen wars, and by the added length cause far more suffering than it would avoid. Thus, one of the avowed purposes of General Sherman's March to the Sea was to bring the pressure of war home to the people of Georgia. Whatever may be the opinion as to incidents of that march, few probably will dispute the rightfulness or wisdom of its general purpose; and yet such a principle as that under consideration would forbid such an expedition entirely, unless it had distinct military purposes as well.

The continuance of the practice of attacking maritime commerce would indicate that governments still consider

the seizure of private property an effective means of pressure on governments.—General Sheridan claims that the loss of property is more apt to bring people to terms than loss of life on the battlefield; and, if this be so, it is often more humane to occasion some sacrifice of property and end the war, than to spare the property and cause the continued loss of life, the expenditure of public funds and the thousand and one injuries necessarily inflicted on private property by the operations of war, no matter what theory of law be followed. Such a theory would do away with commercial blockades, and yet such blockades have been practiced in the most recent wars and are likely to be in the future. When it comes to the question of striking at commerce on the high seas, this reasoning is especially applicable. The influence of the great commercial classes over modern governments is so powerful that effective pressure brought to bear on them is sure to be keenly felt by those holding the reins of government.

A rule that would confine resistance to organized forces might be fatal to national existence.—Even stronger reasons than these militate against the adoption of the view that war is a sort of athletic contest, in which none but the authorized teams must play. At the Brussels Conference in 1874, the attempt was made to convert this into a hard and fast rule of international law, but it was opposed by the able representatives of the smaller powers and aroused in them the utmost indignation, notwithstanding the fact that the Conference had already stretched the rule almost to breaking by the liberal concessions to its opponents. It was admitted that a belligerent might often feel justified in using extreme measures, even where a rising of the population in occupied territory was prompted by the most patriotic motives, but it was thought better to leave such incidents to the unwritten law of nations than by a hard and fast rule to turn over to military justice those who had been willing to sacrifice their all for their country. As it would have been a mistake to introduce any such inflexible rule into an international agreement, so it would be a mistake to introduce it into the unwritten law of nations. At the international conferences the prevailing opinion has seemed to be that the reimbursement of the individual is largely a matter of national rather than international concern, desirable, no doubt, but subject to considerations of expediency and not a matter of absolute right. Likewise it would seem better to run the risk of an abuse of discretion on the part of a Government in entering on irregular warfare than by an artificial rule to prejudge all cases that may arise.

The value in Rousseau's doctrine.—Insofar as there is value in the theory with which the name of Rousseau is associated, it is summed up by Westlake as follows: "The relation of enemies ought to be held to exist (1) between two states at war with one another; (2) between each of those states and those subjects of the other whom for the purpose of the war it may be necessary to affect by acts of force, and so far only as it is necessary so to affect them; but not (3) between individuals."[1]

German doctrine of necessity.—Some of the obvious dangers of the theory that war should be confined to governments themselves are avoided, especially by the German adherents of that theory, by their doctrine of necessity. It is a doctrine like that of self-preservation, of which Hall says: "It would be difficult to say that any act not inconsistent with the nature of a moral being is forbidden, so soon as it can be proved that by it, and it only, self-preservation can be secured. But the right in this form is rather a governing condition, subject to which all rights and duties exist, than a source of specific rules, and properly perhaps it cannot operate in this latter capacity at all."[2] The German writers, however, go further than this with the doctrine of necessity, and apply it, not only where self-preservation is at stake, but in all cases of extreme need when the object of the war cannot be obtained otherwise.[3] In other words the observance of the laws of war is subject to the condition that it is consistent with the attainment of the object of the war. If it is not it is the less important and must give way. Confined to certain extraordinary cases this doctrine is not objectionable, but if given a liberal interpretation it would soon usurp the place of the laws of war altogether. Would it not be better if such an extraordinary occasion should arise to vio-

1 II International Law, 38.
2 Hall, 5th Ed., p. 269.
3 Westlake, Principles, p. 239.

late the law and plead justification, than by announcing such a principle in advance, sanction it almost as law itself?

General influences which have improved war practice.—The foregoing are the most important of the general principles that have been urged as guides for the conduct of belligerents towards each other. But in the last analysis the efficacy of all law depends on its conformity to the public conscience and especially is this true as to the laws of war between belligerents. It is inconceivable that we should use poison even though it might be effective, and the increased care for prisoners and especially the sick and wounded but reflects the philanthropic spirit of the age. Perhaps the last of all to feel this quickening of the public conscience are the courts. They necessarily follow to a very great extent the precedents of a past age and for these reasons it is desirable that many of the incidents of war, such as commercial intercourse with the enemy, should be more fully placed in the hands of the political authorities, who are more responsive to public opinion. Finally the ideals of chivalry, which have always been associated with military life, and the spirit of fair play engendered by personal contact with the enemy, have done much to relieve war of its harshness. During our own civil war the soldiers in the field were much less vindictive than many of the civil authorities at Washington.

CHAPTER II.

BEFORE GROTIUS.

The confusion in the use of the terms "law" and "right."—In a letter quoted later,[1] Count von Moltke denies rather warmly the applicability of the term law to international agreements, as there is no authority to watch over and execute them. He is one of a great number who have considered the essential quality of law to be that of command, so that there can be no law where there is no superior. He represents the opposite extreme from those who would extend the scope of international law to include natural law, and while this view as to what law is, has been regarded by Sir Henry Maine and others as negligible, since Count von Moltke would have undoubtedly recognized the obligation of well-settled usages of war by whatever name called, still it unquestionably produces confusion in the use of the term law and hinders that general consensus of opinion which is so desirable, especially in the relations between belligerents.

Renders the ascertainment of war practice of past ages difficult.—This confusion in the use of terms is not peculiar to our own time, and it renders the ascertainment of the war practice of past ages peculiarly difficult. The most contradictory statements are made as to the existence or nature of a law of war, when the whole difficulty is apt to be a matter of terms. It is probably true, as Montesquieu has said, that "all countries have a law of nations, not excepting the Iroquois themselves, though they devour their prisoners."[2] It is important to bear this in mind, for the statement is frequently made that till recently war broke all legal relations and that an enemy had no rights, a statement that is true only in some of the narrower senses in which the terms "law" and "right" have been used.

[1] *Infra.*, p. 114.

[2] Montesquieu, Spirit of Laws, Bk. 1, Chap. III.

The Aryans early showed high standards of humanity in war.—No one who recalls the wars of extermination waged by the Jews, or the deeds of savagery that disfigure the pages of ancient and oriental history, will care to have them detailed here. Often they involved no suffering to the living, but consisted in savage exultation over the dead; but to us they must be equally revolting. On the other hand, it must be a matter of pride to us that, among the first glimpses we have of the Aryan peoples, we find incidents of humanity in time of war which foreshadow the high standards of war practice in vogue today and form a pleasing contrast to the general current of contemporaneous history. Diodorus Siculus says that, although among the ancient Hindus "the armies on both sides slaughter one another, yet they never hurt the husbandman, as one who is a servant for the common good and advantage of them all; neither do they burn their enemies' country, or cut down their trees or plants."[3] Instances of a like humanity are found among the Persians; and, while we find in Homer incidents of savagery and revenge, these are offset by the many instances of Greek and Roman humanity which are recited in the pages of Grotius; instances which caused him to turn to classic literature with relief from the sickening events of the Thirty Years' War.

Greek and Roman war practice.—In some respects, war was more severe even in the best periods of Greece and Rome than it is today. Prisoners of war were made slaves, the inhabitants of towns taken by assault could expect little mercy, and acts of great severity intended to inspire terror were frequent. On the other hand, declarations of war were very elaborate, the release of prisoners on parole and ransom was not unknown,[4] acts of violence against women and children were denounced and perfidy was condemned.[5]

The few precepts of the Roman Law relating to war made much of by the founders of the Law of Nations.—The

3 The Historical Library of Diodorus the Sicilian, Bk. II, Chap. III, p. 73 (Trans. Booth).

4 Plutarch, Greek questions, Question 17 (Trans. Booth).

5 Grotius, Bk. III, Chap. XI, 9-15 and Chap. IV, 18, quoting numerous Greek and Latin authors.

Digest of Justinian, which is the great source of our knowledge of the Roman Law, and which embodies most of what was best of the great Roman jurists, contains little that pertains to the subjects covered by The Hague Regulations, and, except as to captives, that little consists of incidental remarks; but, like everything else in the Digest, that little was so worked over and elaborated by the jurists of the Middle Ages and their successors that it occupies a prominent place among the sources of the modern law of war.

The law of capture.—Enemy property was placed in the same class with *res nullius*, things belonging to no one, such as animals in a state of nature, from the fact that in both cases title was not derived from someone else but was acquired by mere appropriation.[6] Conquered land became the property of the state;[7] but it was customary to leave the old proprietors in possession of part of what they had owned or even of all of it, subject to a permanent land tax.[8] Other property, unless captured under such circumstances as to make it the individual property of the captor, as in an assault,[9] became part of the general spoil,[10] which, or the proceeds of which, was commonly distributed among the various ranks of the army after a deduction had been made for the public treasury and at times also for the gods.[11] Prisoners of war became slaves, but only on being led into the camp of the enemy. Until then they retained their civil rights.[12] This principle of *intra praesidia,* that firm possession was necessary to give title, occupies a very modest place in the Digest, but it was applied generally to things as well as to persons by Grotius and the other early writers on the Law of Nations; and it played a most important part in limiting the rights of Conquest to places which had been firmly occupied as well as in postponing the vesting of title to cap-

6 Gaius, II, 66-68; Just., II, 1, 17.

7 D, XLIX, 15, 20.

8 Grotius, III, 6, 11; Bluntschli. Revue de Droit International, IX, 519.

Livy, II, 41, VIII, 1.

9 Grotius, III, 6, 18.

10 D, XLIX, 15, 20.

11 Grotius, III, 6, 16, 20.

12 D, XLIX, 15, 5, 1.

tured ships till they were brought to a place of safety, such as a port of the captor or of an ally, or the vicinity of a fleet.

Prisoners did not become slaves in civil wars.—Another important modification of the doctrine that prisoners of war became slaves was that this took place only where the war was solemnly declared;[13] and, as this was impossible in the case of internal war, the opposing forces in such a war did not become formal enemies nor did prisoners of war become slaves.[14] Grotius attributes much of the savagery of the civil wars to this cause, on the supposition that men were more inclined to kill where they had not the right to enslave.[15] In the Middle Ages, when many were inclined to regard those recognizing the authority of the Roman Church as the successors of the Roman people, the modification in question had an important influence, as it gave a legal basis to the doctrine that the wars of Western Europe were civil wars and that accordingly no right of enslaving prisoners of war could arise from them.[16]

The effect of capture on a Roman citizen and of his return to his own country.—The enslavement of a prisoner of war meant the loss of his citizenship, of his position in his family, and of his property rights; but this was subject to the important qualification that his rights revested, and that his old position in his family and in the state revived, on his escape from the enemy and return to his own country. In effect his various rights were suspended for the period of his captivity.[17] A will made during that period was invalid, and his children were released for the time being from obedience to him. If he died in captivity, however, it was provided by a Cornelian law that he should be considered to have died a Roman citizen. The jurists interpreted this to mean that he was considered to have died at the moment of capture, so that those who would have been entitled to succeed to his estate, if he had died at that time, became entitled to it.[18]

Law of reverter or postliminium.—This law of re-

13 D, XLIX, 15, 24.
14 D, XLIX, 15, 21.
15 Grotius, III, 7, 5, 3.
16 Nys, Origines, etc., p. 237.
17 Gaius, I, 129; Ulpian, X, 4.
18 Roby, Roman Private Law, I, 210; D, XLIX, 15, 22.

verter, which changed the effect of capture from an absolute loss of rights to the mere suspension of them, was called the law of postliminium. It applied also to land, slaves, ships of war and horses;[19] but as these are specifically mentioned it is probable that the law did not apply to property in general, but that such property became part of the general booty on recapture. It certainly did not apply to arms, which it was considered a disgrace to loose.[20] It is probable, then, that most kinds of movable property when recaptured, did not vest in the old owners; and by the time of Grotius, at least, this had ripened into a well-recognized rule of international practice, so that the law of postliminium was considered by him and most of his successors to apply to land and territory, but with some exceptions not to movables. This law of war was elaborated in greater detail than any other by the Roman jurists, so that it came to occupy an important place in early works on the Law of Nations, as it has continued to do well into the present century. Its chief function in International Law has been in keeping clear the principle that territory seized by an enemy does not become his in equal right with his old territory till the conclusion of the war. The same result is much more simply worked out in our modern doctrine of Military Occupation; but to a great extent, the results of the old doctrine of defeasible title were the same as those of this later doctrine of mere possession.

The Germanic migrations.—There is no sharp break between the character of the warfare waged by the armies of the later Roman Empire and of that waged by the Germanic tribes which overran it. From the beginning of the fifth century German mercenaries came to be a preponderating element in the imperial armies,[21] and, as each corps was encouraged to keep its own national arms and equipment,[22] there was probably more in common between the warfare waged by the German tribes in the great migrations and the warfare of the later Empire than between the latter and the earlier Roman practice. From the mo-

19 D, XLIX, 15, 2-3; Roby, II, 265.
20 *Ibid.*
21 Oman, the Art of War, p. 16.
22 Oman, p. 43.

ment that these mercenaries came to be employed, their imperfect discipline must have added greatly to the burdens of war; and when the migrations came, the presence of women and children with the armies must have augmented even this increased burden manyfold. Despite this, however, the execration which the supposed conduct of the Vandals called forth, and the detestation which caused the Hun, Attila, to be called "The Scourge of God" show that there were well recognized standards among the Germans which, compared with the reputed standard of the particular tribe, the Vandals, and with that of the Huns, were comparatively high.

The systematic war code of the Saracens.—The Germanic invasion was followed by that of the Saracens. Their law book was the Koran, but it was necessarily incomplete and was supplemented by the decisions of Mohammed and his successors. To meet the needs of the different peoples whom the Saracens conquered, this body of law was codified and the result bears tribute to the brilliant line of jurists who accomplished it.[23] That portion dealing with the law of war is of considerable magnitude. It is the first example we have of a systematic war code.

The waging of war a religious duty.—Once a year holy war was to be made on the unorthodox, on unbelievers and on tributaries who had failed to live up to their obligations.[24] It was possible for tributaries to retain their religion and even the administration of their country, but it was only Jews, Christians and Ghebers who, as tributaries, could have these privileges. To other unbelievers no middle course was offered between Islamism and the sword.[25]

Precepts of kindness and chivalry.—Precepts of kindness and chivalry were not lacking. There were injunctions against making use of incendiary projectiles, and also against cutting trees belonging to the enemy, intercepting his water supply or poisoning wells and water courses, while the killing of women and children or the insane, and the mutilation of prisoners without orders, was absolutely

23 A. Querry Droit Musulman, I, Preface.

24 *Ibid.*, p. 324.

25 *Ibid.*, p. 342.

forbidden.[26] Where an offer of individual combat had been made by an enemy, it was unlawful to render the combatant assistance. The faithful observance of capitulations was obligatory.

Treatment of prisoners of war.—Women, and minors of both sexes, became the immediate property of the captors. The disposition of adult male prisoners was reserved to the commander. They could be sent back, released on ransom, exchanged, or reduced to slavery.[27] The giving of food and drink to prisoners was compulsory. It was recommended that they should not be tortured, nor were their heads to be carried from the field of battle.[28]

Treatment of enemy property.—Cultivated land which was seized became the property of the whole Mussulman community.[29] Booty could not be appropriated except for nourishment, till after a fifth had been taken from it.[30] This fifth was devoted to religious purposes, the care of orphans, of the needy and of strangers.[31]

Comparatively mild treatment of unorthodox Mussulmans.—Against unorthodox Mussulmans, war gave fewer rights than against unbelievers. The object of war against them was their dispersion, and when this could be accomplished without the more serious measures it was wrong to resort to them. Prisoners of war were not enslaved and property was confiscated to only a limited extent.[32]

Actual practice among Mohammedans not uniform.—These rules left much to be desired. Almost unlimited discretion as to the treatment of prisoners of war was left in the hands of the commander, so that the character of the war was largely in his hands, while the immediate enslavement of women and children allowed the worst passions of the Mohammedans to find vent. Still, there were some evidences of a humane disposition, and the Saracens, under whom the first great conquests of Islamism were made, seem to have exercised their power with the greatest consideration. The Turks, however, have always

26 *Ibid.*, pp. 326, 332.
27 *Ibid.*, p. 332.
28 *Ibid.*, p. 333.
29 *Ibid.*, p. 337.
30 *Ibid.*, p. 335.
31 *Ibid.*, p. 178.
32 *Ibid.*, pp. 352-353.

betrayed their Turanian origin, and the West African dynasties which followed that of the Saracens in Spain fell short of the high standard set by their predecessors.[33]

The Eastern Roman Empire.—The Saracens were marvellously successful, but they failed to accomplish the overthrow of the Eastern Roman Empire. That was left for the Turk in 1453 In the meantime the institutions there had retained much of the form impressed on them in the days of the early emperors. The art of war and military discipline and organization had remained while elsewhere they had been forgotten. In the *Tactica* of Leo the Wise, written about the year 900, there is much good counsel "to the effect that no plighted treaty or armistice must be broken, no ambassador or parlementaire harmed, no female captive mishandled, no slaughter of noncombatants allowed, no cruel or ignominious terms imposed on a brave enemy."[34] This is somewhat marred, however, by the approval given to the use of bribes, to the obtaining of information through flags of truce and to other measures in which the East Roman took an unnatural delight as evidence of his cleverness.[35]

The lawlessness of the Middle Ages.—Far different from the state of affairs in the East Roman Empire and among the Saracens was that in the West. The great Carolingians had temporarily checked the tendency towards anarchy that had set in with the Germanic migrations, but on the death of Charlemagne there was no one to take his place, and the tendency towards anarchy was allowed to run its course. The weakness of political power necessitated the castle for protection from neighboring lords as well as from the inroads of Norseman and Saracen, and once built, the castles served to perpetuate the condition of lawlessness which had been the cause of their origin. Kings were able to do little against them and wars came to be petty strifes and knight errant expeditions. In this dark period of the Middle Ages the Church of Rome was the one great institution standing for law and order.

Private Wars.—A proof of the lawlessness of the times is the existence of private wars, which abounded every-

33 Walker, History of the Law of Nations, Vol. I, pp. 125, 129.
34 Oman, The Art of War, p. 201.
35 *Ibid.*, pp. 200, 201.

where but in England. They were probably in part survivals of the old German family feuds and in part outgrowths of the times. In France, especially, they came to be waged with great precision. They could be resorted to only for open and notorious offenses such as homicide, mayhem and battery,[36] and were commenced by the breaking out of an open quarrel or by words of menace or defiance.[37] Relatives of the author of the war of the degree in which marriage was forbidden by the church, were bound to support him under pain of losing their rights of succession.[38] Vassals were held to join their chief, but they could not be attacked except while in actual service. When they returned from the war, they were not to be attacked for simply having performed their duty.[39] The right to wage private war pertained only to gentlemen.[40] The communes obtained it by special concession from the King.[41] The war terminated by a peace, by an appeal of one party to the suzerain, by gage of battle or by the satisfaction of the offense. When one of the parties desired to avoid the war he called on the suzerain to summon his adversary into court and oblige him to give assurance not to injure the appellant further in his person or goods, but to bring the controversy into the suzerain's court and abide by his decision.[42] This the suzerain was obliged to do, although he was bound to exact an assurance from the one making the appeal as well as from the one appealed against. An assurance could be required only on an appeal of this kind. It could not be imposed on the initiative of the seigneur.[43]

Early checks by the temporal powers on private warfare. —One of the early checks imposed on this practice by the kings of France was the requirement of a delay of forty days, after the breaking out of private war, before the relatives of the offending party could be attacked unless they

36 Du Cange, Des Guerres Privées, etc., p. 428; Philippe de Beaumanoir, Les Coutumes du Beauvoisis, Vol. II, p. 354, p. 371. Most of the war practice of the Middle Ages is derived from the scholarly researches of Prof. Nys.

37 Du Cange, p. 430; Beaumanoir, p. 354.

38 Du Cange, p. 433; Beaumanoir, p. 362.

39 Du Cange, p. 441; Beaumanoir, p. 363.

40 Du Cange, p. 426; Beaumanoir, p. 355.

41 Nys, Les Origines du Droit International, p. 84.

42 Du Cange, p. 446.

43 Du Cange, p. 446, *et seq.;* Beaumanoir, pp. 360, 364, *et seq.*

had been present at the opening of the struggle.[44] A century or so before this, however, in 1128, at the Cortes of Najera, Alphonse VII of Castile had gone even further by forbidding all recourse whatever to private wars without a previous defiance, and by requiring a delay of nine days after the defiance before commencing hostilities.[45] In 1187 Frederick Barbarossa made a similar proclamation for the Empire, a respite of three days being required instead of nine.[46]

Checks by the Church.—But at this period the most important checks were those of the Church, especially the famous Truce of God. Originating in the County of Roussilon, in Southern France,[47] it was rapidly taken up elsewhere and in 1095 was solemnly proclaimed by the Council of Clermont. As finally sanctioned by the third Council of the Lateran in 1179, it forbade hostilities from sunset on Wednesday to sunrise on Monday, and on every day from Advent to the octave of Epiphany and from Septuagesima to the octave of Easter, and some of the decrees went even further than this. On days when hostilities were authorized, priests, monks, lay brothers, pilgrims, merchants, laborers and beasts of burden were not to suffer violence. Those who broke the truce were to be excommunicated.[48] This proving insufficient, the interdict was resorted to, special judges were instituted and the Brotherhood of God was formed, one of whose objects was the enforcement of the foregoing rules.[49] Undoubtedly, they were often broken, but they exercised a great influence for good until the occasion for them passed away with the rise of strong temporal powers.

Overthrow of private warfare by the rising power of the state.—The country least troubled by private wars was England. During the War of the Roses, however, she too suffered from them, only to be delivered by the strong hand of Henry VII. In France, as early as 1296, Philip the

44 Du Cange, p. 434.

45 Nys, p. 82.

46 Nys, pp. 86, 178.

47 Dumont, I, 43; Walker, I, 85.

48 Decretalium Gregorii, IX, L. I., tit. 34, De Truega et Pace, CC. 1, 2; Nys, p. 80.

49 Nys, p. 80; Du Cange, Glossarium, Vol. V, p. 2, see also Paciarii and Vol. VI, p. 659; Ward, Law of Nations, II, 24.

Fair had forbidden all private wars while he himself was at war, and, although in the reaction that followed his death, even the forty days' respite for relatives fell into disuse, the power of the state eventually reasserted itself and by an ordinance of 1361 private wars were forbidden altogether, and a century or so later under Louis XI were effectually stopped.[50] In the Empire the weakness of the Imperial Government allowed them to continue long after they were done away with in England and France. They survived longest in Poland and Scotland, lingering in the latter till well on into the eighteenth century.[51]

Reprisals.—Another evil of the Middle Ages was the widespread practice of reprisals, that is, of holding the subjects of another power responsible for the misdeeds or debts of fellow-subjects. This practice was often combined with that of private war. Especially was this true at sea. A notable instance of it occurred near the end of the thirteenth century, between the subjects of two such powerful kings as Edward I of England, and Philip the Fair of France. An English sailor having killed a Norman sailor in the port of Bayonne, certain Normans after applying in vain for satisfaction to their king, seized the first English ship they could find and hung several of the crew and some dogs at the same time, at the mast head. English sailors retaliated and things went so far that alliances were formed between the English, Irish and Dutch, on the one hand, and the Normans, Flemings and Genoese on the other; and a naval engagement was fought in which it is claimed that from eight to fifteen thousand Normans were slain before the two kings finally stepped in.[52]

Approach the character of an ordinary judicial proceeding.—As was the case with private wars, this practice of reprisals soon came to have rules of its own. It was the institution of the law of nations which received the most attention from the great Italian commentators of the fourteenth century, and under them it came to have many of the features of an ordinary legal proceeding.[53] It was usually held, however, that reprisals were an exercise of high

[50] Nys, p. 84.
[51] Ward, Law of Nations, I, 362.
[52] Ward, Law of Nations, I, 295.
[53] Nys, pp. 64, 68.

prerogative and were to be granted by the sovereign and not by the courts,[54] although in France the right was early exercised by the parliamentary courts.[55] Letters of reprisal were not accorded against women, the clergy, students, envoys, pilgrims, witnesses, merchants on their way to a fair, or mariners driven into port or on the coast by tempests.[56] Even within these limits, however, the practice of reprisals was attended with great evils, so that its operation came to be restricted by treaties.

They did not break the peace.—It is to be noticed that while these letters of reprisal were extremely high prerogative writs, they were in strictness nothing more and did not break the peace. They later came to be known as Special Letters of Reprisal to distinguish them from the General Letters which during the English-Dutch conflicts of the seventeenth century came to be granted generally to all subjects irrespective of whether they themselves had suffered or not. Both Special Reprisals and General Reprisals, in the stricter sense of General Letters of Reprisals, have now become obsolete. The General Letters fell with privateering through the Declaration of Paris of 1856 while we meet with few cases of Special Reprisals during the eighteenth century, although such important writers of that century as Bynkershoek and Valin discuss them in great detail as though they were living institutions.

Confusion in Terminology.—In the terminology of these letters there has always been much confusion. The distinction between a letter of mark and a letter of reprisal may have been based originally on the fact that the use of the one or the other was confined to the territory of the power granting it, or it may have been due to the fact that the letter of mark designated the particular individual or property to be seized while the letter of reprisal was not so limited. At any rate they apparently soon came to be used interchangeably and even to be popularly known as letters of mark and reprisal. As time went on, however, it seems to have become customary for letters of reprisal to be granted to particular aggrieved individuals and for letters of mark and letters of mark and reprisal

54 Nys, p. 70.
55 Valin, Traité des Prises, Vol. I, p. 329; Nys, p. 74.
56 Nys, p. 71.

to be used only in case of General Reprisals. Whether the latter could be granted in time of peace was long a subject of controversy between England and the Continental Powers.

Declarations of War.—Early in the Middle Ages, declarations of war came to be recognized as obligatory. It seems likely that this sprang from the necessities of the time, as permanent embassies had not been established; but it is possible that the practice of sending defiances may have been carried over from private warfare, which without them would have descended into brigandage, and it may to some extent, have been an imitation of the old Roman practice. The declarations at first consisted of letters of defiance, but later these were supplemented or supplanted by heralds, who were last employed by Louis XIII against Spain in 1635, and by Sweden against Denmark in 1657.[57]

The dying out of the enslavement of prisoners of war.—For one thing the Middle Ages is especially to be commended, and that is the abandonment of the practice of enslaving prisoners of war. This was partly the cause and partly the effect of the dying out of slavery itself. The times themselves made slavery on a large scale impossible. Strong governments are necessary to the protection of commerce and wealth, especially wealth in slaves; and strong governments were lacking. The old agricultural slaves became serfs; the slaves in the large cities disappeared as the cities themselves disappeared or shrank into insignificance; while from the personal attendants of the nobility sprang the great part of the knights, the under-nobility of a later age.[58] On the revival of trade, the cities, where wealth was greatest, were themselves sticklers for liberty. The times thus worked powerfully against slavery. The demand for slaves died out, and without the demand the continued enslavement of prisoners of war was unlikely. So the dying out of slavery was partly the cause of the abolition of the enslavement of prisoners of war. On the other hand, it was partly the effect. It was inconceivable to reduce a knight to slavery,[59]

57 Twiss, Law of Nations, In Time of War, p. 57 *et seq.*

58 Brunner, Grundzüge der deutschen Rechtsgeschichte, p. 85.

59 Laurent, Histoire de l'humanité, VII, 229.

and thus what had been the great means of recruiting slavery at Rome was lost.

By the time of Grotius.—When Grotius wrote, in 1625, prisoners of war were no longer made slaves so as to be either sold or forced to work or to do other things incident to the condition of slavery.[60] In some of the treaties, even as late as the seventeenth century, there are provisions that prisoners of war shall not be sent to the galleys; but condemnation to the galleys was evidently penal and not the ordinary practice. Thus, by Louis XIVth's famous ordinance of 1681, the captain and crew of an enemy privateer entering a French river were threatened with condemnation to the galleys.[61] Against those who continued to enslave prisoners, however, the practice of enslavement was still kept up. Bynkershoek tells us that the Dutch were in the habit of selling to the Spanish as slaves the Algerines, Tunisians, and Tripolitans who fell into their hands.[62]

The practice of enslavement gave way to that of ransom.—For enslavement was substituted the exaction of ransom. Kings were entitled to the ransoms of persons of high rank, whose ransom exceeded ten thousand livres or crowns, approximately the same sum, on paying that sum to the captor, while the captors themselves were entitled to the ransoms of persons of lower rank.[63] If there were no convention fixing the amount of the ransom, the captor could fix it,[64] although it was customary during feudalism to fix it at the annual revenue of the prisoner's estate, and in later times at a month's pay.[65] Prisoners could be detained till their ransom was paid and even permanently. The lives of those who could not ransom themselves were very insecure. The English prisoners taken at Pontoise in 1441 were chained by their necks like dogs, and those who could not pay were thrown into the Seine. It was also permissible to refuse all ransom. A son of the Emperor Frederick II died a prisoner among the Bolognese twenty-four years

60 Grotius, III, 7, 9.
61 Valin, Traité des Prisès, Vol. I, p. 44.
62 Bynkerschoek, Law of War, p. 21.
63 Nys, p. 244; Walker, p. 249.
64 Grotius, III, 7, 9.
65 Grotius, III, 14, 9, 1; Nys, pp. 245–6.

after his capture.[66] On the other hand, prisoners were often released on their parole not to serve against the captor till they had obtained their ransom and to return to captivity when called upon to do so. Often these agreements were strengthened by hostages, who at times paid with their lives the defalcation of their principals, although the better opinion was that the only right over them was to deprive them of their liberty.[67]

Development of chivalry.—Perhaps even more important than the dying out of the enslavement of prisoners of war was the development of chivalry. Early in the tenth century, when the Emperor Henry I introduced tournaments into Germany, he ordained that no one should be admitted who did not profess Christianity or who had been known to be guilty of perjury, treason, slaughter in cold blood, sacrilege or violation of women.[68] Profession of the Christian religion, honesty, loyalty, fairness, respect for sacred things, and honor were requisites of a true knight, and the necessity of these qualities was so drilled into the aristocracy of the period that they became ingrained in all that was best in the life of Christian Europe and are today what we prize most highly in the qualifications of a gentleman. Often the rules of open and fair fighting led to absurd results. One commander would challenge another to battle, naming the place and time for the conflict,[69] while the offering of aid to a besieged place was regarded as illegal.[70] At Crecy the fight was precipitated by the French forces unexpectedly and unpreparedly coming into contact with the English.[71] Such entire neglect of strategy is hardly comprehensible, but it is now and then a relief to look back on that age of punctiliousness from the sometimes over-ingenious stratagems of today.

Prohibition of certain weapons and the exemption of noncombatants.—A characteristic measure of the age of chivalry was the decretal of Innocent III which forbade

66 Nys, pp. 240, 246; Ward, Law of Nations, Vol. 1, pp. 301 *et seq.*, 308 *et seq.*

67 Nys, p. 247 *et seq.;* Ward, II, p. 179 *et seq.*

68 Ward, II, p. 161.

69 Ward, II, p. 212 *et seq.*

70 Ward, I, p. 264.

71 Oman, Art of War, p. 607, *et seq.*

the use against Christians of the arbalest or cross-bow, and of machines for throwing projectiles, such as the ballista.[72] A gloss, however, restricted the operation of this rule to unjust wars.[73] The prejudice against firearms is shown by the anecdote of Bayard, who, it is said, "when lying mortally wounded of a harquebus shot, thanked God that he had never showed mercy to a musketeer."[74] The provision of the Council of Clermont heretofore cited, which extended a very general exemption to noncombatants in private warfare, seems to have been applied to public warfare also. Some of the leading canonists of the fifteenth century considered it a dead-letter, however, and it was not unusual to hold for ransom wealthy noncombatants as well as soldiers.[75] Merchants were generally allowed a reasonable time to wind up their affairs and depart the country,[76] a provision to that effect, conditioned on reciprocity, being included in the Magna Charta.[77]

The dark side of mediaeval warfare.—While there was thus much that was bright in mediaeval war practice, there was perhaps more that was dark and gloomy. Pillage invariably followed a successful assault. Garrisons of places taken by assault could expect little mercy, and often where terms were granted the commandant and leading citizens were excluded from them.[78] Those who were guilty of obstinate resistance were especially liable to find little mercy at the hands of the enemy. Incomparably the worst feature of mediaeval warfare, however, was the lack of discipline and organization in the armies. Without these, rules of any kind mean almost nothing.

Practice in the English armies.—The numerous English army regulations of the period, however, would indicate a better condition in the English army than elsewhere.[79] Under Henry V the organization was good and the discipline effective, but this was exceptional. Mountague Bernard

72 Nys, p. 192; Decret. Greg., Lib. V, Tit. XV, C. Unicum.
73 Nys, p. 192.
74 Walker, History of the Law of Nations, Vol. I, p. 190.
75 Nys, pp. 193, 197, *et seq.*, 203.
76 Nys, p. 194; Ward, II, p. 356.
77 Stubbs, Select Charters, p. 301.
78 Nys, p. 221; Walker I, p. 132.
79 Nys, p. 204, *et seq.*

gives the following account of the campaigns of Edward III and Henry V: "In the summer of 1346 an English army, under Edward III, landed on the coast of Normandy, amongst a peaceful and industrious people, who, says Froissart, had never heard a battle-cry, or seen an armed man. They took and sacked Barfleur and Cherbourg, and marched on St. Lo. * * *

"Fair and cheerful province-delicious sight to a hungry invader, with its hamlets and church towers, its substantial farms and large sleek cattle, thick orchards and green pastures, sweeping up hill and down dale to the winding margin of the sea! The English scattered themselves over it, *'ardant et exillant le pais,'* and so advanced, burning and destroying—burning and destroying—over the rich flats of the Beauvoisin to the suburbs of Paris. Immense booty was taken; yet the English host, when it met the power of France at Crecy, was reduced to the utmost extremity of want.

"Nearly seventy years had passed from this time, when Henry V appeared before the gates of Barfleur. This time no such scourge was to fall upon the Norman peasantry, who now knew too well the martial sounds so unfamiliar to their ears in the days of his great grandfather. It was the policy of Henry, and was agreeable to his free and kindly disposition, to treat the French as subjects rather than as enemies. Great stores of bread, beef and beer provided at home, followed his army, and he allowed nothing to be exacted from the inhabitants, even when they resisted his passage, but bread and wine. Sir Harris Nicolas, in the Appendix to his Battle of Agincourt, has preserved the General Orders issued on this occasion, which followed pretty closely those published in 1386 by Richard II. They prohibit strictly all bloodshed, insults to women and wanton injury to property. . . . The ordinances of Henry were strictly enforced. The hanging of Bardolph for stealing a pix was a real incident of this campaign and it occurred when the army was in its greatest straits, before the battle of Agincourt."[80] The lack of organization by which, in a

[80] Bernard, Growth of Laws and Usages of War. pp. 97–99 (Oxford Essays, 1856).

land of plenty, Edward III was reduced to want, is typical of the Middle Ages.

War practice of the Swiss and Italians.—Of special interest is the war practice of the Swiss and of the Italians. The former seem to have considered terror one of their most effective weapons, and they have been likened to the Romans for the ferocity which they sometimes displayed.[81] The practice among the Italians, on the other hand, except for the use of poison, was distinctly mild. In the twelfth chapter of the Prince, Machiavelli could not find words too bitter for the mercenaries who had taken the place of all other troops in Italy. He says:

"They endeavored with all possible industry to prevent trouble or fear, either to themselves or their soldiers, and their way was by killing nobody in fight, only taking one another prisoners, and dismissing them afterwards without either prejudice or ransom. When they were in leaguer before a town, they shot not rudely amongst them in the night, nor did they in the town disturb them with any sallies in their camp; no approaches or intrenchments were made at unseasonable hours, and nothing of lying in the field when winter came on; and all these things did not happen by any negligence in their officers, but were part of their discipline, and introduced, as is said before, to ease the poor soldier both of labor and of danger, by which practices they have brought Italy both into slavery and contempt."[82]

War practice at sea.—The anarchy which prevailed on land during the Middle Ages was, if anything, surpassed by that at sea. Piracy was widespread and truces and treaties of peace had little effect on maritime hostilities.[83] Piracy had not been stamped out at the end of the Middle Ages,[84] but a more or less firm control had been gained over the forces avowedly in the service of belligerents by the requirement of privateering commissions and the establishment of institutions similar to the Court of Admiralty in England. At first, the validity of prizes had been ad-

81 Oman, Art of War in the Middle Ages, Lothian Prize Essay, p. 63.
82 Machiavelli, The Prince, Chap. XII (Trans. Morley).
83 Nys, pp. 211–215.
84 Walker, I, p. 165.

judged summarily by the admiral of the fleet, but with the grant of privateering commissions the royal power insisted on judging the conduct of its subjects itself. The Court of Admiralty in England dates back to the reign of Edward III. Under Henry V, private vessels were required to bring their prizes into court before disposing of them and to make a declaration concerning them under penalty of confiscation.[85]

[85] Nys, pp. 259–260.

CHAPTER III.

GROTIUS AND HIS TIMES.

The Renaissance and the outburst of literature on the art and law of war.—In nothing is the change from mediaeval to modern times more noticeable than in the intense interest that came to be manifested in everything the ancients had to teach of the art of war. Especially in Italy and Spain, this resulted in a great output of works on the art of war, which was followed somewhat later by a similar profusion of works on the law of war.

Pierino Belli.—Of the Italian writers, the most notable was Pierino Belli (1502-1575), who occupied a position as military judge in the armies of both Charles V and Philip II, and later was one of the most respected members of the Council of State of Emanuel Filibert of Savoy. His work *De re militari et de bello* appeared in 1563, and was dedicated to Philip II. "His purpose is merely to remind princes of what is permissible and honorable in the declaration of war and conclusion of peace; what should be the treatment of combatant enemies, of prisoners, of the non-combatant population, of property of all kinds, animate or inanimate. Belli's conception of his subject was an admirable one, but he was not so successful in working it out in detail. He seems to be led aside in order to touch upon all the questions which had come before him as military judge, and indeed apologizes for defects due to an active life spent for the most part at a distance from books."[1]

Spanish writers.—In Spain the controversy over the right to enslave the Indians caused special attention to be directed towards the law of war and the rights it gave. Two Dominicans, Franciscus Victoria (1480-1546), a professor at the University of Salamanca, and Dominicus Soto (1494-1560), his pupil, gave scientific form to the claims

[1] Holland, Studies in International Law, pp. 48–49.
See also Nys, Le Droit de la Guerre et les Precurseurs de Grotius, pp. 170–172.

which their fellow-Dominican, Las Casas, so devotedly urged in favor of the aborigines.[2] In his *Relectiones*, Victoria condemned the slaughter of innocents, among whom he included women, children, agriculturists, strangers and the clergy. He considered the seizure of property justifiable only as a means of effectively waging war or of satisfying an injury received, and declared slavery to be no longer a legitimate consequence of war between Christians. He also maintained that hostages, unless they belonged to the arms-bearing class, could not be put to death on a breach of faith by an enemy. He treated the slaying of enemies after victory as lawful only as a punishment for some offense, or where peace and safety could not otherwise be secured. He deemed the plundering of a country permissible only where necessary to carry on the war, to deter the enemy or to rouse the spirits of the soldiers; and concluded by urging the conqueror to exercise his rights over hostile territory with Christian moderation.[3] Soto, Victoria's friend and disciple, followed in the same line. His ability is shown by the fact that he was sent as first theologian to the Council of Trent by Charles V and afterwards became his confessor.[4]

Balthazar Ayala.—Another celebrated name is that of Balthazar Ayala, who was born in Antwerp in 1548, and died in 1584. He was judge in the armies of the Prince of Parma, Alexander Farnese, to whom he dedicated his work from the camp at Tournay in October, 1581. Like Belli, he deals with questions of military discipline as well as with those belonging to the law of nations.[5]

The outburst of military literature in England a little later than in Italy and Spain. Albericus Gentilis.—In England an outpour of military literature took place similar to that in Italy and Spain, but its advent was delayed till the troubles with Spain towards the end of the century.[6] The most notable among the works of this time is that on the Law of War by Albericus Gentilis. He was an Italian by birth, but with his father he early fled from Italy on

[2] Holland, pp. 51–54; Nys, Le Droit, etc., pp. 168, 169, 170.
[3] Walker, I, pp. 227–230.
[4] Nys, Le Droit, etc., p. 169.
[5] Holland, p. 54; Nys, pp. 173–182.
[6] Fortescue, A History of the British Army, I, p. 136.

account of his Protestant beliefs and found his way to Oxford, where he became established in 1581. The first part of his great work De Jure Belli was published in 1588. He freed the treatment of the laws of war from the questions of military discipline so fully discussed by Belli and Ayala, and from the theological associations of Victoria and Soto.[7] He considered in detail and with extensive learning and sound judgment the conduct of war and the causes that justly give rise to it. Walker states that his writings were characterized by "a vigorous style, directness of attack, and a vein of shrewd humor," which lent them "a singularly grateful vivacity, and a high permanent value."[8] His work has been called a juristic commentary on the events of the sixteenth century.[9] The discussion of contemporary events, which earned for it this title added greatly to its practical value, but it must also have raised prejudices against it as a scientific treatise. Similar discussion was accordingly avoided by Grotius.[10]

Early life of Grotius.—Hugo Grotius, the father of international law, was born at Delft, Holland, on April 10, 1583.[11] His ability early attracted the attention of the Grand Pensionary, Barneveldt, and at the age of fifteen he accompanied the latter and Count Justin of Nassau on an embassy to Henry IV of France, who received him with marked favor. He became a lawyer and was so successful that in 1607 he was appointed Advocate-General to the Fisc of Holland and Zealand, and in 1613 was honored with the post of Pensionary of Rotterdam for life. This made him chief magistrate of that important place.

His advocacy of the freedom of the seas.—Grotius' early activity is identified with the advocacy of the freedom of the seas. His Mare Liberum appeared in 1609. It was originally aimed at the monopoly which the Portuguese claimed in the trade with the East Indies, but its special object, when it was actually published, was to strengthen the Dutch against similar claims by the Span-

[7] Holland, pp. 1–39, 57–58.
[8] Walker, I, p. 275.
[9] Nys, Le Droit, etc., p. 185.
[10] Grotius, Prolegomena, 58.
[11] Most of the facts of Grotius' life are taken from his life by Burigny.

iards.[12] Later, Grotius went on an embassy to England to uphold the right of his countrymen to fish in the seas of Greenland, which were included in the widespread claim of the English to jurisdiction over the seas surrounding the British Isles.

His exile.—All this time the Netherlands were divided by a bitter religio-political struggle between the Arminian State Rights party on the one hand and the Calvinist House-of-Nassau party on the other. Grotius took sides with the former, and with two of the other leaders, Barneveldt and Hoogerbetz, was arrested. On May 13, 1619, Barneveldt was executed. The story of Grotius' escape from prison two years later reads like a tale of the Arabian Nights. With the cooperation of his wife, he escaped in a trunk and made his way to Paris, where for a time he received a pension from Louis XIII. There he published his great work, De Jure Belli et Pacis, in 1625.

His last years.—He returned to his native land in 1631, but found it unadvisable to remain; and on the invitation of the Chancellor Oxenstiern he entered the Swedish service as Ambassador to France, a post of the greatest importance in view of the alliance of the two powers in the Thirty Years' War. After a service of some ten years he became dissatisfied and asked for his recall. Queen Christina received him with great honor, but he declined to remain in the Swedish service and set out from Stockholm to Lubeck. Caught in a severe storm at sea, he was compelled to land on the Pomeranian coast and to accept conveyance in an open wagon. Inclement weather overcame him, and at Rostock, sixty miles distant, he was compelled to seek the services of a physician. He died there two days later, on August 28, 1645.

His greatness.—Besides being a great statesman and jurist, Grotius was a commentator on the Bible, the historian of his country, and a dramatist and Latin poet of no mean ability. His works along all of these lines were voluminous. In theology his views were very liberal. He long hoped to bring about a reconciliation between the Protestants and the Catholic Church. His exhaustive learning, his profound philosophy, his literary gifts, his Christian charity and

[12] Westlake, Principles, pp. 37–38.

deep love of mankind mark him as one of the most illustrious ornaments of his race.

Changes for the better between the Middle Ages and the time at which Grotius wrote.—From the period of the domination of feudal ideas to that in which Grotius wrote, some changes for the better had been made in the conduct of war. In 1521 Francis I and Charles V had agreed to exempt from molestation till the following January, each other's subjects engaged in fishing at sea.[13] On land armies had become better organized and drilled. The great gains made in the time of Louis XIV were yet to be realized, but paid standing armies were beginning to be employed, the use of firearms was tending to make personal combats less common and the ransoming of prisoners was giving way to exchange.[14]

Changes for the worse. Civil and religious wars.—In certain ways, however, conditions had become infinitely worse. Such events as the massacre of St. Bartholomew's Day show the depth which religious and civil discord had reached. Walker quotes Montluc as saying: "It is not in this case as in a foreign war, when men fight for love and honor; but in a Civil War we must either be master or man, being as we live as it were all under a roof; and that's the reason why we must proceed with rigor and cruelty."[15] The Civil War in the Netherlands was a veritable struggle to the death. It is well known that a price was placed on the head of William the Silent, and that he was subsequently assassinated. The condition of affairs in the Thirty Years' War was the same.

Grotius' reasons for writing on the law of war.—It was under these circumstances that Grotius wrote: "I, for the reasons which I have stated, holding it to be most certain that there is among nations a common law of Rights which is of force with regard to war, and in war, saw many and grave causes why I should write a book on that subject. For I saw prevailing throughout the Christian world a license in making war of which even barbarous nations would have been ashamed; recourse being had to arms for slight reasons or no reason; and when arms were once taken up

13 Walker, I, p. 190.
14 Nys, Les Origines, etc., p. 246.
15 Walker, I, p. 192.

all reverence for divine and human law was thrown away, just as if men were thenceforth authorized to commit all crimes without restraint.''[16]

Distinction between the law of nations and the law of nature.—In his treatment of the law of war, Grotius distinguished between that which was lawful by the law of nations instituted through the will of all or many nations[17] and that which, while it might go without punishment and in that sense be lawful, was contrary to natural reason and so not without fault.[18] The former, the law of nations, was to be derived from the practice of nations; the latter, natural law, from philosophers, historians, poets, orators, civilians, canonists and Schoolmen.

Grotius' carefulness in not claiming for his own opinions the force of instituted law.—That part of the law of nations which dealt with war was the conventional ''law of war'' of his contemporaries. Grotius seems to have been exceedingly careful not to claim for his own opinions the force of instituted law. He solicitously separated the rules which, from their origin in the Roman Law or in the practice of military courts, had gained unquestioned acceptance from those of less definite authority; and by forbearing to invest the latter, by the mere weight of his assertion, with an authority which they did not otherwise possess, he disarmed opposition and secured a favorable hearing for what he had to say.

His greatest contribution to the law of war included under his law of nature.—His greatest contribution to the law of war was that which he included under the law of nature. The conception of a Natural Law, binding from its very reasonableness, was not a new one. It had come down through the Schoolmen and the Roman jurists from the Stoics. But Grotius so elaborated it, and so distinctly made it his own by applying it to international relations that Rivier has declared him to be justly deemed the father of both the Law of Nature and the Law of Nations.[19] The fundamental principle of the Law of Nature applicable to

16 Grotius, Prolegomena, Par. 28 (Trans. Whewell).

17 Grotius, Bk. I. I, 14, 1.

18 Grotius, III, 4, 2, 2.

19 Holtzendorff et Rivier, Introduction au Droit des Gens, pp. 351, 361.

war, which Grotius laid down, was that "the measures that are necessary (to a lawful end), necessity being taken not in physical exactness, but morally, we have a right to use."[20] In other words, he enunciated the principle that comparatively useless injury should be avoided. In the light of this general principle, Grotius went on to treat the various parts of the law of war in detail.

The right to kill does not extend to noncombatants.—Children are excused from the right to kill by their age, women by their sex. The same rule is to be laid down for men whose mode of life is repugnant to arms, such as the clergy, students, husbandmen and merchants. Captives should not be put to death, and quarter should be given both in battle and in siege.[21] "Exceptions by no means just, to these precepts of equity and natural justice are," says Grotius, "often alleged: Retaliation: the necessity of striking terror: the obstinacy of resistance. It is easily seen that these are insufficient arguments." Where the disarmed have committed a breach of the laws of war, they may be put to death; "but," continues Grotius, "as to Retaliation, nature does not allow it except against the offender himself. Nor is it sufficient, that the enemy is by a sort of fiction, conceived as forming one body. * * * The advantage which is expected by striking terror cannot give a right to kill men; but if we have a right, it may be a reason for not remitting it. An obstinate adherence to one's own party, if their cause be not indecently bad, does not deserve punishment; or at least. not a punishment extending to death; for no impartial judge would so decide. * * * Still less is such killing justified by grief for calamity suffered."[22]

Limits to ravaging.—As to ravaging, "except there be some motive of utility, it is," says Grotius, "foolish, for no good of your own to harm another." Ravaging is tolerable which in a short time reduces the enemy to seek peace. But this will not be the case, first, where, although we be in a country yielding provisions, our possession prevents the enemy from availing themselves of the supply; second, where, although the possession is doubtful, there

20 Grotius, III, 1, 2, 1.
21 Grotius, III, 9–15.
22 Grotius, III, 11, 16.

are strong hopes of victory of which the reward will be both the land and its fruits; third, where the enemy can support himself from other quarters, as if the sea or boundaries on another side be open; and finally, where things are of such a nature that they are of no use in making or carrying on war, such as ornamental works, religious establishments, monuments for the dead and burial places.[23] "It is also most true," observes Grotius, "as some theologians have noted, that it is the duty of rulers and leaders, who wish to be reckoned Christians by God and by men, to abstain from storming of cities, and other like violent proceedings; which cannot take place, without great calamity to many innocent persons, and often do little to promote the ends of war; so that Christian goodness almost always, justice mostly, must inspire a repugnance to them."[24]

Right of acquiring property from the enemy.—As to the right of acquiring property from the enemy, this, according to Grotius, is limited by the extent of the enemy's debt to you, "except that beyond this, things necessary to your safety may also be detained, but are to be restored when the peril is over, either in themselves or in their price."[25] But Grotius makes a distinction between civil debts, those due to rectify an existing inequality, and those due as a penalty for wrong-doing. For the first kind, the property of the subjects may be treated as security, as where reprisals are ordered, and so many be taken,[26] but "such an obligation, imposed on the property of another, is" he says, "an odious rule, and therefore ought not to be carried further than it appears to be actually settled."[27] With debts due to rectify an existing inequality are classed those arising from war undertaken to rectify such inequality.[28]

Exhortation to respect private property.—"But," says Grotius, "the rules of charity are wider than those of justice" and "humanity requires that we should leave, to those who are not in fault in the war, and who are only

23 Grotius, III, 1–4.
24 Grotius, III, 12, 8, 4.
25 Grotius, III, 13, 1, 1.
26 Grotius, III, 13, 1, 2.
27 Grotius, III, 13, 2.
28 Grotius, III, 13, 3.

bound as sureties, the things which they cannot do without better than we can, especially if it appear that they will not recover from their city what they thus lose;" and "this also is to be noted, that so long as we have a hope of receiving our debt from the original debtor, or from those who have made themselves debtors by not yielding our right, to come upon those who are free from fault, although it may not be at variance with strict law, is contrary to humanity."[29]

Ransom.—Prisoners of war no longer being made slaves, "it will," declares Grotius, "be the best course to exchange the prisoners; and next to that, to let them be ransomed at a reasonable price. What this is, cannot be precisely defined, but humanity teaches us that it should not be stretched so far that it leaves the prisoner without the necessaries of life."[30]

Moderation in Conquest.—In Conquest, it is often not only a measure of humanity but also one of prudence to permit the vanquished to retain their power of government, if not wholly, at least in part; but, even when all authority is taken from them, they should, so Grotius maintains, be allowed to retain their own laws with regard to public and private property, their own customs and magistrates, and, as part of this indulgence, the observance of their own religion, except so far as they may be persuaded to change.[31]

Conclusion.—In conclusion, Grotius says: "May God write these lessons,—he who alone can,—on the hearts of all those who have the affairs of Christendom in their hands: and may he give to those persons a mind fitted to understand and to respect Rights, divine and human; and lead them to recollect always that the ministration committed to them is no less than this; that they are the governors of Man, a creature most dear to God."[32]

Influence of Grotius' work.—The work of Grotius made a tremendous impression. Gustavus Adolphus, the greatest captain of his age, expressed the highest admiration for the author and recommended that he be taken into the

29 Grotius, III, 13, 4.
30 Grotius, III, 14, 9.
31 Grotius, III, 15, 7-10.
32 Grotius, III, 25, 8.

Swedish service.[33] It is said that he always carried a copy of the De Jure Belli et Pacis with him. Editions, translations and commentaries multiplied on every hand and the recognition it had gained for the law of nations and of nature in the field of jurisprudence was manifested by the establishment of a chair in that subject at Heidelberg by the Elector Palatine, Charles Lewis, in 1661.[34]

Samuel Pufendorf.—The first incumbent of that chair was Samuel Pufendorf. His contributions to the laws of war, however, were comparatively unimportant. They occupy but a small part of his immense work.

Conduct of the Thirty Years' War.—Great as was the influence of Grotius' work, it could not be expected to restore to its normal condition a war such as that of the Thirty Years, which had been commenced in civil and religious strife and carried on with cruelty and bitterness. Gustavus Adolphus was so high-minded and maintained such excellent discipline that he was able to preserve in his army a high standard in the observance of the laws of war, but other commanders had neither his power nor his good-will. Six years after the publication of Grotius' work occurred the horrors of the siege of Madgeburg.

Oliver Cromwell.—A notable instance of the old practice of using terror as a means of warfare was the refusal of quarter at Drogheda by Cromwell. "It will tend to prevent the effusion of blood for the future,"[35] he said. Possibly it did this temporarily, but it is also said that its "memory still helps to separate the two races Cromwell wished to unite."[36] From these events we turn with relief to a newer and better era. The Treaty of Westphalia (1648) marks roughly the end of the old.

33 Burigny, Life of Grotius, p. 135; Hely, Etude sur le Droit de la Guerre de Grotius, p. 30.

34 Walker, I, 337.

35 Morley, Oliver Cromwell, p. 301.

36 Firth, Cromwell, p. 261.

CHAPTER IV.

WARS OF PRINCES.

Commencement of a new era.—From the Dutch wars of Louis XIV to the present time the character of war has been much the same. If anything, the wars of the early part of this period were less severe than those of more recent times. They lacked the religious and civil element of the wars which had preceded them and were essentially struggles between princes, who regarded with disdain the participation of the masses in politics or war. The armies were small, paid, highly-trained bodies. Their leaders took pride in their knowledge of the art of war, and strategy in particular, and for the purposes of strategy, the husbanding of their own resources and those of the country through which they were marching was absolutely necessary. Furthermore, the work of Grotius had crystallized public sentiment and it was not unnatural that the admirers of Gustavus Adolphus, as all the great generals of the period seem to have been, should also have admired the great work which had been his constant guide.

The place of the herald-at-arms taken by the permanent embassies.—With the establishment of permanent embassies, the sending of heralds-at-arms to declare war grew to be incongruous, and as we have seen, the last instance of that custom was in 1657.[1] It had served as a warning to the enemy and as the test of full legal war. As a warning to the enemy, its place was taken and much more than taken by the establishment of the permanent embassies, which facilitated the presentation of demands, allowed of the continuance of long negotiations, and served as a source of information of the preparations of a possible enemy. Even such writers as Bynkershoek and Ward, who did not believe in the necessity of a formal declaration, thought it necessary that there should be a demand of satisfaction for the injury complained of, and a denial or delay of the same before recourse to arms. Formal dec-

[1] See *supra*, p. 19.

larations as warnings to the enemy were superseded by ultimatums, or the rupture of diplomatic relations under such circumstances as to leave little doubt of the intentions of the parties. Practice under the new order of things was far from what might have been desired, but the new institution in itself was far better calculated to guard against surprise, treachery and disloyalty than the old.

The old declaration a test of legal war rather than a warning to the enemy.—But the old declaration of war had served as a test of full legal war, as well as a warning to the enemy, and this, according to Grotius, was its real significance. He says that the reason for it was "that it might be clearly known that the war was undertaken, not as a venture of private persons, but by the will of the two peoples, or their heads; for from this public character arise peculiar effects, which do not take place either in a war carried on against pirates, or in one which a king makes against his subjects."[2] It is in this sense that the declaration continued for a long time to have a more or less obligatory character, and it is mainly in this sense that it has been revived today by The Hague Convention. It may be interesting to note how from a necessary preliminary to war it came to be little more than a public recognition of its existence.

Declarations were not necessary against those joining the enemy.—In the first place it must be remembered that Grotius himself held that no declaration was necessary against those who joined themselves to the enemy.[3] Nor did the mere giving of aid to one of the belligerents require a declaration. Many of the earlier cases of war without declaration were cases of this kind. Elizabeth justified her not declaring war against Philip of Spain on the ground that she was merely aiding The Netherlands in accordance with ancient treaties, and Gustavus Adolphus justified his failure to declare war against the Emperor by the fact that the year previous the Emperor had aided the King of Poland against him without declaration. Many of the cases given by Colonel Maurice in his Hostilities without Declaration of War are of this kind. Numerous instances of this occurred in the War of the Austrian Succes-

[2] III, XI.
[3] III, IX.

sion, in the Seven Years' War, and in the War for American Independence. All the old rule required was that war should be commenced by a declaration. When once commenced, others might be embroiled in it without declaration. It is easy to see how important this exception was, especially during the eighteenth century, when a large part of Europe eventually came to be involved in the numerous wars that occurred.

Nor where a war was commenced under pretext of title.—In a number of other cases wars were commenced under pretext of title. They were ostensibly civil wars, and so came within another exception to the old rule, that declarations were not necessary in civil war. It was thus that the War of Devolution was commenced in 1667 by the claim of Louis XIV to the Spanish Netherlands, the War of the Spanish Succession in 1701 by the claim of the Emperor Leopold to Lombardy, and the War of the Austrian Succession in 1741 by Frederick the Great's claim to Silesia. Frederick likewise disclaimed all hostile intention in his seizure of Saxony in 1756. Ostensibly then these were not violations of the old rule as to the necessity of declarations of war.

Influence of maritime pretensions and struggle for trade and territory in the colonies.—The above cases, then, did not mark any change in formal practice. Of more importance were the informal hostilities growing out of (1), the maritime pretensions such as those of the English in the four seas and those of Spain in America and (2), the struggle for trade and territory in the colonies. The action of men like Drake had little or no direct effect on the laws of war, as their actions were but little, if any, removed from piracy, but the example of their lawless depredations was not without its effect when the race for colonial possessions commenced. Thus the expedition sent by Cromwell to the West Indies in 1654, which resulted in the acquisition of Jamaica, was little better than a filibustering expedition, while not much more can be said of the expedition to Africa and America of Admiral Holmes in 1664, which finally resulted in open war between the English and the Dutch. Of not quite so objectionable nature were the colonial hostilities carried on between the Dutch and the Portuguese, which resulted in a declaration of war in

1657, as Portugal's independence of Spain had not yet been generally recognized, so that any action by or against her was of an exceptional nature. These hostilities, as well as the blockade of Porto Bello in 1726 by Admiral Hosier, and the fighting which commenced in America in 1754 between the French and English had a perceptible influence on the European practice of commencing hostilities. For instance, the blockade of Porto Bello in 1726 was followed by the siege of Gibraltar in 1727, without formal declaration, and the fighting between the French and English in America in 1754 and 1755, was followed by the expedition against Minorca in 1756, also without a declaration. But their importance is likely to be exaggerated, as the colonies have always held an exceptional place in the public law of Europe.

The sequestration of property and the issuance of general letters of marque and reprisal prior to a declaration the determining factor in making prior declarations unnecessary.—Whatever importance incidents like the above did have in accustoming the public mind to hostilities without declaration of war, the determining factor that led to the quite general acceptance of the doctrine that a formal declaration was not necessary to constitute war in its full legal sense, was the practice which became general from the middle of the seventeenth century, of sequestrating property, and of granting general letters of marque and reprisal, in contemplation of war. One of the early instances of this practice occurred in 1664, in connection with the war between the English and the Dutch. On the sixteenth of December, 1664, Charles II issued a proclamation empowering his subjects to make reprisals on all Dutch ships. This was followed by a similar declaration on the part of the Dutch on January 24, 1665, although no declaration of war was made till the following March.[4] It is probable that it was in connection with this that De Witt made his famous statement that "he saw no difference between General Reprisals and Open War," rather than in connection with the grant of letters to the agent of the Knights of Malta, two years earlier as supposed by Twiss.[5] The reason for this action on the part of the Eng-

[4] Lediard, The Naval History of England, 575.

[5] Twiss, I, 31.

lish King is very quaintly put in Kennet's Collection of English History,[6] where he says: "It is, however, a justice to observe, that this way of dealing with our friends before we had pronounced them enemies, was not merely a trick of France, or an intrigue of our own ministry (as some have labored to represent it), but it was the very voice of the English people, and especially the cry of all our merchants and traders. The city of London was so full of all resentments against the Dutch for engrossing and usurping upon navigation and commerce, that they not only lent a hundred thousand pounds (as before remembered) for expedition of the fleet, but when the king still wanted another like sum, they advanced it with the same readiness." It was the granting of the general letters at this time that Lord Hale instanced as an example of war commencing without a solemn declaration.[7] England, however, was not the only offender along these lines, for while the seizure of the goods belonging to the Dutch in 1657 by the French may be considered as an instance of reprisals properly so-called, as distinguished from reprisals in contemplation of war, the same cannot be said of the seizure of the goods of the Dutch by Louis XIV in 1688.[8]

The memory of the old rule lingered on.—The number of examples of these seizures in contemplation of war was the principal basis for the contention of Bynkershoek in 1737 that Grotius' assertion that the customary law of nations required a declaration of war, could not be sustained.[9] But despite the frequency of these sequestrations and grants of general letters of marque and reprisal prior to the declaration of war, it was long felt that seizures made prior to a declaration were void, and that the ships seized should be handed back. Thus in the negotiations between Stanley and Bussy in 1761, looking to the termination of the Seven Years' War, it was demanded that all private ships taken prior to the declaration of war should be restored or compensated for, because taken contrary to

6 2, 251.
7 Pleas of the Crown, 162–163.
8 Bynkershoek, pp. 16–17.
9 P. 6, *et seq.*

the law of nations.[10] And although in the final treaty nothing was said on this subject with regard to French ships, it was agreed with Spain that the decision of prizes made in time of peace by the subjects of Great Britain should be referred to the British Admiralty, to be judged according to treaties and the law of nations.[11] Even as late as August 12, 1778, Lord Chancellor Thurlow wrote: "I find a doubt hath been started whether it be correct to make a prize or to condemn it as confiscate, and still more to distribute it to the captors, before a Declaration of War. Upon the last it is insisted that the goods of nations not declared Enemies can at most be taken as Reprisal, and detained only as pledges for satisfaction. It is said that this was done in 1754, and that no prizes were actually condemned or distributed before Declaration of War at that period."[12] This was written in a letter to Philip Stephens, Secretary of the Admiralty, requesting that a careful search should be made for precedents in these matters subsequent to the Revolution.

The question put at rest for Anglo-American courts, at least, by Lord Stowell.—All doubt of the legality of the seizure of private property of the enemy before the declaration of war was finally settled for British and American courts, at any rate, by Lord Stowell, in the case of The Boedus Lust[13] when he held that the seizure of Dutch property under an embargo in 1803 was at first equivocal, but that as the transaction ended in hostilities, these had the retroactive effect of making the original seizure hostile, and the property seized good prize. In other words, he held that acts of force used against another nation might not constitute war in themselves, but that if war followed, it had a retroactive effect and constituted the first acts of force, the commencement of the war. From Lord Stowell's time this view that war declarations might have a retroactive effect, and did not necessarily precede the capture of private property, was generally sustained, especially in England and the United States.

Embargoes and letters of marque and reprisal now things

10 Ward, p. 38.
11 Ward, p. 39.
12 II Twiss, 67.
13 5 Rob., 246.

of the past.—It is interesting to note that the practices which had been the special occasion of the incorporation of the retroactive effect of declarations of war into the law did not long survive Lord Stowell's decision. Grants of letters of marque and reprisal, and embargoes in contemplation of war, soon became things of the past. The former were in effect abolished by the Declaration of Paris, and from the Crimean War it has been customary to allow a certain time after the outbreak of hostilities for the departure of merchant ships belonging to the nationals of the enemy. It is for this reason that some have claimed that the rule laid down by Lord Stowell itself had changed, but the careful study of the wars of the last fifty years by M. Dupuis shows this not to have been the case.[14]

No special form for declarations.—Since the old sending of heralds-at-arms, there has been no particular form for making declarations. Most of those of the seventeenth and eighteenth centuries seem to have been printed declarations published at home. An interesting survival of a part of the old custom of declaration by herald was that of England against France in 1778, as described by the Russian envoy to London.[15] "A herald, drawn from the mounted guard of the king, read the declaration of war to the noise of trumpets and timbals, before the palace of St. James, where the king stood in the embrasure of an open window, hat on head and sword in hand; this sword, like the temple of Janus, which remained open among the Romans till peace, remains unsheathed in the church till the end of hostilities."[16] In the United States declarations of war have taken the form of acts of Congress, and have been declarations of the existence of war rather than declarations of future war.

Substitution of contributions for pillage.—One of the greatest advances ever made in the conduct of warfare was the substitution, during this period, of contributions for pillage. Gustavus Adolphus had ransomed towns from pillage during the Thirty Years' War,[17] and the generals of the period of Louis XIV followed in this as in other

14 13 R. G. D. I. P., 725.
15 II Rivier, 224.
16 Martens, 9 Recueil des Traités conclus par la Russie, 290.
17 Hall, International Law, p. 442.

branches of war the footsteps of their great master. Of the early practice of contributions, Vattel says: "The long wars of France in the reign of Louis XIV furnish an instance which can never be too much commended. The sovereigns being respectively interested in the preservation of the country, used on the commencement of war to enter into treaties, for regulating the contributions on a supportable footing: both the extent of the country in which each could demand contributions, the amount of them, and the manner in which the party sent for levying them were to behave, were settled. In these treaties it was expressed that no body of men under a certain number, should advance into the enemy's country beyond the bounds agreed upon under the penalty of being treated as *parti bleu* (marauders or robbers). This was preventing a multitude of disorders and enormities, committed on quiet people, and generally without the least advantage to the sovereigns at war."[18]

Marshal Saxe's method of levying contributions.—Marshal Saxe describes the methods pursued by him: "An experienced general, so far from maintaining the troops under his command, at the expense of their sovereign, will, by raising contributions, secure their subsistence for the ensuing campaign, so that being well lodged, clothed and supported, they will consequently be easy, contented and happy. In order to accomplish this, it will be necessary to fall upon a method of drawing supplies of provisions and money from remote parts of the country, but without fatiguing thereby the troops too much; large detachments are exposed to the danger of being cut off by the enemy; are likewise detrimental to the service, and rarely productive of those advantages which are expected from them; the best way is to transmit to those places from which contributions are required, circular letters, threatening the inhabitants with military execution, on pain of their refusal to answer the demand made from them; which ought at the same time, to be moderate and proportionable to their several abilities; after which, intelligent officers must be selected, and detached with parties of twenty-five or thirty men, allotting to each a certain number of villages,

[18] Vattel, Bk. III, Chap. IX, Sec. 165; see also Bernard, History of the Laws and Usages of War, pp. 101–103.

and giving them strict orders to march by night only, and not to plunder, or commit any manner of outrage on pain of death. When they arrive at their appointed places they must send a noncommissioned officer and two men in the evening to the chief magistrate to know if he is prepared to take up his acquittance, which will be given under the hand and seal of the commander in chief of the army; if he answers in the negative, the commanding officer is not thereupon either to plunder the place, or to take the sum required, but must discover himself, and his party, set fire to some detached house, and afterwards march away again, threatening at the same time to return and burn the whole village.

"All these parties are to be assembled at some rendezvous, before they are dismissed, where a strict enquiry must be made into their conduct, and those who are found guilty of the least rapine, be hanged without mercy; if any officers likewise are convicted of having taken or received money from the villages they must be punished with death, or cashiered at least. But if, on the other hand, it appears that they have properly executed their orders, they must be rewarded accordingly; this method of raising contributions will thus be rendered familiar to the troops and all the places that have been summoned within a hundred leagues in circumference, will not fail to bring their stipulated quantities of provisions and money; for the calamities they have been threatened with, in case of their delay, will augment their fears to such a degree that they will be very glad to purchase their security, by discharging the demand made upon them, notwithstanding any prohibitions which may have been issued by the enemy to the contrary.

"Twenty parties detached monthly will be sufficient to accomplish the whole affair, neither will it be possible for the enemy to discover them, notwithstanding his most diligent endeavors for that purpose, provided they make use of the proper precautions on their march, and adhere to their instructions.

"Large bodies of troops detached on these duties encompass in the execution only a small tract of country, and spread distress in every place where they appear; the inhabitants conceal their cattle and effects from them, and can hardly be compelled to surrender up anything, because they are very sensible, that their stay can be but short; and that, as they take care to send the earliest intelligence of their situation to the enemy, he will soon relieve them; a circumstance by which such large parties have frequently been obliged to retreat with all the expedition they could, after having totally miscarried in their undertaking, and left several of their men behind them; but even when they meet with no interruption from the enemy, the commanding officers, either influenced by fear, necessity or self-interest, generally enter into some composition with the inhabitants, and return with only a small part of what was demanded, and with the troops much harassed and out of condition.

"This is the usual consequence attending this method of raising contributions, while, on the other hand, that which I have been proposing, cannot fail of success.

"In order, moreover, to render the payment as easy as possible to the inhabitants, they must only be required to make it monthly, in such shares and proportions as the commander in chief shall appoint; in consequence of which indulgence, added to their apprehensions of having their habitations burnt, unless they comply therewith, they will assist one another and be able to advance the whole with much less inconvenience and distress; those who are at the greatest distance disposing of their properties in order to bring their respective contributions in money, and those which lie contiguous, furnishing theirs in provisions.

"These parties must either be very unfortunate indeed, or else very imprudently conducted, if they fall into the hands of the enemy; because with twenty-five or thirty men on foot, one may traverse a whole kingdom with security; when they find themselves discovered they must immediately march off the ground; for the enemy will be deterred from pursuing them far, particularly in the night-time, by the apprehension of falling into an ambuscade; a circumstance which might very well come to pass, especially when several of the parties have agreed together upon certain places of appointment to assemble at, in case of such accidents.

"Nothing can be more entertaining than these incursions, and the soldiers themselves will certainly take pleasure in them."[19]

[19] Marshal Saxe, Memoirs upon the Art of War, p. 94–97.

Requisitions older than Washington.—It has sometimes been claimed that Washington was the first to make use of requisitions. The above passage and other passages from the Memoirs of Marshal Saxe show that this could not have been so, but that contributions included contributions in kind as well as money.

Dislike for irregular troops.—The dislike for irregular troops, which has been shown in all ages by military commanders, was especially manifested during this period. In a cartel for the exchange of prisoners entered into between the Emperor Leopold and Louis XIV on May 2, 1692, it was agreed that bodies of less than fifteen horse or nineteen foot should not be allowed to go against the enemy without officers on pain of being treated as robbers;[20] and such an agreement was not uncommon. As to the use of militia, Moser says, however, that sovereigns did not hesitate to condemn and punish in others what they made no scruple of doing themselves.[21]

Dying out of ransom.—The practice of ransom died out in the eighteenth century. Hall cites the cartel of 1780 between France and England as the last instance of an agreement fixing the rates of ransom for military officers and men, and states that "since that time no prisoners have probably been ransomed except sailors captured in merchant vessels which have subsequently been released under a ransom bill."[22]

Increased care for the sick and wounded.—Beginning with the wars of Louis XIV, cartels often provided for the release of the medical and clerical staff and often of other branches of the noncombatant service without ransom, long before the practice of ransoming had been abandoned.[23] Provision was also made that money expended for the care of the sick and wounded should be repaid.[24] A notable arrangement was that entered into in 1759 between Maria Theresa and Frederick the Great, in which they agreed that the health resorts Landeck and Warmbrunn, in Silesia, and Teplitz and Carlsbad, in Bohemia,

20 Dumont, Tome, VII, Part II, p. 315.
21 Moser, Versuch, IX, p. 267.
22 Hall, Inter. Law, p. 428.
23 Hall, Inter. Law, p. 422; and see Gurlt, Krankenpflege im Kriege.
24 Gurlt, *Ibid.*, p. 17, *et seq.*

should be safeguarded.[25] Conventions providing for special protection to the sick and wounded were not uncommon.[26]

Growth of an effective public opinion.—While instances of cruelty were not lacking, the following quotation from Vattel in reference to the devastation of the Palatinate in 1674 and 1689 shows that an effective public opinion had been developed. He says: "All Europe resounded with invectives and reproaches on this manner of making war. The court vainly covered it with the design of securing its frontiers. This was an end which could be little answered by laying waste the Palatinate. It was well known to be the revenge and cruelty of a haughty and implacable minister."[27]

Vattel and Rousseau on the warfare of their time.—Such incidents seem to have been exceptional. Vattel, writing in 1758, eulogizes the conduct of warfare in his time in words which contrast vividly with those used by Grotius a century and a quarter before. In one passage, remarkable for its likeness to the famous passage of Rousseau written four years later, Vattel says: "It is against one sovereign that another makes war and not against the quiet subjects. The conqueror lays his hands on the possessions of the state, on what belongs to the public, while private persons are permitted to retain theirs. They suffer but indirectly by the war; and to them the result is that they only change masters."[28] The words of Rousseau are: "War, then, is not a relation of man to man, but a relation of state to state, in which individuals are enemies only accidentally, not as men, nor even as citizens, but as soldiers; not as members of the country, but as its defenders. Finally, each state can have for its enemies only other states and not men, seeing that between things of a diverse nature no true relation can be fixed."[29]

The statements of both were rough generalizations of the practice of their time.—Vattel was without question merely generalizing the practice of his time. He was not laying

25 *Ibid.*, p. 113, *et seq.*
26 *Ibid.*, p. 101, *et seq.*
27 Vattel, Bk. III, Chap. IX, § 167.
28 Vattel, Bk. III, Chap. XIII, § 200.
29 J. J. Rousseau, Du Contrat Social, L. I, Chap. IV.

down a philosophical principle which should serve as a basis for a law of war; nor did Rousseau consider himself to be laying down a principle which might in the future become a living principle of that law; for, after the passage that has just been quoted, he goes on to say that this principle is conformable to the practice of all civilized nations. He was merely drawing an argument against slavery from the practice of his times, and was evidently not conscious of what bearing it would have if applied in detail to the varied incidents of war.

Vattel.—Of Vattel a few words must be said; and they cannot be better said than in the language of Prof. Westlake. "Vattel," says Westlake, "was a native of the principality of Neuchâtel, then belonging to the king of Prussia, but served the elector-king, elector of Saxony and king of Poland, successively, as *conseiller d'ambassade*, minister in Switzerland, and *conseiller privé du cabinet.* His famous work was published in 1758, under the title of *Le Droit des Gens, ou principes de la loi naturelle appliqués à la conduite et aux affaires des nations et des souverains.* Its philosophical principles are those of Wolff, of whom Vattel was a great though not a servile admirer, but its chief merit is on the practical side. It presents the law of nations as it then stood with a fulness of which there had been no previous example, including the topics which had grown up since the time of Grotius or on which Grotius had not dwelt, and on which Wolff had had little or nothing to say; and it does so from the point of view of a man versed in affairs, familiar with the customs which had been taking shape since the Peace of Westphalia, and duly appreciating their value. Its reputation was therefore as well deserved as it was immediate, and it must remain of lasting importance in the study of international law, as the focus in which the schools of reason and custom were first brought together, and from which the succeeding divergences may be traced."[30]

Bynkershoek.—In striking contrast to the fascinating Vattel was the mercilessly legal Bynkershoek, who preceded him by only a few years. Bynkershoek was a Dutch lawyer and jurist, and was president of the High Council of Holland. His most important work on public law, of

[30] Westlake, Principles, p. 76.

which his Law of War was a part, was published in 1737. He was one of the clearest thinkers who have ever written on the laws of war, and his opinions on maritime warfare have had great influence on the British Admiralty Courts; but his cruel logic shows the great danger to which men removed from the actualities of war are liable. Prof. Nys declares that none even of the precursors of Grotius was as pitiless as Bynkershoek.[31]

[31] Nys, Origines, etc., p. 193.

CHAPTER V.

THE REVOLUTIONARY AND NAPOLEONIC STRUGGLES.

The change from wars of princes to wars of peoples.—The wars of which Vattel and Rousseau wrote were wars of princes. Except at sea, they were almost all that those who make the words of Rousseau their creed could desire. Probably at no other time had guerilla fighting been so scarce, or had private persons suffered less from the burdens of war. But, in making the statements above quoted, Vattel and Rousseau were historians rather than prophets. The next war of importance to follow the publication of Rousseau's work was that for American Independence; and there have been few wars since but have been strongly tinged by popular sentiment. With strong popular sentiment irregular fighting has been frequent, and with the great national armies, the burdens of private individuals have been increased many fold.

Rules said to have been laid down by Great Britain in the war for American Independence.—In the War for American Independence, G. F. de Martens says that Great Britain promulgated the following rules as recognized laws of war: "First, an army which occupies the country of an enemy may demand provisions there and levy contributions and to force the inhabitants to satisfy these demands, may resort to military execution, that is, ravage and destruction; second, when the enemy, being in his own country, finds it to his advantage to prolong the war and evade coming to action, it is permissible to ravage the country in his presence, to make him expose himself in attempting to protect the country; third, when, in war, one is not able to destroy the adverse party or to lead him to reason without reducing his country to distress, it is permitted to carry distress into his country; fourth, when the inhabitants are themselves the principal parties to the war, which happens in the case of a revolt or of a rebellion, they are themselves the principal objects of hostilities, which one is under the necessity of directing against them to attain the end of the war.'"[1]

Probably no public declaration of these rules.—Just in what way these principles were announced by the British Government is not stated. There was probably no public announcement, or it would have been noticed in the debates in Parliament where the whole conduct of the war was so vigilantly scrutinized. Possibly they were generalizations drawn from the apparent mode of its conduct.

The employment of Indian allies and the confinement of prisoners of war in prison ships.—The excesses of the Indian allies of Great Britain during the war caused the famous protest of Lord Chatham against their use;[2] and this example has ever since led publicists and statesmen to denounce the employment in war of peoples of a lower civilization whose manner of life makes it improbable that they will follow the rules of civilized warfare. The confinement of prisoners of war in prison ships, in this and the Napoleonic wars, also led to grave abuses against which The Hague Regulations provide.

The hanging of Major Andrè.—The hanging of Major Andrè as a spy has been characterized by Sir Robert Phillimore as a blot on the escutcheon of Washington,[3] but the characterization is not justified. Major Andrè's excuse for himself was that he was *"betrayed"*[4] (being adjutant general of the British army) "into the vile condition of an enemy in disguise within your posts."[5] When captured he had not regained his own lines and had on his person intelligence as to the forces, ordnance and works at West Point. There seemed to be in his own mind no question that he was technically in the position of a spy. The only plea that his friends made for him was that he had landed under a flag of truce. If this had been true, as it seems not to have been, his assumption of a disguise within the lines would have placed him in the same position as if he had been disguised from the first. However much compassion we may feel for him, the fact of his having been

1 Martens, Precis du Droit des gens, Bk. VIII, Chap. IV, § 280.
2 Hansard's Parl. Debates, Vol. XIX, 487–489.
3 Phillimore, Int. Law, Vol. III, p. 175.
4 The italics are the author's.
5 Minutes of a Court of Inquiry upon the case of Major Andrè, p. 12.

betrayed into the position of a spy does not make his hanging unjustifiable. He was engaged in completing arrangements for the subornation of a prominent American officer and the betrayal of an important American post. The circumstances as a whole, instead of mitigating the situation in which he was found, distinctly pointed to the necessity of making his fate an example to those who should seek to engage in similar enterprises in the future.

Principal effect of the Revolutionary and Napoleonic Wars on the Law of War was in connection with the Law of Conquest.—Turning again to the shores of Europe, we come on another Revolutionary War, that of the French. Its principal effect on the law of war between belligerents was in connection with the Law of Conquest, which occupied an important place in the treatises on the Law of Nations previous to the French Revolution, a place which it occupies no more. The questions discussed are as important now as they were before, but they are now treated under the head of Military Occupation, while Conquest is usually confined to the case of wars ending without treaties of peace, either through the subjugation of one of the belligerents or the mere cessation of hostilities.

The old doctrines of Conquest and Postliminium.—The old doctrine of Conquest was that territory and lands, like other forms of property, passed to the belligerent who had taken them securely into his possession. To constitute secure possession, the end of the war was not essential, the most common test of firm possession being that the territory possessed should be so guarded by permanent fortifications as to necessitate taking them to repossess the land.[6] Thus far the rules as to the taking of all kinds of property were alike. With regard to territory and land, however, the theory of conquest was profoundly modified by the doctrine of Postliminium, which was based on the old Roman doctrine from which it derived its name. According to the doctrine of Postliminium, the recovery of territory before the conclusion of peace, or its reconveyance under the treaty of peace, reestablished as far as possible the legal and political relations existing before the conquest. Grants of land made in the meantime were rendered null; debts discharged by the conqueror were re-

[6] Grotius, III, 6, 41; Bynkershoek, p. 45.

vived, except insofar as there had been actual compulsory payment; and in general the condition of things preceding the conquest was restored. Furthermore, it was immaterial whether it was the subject of an enemy who had benefited in the meantime, or the subject of a neutral power, or even a neutral power itself. An enemy or the subject of an enemy could give no better right than he himself had, and the right he had in the property taken was subject to the right of the enemy to retake it at any time before the conclusion of hostilities. This right to retake territory and lands was a different right from that to retake movables. They in general became the absolute property of the captor and could be disposed of in the same way as property originally his. A third party got good title to them, even as against the original owner, and his acceptance of them involved no breach of his neutrality. But the acceptance of conquered territory during war was a different matter. It involved cooperation with the conqueror, in depriving the original holder of his property and so was a distinctly hostile act. In the few cases where conquered territory was transferred before the conquest had been confirmed by a treaty of peace, war actually followed, or it was expected at the time of the transfer that it would.

The doctrine of Postliminium prevented the conqueror becoming the definitive owner of territory seized by him till the conclusion of hostilities.—So far as the alienation of conquered territory went, then the conqueror was not its definitive owner till the conclusion of hostilities. He had merely a possessory right, good as against third parties. This was early recognized by the jurists. Pufendorf said: "It is to be observed that the Right to Acquisitions of War is of Force only against any third disinterested Party. But to give the Conqueror a Right of Propriety that will hold good against the Conquered there must of Necessity be a Pacification and Agreement between both the parties, otherwise the Right is supposed to continue still in the old Proprietor, and whenever he is strong enough he may justly struggle to recover it."[7]

So Vattel: "Immovables, lands, towns, provinces, etc., pass under the power of the enemy who makes himself master of them; but it is only by the treaty of peace or

[7] Pufendorf, De Jure Naturae et Gentium, VIII, 6, 20.

the entire submission and extinction of the state, to which these towns and provinces belonged, that the acquisition is completed, and the property becomes stable and perfect.

"Thus a third party cannot safely purchase a conquered place or province till the sovereign from whom it was taken has by a treaty of peace renounced it, or being irrecoverably reduced, has forfeited its sovereignty; for while the war continues, while the sovereign has still hopes of recovering his possessions by arms, is a neutral prince to come and deprive him of such liberty by purchasing of the conqueror this place or province? The first proprietor cannot forfeit his rights by the action of a third person, and if the purchaser is for maintaining his purchase, he will find himself engaged in a war. Thus the king of Prussia put himself among the enemies of Sweden, by receiving Stettin from the hands of the king of Poland and the Czar, under the title of sequestration."[8]

The case of the transfer of territory seized in war to a third party before the conclusion of hostilities seems not to have occurred to Grotius.—This solution of the question as to territory transferred to a third party during war does not appear to have occurred to Grotius, although as arrived at by his successors, it would seem logically to follow from what he laid down on the subject of Postliminium.[9] Perhaps it was suggested to Pufendorf by the sale of Dunkirk by Charles II to Louis XIV in 1662.[10] Dunkirk had been taken by England from Spain a few years before, but the death of Cromwell had prevented the conclusion of a treaty of peace confirming the English possession; and on the Restoration, Spain had resumed peaceful relations with England with only a formal protest against Dunkirk's retention.[11] In the treaty of sale, however, elaborate provision was made against the possible attempt of Spain to retake the place;[12] and one of the main reasons given for Louis' insistence that no higher price should be paid was the imperfect title of the English, resting as it did on the Rights of Arms alone, unfortified by Treaty.[13]

[8] Vattel, Bk. III, Chap. XIII, §§ 197, 198.
[9] Grotius, III, 9, 6, 2.
[10] Comte d' Estrades, Lettrès, Memoires et Negociations, I, 346.
[11] The Life of Edward, Earl of Clarendon, I, p. 503, *et seq.*
[12] Dumont, Tome VI, Part II, p. 432.
[13] Comte d'Estrades, Lettrès, etc., I, 346.

The sale attracted a great deal of attention, and could hardly have failed to receive the careful consideration of Pufendorf. Possibly, if a similar circumstance had occurred earlier, it would have called Grotius' attention to the possessory nature of the right of the conqueror and caused him to give the great weight of his authority to some doctrine more nearly resembling the modern doctrine of Military Occupation than did the doctrine of defeasible title, which he taught.

As a principle of property law the doctrine of Conquest and Postliminium was exceedingly cumbersome.—In the light of what Pufendorf and Vattel said, it would seem strange that the old doctrine of defeasible title continued to survive but for the fact that the relation of the conqueror to the inhabitants was involved in it, as well as the relation of the conqueror to the territory. As a principle of property law, it was bad; but, as a principle requiring the general recognition of the authority of the conqueror, it had many advantages.

But on the other hand it supplied the need for some recognized authority in occupied territory.—The need of some recognized authority in a country occupied by an enemy is apparent. Without authority there can be little law, and without law the life of a highly developed community must be paralyzed. But, the recognition of authority implies the duty of obedience, and what duty of obedience is there towards an enemy? The answer is by no means easy. It was avoided by the doctrine of defeasible title, for with title went sovereignty, and with sovereignty protection; and, in return for protection, the inhabitants owed allegiance. The whole theory was simple and clear, and, as it was of daily use in making plain to the inhabitants of conquered territory their duty to the conqueror, while on the other hand the alienation of conquered territory was exceedingly rare, it is not surprising that the doctrine of defeasible title continued to be maintained.

The change of allegiance of the inhabitants of firmly occupied territory during war was well settled.—The doctrine that allegiance changed on conquest and that conquest could take place before the cessation of hostilities was well settled. Thus, Pothier, writing shortly before the French Revolution, affirmed that the inhabitants of conquered territory became French citizens from the moment of conquest, but that they were restored to the condition of aliens by the handing back of the territory by the treaty of peace.[14] This doctrine of change of allegiance had, however, certain unfortunate results. It sanctioned both the exaction of an oath of allegiance to the conqueror and compulsory service in his army; and we accordingly find that oaths of allegiance and military service both were required of the inhabitants of occupied territory during the period of Frederick the Great. These things seemed so natural to G. F. de Martens, the first edition of whose work appeared in 1788, that he referred to them as instances of the moderation of conquerors rather than of their severity.[15]

Work of Prof. Lameire.—Within the last few years we have had the privilege of observing the workings of the old law of Conquest in great detail in the interesting studies of Irénée Lameire, Professor of the History of Public Law in the University of Lyons. He depreciates the practical importance of the Law of Postliminium, and well he may in the fields on which he has shed so much light. As between the conqueror and the inhabitants it had very little application. The effects of conquest, even perfected by treaty, except in making the inhabitants the subjects of the conqueror and as such liable to the obligations of subjects, were so slight in the eighteenth century that Professor Lameire is continually tempted to compare them with the effects of military occupation in the nineteenth century, much to the advantage of the former. What he fails to notice is that the doctrine of Postliminium was essentially a doctrine of the law of property and marked a profound difference between movables and immovables. Third parties could get good title to the former during war. They could not to the latter.

Causes that led to the modern doctrine of occupation.—Such was the state of the law at the outbreak of the French Revolution. The chief causes that led to the change in the law were the doing away with the presumption that a belligerent always had the intention to appropriate all

14 Pothier, Traité des Personnes, Titre II, Sec. 1.

15 Martens' Summary of the Law of Nations, Bk. VIII, Chap. III, Sec. 8.

the territory he could lay his hands on, and the clearer application of the principle of the *de facto* nature of the right of a belligerent to seize the debts of the subjects of his enemy in the enemy's country, to the general relations between the belligerents and the occupied country. The former was due to the disapproval of conquest by Rousseau and others; the latter, to the decision reached as to the confiscation of the debts of the Elector of Hesse-Cassel by Napoleon.

Under the old doctrine the intention to appropriate territory without limit had been presumed.—Under the doctrine of the defeasible title, the intention to appropriate territory seized was always presumed. Bynkershoek went so far as to say: "The intention of the conqueror is not merely to invade one district, but the whole of the hostile empire, and to make his own all the countries belonging to it."[16] Practice was in accord with this view. Princes desired land, as they did other property, in order to enlarge their estates; and it mattered little whether the territory was fitted to form part of the national domain or whether the inhabitants were fitted to become members of the conquering state.

This presumption was shattered by the French Revolution.—This presumption the French Revolution shattered. Pufendorf and Locke had already preached the doctrine that might could not make right. Rousseau followed them and burned into the consciousness of the French nation the fact that the so-called right of conquest was only the law of the strongest. The revolutionary leaders proclaimed this view with characteristic fervor and embodied a renunciation of wars of conquest in the Constitution of 1791.[17] As a result of this renunciation, territory which would formerly have become a part of France by the fact of seizure did not become so until definitely incorporated.

This change in the law reflected in a decision of the Court of Cassation in 1818.—This change in the law is reflected in a decision of the French Court of Cassation in 1818. A person was held for trial before one of the French courts of assize for the assassination of a Catalan, in Catalonia, Spain, in 1811, on the ground that as Catalonia was

16 Bynkershoek, Law of War, p. 48.
17 Title VI.

then occupied by the French forces and administered by French authorities it was to be considered a French territory. The Court of Cassation, on appeal, rejected this view, holding that "this occupation and this administration by the French troops and authorities had not communicated to the inhabitants of Catalonia the title of French, nor to their territory the quality of French territory; that such communication could only have resulted from an act of union emanating from the public authority, which act had never existed."[18] In other words, the law as stated by Pothier, had been reversed.

The confiscation of the debts and domains of the Elector of Hesse-Cassel by Napoleon gave rise to a decision of similar tenor by one of the German Universities.—Another influential decision of the same tenor was rendered by one of the German Universities, on the question of the lawfulness of the confiscation of certain domains and debts of the Elector of Hesse-Cassel by Napoleon. It brought out, more clearly than had hitherto been done, the profound modification of the doctrine of Conquest by that of Postliminium; distinguished between the permanent conqueror and "the mere transient conqueror;" and ascribed to the acts of the latter the mere *de facto* effect which had always been exemplified in the confiscation of debts in territory the title to which had not been perfected by the cessation of hostilities. Confiscation of debts by "a transient conqueror" had always been considered valid, but only to the extent of actual payment made under compulsion. A mere release of the debt, which would have been sufficient if the conqueror had been considered the legal successor of the power he had dispossessed, was always considered a nullity. Bynkershoek, the great expositor of the doctrine of defeasible title, was led by this consideration to say that the "occupation which is had in war consists more in fact than in law."[19]

In accordance with this principle, the German University, which delivered the final judgment, "rightly said that the real question was, whether Napoleon had, or had not, become the true creditor of the Hesse-Cassel funds. They drew a broad distinction between the validity of acts done

[18] Ortolan, Diplomatie de la Mer, I, 291–292.
[19] Bynkershoek, Law of War, p. 56.

by a mere transient conqueror and acts done by him after the kingdom had been wholly subdued, and the subjects had either expressly or by implication, accepted him as their ruler.

"In the former case the Conqueror's right was confined to the effect of his private acts, to the *occupatio bellica,* and required actual seizure and possession for its valid exercise.

"In the latter case the rights and title of the Conqueror had been ratified by the Public Act of the State." Napoleon's case,[20] they decided, was one of the latter kind.

Changes which made the old doctrine of defeasible title unnatural even to the lay mind.—These two decisions brought with great clearness to the juristic mind the essentially temporary and provisional character of the right of a belligerent during hostilities over occupied territory. But there were yet other forces at work that made the passage of title during war seem unnatural and odious even to the lay mind, and these were (1) the change in the conditions of warfare and (2) the growth of national sentiment.

The change in military science.—Warfare itself had changed. The immense armies of the Revolution rendered it possible to strike blows directly at the source of the enemy's power and to dictate terms of peace at his capital. This made the terms of peace all-important and the military events important only as leading up to them, whereas formerly the treaty of peace had been important mainly as confirming the changes brought about by the war itself. The object of campaigns had been the seizure of small coveted provinces,[21] and once taken they were not liable to be retaken or restored. But, henceforth, what was taken was not so important as what was retained. Whole countries passed under the control of the French armies, to be handed back by the treaty of peace, so that it became more natural to treat military occupation as effecting a temporary change which might become permanent than as effecting a permanent change which events might prove to be only temporary.

The growth of national sentiment.—The growth of national sentiment had a similar effect. No matter how satisfactory in theory may have been the old doctrine that

20 Phillimore, Inter. Law, III, 846.

21 Jomini, Art of War, p. 150.

the conqueror had the right to require an oath of allegiance and military service from the conquered, it must always have been galling to the loyal subject of a worthy sovereign, and it became absolutely intolerable when conceptions of voluntary allegiance and national patriotism, took the place of the old feudal ideas of reciprocal protection and obedience. The individual was no longer the involuntary subject of the lord of the soil. His loyalty was based on an intelligent and voluntary adherence to a fatherland, of which he was a member, and to which he was attached by all the ties of kinship, language and association. This new patriotism was perhaps never higher than at the close of the Napoleonic wars. It made the continuance of the old doctrine as to the rights of the conqueror impossible, and rendered inevitable the rule which has since been accepted without question, that as long as hostilities last it is illegal to demand from the inhabitants of occupied territory either oaths of allegiance or military service.

The changes find scientific expression in the work of Heffter.—The changes in conditions and in thought thus brought about found scientific expression in 1844 in the work of the constructive German jurist, Heffter, who discarded the old doctrine of Conquest, and demonstrated the provisional nature of the rights of a belligerent over occupied territory till the conclusion of hostilities.[22] Since then, such rights have been classified and discussed under the technical head of Military Occupation, which has come to be treated more and more in detail, while Conquest and Postliminium have sunk to a position of insignificance. Conquests are still effected, but only where, because the enemy's power is annihilated, or for some other reason, hostilities end without a treaty of peace.

Survival of the old doctrines in dicta of the Supreme Court.—Traces of the old doctrine, however, survive in *dicta* of the Supreme Court in the cases of *United States v. Rice*[23] and *Fleming v. Page*.[24] The actual decision in neither case can be shaken; but in the former case Mr. Justice Story, in discussing the subject of Conquest, made certain

22 Heffter, Le Droit Inter. Public, Secs. 132–133.
23 4 Wheaton, 246.
24 9 Howard, 603.

sweeping statements which left out of account the essential limitations imposed on conquest by the law of Postliminium, and these statements Chief Justice Taney repeated in *Fleming v. Page.* But, while Chief Justice Taney considered the title of the United States to Tampico to be good, according to the law of nations, in consequence of the mere occupation of the place by the American forces, yet he rejected, on principles of constitutional law, the contention that it had become American territory. The modern doctrine had been stated by Chief Justice Marshall, in 1828, in the case of the *American Insurance Company v. Canter,* in which he said: "The usage of the world is, if a nation be not entirely subdued, to consider the holding of conquered territory as a mere military occupation, until its fate shall be determined at the treaty of peace. If it be ceded by the treaty, the acquisition is confirmed, and the ceded territory becomes a part of "the nation to which it is annexed.""[25]

Seizure of art treasures—by Napoleon.—The influence of France on the change from the doctrine of Conquest to that of Military Occupation was her most important contribution to the law of war between belligerents during the Revolutionary and Napoleonic Wars. On the other hand, some of Napoleon's acts tended to create fixed international sentiment by the disapprobation they provoked, as in the case of his seizure of art treasures of the different countries which he occupied.

Prior to Napoleon.—Prior to the Renaissance the seizure of art treasures by the various Italian cities seems not to have been uncommon, and while the Renaissance seems to have inaugurated a better era among the Italians themselves,[26] its effect was not so marked or at least was felt later in the conduct of the earlier French invaders of Italy. Charles VIII and Louis XII both seized notable libraries, and circumstances alone prevented their taking other treasures as well.[27] Francis I, however, abstained from such action, much as he coveted works of art,[28] and there were

25 1 Peters, 542.

26 Eug. Müntz, Les Annexions de Collections d'Art ou de Bibliotheques et Leur Role dans les Relations Internationales, VIII Revue d'Histoire Diplomatique, 487.

27 *Ibid.*, 488.

28 *Ibid.*, 492.

few subsequent examples of the seizure of art treasures by the French kings.[29] A notable case in the Thirty Years' War was the seizure of the library of the Elector Palatine, in 1622, and the subsequent sending of the books to Rome,[30] but this act aroused the indignation of Gustavus Adolphus, and was made the subject of reprisals in kind by him.[31] During the eighteenth century the spoliation of art museums and libraries had fallen into desuetude.[32] The public archives were not always safe, especially where a claimant to a disputed province wished to secure his position by deeds of title. Professor Nys gives two instances of the seizure of title deeds and similar documents, one by Louis XIV, in 1678, the other by his successor, in 1747,[33] but in each case the seizure was contrary to express stipulations in capitulations and can hardly be given as instances of what was then considered correct practice.

Heavy burden of Napoleon's armies.—During the days of the French convention, the war threatened to take on the bloody aspect of the Reign of Terror, but, says Mountague Bernard, "the sanguinary decrees of the Convention, which directed that no quarter should be given to English or Hanoverians and that neutral sailors found on board of British ships should be put to the sword, were execrated and disobeyed."[34] Perhaps the heaviest burden of the subsequent war was due to the extended use of requisitions to support the immense forces which Napoleon kept under arms. They were largely responsible for the uprisings that caused his downfall.

Burning of the public buildings at Washington.—In this relation, the incident of chief importance in the war of 1812, between Great Britain and the United States, was the burning of the public buildings at Washington. Otherwise, especially in the respect shown for private property, the conduct of the British commanders was generally commendable, and it is hard to determine on just what principle they acted at Washington. Admiral Cockburn, in his

29 *Ibid.*, 494.

30 *Ibid.*

31 Harte, II Gustavus Adolphus, 65.

32 Müntz, IX R. H. D., 375.

33 III Nys, 314.

34 Bernard, the Growth of Laws and Usages of War, p. 112 and p. 134.

report, excused the burning of the Capitol as an act of reprisal for shots fired from it,[35] but General Ross made no such explanation,[36] and for the burning of the public buildings other than the Capitol no excuse at all was offered. Afterwards, when the burning of the buildings had been the subject of so much censure, the attempt was made to justify it as an act of retaliation for the alleged burning of the public buildings at York (now Toronto) by the Americans earlier in the war; but there was clearly no such idea in the mind of either Admiral Cockburn or General Ross at the time. That old score had been wiped out, and the reprisals which Admiral Cochrane threatened to make soon afterwards were for an entirely different cause.[37] The orders that Admiral Cochrane issued were directed to the naval forces alone, and had nothing to do with the expedition against Washington under General Ross.[38] The burning of the buildings was almost universally condemned, and there has since been no question that the rights of a belligerent over the nonmilitary immovable property of his enemy do not extend to its destruction. In considering the burning of Washington, however, it is only fair to mention the remark of an English writer, that the public buildings at that time were comparatively insignificant, the Capitol being the only one of any considerable architectural pretension.[39]

35 James, History of the War in America, II, 494.
36 *Ibid.*, p. 497.
37 Henry Adams, History of the United States, IX, 125.
38 *Ibid.*, p. 128.
39 Gleig, Campaigns at Washington, p. 138.

CHAPTER VI.

THE PERIOD OF PEACE AND THE DECLARATION OF PARIS.

Changes wrought during the period of peace.—The exhausting wars of the Napoleonic period were succeeded by almost forty years of peace. The great inventions were followed by an industrial revolution, and this, with the spread of the doctrines of free trade and the brotherhood of man, led to ideas of a world-economy and world-peace that found expression in the great International Exposition of 1851. The condition of society at that time was well described by Mountague Bernard, who, writing in 1856, said:

"Forty years of peace, during which the inventive and constructive faculties have been stimulated to the utmost, have altered the face of society, and the change has been such as to make the contrast sharper and the plunge more abrupt. We live in times not of excessive luxury, but of elaborate comfort and ease, of order in things great and small, of vast mechanical enterprises, diffused though superficial knowledge, fluent benevolence, and tolerably active charity. We have attained remarkable success in avoiding and putting out of sight all that would hurt the bodily senses or distress the mind. The current of thought among good men and their disciples and imitators sets in the direction of social improvement. The prejudices and antipathies of race are smoothed down, the ties of country and of home weakened; and we have accustomed ourselves to divide society into classes rather than into peoples, and to study the component strata more than the superficial plan. At the same time the extension of trade has knit closer the mutual dependence of nations, so that the stoppage of a single avenue of intercourse, the smallest rise in the price of any necessary article, is felt with electric rapidity in places most remote from each other. As all these things seemed to remove indefinitely the danger of war, so it was reasonable to expect that they would modify its character when it came."[1]

[1] Bernard, The Growth of Laws and Usages of War, p. 88.

Find expression in the Declaration of Paris.—And so they did. The desire for improvement found expression in the four articles of the Declaration of Paris of 1856, which embodied the principles which the allied powers had followed during the war with Russia. They mark the most important modification of the laws of war that has ever resulted from convention. The four articles are:

1. *Privateering is and remains abolished.*

2. *The neutral flag covers enemy's goods, with the exception of contraband of war.*

3. *Neutral goods, with the exception of contraband of war, are not liable to capture under the enemy's flag.*

4. *Blockades in order to be binding, must be effective, that is to say, must be maintained by a force sufficient really to prevent access to the coast of the enemy.*

The last three articles concern neutrals primarily; but the relation of the second to the general abolition of the capture of private property at sea, as well as the insistence of Great Britain that the first and second articles should only be considered together, necessitates the examination of the Declaration as a whole, and of the first two articles in particular, in some detail.

The Congress of Paris.—The Declaration was the work of the Congress of Paris, composed of representatives of Austria, France, Great Britain, Prussia, Russia, Sardinia, and Turkey, who had assembled to arrange terms of peace at the end of the Crimean War. Count Walewski, the French representative, considered the time opportune for a declaration of principles of maritime warfare, and on April 8, 1856, proposed the four articles above mentioned.[2] Lord Clarendon immediately announced the willingness of the British Government to accept them, on condition that the first two articles should be inseparable;[3] and at the following meeting of the Congress the other representatives announced the adhesion of their governments.[4] On April 16, the representatives of all the seven powers signed the Declaration, with the understanding that no signatory or adhering government should ever enter into an arrangement,

[2] British and Foreign State Papers, Vol. XLVI, p. 125.

[3] *Ibid.*, p. 128.

[4] *Ibid.*, p. 133.

involving the rights of neutrals, that did not rest on all the four principles.[5]

The change in the attitude of Great Britain.—The Declaration marked a revolution in the maritime policy of Great Britain. Hitherto, she had insisted on her right to seize enemy property on the high seas, whether found in neutral bottoms or not, and had combated the doctrine of free ships, free goods, as designed to cripple her power at sea by allowing enemy commerce to be carried on in neutral bottoms without molestation. Therefore, in adopting the second article, she accepted the very principle which she had so long opposed. The reason for the change of policy was explained in Parliament by Lord Clarendon, who, while holding the post of Secretary of State for Foreign Affairs, had represented his government at the Congress. "It was evidently impossible," declared his Lordship, "that we should revert to our former policy—the great changes which had taken place in our commercial policy forbade that we should ever have recourse to that policy again. The Government therefore thought that it would be wise and politic and expedient that when we were under no compulsion and our motives could not be misunderstood, we should make the declaration we have made, that we will not recede but will abide by what we have done in the hope that we should thereby mitigate the evils of war and produce a friendly feeling among the nations of the earth."[6]

At another time he said:

"It has been, and still is, the great object of modern civilization to mitigate the miseries of war, and to define and extend the rights of neutrals. This has been done with respect to war by land, but not with respect to war by sea. By land we should think it disgraceful to seize the property of neutral and peaceful persons even subjects of the enemy; but that is not the case by sea; and we even give licenses to buccaneers to seize the property of peaceful merchants on the ocean. There is no assignable reason for this difference, except, perhaps, that the acts committed by sea are less under observation than those committed on land, and the force of opinion is, consequently, less

[5] *Ibid.*, p. 137.

[6] Hansard's Parliamentary Debates, Third Series, Vol. CXLII, column 498.

brought to bear on the former. The present state of the maritime war shows, indeed, but little improvement upon the customs of the most barbarous ages.'"[7]

England was acting on the principle that the capture of private property at sea might well be done away with altogether.—Evidently the British government was acting on the belief that the capture of private property at sea might well be done away with altogether; and Lord Palmerston, then Prime Minister, even expressed himself to that effect in his Liverpool Address of November 7, 1856.[8]

The position of the United States.—The United States, with other nonsignatory governments, was asked to accede to the Declaration. Secretary Marcy expressed the willingness of the United States to adhere, but only on condition that the first article be so amended as to exempt all private property at sea from capture, except in case of contraband or of blockade. He stated that the United States, with her small regular navy, would not feel able to agree to the abolition of privateering, unless the occasion for privateering, the capture of private property at sea, were also done away with.[9] The success of this proposal seemed likely. Lord Palmerston and Lord Clarendon might be expected to favor it; Russia even intimated a desire to take the initiative; and France, Piedmont and Holland also expressed their approval;[10] but, before the proposed amendment was acted on, a change of administration placed Mr. Buchanan in the Presidential chair, and the negotiations were by him suspended, as some conjectured, in order to widen the amendment so as to include a prohibition of commercial blockades. But the negotiations were, in fact, dropped.[11]

There is little likelihood that even the nonsignatory powers will fail to respect all the rules laid down in the Declaration.—Spain and Mexico were the two principal powers, besides the United States, to withhold their adherence to the Declaration, but at the Second Peace Conference they also adhered. In the wars in which the United States

7 *Ibid.*, 490.

8 Aegidi und Klauhold-Frei Schiff unter Feindes Flagge, p. 25.

9 Mr. Marcy to Count de Sartigés, Sen. Ex. Doc., 104, 34th Cong., 1st Sess.

10 Laveleye in the Revue de Droit International VII, pp. 569–570.

11 Stark, The Abolition of Privateering and The Declaration of Paris, p. 151.

is engaged the Declaration is not binding, but, as to the second, third and fourth articles, this fact is of no practical importance, since they are all now recognized as principles of international law. The question of privateering is more doubtful, but it has not since assumed a serious practical aspect. President Lincoln was authorized to commission privateers during the Civil War,[12] but he forbore to do so; and although a few commissions were issued by the Confederacy, the results were unimportant, the great damage done to Northern commerce being inflicted by the regularly commissioned Confederate cruisers.[13] On the outbreak of the war with Spain, the United States declared it to be her policy not to resort to privateering, and although Spain reserved the right to do so she did not afterwards avail herself of the reservation.[14]

Early efforts to secure the exemption of private property at sea from capture.—The effort made in connection with the Declaration of Paris to abolish not only privateering but also the capture of private property at sea, was not wholly new. About the middle of the eighteenth century the Abbe Mably had lamented the difference in treatment of private property at sea from that on land[15] and towards the end of the century the distinguished Italian jurists, Galiani[16] and Azuni,[17] had followed his example.

The views of Benjamin Franklin.—Similar views were held by Benjamin Franklin, and he sought to embody them in the Treaty of Peace of 1783 between Great Britain and the United States. In a letter to Richard Oswald, the British Commissioner, reducing his views to writing, he said:

"It is for the interest of humanity in general that the occasions of war and the inducements to it should be diminished.

"If rapine is abolished, one of the encouragements of war is taken away, and peace therefore more likely to continue and be lasting.

12 Wharton, Inter. Law Digest, III, p. 491.

13 Dana's Wheaton, p. 456.

14 J. B. Moore—Maritime Law in the War with Spain—Naval War College—Inter. Law Solutions, 1901—pp. 150–151.

15 Mably, Le Droit Public de L'Europe, II, 407.

16 Galiani, Recht der Neutralität (trans. Cäsar), II, 218, *et seq.*

17 Azuni, The Maritime Law of Europe, II, 232.

"The practice of robbing merchants on the high seas, a remnant of the ancient piracy, though it may be accidentally beneficial to particular persons, is far from being profitable to all engaged in it, or to the nation that authorizes it. In the beginning of a war some rich ships, not upon their guard, are surprised and taken. This encourages the first adventurers to fit out more armed vessels, and many others to do the same. But the enemy at the same time become more careful, arm their merchant ships better, and render them not so easy to be taken; they go also more under protection of convoys; thus, while the privateers to take them are multiplied, the vessels subject to be taken; and the chances of profit are diminished, so that many cruises are made wherein the expenses overgo the gains, and, as is the case in other lotteries, though particulars have got prizes, the mass of adventurers are losers, the whole expense of fitting out all the privateers, during a war, being much greater than the whole amount of goods taken. Then there is the national loss of all the labor of so many men during the time they have been employed in robbing; who, besides, spend what they get in riot, drunkenness and debauchery, lose their habits of industry, are rarely fit for any sober business after a peace, and serve only to increase the number of highwaymen and housebreakers. Even the undertakers who have been fortunate are by sudden wealth led into expensive living, the habit of which continues when the means of supporting it ceases, and finally ruins them; a just punishment for their having wantonly and unfeelingly ruined many honest, innocent traders and their families, whose subsistence was employed in serving the common interests of mankind."[18]

Article proposed by Franklin for the Treaty of Peace between Great Britain and the United States.—Accordingly, Franklin proposed the following article: "If war should hereafter arise between Great Britain and the United States, which God forbid, the merchants of either country then residing in the other shall be allowed to remain nine months to collect their debts and settle their affairs, and may depart freely, carrying off all their effects without molestation or hindrance. And all fisherman, all cultivators

[18] Works of Benjamin Franklin (Bigelow), Vol. VIII, pp. 246–247.

of the earth, and all artisans or manufacturers unarmed, and inhabiting unfortified towns, villages or places, who labor for the common subsistence and benefit of mankind, and peaceably follow their respective employments, shall be allowed to continue the same, and shall not be molested by the armed force of the enemy in whose power by the events of war they may happen to fall; but, if anything is necessary to be taken from them, for the use of such armed force, the same shall be paid for at a reasonable price. And all merchants or traders with their unarmed vessels, employed in commerce, exchanging the products of different places, and thereby rendering the necessaries, conveniences, and comforts of human life more easy to obtain and more general, shall be allowed to pass freely unmolested. And neither of the powers, parties to this treaty, shall grant or issue any commission to any private armed vessels, empowering them to take or destroy such trading ships, or interrupt such commerce.''[19]

Its embodiment in the Treaty with Prussia.—This article was not included in the treaty with Great Britain, but almost its exact counterpart was embodied, as Article XXIII in the Treaty of Amity and Commerce of 1785, which Franklin negotiated with Frederick the Great. In 1823 the French Government announced its intention to adhere to the same principle in its expedition against Spain;[20] and President Monroe and his Secretary of State, John Quincy Adams, sought to use the occasion to bring about an international agreement to the same effect,[21] but in this they were not successful.[22]

It is not improbable that the ''psychological moment'' for effecting the reform in question through international agreement was when the Declaration of Paris was signed. At no other time have the evils of war been more palpable and its benefits less apparent. The reaction which afterwards took place is illustrated by Lord Palmerston's change of position. In 1856, as we have seen, he was ready to abolish the capture of private property at sea altogether.

19 *Ibid.*, pp. 248–249.

20 Laveleye Revue de Droit International, VII, p. 565.

21 Am. State Papers, For. Rel., V, 246.

22 Stark, The Abolition of Privateering and the Declaration of Paris, p. 41.

In 1862, in the House of Commons, he declared that his former views were immature, and that he had come to believe such abolition would be dangerous.[23] The United States, however, has continued to follow the lead of Franklin, Monroe, and Adams, and proposed at the First Peace Conference a Declaration that private property at sea should be inviolable. As the subject was not embraced in the powers of the delegates, the Declaration was not adopted, but the wish was expressed that it be referred to a future conference for consideration.[24] For the action of the Second Peace Conference the reader is referred to the account of that Conference.[25]

Dana's argument against such exemption.—That such an agreement will be reached in the near future seems unlikely, for there appears to have been a growing disinclination to forswear any of the effective means of belligerent action. Dana has perhaps best stated the argument against an agreement, in a note to Wheaton, in which he says:

"The truth is the most humane and often the most efficient part of war is that which consists in stopping the commerce and cutting off the material resources of the enemy. If cutting off our commerce with him, and his with us, cripples and embarrasses him, it must be done. Driving his general commerce from the sea, and blocking his ports to keep neutral commerce from him, must diminish his resources, and tend to coerce him. It is the least objectionable part of warfare.

"It takes no lives, sheds no blood, imperils no households; has its field on the ocean, which is a common highway; and deals only with persons and property voluntarily embarked in the chances of war, for the purpose of gain, and with the protection of insurance. War is not a game of strength between armies or fleets, nor a competition to kill the most men and sink the most vessels, but a grand national appeal to force, to secure an object deemed essential, when every other appeal has failed. The purpose of using force is to coerce your enemy to the act of justice assumed to be necessary. It is hazardous to lay down

23 Hansard's Parliamentary Debates, Third Series, CLXV, 1692.

24 Holls, The Peace Conference at The Hague, p. 306, *et seq.*

25 See *infra*, p. 188.

absolute rules in advance for all nations, under all circumstances, limiting possible means of coercion.''[26]

Hope for such exemption lies rather in international practice than in international agreement.—That the capture of private property at sea is often utterly futile can hardly be questioned. The solution of the question would seem to be to class such captures among those ''ulterior measures of government,''[27] of which Chief Justice Marshall speaks, which, not following from the fact of war itself, are only carried out when the proper political authority thinks them necessary. If, on the occasion of war, each nation should announce its intention not to avail itself of this right at all, or on condition of reciprocity, as Austria and Prussia did in 1866, or should reserve the right, as Spain did with regard to privateering in 1898, it is possible that eventually a practice of abstention would grow up that would render an agreement possible or superfluous.

26 Dana's Wheaton, p. 401.
27 United States v. Brown, 8 Cranch, 126.

CHAPTER VII.

THE CIVIL WAR IN THE UNITED STATES.

The Instructions for the Government of Armies of the United States in the Field.—The Civil War in the United States will be remembered in the annals of the Laws of War for the issuance of the Instructions for the Government of Armies of the United States in the Field, prepared by Dr. Francis Lieber and revised by a board of officers of the United States Army. The circumstances that led to their preparation are narrated by Brigadier-General George B. Davis in his work on the Elements of International Law. "The need of a positive code of instructions was," says General Davis, "severely felt during the early part of the Civil War in the United States. During the first two years of that war the Federal Government had succeeded in placing in the field armies of unexampled size, composed in great part of men taken from civil pursuits most of whom were unfamiliar with military affairs, and utterly unacquainted with the usages of war. These armies were carrying on hostile operations of every kind over a wide area, and questions of considerable intricacy and difficulty were constantly arising, which required for their decision a knowledge of international law which was not always possessed by those to whom these questions were submitted for decision. Conflicting decisions and rulings were of frequent occurrence in different armies, and at times in different parts of the same field of operation and great harm not infrequently resulted before these decisions could be reversed by competent authority.

"To remedy this difficulty, Professor Francis Lieber, an eminent jurist, who had been for many years an esteemed and honored citizen of the United States, was requested by the Secretary of War to prepare a code of instruction for the government of the armies in the field. This code while conforming to the existing usages of war on land, was to contain such modifications as were necessary to adapt those usages to the peculiar circumstances of the contest then prevailing. The rules prepared by Dr. Lieber were submitted to a board of officers, by whom they were approved and recommended for adoption. They were published in 1863, and were made obligatory upon the armies of the United States by their publication in the form of a General Order of the War Department.''[1]

They were the first comprehensive codification of the laws of war.—The Instructions were of special importance as the first comprehensive codification of the laws of war. At the Brussels Conference of 1874, the President, Baron Jomini, declared it was they that had suggested the idea of an international war code and had thus led the Russian Emperor to convoke the Conference,[2] and as the Project of Declaration adopted at Brussels served as the basis of The Hague Regulations relating to the Laws and Customs of War on Land, the historical importance of the Instructions is evident.

Their defects.—But it was a first attempt. It embodied extreme views of the rights of the military occupant over the inhabitants of occupied territory,[3] followed too closely the hard precedents of earlier wars,[4] and was in general diffuse and academic. Written by a nonmilitary man, it lacked the clearness which actual experience would have afforded, and omitted much that might have occurred to one who had seen responsible service in the field. Furthermore, it was the work of an individual and not of a collective body. The advantage of the latter in legislative work of any kind is not easily over-estimated. Prof. Holland has noticed this in connection with the drawing up of the Manual of the Laws of War of the Institute of International Law. "I was much struck," he says, "by the advantage of getting a number of competent persons to work simultaneously upon one subject, even when oral discussion of their differences of opinion was only partially possible. It was surprising to see how, when a phrase had carefully been considered for months, it was still possible for a fresh mind to make a suggestion for its amendment, which every one at once saw to be an improvement.''[5]

1 Davis, Elements of International Law, pp. 499–500.
2 Protocol 2 of Full Conf., Parl. Papers, 1875, Misc. No. 1.
3 Articles 26, 52, 82, 85.
4 Articles 36, 60.
5 Holland, Studies in International Law, p. 94.

The Confederate Act of Sequestration.—Early in the war, on August 6, 1861, the United States Congress passed an act subjecting "to seizure and forfeiture all property of every kind, used or intended to be used, in aiding, abetting or promoting the insurrection,"[6] or allowed or permitted to be so used, including slaves employed in military operations.[7] This was clearly within belligerent right at that time. Property specially adapted to such purposes when on the sea would be classed as contraband of war and confiscated even in the hands of neutrals. But exaggerated ideas of the effect of the statute appear to have been held by the Confederate authorities, who replied by the Act of Sequestration of August 30, 1861, which subjected to sequestration all property of the inhabitants of the Northern States, including debts owed to them by Southerners, in order to indemnify those aiding the Confederate States for losses incurred under any confiscation acts of the United States or of any of the States thereof.[8] This act could have been justified only as a measure of retaliation for the Federal Confiscation Act, but, as that act was within belligerent right, it furnished no excuse for the seizure of private property and especially of debts, which by this time had come to be recognized as inviolable. Mr. Blaine states that the Sequestration Act was largely responsible for the Confiscation and Captured and Abandoned Property Acts passed later in the North.[9]

The Federal Confiscation Act of July 17, 1862.—The Federal Confiscation Act of July 17, 1862, directed that proceedings *in rem* be taken against all property of those who did not cease after sixty days to aid and abet the rebellion.[10] The act was directed at private property generally and can be defended only as a retaliation for the Sequestration Act or as an exercise of sovereign power in suppressing rebellion, not as an ordinary exercise of belligerent right. As a matter of fact, however, the requirement that the proceedings for confiscation must be brought in the district or territorial court of the United States, at the

6 United States v. Klein, 13 Wallace, 130.
7 McPherson, History of the Rebellion, p. 195.
8 McPherson, p. 203.
9 Blaine, Twenty Years of Congress, I, 349.
10 McPherson, pp. 196–197.

place where the property was found, limited its operation to Northern States, or to places where the power of the United States was firmly established. As a result, the act netted only $408,008.03 into the United States Treasury. The returns of the operation of the Confederate Sequestration Act are very meagre, but from January 1, 1863, to September 30, 1864, they amounted to $6,102,070.39 in Confederate currency, equivalent to perhaps $380,000 in gold at the time of collection.[11]

The Captured and Abandoned Property Act.—Much more important was the Captured and Abandoned Property Act of March 12, 1863. It declared that all captured and abandoned property not used or intended to be used for waging or carrying on war against the United States should be turned over to agents of the Treasury, and the proceeds turned into the Treasury, subject to claim by the owner till two years after the suppression of the rebellion.[12] "The act was undoubtedly intended to apply particularly to cotton and the other staple products of the Southern States. To such products only was it in practice applied."[13] They constituted the sinews of the South, her mainstay in the war. From the sales under this act, $31,722,466.20 was realized.[14]

It was the general impression and such was the literal wording of the act that only those owners who had never given any aid or comfort to the rebellion would be entitled to claim the proceeds of the property. Accordingly few who had participated in the rebellion even though they had been pardoned, put in any claim under the Act and when, in the December Term of 1871, the Supreme Court decided that the property had not been confiscated, but had been held in trust not only for those who had been loyal, but for those who had been pardoned as well[15] the two years for presenting claims had passed. Congressional Committees have continued to make efforts to have the period for presenting claims revived, but so far unsuccessfully, so that at last accounts $10,512,007.96 was still held

11 Schwab, The Confederate States of America, p. 120.
12 13 Wallace, 130.
13 Moore, International Arbitrations, Vol. 4, p. 37–45.
14 House Report 784, 51st Congress, 1st Sess.
15 United States v. Klein, 13 Wallace, 128.

in trust by the United States Government for beneficiaries who had no means of reaching it.[16]

Treatment of private property by the federal forces.—The federal forces did not, as a rule, live off the country. One of the first to do this was General Pope. On July 18, 1862, he gave orders that his troops should, as far as possible, subsist on the country. He carefully regulated the gathering of supplies and ordered vouchers to be given for the reimbursement of loyal citizens after the war.[17] Later on there were other instances of living off the country, that of General Sherman, on his March to the Sea being the most notable. Of that march General Sherman says: "No army could have carried along sufficient food and forage for a march of three hundred miles; so that foraging in some shape was necessary. The country was sparsely settled, with no magistrates or civil authorities who could respond to requisitions, as is done in all the wars of Europe; so that this system of foraging was simply indispensable to our success."[18] Where the officer in command thought proper written certificates of the facts but no receipts were to be given.[19]

General Sherman's action at Atlanta.—General Sherman's action at Atlanta in expelling the inhabitants and destroying a good part of the town seems hard to justify. In defense of his action General Sherman said he wished all the houses for military storage and occupation; that he desired to contract the lines of defense to the narrow and vital parts of the city; that if the poor had been allowed to remain they would eventually have had to be fed, and that the continued residence of the inhabitants would have been liable to result in correspondence dangerous to the cause.[20]

The devastation of the Shenandoah Valley by General Sheridan.—Another noted incident of the war was the devastation of the Shenandoah Valley by General Sheridan. The valley had been of immeasurable value to General Lee in furnishing him with men and supplies. The raid

16 House Report 784, 51st Congress, 1st Sess.
17 Ropes, The Army under Pope, p. 174.
18 Sherman's Memoirs, Vol. II, p. 183.
19 *Ibid.*, p. 176.
20 *Ibid.*, p. 118.

was made under orders from General Grant, who, on August 16, 1864, wrote:

"If you can possibly spare a division of cavalry, send them through Loudoun County to destroy and carry off the crops, animals, negroes, and all men under fifty years of age capable of bearing arms. In this way you will get many of Mosby's men. All male citizens under fifty can fairly be held as prisoners of war, not as citizen prisoners. If not already soldiers, they will be made so the moment the rebel army gets hold of them."[21] The order was an extreme one, but aimed as it was at a population composed largely of guerillas, as Mosby's men were, it cannot be said to lack justification.

General Sheridan's views on the fundamental principles of the laws of war.—General Grant's orders were the occasion of the following comment on the part of General Sheridan:

"Hence, as I have said, I endorsed Grant's programme, for I do not hold war to mean simply that lines of men shall engage each other in battle, and material interests be ignored. This is but a duel, in which one combatant seeks the other's life; war means much more, and is far worse than this. Those who rest at home in peace and plenty see but little of the horrors attending such a duel, and even grow indifferent to them as the struggle goes on, contenting themselves with encouraging all who are able-bodied to enlist in the cause to fill up the shattered ranks as death thins them. It is another matter, however, when deprivation and suffering are brought to their own doors. Then the case appears much graver, for the loss of property weighs heavy with the most of mankind, heavier often than the sacrifices made on the field of battle. Death is popularly considered the maximum of punishment in war, but it is not; reduction to poverty brings prayers for peace more surely and more quickly than does the destruction of human life, as the selfishness of man has demonstrated in more than one great conflict."[22]

Similar views of General Sherman.—General Sherman had written in a similar strain from Savannah to General Halleck, December 24, 1864. He said:

21 Sheridan's Memoirs, Vol. I, p. 486.
22 *Ibid.*, pp., 487–488.

"I attach more importance to these deep incisions into the enemy's country, because this war differs from European wars in this particular; we are not only fighting hostile armies, but a hostile people, and must make old and young, rich and poor, feel the hard hand of war, as well as their organized armies. I know that this recent movement of mine through Georgia has had a wonderful effect in this respect. Thousands who have been deceived by their lying newspapers to believe that we were being whipped all the time now realize the truth, and have no appetite for a repetition of the same experience."[23]

The main features of the March to the Sea and of General Sheridan's action in the Shenandoah above sound criticism.—The opinions of two such generals is not to be regarded lightly. Expressions in them may undoubtedly be interpreted to justify acts which none would have more forcibly condemned than they. But in judging such expressions they can only be understood in the light of the circumstances that occasioned them. These were Sheridan's action in the Shenandoah and Sherman's March to the Sea. Any theory which would condemn the essential features of either would need strong arguments in its favor.

The resort to guerilla warfare by the Confederate authorities.—In April, 1862, the organization of Partisan Rangers was authorized by the Confederate Government,[24] although previously to that time isolated bands of men had been recognized by Confederate commanders as soldiers. Their excesses, or often the excesses committed by others under the protection of their name, gave rise to repeated correspondence on the part of the opposing generals. On July 3, 1862, when in command of the army in West Tennessee, General Grant had occasion to issue the following order:

"The system of guerilla warfare now being prosecuted by some troops organized under the authority of the so-called Southern Confederacy, and others without such authority, being so pernicious to the welfare of the community where it is carried on, and it being within the power of

23 Sherman's Memoirs, Vol. II, p. 227.

24 Official Records of the War of the Rebellion, Series IV, Vol. I, p. 1094, *et seq.*

the communities to suppress this system, it is ordered that wherever loss is sustained by the government, collections shall be made by seizure of a sufficient amount of personal property from persons in the immediate neighborhood sympathizing with the rebellion to remunerate the government for all loss and expense of collection.

"Persons acting as guerillas without organization and without uniform to distinguish them from private citizens are not entitled to treatment as prisoners of war when caught and will not receive such treatment."[25]

Its failure.—But it was not the Northern commanders alone who had cause to complain. In his report of November 26, 1863, James A. Sedden, the Confederate Secretary of War, said that their Rangers when under inefficient officers and within the Confederate lines had come to be regarded as more formidable and destructive to their own people than to the enemy.[26] Accordingly on February 17, 1864, the act organizing Partisan Rangers was repealed, permission being given the Secretary of War to except from such act companies acting within the lines of the enemy.[27] In the first of the following April, General Lee wrote to the War Department saying that he would see to the transfer of the partisans connected with his army into the regular service, but that if it were not possible to do that with Mosby's men, he would recommend the retention of that battalion as partisans. He was inclined to believe Mosby's discipline had been strict, but added:

"Experience has convinced me that it is almost impossible under the best officers even, to have discipline in these bands of partisan rangers, or to prevent them from becoming an injury instead of a benefit to the service, and even where this is accomplished, the system gives license to many deserters and marauders who assume to belong to these authorized companies and commit depredations on friend and foe alike. Another great objection to them is the bad effect upon the discipline of the army from the constant desire of the men to leave their commands and enjoy the great license allowed in these bands. With the

25 *Ibid.*, Series I, Vol. XVII, Part II, p. 69.
26 *Ibid.*, Series IV, Vol. II, p. 1003.
27 *Ibid.*, Vol. III, p. 194.

single exception mentioned, I hope the order will be issued at once, disbanding the companies and battalions serving in this department.''[28]

The general inefficiency and undesirability of guerilla warfare.—The experience of Generals Grant and Lee and of the other generals of the war seems to coincide with that of commanders in all time as to the inefficiency and undesirability of irregular troops under ordinary circumstances.

The ''Fort Pillow Massacre.''—Threats of ''no quarter'' were at times made during the war, but apparently not carried out. Notice, however, must be taken of what is known as the ''Fort Pillow Massacre.'' As over three hundred out of a total garrison of five hundred and fifty-seven men survived, it is seen that no such general slaughter could have taken place as has sometimes been claimed. Of the prisoners, two hundred and twenty-six were able to march away with their captors.[29] The rest were received on board the United States Steamer *Silver Cloud* on the following day. It is a significant fact that about half of those received on board were negroes. Considering the circumstances of the case, the number of killed does not seem extraordinary. After a stubborn resistance the garrison endeavored to escape over the bluff to a United States gunboat which was lying in the river. They did not lower the flag and the Confederate soldiers below the bluff had no means of knowing that the fort was taken till the halyards of the flag were cut by one of General Forrest's officers.[30] General Forrest seems to have acted with great promptness in bringing the firing to a close. In his official report he says that twenty minutes after the bugle had sounded the charge, firing had ceased.[31] General Sherman testifies that General Forrest was usually very kind in his treatment of prisoners on other occasions.[32] The contemporary reports of the affair must be attributed to the tremendous excitement and passion under which everyone at the time was laboring.

[28] *Ibid.*, Series I, Vol. XXXIII, p. 1252.
[29] Wyeth, Life of Gen. Forrest, p. 359.
[30] See Wyeth, Life of Gen. Forrest, and Mathes, General Forrest.
[31] Wyeth, p. 365.
[32] Memoirs, Vol. II, pp. 12–13.

Treatment of prisoners of war.—The treatment of prisoners of war left much to be regretted, but little can be gained by going into its details. Early in the war persons captured on Confederate privateers were sentenced to death as pirates, but, whether from fear of retaliation or a sense of justice, their sentence was never executed. Henceforth, persons so captured were allowed the privileges of prisoners of war, and the armies in the field in their conduct towards each other acted according to the principles of international warfare.

The Confederacy a de facto government.—An important distinction was drawn between acts done in obedience to the Confederate Government as a *de facto* government, and acts done in aid of the rebellion. The distinguishing characteristics of a *de facto* government of the type of the Confederacy, Chief Justice Chase declared to be (1), "that its existence is maintained by active military power, within the territories, and against the rightful authority of an established and lawful government; and (2), that while is exists, it must necessarily be obeyed in civil matters by private citizens who, by acts of obedience, rendered in submission to such force, do not become responsible, as wrongdoers, for those acts, though not warranted by the laws of the rightful government. * * * To the extent then, of actual supremacy, however unlawfully gained, in all matters of government within its military lines, the power of the insurgent government cannot be questioned. That supremacy did not justify acts of hostility to the United States. How far it should excuse them must be left to the lawful government upon the reestablishment of its authority. But it made obedience to its authority, in civil and local matters, not only a necessity but a duty. Without such obedience civil order is impossible."[33] So, "a contract for the payment of Confederate States treasury notes, made between parties residing within the so-called Confederate States" was enforced "in the courts of the United States, the contract having been made on a sale of property in the usual course of business, and not for the purpose of giving currency to the notes or otherwise aiding the rebellion."[34]

[33] Thorington v. Smith, 8 Wallace, 9–11.
[34] Thorington v. Smith, 8 Wallace, 1.

The United States Sanitary Commission.—One of the most hopeful features of the war was the creation of the United States Sanitary Commission, a voluntary organization, for the purposes "of inquiry and advice in respect of the sanitary interests of the United States forces." It was one of the many instances of the increased attention to the care of the troops which had commenced with the work of Miss Nightingale and the Sanitary Commission in the Crimean War.

CHAPTER VIII.

THE GENEVA CONVENTION OF 1864 AND THE DECLARATION OF ST. PETERSBURG.

The seed that developed into the Geneva Convention.—Independently, and almost simultaneously, as the result of their experiences in the Italian War of 1859, Dr. Palasciano in Italy, M. Henri Arnault in France, and M. Henri Dunant in Geneva, called attention to the need of greater care for the sick and wounded.[1] The efforts of M. Dunant bore fruit. That this was so, or at any rate that the fruit was so abundant, was largely due to the humanity, energy and diplomacy of his friend, M. Gustave Moynier. Among the names that have stood for the betterment of mankind his deserves a high place.

The work of the Geneva Society of Public Utility.—As President of the Geneva Society of Public Utility, M. Moynier set about devising ways and means for the carrying out of the ideas of M. Dunant, and as a result succeeded in gathering together at Geneva a semi-official conference of military men and doctors, about half of whom were representatives of the war departments of the different governments. The Conference sat from the 26th to the 29th of October, 1863. It decided on the creation of a network of committees of succor for the sick and wounded in all countries, and expressed the wish "that neutrality be proclaimed in time of war, by belligerent nations, for ambulances and hospitals, and that it be equally admitted in the most complete manner for the official sanitary personnel, for volunteer nurses, for the inhabitants of the country succoring the wounded, and for the wounded themselves; that some identical, distinctive sign be adopted for the sanitary corps of all the armies, or at least for the persons of the same army attached to that service; and that an identical flag be adopted in all countries for ambulances and hospitals."[2]

1 Moynier, Etude sur la Convention de Genève, p. 49, *et seq.*
2 Moynier, *Ibid.*, p. 59.

Work of the Conference of 1863.—It will be observed that the work of the Conference consisted of two parts, the decision to create Red Cross Societies and the expression of the wish for the neutralization of the sick and wounded and of the persons and property connected therewith. The one led to the Red Cross Societies, the other to the Geneva Convention of 1864, two things commonly associated but which were entirely distinct. The Convention of Geneva, which was adopted in the following year, did not extend the protection which it offered the official staff to volunteer societies. At the Conference of Brussels of 1874, it was the opinion that such protection should be so extended, and this has now been done by the Revised Convention of 1906. Into the history of the Red Cross Societies it is not the purpose of this work to go, though it might be done with great profit. The ability of the President of the International Committee at Geneva, M. Gustave Moynier, has taken the society out of the category of a mere private association and placed it in a position where it deals directly with governments.

The International Congress of 1864.—The Conference of 1863 was not diplomatic as most of its official members represented their war departments rather than their governments; but it invested the Geneva Committee with power to take steps towards the calling of a Congress which should represent the governments themselves. The committee sounded its various correspondents as to the disposition of their respective governments, and finding their answers favorable, secured the cooperation of the Swiss Federal Council, which, on June 6, 1864, addressed invitations to most of the States of Europe and America to attend an International Congress. Sixteen states, including Prussia, Spain, the United States, France, Great Britain, Italy and Norway and Sweden responded by sending delegates. The Congress met on August 8, and on August 22, 1864, a treaty was signed along the general lines of the views expressed by the Conference of the preceding year. This treaty has since become famous as the Geneva Convention.[3]

As already stated, this Convention gave no recognition to what have since become known as the Red Cross Societies, it being feared that such recognition might result

[3] Moynier, Etude sur la Convention de Genève, p. 60, *et seq.*

in interference with military operations. It, however, declared that places used exclusively for the sick and wounded should not be made the scene of hostile operations; that ambulances, or field hospitals, in actual service should be returned on the recovery of the sick and wounded in them; and that prisoners incapable of further service should be sent back, as should the medical and religious staff of the army, on the completion of the duties in which they were engaged at the time of the capture. The Convention further emphasized the obligation to care for the sick and wounded, no matter to what nation they should belong; declared that the inviolability of noncombatants should not be forfeited for sheltering the sick and wounded, but that they should be exempt from quartering and freed from a portion of the war contributions imposed. As a compliment to the Swiss Republic, the Congress chose the design of its national flag with the colors reversed, a red cross on a white field as a mark to distinguish the medical and religious personnel and the places set aside for the care of the sick and wounded.

The cordial reception given the Convention.—The reception given to the Convention was very cordial. In less than four years all Europe had adhered to it, including even Turkey, which adhered July 5, 1865. Persia was the first of the purely Asiatic nations, and Salvador the first of the American, to follow the example of those of Europe. Both signed the Convention in 1874. Salvador was followed by Bolivia, Chili and the Argentine Republic, in 1879; by Peru in 1880, and by the United States in 1882. In Asia, the example of Persia was followed by Japan, June 5, 1886; by Siam, June 29, 1895; and by China, June 29, 1904.

The significance of the Convention.—The significance of the Geneva Convention lay not in the novelty of its ideas, as most of its requirements had already come to be recognized as usages of war, but in the fact that it crystallized the intense humanitarian spirit of the age which called it into being, reacted on and helped to make more intense that spirit and preserved the expression of it for an age which seems likely to be a sterner one than that which preceded it.

Additional Articles of 1868.—The experience of the Austro-Prusian War of 1866 soon made the need of certain revisions evident. The Swiss Federal Council convoked a Congress at Geneva, which met there in October, 1868, and voted what have since been known as the Additional Articles of 1868, Nos. VI to XV of which related exclusively to maritime warfare. They never became binding through lack of unanimity in their ratification, but during the Franco-German War and the Spanish-American War, they were adopted as a *modus vivendi* pending hostilities. The articles relating to land warfare had an especial value as interpretations of the Convention of 1864.

The Declaration of St. Petersburg.—Almost simultaneously with the Additional Articles of 1868 there was drawn up the famous Declaration of St. Petersburg. Early in 1863, there was introduced into the Russian army, for the purpose of destroying caissons of ammunition, a bullet, much used in hunting the tiger and elephant in India, which was furnished with a percussion cap, and on coming into contact with hard surfaces exploded. In 1864, the Minister of War, deeming it improper that these bullets should be used against men, ordered that they should be distributed only to the under-officers of sharp-shooters, who were never to have more than ten at their disposal and were to use them with great care. Similar bullets were also in use in other countries.[4]

The use of a new explosive bullet proposed to the Russian Government in 1867.—In 1867 another explosive bullet, without the cap, but which exploded by contact with a substance even as soft as the human body, and which was shattered by such explosion—an effect which the percussion cap had not produced—was proposed to the Russian Government. General Milutine, the Minister of War, feeling that the use of such bullets would unnecessarily increase the miseries of war, proposed to the Emperor Alexander either completely to renounce the use of explosive bullets or to use only those with percussion caps which exploded only on contact with a hard substance. The idea of the Minister was approved by the Emperor, who, to give it wider application, convoked a conference of the powers at St. Petersburg.[5]

[4] Moynier, pp. 313–314.
[5] *Ibid.*, pp. 314–319.

The International Military Commission.—The International Military Commission, as the Conference called itself, included representatives of most of the European powers, and late in the session the representative of Persia also. Previous correspondence had shown a unanimous sentiment in favor of the prohibition of all explosive bullets. It was felt that a rule that merely distinguished between different varieties of them would be illusory.[6] Prussia even wanted to go further and extend the prohibition to numerous projectiles, such as chain and bar shot, which German writers, especially, had usually condemned. England and France, however, were not willing to go into any general consideration of the subject and so the matter was dropped,[7] although the request of Switzerland that inflammable bullets be included in the prohibition was acceded to. There are not the same objections to the use of explosives in shells as in bullets, and so the prohibition was confined to projectiles of less weight than four hundred grammes or fourteen ounces avoirdupois. The Declaration finally drawn up bears the date of November 4-16, 1868. It has been acceded to by most of the European States.

6 *Ibid.*, pp. 319–322.

7 Pradier-Fodere, Droit International Public, VI, pp. 935–937.

CHAPTER IX.

THE FRANCO-GERMAN WAR.

The importance of the Franco-German War in the development of the laws of war.—The Franco-German War was prolific of controversies both as to law and as to fact. Driven to desperation by the catastrophes that had befallen them, the French people, or at least individual Frenchmen, resorted to an irregular warfare which gave rise to recriminations on the part of the Germans and caused the war to assume a bitterness that made controversy inevitable. Much of the modern law of war accordingly dates from that period, and much that was not brought out directly in connection with the war was afterwards developed, especially at the Brussels Conference of 1874, as a result of the experience gained therein.

Observance of the Geneva Convention, the use of explosive bullets and the bombardment of towns.—In the Franco-German war, all the belligerents were parties to the Geneva Convention of 1864 and the St. Petersburg Declaration of 1868, and, as has been seen, they adopted the Additional Articles of 1868 as a *modus vivendi.* In the use of explosive bullets and the bombardment of undefended towns, there appears to have been little to criticise, although grave charges were made on both sides. In most cases of bombardment, previous notice was given by the German commanders, but in the bombardment of Paris this was not the case. The lack of notice at Paris was made the subject of protest by the diplomatic corps within the city[1] in answering whom Bismarck took the position that notice was not obligatory.[2] Such a position would now be untenable, except in cases of assault, by H. XXVI. The shelling of the residence portion of Paris and other towns has been condemned on account of the misery caused thereby to noncombatants, but at Brussels General Voigts-Rhetz was utterly opposed to admitting the illegality[3] of the practice

1 Archives Diplomatiques, 1871–1872, Vol. IV, p. 1340.
2 Archives Diplomatiques, 1871–1872, Vol. IV, p. 1366.
3 Protocol 2 of Committee, Parl. Papers, 1875, Misc. No. 1, p. 196.

and there is little reason to suppose a different view will be taken in the future in view of its effectiveness.

Employment of savage troops.—The question of the use of savage or semi-civilized troops has arisen frequently in recent warfare, and it did here. In his note of January 9, 1871, Bismarck gave instances of cruelties committed by the Algerian troops who formed a small part of the French army[4] and Count Chaudordy's reply was unsatisfactory.[5] Rolin-Jaequemyns, the most impartial commentator on the events of the war, condemns in severe terms their use then, as in 1859.[6] Calvo, who is inclined to be favorable to the French, on the other hand, thinks it contestable that the French Government allowed any of the improper practices to which the Africans were accustomed in their own warfare, as those who had been enrolled had come constantly in contact with French soldiers, were commanded by French officers and subject to the same discipline as the rest of the army.[7]

The francs-tireurs.—But of far more importance than the question as to whether the Algerians were entitled to the quality of soldiers was the question whether the francs-tireurs were. After the first disasters the French Government took steps to increase the strength of the army, and with this end in view authorized the organization of corps of francs-tireurs, detached bodies which should act on the flank and rear of the enemy and thus threaten his lines of communication, keep a considerable body of the enemy from the front, and annoy him generally. Where a nation is fighting a war to the death, say for national existence, guerilla fighting of this kind may be even to the highest degree commendable, but otherwise experience would seem to teach that it is very much to be deplored. The experience with the francs-tireurs seems to have been the same as that with the Partisan Rangers of the South. They were more of a scourge to friend than to foe, and were the cause of innumerable acts of irregularity done in their name and often amounting to crimes, which gave rise to strong recriminations on the part of the Germans and resulted in

[4] Archives Diplomatiques, 1871–1872, IV, p. 1322.
[5] *Ibid.*, p. 1408.
[6] Revue de Droit International, II, 659.
[7] Calvo, Le Droit International, IV, 139.

the war assuming a character of bitterness which it need never have taken on.

German proclamation as to franc-tireurs.—The following proclamation was early published by the German forces in the regions occupied by them in France:

"The commander-in-chief hereby notifies the inhabitants of the arrondissement that a prisoner to be treated as a prisoner of war ought to make good his quality as a French soldier by establishing that, by an order emanating from legal authority and addressed to his person, he has been called to the service and enrolled on the lists of a corps militarily organized by the French Government. At the same time his quality of soldier, he being a part of the active army, ought to be indicated by military and uniform insignia, inseparable and recognizable by the naked eye at rifle shot.

"The individuals who have taken up arms without having complied with the conditions above cited, will not be considered as prisoners of war. They will be judged by a council of war, and unless they have rendered themselves culpable of action which carries with it a more severe penalty, will be condemned to ten years of hard labor and detained in Germany till the expiration of the sentence."[8]

The corresponding provisions of The Hague Regulations.—The first paragraph of this proclamation covers the same ground as the first two clauses of Article I of The Hague Regulations. These are:

"The laws, rights, and duties of war apply, not only to the army, but also to militia and to corps of volunteers, which satisfy the following requirements:

"1. That of being commanded by a person responsible for his subordinates;

"2. That of having a distinctive mark, fixed and recognizable at a distance."

The German proclamation went further than The Hague Regulations would allow.—As tested by this later standard, the German proclamation certainly demanded too much. In accordance with the theory that fighting should be confined to the authorized forces of the two belligerents, it required the authorization of the French Government and a call to service from it addressed to the individual him-

[8] Revue de Droit International, II, 663.

self. Similar requirements were proposed at the Brussels Conference in 1874, but there the injustice of such requirements in a section of the country cut off from the central authorities was pointed out, and the requirement of command by a person responsible for his subordinates was adopted instead. Such person need not be a military officer, but may be any one, who, through official position or influence in the community, can be effectively held to account for the misdeeds of those under him.

The main point of controversy as to the francs-tireurs one of fact.—As to the uniforms of the francs-tireurs, Bismarck claimed that the blue blouse they wore was the national costume and that the red cross on the arm was only discernible at a short distance, and could be instantly taken off and replaced, so that it became impossible for the Prussian troops to distinguish combatants from non-combatants. The French authorities denied that any such confusion could in good faith arise,[9] so that we have on this point a square issue of fact which it is impossible for us to decide. If Bismarck's claim was correct, the Germans were justified in many of the severer measures they took later in the war, while, if the contention of the French authorities was correct, they were not. The probabilities are that the organization of the francs-tireurs was one of those measures "in the twilight zone" between what was permissible and what was not permissible, and so led to the inevitable controversies and bitterness which all such measures produce. Except in the utmost straits they should never be resorted to. The requirement that the soldier should be distinguishable as such by the naked eye at rifle shot would not be recognized today. As Hall says, with our modern guns, it would require not only a uniform but a conspicuous one.[10]

The Germans apparently did not resort to fictitious occupation.—It has sometimes been said that the Germans resorted to fictitious occupation; that they claimed the authority of the occupant where they had not the force to support it; and that the Brussels Declaration was a condemnation of their action. None of these assertions can be shown to be well founded. It is true that occupation

[9] Archives Diplomatiques, II, 436.
[10] Hall, International Law, 544.

was established by flying columns, and that one could go for miles within occupied territory without seeing a single Prussian soldier, but the test of effective occupation is the ability to suppress insurrection and not the visible presence of the occupant everywhere within the occupied territory. Subjected to this test, the German occupation was not, at any rate, shown to be ineffective, as no successful uprisings occurred.

Their conduct in this regard was not condemned by the Brussels Conference.—Nor did the Brussels Conference condemn the German action. It is probably the case that the position that General Voigts-Rhetz, the German representative at that Conference, took, was in line with the German action during the war, but it is a mistake to suppose that he contended that occupation need not be effective. He was as thoroughly in accord with the article of the Declaration requiring occupation to be effective as were the other delegates. What he objected to was the attempt to treat military occupation as analogous to blockade, and in this he was apparently right.[11]

The Germans did go too far, however, in requiring the cooperation of the inhabitants in the prevention of such acts as the escape of persons intending to join the French army from the occupied territory.—It is entirely proper to require the cooperation of the inhabitants and local authorities of occupied territory in the suppression of acts of lawlessness, even though such acts be committed with patriotic intent. It is also proper for the occupant to take measures to prevent the enemy from deriving support from the occupied territory, either in supplies or men. But it is not proper for the occupant to require the cooperation of the inhabitants in this latter case as in the former. Acts of lawlessness are directed against society itself, and it is even more to the interest of the inhabitants than to that of the occupant that they should be suppressed, while acts such as quitting the occupied territory to join the national army, do not affect society, are prompted by the highest motives, and are prohibited only because they are inimical to the interests of the occupant. To require the cooperation of the inhabitants in the suppression of such acts would do violence to every feeling of patriotism. Accordingly,

[11] See *infra*, p. 106.

requirements such as were made by the Germans, that mayors should furnish lists of persons liable to serve in the French army, so that those joining might be punished,[12] went beyond the proper bounds of the occupant's authority.

The burning of houses or villages as a penal measure is to be generally condemned.—Much complaint was caused during the war by the frequency with which the burning of houses and even of whole villages was resorted to. As punishment for the most severe offenses, it is possible that such burning may sometimes be justified, but, if there is one lesson taught by the Franco-German war and the South African war alike, it is that such a practice, instead of curing evils, makes them tenfold more virulent. Driven to desperation by the loss of all they possess, they who suffer become apostles of revenge and put new life in a struggle in which they have now no more to lose. Once entered upon, the policy of burning becomes so easy and the exasperations that prompt it become so multiplied, that until the end of the war outrage and violence are inevitable.

The placing of notables on trains to protect the trains from hostilities.—Another measure which has called forth much criticism was the use made by the Germans of notable citizens on railroad trains in order to protect them from acts of hostility. It has been claimed on analogy to the case of hostages, against whom violence cannot be used, that this was improper; but the case is quite different. The punishment of hostages would be a punitive measure while the use of citizens in this way was a preventative measure and a most effective one. Granted that the acts against the railroads were unlawful, the measure would not seem to have been an unduly harsh one. But there lay the difficulty. Such acts were not unlawful when committed by the regular forces, so that if the francs-tireurs were to be considered as regular forces, the measure was an improper one, and it was against them primarily that it was aimed. Like so many other questions of the war, it turned on whether or not the francs-tireurs were entitled to the quality of soldiers.

The provision in the German Military Penal Code as to the necessity of trials.—The Germans themselves rendered impossible the repetition by their officers of such orders

12 Archives Diplomatiques, IV, 1201.

as that of August 31, 1870, in which the commanding general declared that francs-tireurs and other individuals committing flagrant acts of hostility should be hung or shot without process,[13] by the German Military Penal Code of 1872, which provided that, for the infliction of all penalties provided for by the Code, a judicial proceeding should be necessary.[14]

Severity against persons attempting to join the French army.—Perhaps the most severe decree the Germans issued was that declaring that inhabitants of Alsace and Lorraine joining the French army should suffer the confiscation of their goods and ten years' banishment, and that absence from home for eight days without permission should be conclusive as to enrollment. This decree was published late in the war. It was condemned as excessive by the able German writer, Loening, who says that only five condemnations were enforced under it.[15] Rolin Jaequemyns criticises the decree, first, on the ground of the general odiousness of confiscation, and second, on the ground that it rendered liable to punishment those who had succeeded in making their escape from the occupied territory and had thus wiped out their offense by its successful consummation on the analogy to spying and blockade running.[16] Both criticisms appear to be sound.[17]

Treatment of persons residing in the territory of the opposing belligerent at the outbreak of war.—At the beginning of the war each government manifested a general intention to allow the subjects of the other, residing in its territory, to remain during good behavior. Measures were even taken in France to prevent the withdrawal of Germans liable to active military service. The feeling against German spies, however, soon ran so high that finally, on very short notice, all the Germans in the Department of the Seine were required to leave France or to retire south of the Loire.[18] The act was one very much to be deplored, but it was not altogether unnatural under the circumstances.

13 Archives Diplomatiques, IV, 1163.
14 Revue de Droit International, V, 83–84.
15 Revue de Droit International, V, 84, *et seq.*
16 Revue de Droit International, III, p. 516, *et seq.*
17 See *infra*, p. 303.
18 Archives Diplomatique, II, 425.

Treatment of balloonists.—The question of balloonists gave rise to much controversy. Bismarck threatened to treat them as spies, on account of the intelligence they were able to obtain, but he does not appear to have carried his threats into execution. H XXIX does not specifically cover the case of balloonists sent to obtain information, but by making the obtaining of information within the lines of the enemy *secretly,* the gist of spying it makes Bismarck's position no longer tenable.

Use of requisitions and contributions.—In providing for the army the Germans made extensive use of requisitions and contributions. Féraud-Giraud cites a report to the French Minister of Foreign Affairs in which it is stated that war contributions levied by the Germans amounted to 39,000,000 francs, the taxes collected by them to 49,000,000, and the requisitions to 327,000,000.[19]

Nor did this take into consideration the contribution of 200,000,000 francs charged to the city of Paris in the armistice of January 28.[20] The levying of these contributions and requisitions raised a great outcry in England, but the general principle involved in them has been approved by The Hague Conferences. It could never have been atacked, save through the inadmissible theory that private citizens are not to bear any of the direct burdens of war.

Treatment of French forests.—The treatment of the French forests by the German authorities has often been condemned, but, as it would appear, unjustly. The unfavorable opinion has been based on a decision in which the Court of Cassation enunciated the broad, general doctrine that large trees which nature and legislation had assimilated to the domain itself should not be cut by the occupant.[21] This was the position taken by the Austrian delegate at Brussels, but his contention that the large trees should not be cut at all was overruled,[22] and the work of the Brussels Conference in this respect was ratified at The Hague. The occupant now has the rights of a usu-

19 Féraud-Giraud, Recours à Raison des Dommages Causés par la Guerre, Sec. 32.

20 Archives Diplomatiques, IV, 1422.

21 Féraud-Giraud, Sec. 27.

22 Protocol 12 of the Committee and 4 of the Full Conference.

fructuary, and may cut such of the large trees as are marked for the purpose by the regular authorities; or, where that is impossible, he may follow any rules of good forest administration.

The German Government did not subsequently admit that it had gone beyond its rights in the treatment of the French forests.—It has sometimes been suggested that the German authorities afterwards admitted that they had gone beyond their rights, because they did not interfere to secure to the contractors wood which, though cut during the occupation, had not been carried away at its termination. But the ground of their action evidently was that the occupant is a *de facto* authority; that he has the right to appropriate some forms of public property, but has not the title thereto; and that, if his appropriation is not complete at the termination of the occupation, all his right to the property then ceases. Of course, if the occupant himself has no right to complete the appropriation of property after occupation is over, he can give no such right to a third party. Executory contracts for the exploitation of the public domain must, therefore, cease to be operative with the occupation itself.

The weight of authority shows that the Germans acted within their rights.—As the opinion adverse to the action of the Germans has been almost wholly based on the decision of the French court, the invalidating of the principle of that decision by the subsequent action at Brussels and The Hague leaves practically no authority for such opinion. On the other hand, Loening and Bluntschli,[23] both of whom, although Germans, were free in their criticism of German conduct, consider that the action of the Germans in the management of the French forests was a model of what the forest administration of an occupant should be. Loening was a professor at the University of Strasburg, and so had exceptional means of knowing the truth. He said that he had authentic information that the number of mature trees cut by the Germans was not greater than the French had planned to cut themselves, although they were not in all cases the same.[24]

Treatment of private property at sea.—Early in the war

[23] Bluntschli, Le Droit International Codifié, Sec. 646.
[24] Revue de Droit International, V, 104.

the Germans announced their intention to respect private property at sea, but there the French were the more powerful and they refused to reciprocate. On their making the captains of certain merchant ships prisoners, the German authorities resorted to reprisals and seized prominent citizens of different towns as hostages. This action of the German authorities was improper, as the legality of the French action is unquestionable.[25] The organization of a volunteer navy by Prussia gave rise to the question as to just what was meant in the Declaration of Paris by the abolition of privateering. That question is now the subject of a Convention drawn up at the Second Peace Conference.[26]

Treatment of prisoners of war.—Although there were occasional charges of the ill-treatment of prisoners of war, the care taken of them on both sides was very commendable. In Germany postal cards were distributed to the soldiers, a bureau of information was established to give information as to officers, and lists of prisoners were prepared, by order of the Minister of War. In addition private committees saw to the distribution of reading matter, and established a bureau for the forwarding of letters to the sick and wounded, and for furnishing information about them to their friends and relatives.[27]

Administration of occupied territory.—Early in the war the Germans established seats of government for Alsace at Strasburg and for Lorraine at Nancy. Then a third government was established at Versailles and finally in December a fourth at Rheims.[28] Over each division was placed a military governor-general with a civil commissioner as associate.[29] The municipalities in general continued their functions during the war, but the employees of other services generally refused to serve under the enemy, so that in the Railroad and Postoffice Departments the Germans had to take the whole administration of affairs on their own shoulders, and in levying taxes could only roughly approximate what the amount of the taxes

25 Rolin-Jaequemyns Revue de Droit International, III, 339.

26 See *infra*, p. 235.

27 Rolin-Jaequemyns, Revue de Droit International, II (1870), p. 689, *et seq.*

28 Brenet, p. 146.

29 II R. D. I., 691.

would have been. After the fall of Napoleon III the Germans, in their desire to avoid recognition of the provisional government in France, refused to permit the courts to discharge their functions except in the name of the Emperor, with the result that most of the courts declined to act; for, being required by law to exercise their powers in the name of the sovereign, they felt that Napoleon III was no longer to be considered as holding that place.[30] It is much to be regretted that the German authorities did not devise some means of enabling the courts to act in conformity with their sense of legal obligation, without appearing on their own part to recognize the provisional government.

30 Bray, Le Droit, etc., p. 311, *et seq.*

CHAPTER X.

THE CODIFICATION OF THE LAW OF WAR.

The organization of the Institute of International Law.—Not long after peace between France and Germany had been declared, Dr. Lieber, in a letter to Rolin-Jaequemyns, founder and editor-in-chief of the Revue de Droit International, suggested the organization of an institution which should include among its members the leading exponents of International Law. About the same time Gustave Moynier and Bluntschli made similar recommendations. Rolin-Jaequemyns acted on the suggestion, and in March, 1873, sent invitations to representative jurists. In September eleven of these met at Ghent and founded the Institute of International Law. M. E. de Laveleye, in a memoir which he wrote on the occasion, declared the object of the Institute to be the collective scientific investigation of the rules of justice which should seem to the members to be the rightful base of the relations of people to people.[1]

The Institute cannot have a session oftener than once a year, nor can the interval between sessions be more than two years. At each session the Institute designates the place and time of the next. It is composed of members, associates and honorary members, the members not exceeding sixty and being chosen by the Institute from among the associates.[2] The first annual meeting was held at Geneva in 1874, and meetings have since been held at The Hague (twice), Zürich, Paris (twice), Brussels (thrice), Oxford, Turin, Munich, Heidelberg, Lausanne, Hamburg, Geneva, Cambridge, Venice, Copenhagen, Neuchatel and Ghent. The office of President has been held by M. M. Mancini, of Rome; Bluntschli, of Heidelberg; de Parieu, of Paris; Rolin-Jaequemyns, of Ghent; Bernard, of Oxford, Pierantoni, of Rome; von Holzendorff, of Munich; von Bulmerincq, of Heidelberg; Rivier, of Brussels; von Bar,

[1] Holland, Studies in Inter. Law, p. 88.

[2] Annuaire, XIX, Articles II, III, IV of the statutes.

of Göttingen; Moynier, of Geneva; Renault, of Paris; Westlake, of Cambridge; Brusa, of Turin; Goos, of Copenhagen; Asser, of The Hague; Lardy, of Paris; Descamps, of Louvain; Lord Reay, of London; and Alberic Rolin, of Ghent.[3] The next meeting is to be held in Florence, in 1908, under the presidency of Gabba, of Pisa. The indirect influence of such an association must almost necessarily be even greater than its direct. The personal contact of the leaders of international juristic thought can hardly help being a powerful factor in the development of common ideas of right and duty.

First steps towards the Brussels Conference.—In March, 1874, Count de Houdetot, President of the Society for the Amelioration of the Condition of Prisoners of War, which had been formed in Paris, in 1872, communicated with the diplomatic representatives of the various countries at Paris, requesting that delegates be sent to a Conference to be held in Paris, in May, 1874, to consider means for alleviating the condition of prisoners of war and to prepare the way for an official Congress, which should formulate an international treaty. He was evidently following the course which had led successfully to the Geneva Convention.[4]

Action of the Russian Government.—Little would probably have come of this, as the Earl of Derby, then British Foreign Secretary, had determined not to take any such action on the initiative of a private society,[5] if the Russian Government had not stepped in and carried on the undertaking. Alexander II had already given orders that a project be drawn up covering practically the entire war practice on land, when the French society came forward with its scheme.[6] At the suggestion of the Russian Minister of Foreign Affairs, Count de Houdetot consented to the absorption of the project of his society into the greater one of the Russian Emperor, and the movement was thereafter carried on by the Russian Government. The project which the latter submitted was drawn up with great care and ability, beginning with a declaration of general prin-

[3] Holland, Studies, p. 89, adapted.

[4] Parl. Papers, 1874, Misc. No. 1, pp. 1–3, 17–18.

[5] *Ibid.*, p. 19.

[6] *Ibid.*, p. 21.

ciples and then proceeding to the statement of detailed rules.

Attitude of the British Government.—It was from Great Britain that the least cooperation was to be expected. The father of the Earl of Derby had been one of the leaders in the opposition to the Declaration of Paris, and, even without this personal equation the criticism to which that measure had been subjected in England was calculated to make a British official wary of assenting to any limitation of belligerent action. Before committing his government, Lord Derby sent a long despatch to Lord Loftus, at St. Petersburg, in which, while expressing his sympathy with the feelings of humanity which had moved his Imperial Majesty, he said that the British Government was not convinced of the practical necessity for such a scheme for the guidance of military commanders in the field and feared that the Conference might give rise to the discussion of questions which would lead to recriminations between the delegates. He intimated, however, that the British Government since it was desirous of joining in any measure which would prevent unnecessary suffering, would not object to the Conference, if there should be no discussion of the general principles as to the relations between belligerents and no attempt to undertake new obligations with regard to such general principles.[7] Lord Derby stated that he must require the assurance of every government that naval matters would not be discussed.[8] Such an assurance having been given, Major-General Horsford was appointed as a military delegate, Great Britain following the example of the German Empire[9] in not sending a diplomatic representation with full powers, but merely a military delegate, so that the action of the government should in no way be forestalled.[10]

Practically all Europe was represented in the Conference before the close of its sessions. The United States declined its invitation, as coming too late.[11] The first meeting was held on July 27, and Baron Jomini, the Russian

[7] *Ibid.*, p. 27.
[8] *Ibid.*, p. 28.
[9] *Ibid.*, p. 24.
[10] Parl. Papers, 1874, No. 2, p. 19.
[11] *Ibid.*, p. 8.

diplomatic delegate, and son of the famous author of the Art of War, was elected President.[12]

Rules adopted by the Conference.—At his suggestion it was agreed that only those points should be entered in the Protocol on which opinion was unanimous, and that no mention should be made of divergence of opinion, with the reservation that if a delegate should express a wish that some special position should be noted his wish should be complied with.[13] This rule was observed during the earlier discussions, in which only comparatively slight differences of view were exhibited; but, when the more controverted points came to be discussed, it was felt that, as the Conference was only preparing the way for a future agreement, it would be best to enter in the Protocols the various positions advanced so that the governments might be able to act upon the final Declaration with full knowledge of the bearings of the rules laid down.[14] It is unfortunate that this mode of procedure did not prevail from the first, as the discussions on the later points furnish an invaluable commentary on the text. That it did not was probably due to the feeling that is sometimes manifested against the publication of dissenting opinions by Supreme Court Judges, on the ground that they detract from the authority of the court and of the decision. The departure from the original procedure was, however, in one way unfortunate, in that it furnished to Lord Derby's mind indubitable proof that applications of principles not generally recognized had been introduced into the Declaration, and thus led the way to Great Britain's final refusal to ratify the acts of the Conference.[15] Another rule of the Conference was that the proceedings should be secret.[16] This was faithfully observed till within a few days of the end of the Conference, when a partial garbled account of the proceedings appeared in a French newspaper.[17]

The organization of the Conference.—It was at first proposed that two committees should be appointed, one mili-

12 Parl. Papers, 1875, Misc. No. 1, Protocol No. 1 of the Full Conference.

13 *Ibid.*

14 Protocol 12 of the Committee; Protocol 4 of the Full Conference.

15 Parl. Papers, 1875, Misc. No. 2, p. 4.

16 *Ibid.*, Misc. No. 1, Protocol 1 of the Full Conference.

17 *Ibid.*, Protocol 5 of the Full Conference and p. 157.

tary, the other diplomatic, to consider in a preliminary way the questions most appropriate to each; but the difficulty of dividing the work so as to meet the requirements of such a scheme soon became evident, and it was decided to have only one committee, composed of one delegate from each country; the military, diplomatic and juristic members of each delegation replacing each other, if desired.[18] Throughout the Conference the military element greatly predominated, although in the consideration of military occupation the diplomatic element was more largely represented than at other times. M. Lansberge, from The Netherlands, and Baron Lambermont, from Belgium, were the only diplomatic delegates who represented their countries regularly on the Committee, although Baron Jomini had a regular place on it, as chairman. The diplomatic delegates, however, by their ability and force of conviction largely overcame the advantage that the military delegates had in numbers.

Rights of members.—The members of the Conference not on the Committee had the right to attend, though not to speak or vote.[19] As they must have been consulted by the active members of the delegations, their influence is not to be estimated by the number of times their names appear in the Protocols. Dr. Bluntschli, and later Prof. Martens, were members of the Conference, and participated in the discussions during the two days when the project was before the whole Conference, but they were never members of the Committee, and took no active part in its nineteen sittings.

The original project drew a sharp line between combatants and noncombatants.—The original Russian project had defined certain conditions compliance with which would entitle persons engaging in hostilities to treatment as prisoners of war. It went further, however, and declared that persons not satisfying these conditions should be handed over to military justice.[20] The first provision standing by itself was, on the whole, not objectionable, as it merely stated affirmatively that persons of a certain kind should be treated as soldiers, without excluding anyone; but,

18 Protocol 2 of the Full Conference.
19 *Ibid.*
20 Parl. Papers, 1874, Misc. No. 1, p. 13.

coupled with the second, it created a hard and fast rule, which, if it had been in force in the past, would have handed over to military justice perhaps many of the world's greatest patriots. The attempt thus to confine war to the regular forces of the belligerents, though no doubt prompted by the highest motives of humanity, aroused the deepest opposition on the part of the delegates from Belgium and The Netherlands, who declared at the first meeting of the Committee that, while they wished to diminish as far as possible the calamities of war, they could consent to no provision having "a tendency either to weaken national defense or to detach citizens from their duty towards their country."[21] This declaration was subsequently supported by the delegates from Spain, Switzerland, Portugal and Turkey. The British delegate did not join in it, but, by abstaining from the discussion, indicated that in his opinion it concerned questions involving principles not generally recognized.

The Russian argument in favor of this.—The Russian delegates, on the other hand, earnestly urged that the apprehensions of the smaller powers were unfounded. They claimed that the project left the right of defense intact, and that its only effect was to make it the duty of each government so to organize its defenders that in time of war they could be distinguished as part of the regular military force and needless recriminations thus avoided. At the same time they argued that this was not only the duty of governments but also their interest, since it was only organization that could bring out a people's full defensive strength.[22] To the Russian delegates, as well as to the delegates of other governments which had adopted the practice of conscription, the performance of such a duty seemed a slight thing, in view of the increased efficiency it would give to national forces and the irregularities it would avoid. To them it meant practically nothing, as they already had a far more complete organization than the proposed rules would have required; but they did not reckon with the opposition that anything approaching compulsory military service would arouse in countries like Great Britain.

[21] Parl. Papers, 1875, Misc. No. 1 Protocol 1 of the Committee.
[22] Protocol 4 of the Full Conference.

As a result of the discussion the negative provisions, excluding from the category of belligerents all persons not exhibiting certain specified qualifications, was dropped. As finally drawn up, the Declaration merely enumerated certain conditions under which those in arms should be entitled to treatment as soldiers. These conditions were very liberal, and as it was expressly understood that they were not to be treated as exclusive, the final Declaration was entirely free from the objections that were urged against the original project.[23]

Treatment of military occupation.—An almost equal interest was aroused by the attempts to define occupation and to limit requisitions and contributions. Both these points are of vital importance: the definition of occupation, because on it depends the beginning and termination of the tremendous penal powers of the military occupant; the limitation of contributions and requisitions, because they constitute the heaviest burden the private citizen has to bear. On one point with regard to occupation the Conference was in entire accord, and that was that it must be effective, that is, that the occupant must have such force under his control as to suppress insurrection. The Swiss and Swedish delegates wished to make this definition more tangible by assimilating occupation to blockade, but to this the German delegate, as has been seen,[24] vigorously objected, not on the ground that occupation need not be effective, but on the ground that unlike blockades, occupation cannot be everywhere visible and that accordingly the analogy between the two is false.[25] The objection was apparently well taken. The general principle of the necessity of effective control being established, it would seem best to leave the application of the principle to the governments concerned. The sanction of the laws of war is so indefinite that it is above all necessary that the rules should not be arbitrary or technical, but that they should be simple and reasonable and thus appeal immediately to the minds and wills of the military commanders to whom their observance is entrusted.

The final limitation of contributions and requisitions to

23 Protocol 4 of the Full Conference.
24 *Supra*, p. 93.
25 Protocol 10 of the Committee.

Contributions and requisitions were the subject of much debate. It was at first attempted to limit those which the army of occupation might levy to what the army of the country occupied would have had the right to demand, or to what the occupying army would have had the right to demand in its own country, but as these limitations appeared to be impracticable and to overlook the element of military necessity they were both dropped.[26] It was further attempted to create a limitation by requiring the receipts given for money or supplies not only to certify the fact of the taking but also to promise indemnity. One objection made to this proposal was the likelihood of its giving rise to fraud; but the principal objection was that, if the receipts should be required to convey a pledge of indemnity the successful belligerent would in the end impose the burden of payment on his vanquished antagonist, who would thus be compelled to reimburse some of his subjects in full for requisitions and contributions, possibly at the cost of other subjects who had suffered loss in other ways and who were equally entitled to indemnity. It was further apprehended that, if an attempt should be made to equalize the treatment of the two classes, by a ratable diminution of what was due to both, a pretext would be afforded to the successful belligerent for interfering between the vanquished and his subjects.[27] No satisfactory conclusion was come to on this point, and it was left to the unwritten law of nations.

The attempt to abolish contributions.—The attempt was also made to do away with contributions altogether. It was urged that, while supplies might be necessary to the support of the army, there was not the same necessity for money, as the army could take what supplies it needed without payment. But it was pointed out that a rule by which supplies could be taken but not money would work greater hardship than it would avoid, by confining levies to nearby districts from which supplies could easily be transported and by casting on agricultural districts burdens which rich cities would often be better able to bear.[28]

The final limitation of contributions and requisitions to

[26] Protocol 15 and 16 of the Committee.

[27] *Ibid.*

[28] Protocol 16 of the Committee; see *infra*, p. 315.

the necessities of war.—As a result of the discussion, it was provisionally agreed that both contributions and requisitions might be levied, but that they should be limited to the necessities of the war. By those who had been most anxious to check altogether the abuses connected with contributions and requisitions, this limitation was not thought to be very substantial, but it was in fact by no means unimportant, since it rendered illegal contributions levied for the purpose of enriching the occupant, which had been one of the gravest abuses of the Napoleonic wars.

Proposed revision of the Geneva Convention.—During the course of its proceedings with only military delegates as members, the Committee also considered the question in what ways the revision of the Geneva Convention and of such of the Additional Articles as applied to warfare on land was desirable.

Notable members of the Conference.—The Conference was a singularly able body of men. Among the delegates, however, there stand out especially M. Landsberge, of The Netherlands; Baron Lambermont, of Belgium; Col. Hammer, of Switzerland, and General Voigts-Rhetz, the German delegate. The experience of the latter, acquired in the Franco-German War, made his views especially valuable. In no sense can the Conference be said to have condemned the conduct of that war. On the other hand, its results were valuable largely from the experience gained therein.

Adverse report of the British delegate.—It might have been expected that the declaration as finally drawn up would be acceptable to all the parties concerned. It was so worded that disputed points were left to the unwritten law of nations, and was so guarded by reservations that its gains could not be said to be counterbalanced by concessions. The report, however, of the British delegate, Major-General Horsford, was adverse, and it was also misleading. It conveyed an impression of disagreement as to the final result which was by no means correct, while it so seriously misconstrued the positions taken and the results reached by the larger powers on controverted points, as to lead to the conclusion that its author was so biased against the whole scheme from the beginning as to be unable to exercise towards it an impartial judgment.

The British Government refuses to ratify the work of the Conference.—In view of this circumstance and of the previous unfavorable attitude of the British Government, it is not surprising that Lord Derby refused to proceed further with the work of the Conference. In a despatch of January 20, 1875, to Lord Loftus, he said: "It, however, soon appeared, when the more important Articles of the Project came to be examined and discussed, that the attitude of reserve which Her Majesty's Government had held towards it, and the caution of the British delegate were fully justified. Instead of mere rules for the guidance of military commanders based on usages, upon which a general understanding could be shown to be desirable in the interests of humanity, the Articles of the Project were seen to contain, or to imply, numerous innovations, for which no practical necessity was proved to exist, and the result of which, if adopted, would have been greatly to the advantage of the Powers having large armies constantly prepared for war, and systems of universal compulsory military service." Lord Derby also declared that the definition of military occupation had been adopted to reconcile opposing views and would lead to recrimination, and that the same thing was true of the provisions as to belligerent character and as to requisitions and contributions. He further criticised the Declaration because the articles on Reprisals had been dropped. And in conclusion he said: "It will have been seen from the foregoing observations that Her Majesty's Government regard the result of the Brussels Conference to have been to demonstrate that there is no possibility of an agreement upon the really important Articles of the Russian Project; that the interests of the invader and the invaded are irreconcilable; and that, even if certain rules of warfare could be framed in terms which would meet with acquiescence, they would prove to exercise little more than that fictitious restraint deprecated by the Russian Government at the opening of the Conference." One cannot help feeling in reading this despatch that he is reading the argument of a man who had made up his mind from the very first.[29]

The reply of Prince Gortchacow to Lord Derby.—Prince Gortchacow made a lengthy reply. He pointed out that

[29] Parl. Papers, 1875, Misc. No. 2, pp. 2–7.

what the Conference had done was to declare that a population organized in a way falling far short of compulsory military service and observing the laws of war should be treated as belligerents, and that in no respect could it be said that the rights of defense would be weakened. He also stated that the discussions which had arisen had shown how uncertain were the laws of war, and how necessary was some general agreement upon them.[30] This closed the official correspondence. That the objections of Lord Derby were unfounded is shown by the action of the Government headed by Lord Salisbury in ratifying The Hague Convention, containing most of the provisions which Lord Derby had so severely condemned.

The Institute of International Law approves the work of the Conference.—At the Geneva meeting of the Institute of International Law, in 1874, a committee was appointed to study the results of the Brussels Conference. Rolin-Jaequemyns, acting as secretary to the committee, drew up a long list of questions concerning the Declaration, and the answers which he received and his own report make an interesting commentary on the project.[31] William Beach Lawrence had already questioned the propriety of denying to belligerents the choice of any means which might enable them to shorten wars.[32] Travers Twiss doubted the wisdom of codification, lest it might stereotype the law;[33] while Mountague Bernard, although he admitted the value of the recorded discussions of the conference, considered the acceptance of the Declaration undesirable. He admitted, however, that some of its provisions might profitably be embodied in a code of instructions drawn up by particular countries for the use of their armies.[34] With these exceptions, all the members of the committee whose opinions Rolin-Jaequemyns gathered, were agreed in hailing the Declaration as an advanced embodiment of enlightened public sentiment.[35] Accordingly, the Institute passed resolutions approving it and expressing the wish that govern-

30 Parl. Papers, 1875, Misc. No. 3, pp. 5–9.

31 Rolin-Jaequemyns, Revue de Droit Inter. VII (1875), pp. 87–111, 438–552.

32 *Ibid.*, pp. 526–529, p. 450.

33 *Ibid.*, p. 451.

34 *Ibid.*, pp. 467, 523.

35 *Ibid.*, pp. 463–465, 466–469.

ments generally might incorporate its rules in the instructions for their armies. The Institute also approved the proposition of General Arnaudeau, one of the French delegates, in favor of an agreement between the powers for the purpose of establishing uniformity in the penal codes used in war, as well as the proposition of the Italian delegates, Baron Blanc and Colonel Count Lanza, in favor of a similar agreement for the unification of the rules of intercourse between the belligerents. Finally it expressed its approval of the proposal of Colonel Brun, one of the Danish delegates that "after a contest, the belligerents are held to communicate to the adverse party the list of dead fallen into their power. To render this easier it will be desirable that each soldier be furnished with a mark indicating his number (his name), the number of his regiment and that of his company."[36]

The approval richly deserved.—The approval given by the Institute to the work of the Conference was richly deserved. It had been feared that the predominance of the military element among the members would result in retrogression rather than advancement.[37] Exactly the opposite actually happened. The practical knowledge of the conditions of warfare which the military men possessed enabled them to deal at first hand with questions which men of other training would have had to resort to treatises on International Law to decide. Depending solely on books, they would have been almost certain to allow undue weight to the precedents of a bygone age or the generalizations of scientific writers, so that their work would have fallen short of the spirit of the age or have embodied principles which did not truly incorporate the experience of the past.

The moral tone of the Conference was high.—As it was, the delegates, while not losing sight of military necessity, showed that they had imbibed the humane spirit of the age and that they had a full appreciation of the power for good or evil which they held in their hands. Their proposals were clear cut and practical, and the questions were argued with great ability and with consideration for the feelings of other delegates.

It is fortunate that the Declaration of the Conference was

[36] *Ibid.*, p. 287.
[37] *Ibid.*, p. 91.

so largely the work of military men.—Finally, it is fortunate that the Declaration was so largely the work of military men. This circumstance has tended to add to its authority as a practical measure, as well as to the authority of The Hague Regulations, which are based on it. The necessities of war are capable of such a liberal construction that the Regulations would be of little use in ameliorating belligerent practices in the hands of men antagonistic to it; and such a feeling of antagonism might well have existed among military men had the declaration been drawn for them by men of other training whom they believed to be unacquainted with the conditions for which they were legislating. The danger of hostility to The Hague Regulations is therefore now avoided by the fact that military men had so large a share in their creation. That military men on that occasion showed themselves so thoroughly imbued with the humanitarian spirit of the age is evidence that they may in the future be entrusted with the leading part in the development of the laws of war that they have had in the past.

The Russo-Turkish War of 1877.—During the Russo-Turkish War of 1877 the Russian Government endeavored, by the publication and distribution of a sort of military catechism, to acquaint its soldiers with the laws of war; and it also issued a most humane regulation for the treatment of prisoners of war.[38] The Turkish Government took no such steps. Only on the representation of neutral powers was a translation made of the Geneva Convention into Turkish. Late in 1876 the Turkish Government had found that the Red Cross violated the susceptibilities of Mohammedans. It accordingly made known to the Swiss Government its intention to substitute the Red Crescent for the Red Cross. After some negotiations between the signatories of the Geneva Convention it was suggested by the German Government that the substitution be agreed to as a *modus vivendi* for the war. Both parties agreed to this, Russia's consent being conditioned on the promise of Turkey to instruct her troops to respect the Red Cross.[39]

Nevertheless, numerous complaints arose, and mutual recriminations added to the difficulty of ascertaining the facts.

38 Holland, Studies in Inter. Law, pp. 86, 164.

39 Pradier Fodere, Droit Inter. Public, VII, pp. 399–405.

That the irregular troops of the Turks, such as the Bashi-Bazouks and Kurds, continually committed outrages, and that prisoners were subjected by the Turks to slaughter and mutilation can, however, scarcely be questioned.[40]

The Manual of Oxford.—At the meeting of 1875 the Institute of International Law, as we have seen, passed resolutions recommending that governments instruct their armies in the rules of International Law.[41] In order to ascertain what was being done in that direction, the Secretary-General, Rolin-Jaequemyns, in his annual report of 1878, suggested a study of the different codes which various countries had adopted for their armies. The result was a report by Gustave Moynier, and as comparatively little was found to have been done it was agreed that he should draft a code, or manual, to be proposed to the various governments. Great care was taken that the completed work should fairly represent the opinion of the Institute. To secure this copies of the first draft were sent to all the members. Criticisms of all kinds poured in. A second draft was made and submitted to a committee, which sat for several days at Dr. Bluntschli's home, in Heidelberg. Early in September, 1880, the final draft was made, and it was accepted by the Institute at Oxford soon afterwards. Copies of the manual were then sent to the various governments, with a letter representing it to be the duty of each government to issue some such instructions to its troops. The provisions of the new code followed very closely those of the Declaration of Brussels. The subject of Reprisals, however, is briefly included. The substance of the manual is in most cases the same as that of the Declaration of Brussels, but the form is quite different. The general arrangement is different, and the provisions are so worded, with explanatory passages in small type between, as to render them easy of comprehension by the soldier. The work was ably done, but the direct results were not so great as were hoped for.

Correspondence between Dr. Bluntschli and Count von Moltke following the publication of the Manual of Oxford.—An interesting correspondence followed the publication

40 *Ibid.*, p. 165.

41 This account of the compilation of the Manual is taken from Holland, *Ibid.*, p. 89, *et seq.*

of the Manual between Dr. Bluntschli and Count von Moltke, to whom he sent a copy. In the course of his observations Count von Moltke said:

"In the first place, I appreciate fully the philanthropic efforts made to lessen the evils incident to war. Perpetual peace is a dream, and not even a good dream. War is an element of the world's order established by God. The noblest virtues of man are developed there: courage and self-effacement, the fidelity to duty and the spirit of sacrifice; the soldier gives his life. Without war the world would stagnate and lose itself in materialism.

"I am further absolutely in accord with the proposition announced in the introduction; that the gradual softening of manners ought to be reflected in the manner of making war. But I go further and I believe that the softening of manners alone can lead to that end, which would not be attained by means of a codification of the law of war. All law supposes an authority to watch over and execute it, and it is this power that is lacking in the observation of international agreements. What third powers will ever take arms for the sole motive, that, two powers being at war, the laws of war have been violated by one or both of them? For this kind of infractions there is no judge here below. Success can come only of the religious and moral education of individuals, of the sentiment of honor and of the sense of justice of the chiefs, who impose on themselves the law and conform thereto as far as the abnormal conditions of war allow.

"This being so, it is also necessary to recognize that the progress of humanity in making war has really followed the general softening of manners. Only compare the horrors of the Thirty Years' War with the struggles of modern times!

"A great step has been made in our day by the establishment of compulsory military service, which compels the educated classes to enter the army. The gross and violent elements without doubt always make a part, but they are not the only elements as formerly.

"Besides, governments possess two powerful means to prevent the worst excesses; rigorous discipline, maintained in time of peace and of which the soldier has gotten the habit, and the vigilance of administration which provides for the subsistence of the troops in the field.

"The greatest benefit in war is that it be terminated promptly. It ought to be permitted in view of this end, to use all means, save those which are positively condemnable. I by no means agree with the Declaration of St. Petersburg, when it pretends that the enfeebling of the military forces of the enemy constitutes the only legitimate mode of proceeding in war. No, it is necessary to attack all the resources of the enemy's government, his finances, his railroads, his provisions, his prestige. * * *

"I believe that in war, where all must be considered individually, the only articles which will prove to be efficacious are those which address themselves essentially to the chiefs. Such are the prescriptions of the manual concerning the wounded, the sick, the physicians and the sanitary material. The general recognition of these principles, as of those which concern prisoners, will constitute in itself an essential progress towards the end which the Institute of International Law pursues with so honorable a perseverance."[42]

Wholesome effect of Count von Moltke's letter.—There is much in this letter that will not be generally accepted, but Count von Moltke stated so clearly and forcibly the most important forces which make for the betterment of the conditions of warfare that his letter has been extensively quoted. Its effect was not so much to make questionable the advantage of written agreements as to emphasize the far greater importance of other things. The exaggerated importance sometimes ascribed to international agreements by international jurists today is the excuse for what he said.

The adoption of manuals by various governments.—In his report to the Institute of International Law, as has been observed, Moynier found that little had been done by the various governments for the instruction of their troops. He found, however, that the Dutch and French Governments had adopted unofficial manuals for use in the schools for the instruction of officers; that the German Government, even as early as 1870, had issued confidential instructions as to conduct in warfare to its officers; that a draft of such rules had been drawn up for the Swiss Government, and that other governments had had the subject

[42] Revue de Droit Inter., XIII, pp. 80–82.

under discussion. The best known of the manuals is the French, the first edition of which appeared in 1877, and which is a very able work. Other manuals that may be noticed are that of the Servian Government, issued in 1878, that of the Spanish Government, issued in 1893, which was founded mainly on the work of a congress of officers representing the armies of Spain, Portugal and the various Latin states of South and Central America, held in Madrid, in 1892,[43] and finally that issued by the British war office, in 1903, consisting of The Hague Regulations of 1899, with supplementary matter and notes by Professor Holland.

Notable army regulations.—Notable army regulations are those of Spain approved by a law of January 5, 1882; of Italy, of September 16, 1896; of Switzerland, of March 31, 1904; of Russia, of June 14-27, 1904; and of Portugal and Columbia.[44]

The publication of the German staff.—The German staff published a work in 1902 entitled Kriegsbauch im Land Kriege—the laws of war on land. It is one of a series of monographs, which the staff considers of the first importance, intended to make the German officers profit by the recent wars.[45] Its historical character is possibly responsible for its partisan references to the Franco-German War which detract from its scientific value, but it is a work of great ability, is clear and well thought out and of great practical value. It is largely based on the work of Lueder, and through him on the Brussels Project of Declaration and so unfortunately lays less stress on The Hague Regulations than the international character of the latter would call for.

43 Holland, Studies in International War, pp. 85–87.

44 Merighnac, Les Lois de la Guerre Continentale Suivant le Grand Etat-Major Allemand, 14 R. G. D. I. P., p. 199.

45 *Ibid*, p. 203.

CHAPTER XI.

WARS IN THE EAST AND WEST.

Progress shown by Japan in the Chino-Japanese War.—The Chinese-Japanese War was noteworthy for the progress Japan was shown to have made in the observance of occidental standards in the conduct of warfare, and for the high tone which she took in observing those standards against an enemy which failed to recognize their binding force. One of the first questions that confronted her was the treatment of Chinese resident in Japan. By a decree of August 4, 1894,[1] she allowed those who wished to remain to do so during good behavior on condition of registering within twenty days. Mr. Ariga, in his able work entitled La Guerre Sino-Japonaise, says that about half the Chinese resident in Yokohama and Kobe took advantage of this act. Registered Chinese were to continue in their employments, including commercial intercourse with China. As an incident to this continued right of residence and of commerce, the Japanese courts remained open to the Chinese who remained.[2]

Care in restricting hostilities to the regular combatants.—Great care was taken that those not entitled to combatant privileges should not engage in hostilities. It was feared that the volunteers who offered themselves at the beginning of the war might not live up to the high standard which the Empire had set for itself, and their services therefore were refused.[3]

Afterwards, on the invasion of Chinese territory, it was found that the coolies, contract laborers attached to the army, were committing depredations, and as a consequence their arms were taken from them. As a result, ten days later, a large number of them were killed while transporting provisions for the army. Notwithstanding this, the order forbidding them to bear arms was not withdrawn.[4]

[1] Ariga, La Guerre Sino-Japonaise, p. 23.
[2] *Ibid.*, pp. 28–29.
[3] *Ibid.*, pp. 34–38.
[4] *Ibid.*, pp. 45–50.

H XXVI provides that a commander, before commencing a bombardment will do all in his power to warn the inhabitants unless it accompanies an assault. The bombardment of Kinchau came within the exception being simultaneous with the assault, and accordingly no notice was given the inhabitants.

The taking of Port Arthur.—The taking of Port Arthur was the one regrettable incident of the war on the part of the Japanese. The occurrences there are well summed up by Prof. Holland, who says:

"It was the torture and mutilation of those Japanese who happened to be made prisoners during the operations against Port Arthur which stung their fellow countrymen into madness, and explains, though nothing can excuse, the massacres which were carried on by them for four days after the place was taken."

The account of the taking by Marshal Oyama.—In his official response to the inquiry of the General Staff as to what happened at Port Arthur, Marshal Oyama replied:

"(a) The facts disclosed below will make it evident that the confusion of the soldiers and of the civil population was necessary:

"1. The city of Port Arthur, which was a military port, was composed of a great number of soldiers and workers.

"2. The retreating soldiers fired on the Japanese from the interior of the houses.

"3. Arms, bullets and powder were left in each house.

"4. The entry of the Japanese army into the city took place towards sunset.

"(b) Those, among the soldiers, who were killed after the 21st, had all opposed an obstinate resistance or attempted to escape. Death was therefore a necessary punishment.

"(c) The pillage of the property of the civil population is an accusation without foundation. It may be that the Japanese army, which passed the night in the city, exacted certain objects of which it had need, such as tables, benches, candle-sticks, cups, firewood, coal, etc.; but, as to pillage, I am able to affirm that it never existed. Some rare infractions under this head were condemned, conformably to establish laws."[5]

[5] *Ibid.*, pp. 88–89.

Criticism of this account.—As to (a), Mr. Ariga considers that Marshal Oyama has made good his point provided the assault of the city and the fighting in the streets was necessary at all;[6] and as to (b), that the Marshal is not sufficiently precise as to whether the prisoners were shot in endeavoring to prevent their escape, or after their recapture for having attempted to escape.[7] In the former case the killing would have been justified, in the latter, not. If the obstinate resistance of the prisoners amounted to insubordination, then it may have justified their being killed; but if it occurred, not after they were made prisoners, but before, it must certainly be condemned, their punishment therefor being something that would have occasioned the severe rebuke of even Bynkershoek.[8]

Treatment of the dead.—No attempt was made by the Japanese to identify the Chinese dead, as it was practically impossible to do so on account of the Chinese military authorities having taken no notice of the civil status of the soldiers. If it had been possible to identify them, one of the great reasons for identification, the right of the family of the deceased to a pension, did not exist among the Chinese.[9] In disposing of the dead, regard was had to the prejudice of the Chinese against cremation, and at first they were usually buried, although the icy condition of the ground made the digging of graves very difficult. Later, however, it was found that the Chinese in the neighborhood regarded the soldiers as strangers and so cared little what was done with the dead bodies. Accordingly less care was taken in this regard.[10]

Treatment of prisoners of war.—Little complaint can be made as to the treatment of prisoners of war, except in the case of Port Arthur. The Geneva Convention was not always observed, but this question presented peculiar difficulties. While Japan had adhered to the convention, China had not. Moreover, the Chinese had no organized medical staff, and their knowledge of medicine was so imperfect as to make reciprocity of treatment impossible.[11] Consequent-

[6] *Ibid.*, pp. 89–92.
[7] *Ibid.*, pp. 92–93.
[8] Bynershoek, Law of War, p. 22.
[9] Ariga, pp. 98–99.
[10] *Ibid.*, pp. 101–104.
[11] *Ibid.*, p. 111.

ly, the convention was not so perfectly observed, even in respect of aid to the sick and wounded in the field as might have been desired,[12] although the general standard maintained by Japan was by no means low.

In this relation the illustrious work of an Englishman, Dr. Daly, at Incau must be mentioned. In the hospital established there by himself and others were gathered more than a thousand wounded Chinese, while in the Japanese hospital at the same place, out of thirty in all, only one was a Chinese, though the number later increased to five.[13] Except in special cases, the Red Cross Society was not allowed to carry on its work within the scene of active operations. This, Mr. Ariga considers to have been unfortunate, as the regular staff was not able to attend to all that was to be done.[14]

Treatment of private property.—In the treatment of private property, the action of the Japanese seems to have been all that could be desired. Goods requisitioned were paid for, no imposts or fines were exacted, nor, to Mr. Ariga's knowledge, were any contributions.[15] The rate of exchange and the price to be paid for provisions were settled by the military authorities.[16] Among the services requisitioned were those of guides and of drivers, with their wagons and teams.[17] Little aid in the execution of requisitions was given by the local functionaries, as most of them had fled. In Kinchau, however, a body of merchants, which had been made use of by the Chinese authorities, was made use of by the Japanese also.[18]

The administration of the occupied territory.—The administration of the occupied territory was at first entrusted to civil officials, most of them being the old consuls or secretaries of legation, or secretaries of provinces having a port open to strangers; but the friction that this brought about between them and the army caused them to be superseded later by purely military men.[19] The local function-

[12] *Ibid.*, p. 117.
[13] *Ibid.*, p. 119.
[14] *Ibid.*, pp. 138–147.
[15] *Ibid.*, pp. 163–164.
[16] *Ibid.*, pp. 167–172.
[17] *Ibid.*, pp. 165–166.
[18] *Ibid.*, p. 165.
[19] *Ibid.*, pp. 178–179.

aries having fled, it was necessary to get others to take their places. The city of Kinchau, for example, was divided into four districts, over each of which some popular citizen was placed while two citizens of similar standing were placed over the entire city. Finally it was decided that mayors should be placed at the head of each village and elections were held for that purpose.[20] A notable feature of the occupation was the effort made to improve the sanitary condition of the territory occupied.[21] Of penal measures the most noteworthy was that of holding the villages to collective responsibility for offences committed against the law of nations, after the manner of the Germans in France in 1870.[22]

The conduct of the Chinese.—At the beginning of the war, the Chinese Government, through the American Ministers at Pekin and Tokio, proposed to the Japanese Government the exemption of private property at sea from capture. This was accepted. Later the Chinese Government refused to exempt Japanese vessels entering Chinese ports from capture, but as this was only the enforcement of the rule of non-intercourse, it can not be held to be in contradiction to China's previous action with regard to the exemption of private property at sea.[23] In other respects the action of the Chinese does not seem to have materially improved over that of previous times. Prices were offered for heads and hands, heads actually were cut off and exhibited in triumph, and bodies were sadly mutilated.[24]

The Graeco-Turkish War of 1897.—The Graeco-Turkish War of 1897 is especially interesting for the care which the Turkish authorities took to show the world their intention to live up to modern standards in the care of prisoners of war[25] as well as to the obligations of the Geneva Convention. Elaborate orders were issued in accord with the latter, special envoys of the Sultan visited the hospitals and ambulances and it is said that the members of his harem

[20] *Ibid.*, pp. 195–196.

[21] *Ibid.*, pp. 97–201.

[22] *Ibid.*, pp. 207–209.

[23] But see Takahashi, International Law during the Chino-Japanese War, pp. 9–11.

[24] Holland, Studies in International Law, pp. 116, 128; Ariga, La Guerre Sino-Japonaise, p. 87.

[25] Nicolas Politis, Chronique des Faits Internationaux, 4 R. G. D. I. P., 697.

themselves prepared linen and other material for the care of the sick and wounded.[26] In the large centers, at least, quittances were given for requisitions.[27] On the other hand violence to noncombatants was not infrequent and in Thessaly the Greeks were ordered to return to their homes under penalty of the confiscation of their goods.[28] In the administration of the occupied territory perhaps the most notable measures were the imposition of the Turkish imposts on sheep, salt and tobacco[29] and the direction of the Greek Government to its functionaries to resign their positions.[30]

Expulsion of Greeks from Turkey.—Immediately after the declaration of war a decree of the Sultan pronounced the expulsion *en masse* within fifteen days of the Declaration of all Greeks residing in Ottoman territory. There were then nearly 200,000 of these, most of them merchants.[31] The fifteen days of grace were confined to merchants and other Greek subjects having a permanent occupation. All other Greeks were ordered to quit in three days, and at Smyrna, for instance, Greek subjects were forcibly embarked from the first day of the war. Scarcely eight days after the declaration of war 15,000 of them had left Turkey.

By a special decree of May 2, the Imperial Government declared that until the reestablishment of relations with Greece, the process of Greek subjects pending before Ottoman tribunals would be suspended, that those owing debts either to the fisc or to individuals should, before quitting the Empire, furnish sufficient guarantees of solvency, and that those who possessed immovables would not be able to sell them. Special commissions were instituted in most of the provinces composed of four Turkish functionaries. They were to agree to the request of the Greeks to remain on condition of their changing their nationality.

Against this decree the ambassadors of the great powers protested. They said it would give rise to regrettable disorders and that especially it should not be applied to Greeks employed in foreign houses, in hospitals, embassies and consulates. They demanded a prolongation of the fifteen

26 *Ibid.*, p. 699.
27 *Ibid.*, 706.
28 *Ibid.*, pp. 701–702.
29 *Ibid.*, 710.
30 *Ibid.*, 709.
31 *Ibid.*, 525.

days of grace, and while the Porte acceded to this by granting an extension of a week he expressly refused to except the employees of consulates, hospitals and foreign houses from the decree. This brought out another protest from the ambassadors, and henceforth such employees do not seem to have been molested. The last day of grace was finally fixed at May 25, but before that time hostilities had ceased.[32]

Spanish-American War principally maritime.—The Spanish-American War was largely maritime in character. As already noticed, the Additional Articles to the Geneva Convention of 1868 had not received the unanimous approval of the signatories of the Geneva Convention and so had not become binding. On the suggestion of the Swiss Government, however, the practice of the Franco-German War was followed and they were adopted so far as they related to naval warfare, as a *modus vivendi* for the war.[33] Nor was the Declaration of Paris binding on either of the parties. However, immediately on the outbreak of hostilities the United States declared that its "policy" would be not to resort to privateering, and although Spain reserved the right to make use of letters of marque she did not avail herself of the reservation. To the second, third and fourth articles of the Declaration of Paris, the United States adhered, as "recognized rules of international law."[34] Spanish vessels in ports of the United States were allowed thirty days from the outbreak of hostilities to load their cargoes and depart, and were assured of exemption from seizure during their home voyage, on condition, however, of not carrying coal, contraband or analogues of contraband, such as despatches or Spanish officers. Spanish vessels sailing from a foreign port to a port in the United States, before the outbreak of hostilities, were likewise allowed to enter, discharge their cargo and leave without fear of capture during the remainder of the voyage. The Spanish decree made no such provision with regard to vessels sailing for a Spanish port, and instead of thirty days for the departure of vessels already in port allowed five.[35]

32 *Ibid.*, pp. 525–532.

33 J. B. Moore, Maritime Law in the Spanish War, in Inter. Law, Situations—Naval War College—1901, pp. 144–145.

34 *Ibid.*, p. 152.

35 *Ibid.*, p. 153.

Neutral ships allowed to clear for Spanish ports.—"On April 27, 1898, the Treasury Department issued to collectors of customs certain instructions, which were prepared in consultation with the Department of State. These instructions forbade the clearance of an American vessel for a Spanish port, but the only restriction they placed upon the clearance of any other vessel for such a port was that the vessel should not carry cargo of contraband of war or of coal. Thus the clearance of a neutral ship with an American-owned cargo for a Spanish port was permitted, and to this extent trading between enemies was allowed."[36]

The decision of the Supreme Court in the case of the Paquete Habana.—The decisions of the Supreme Court belong rather to the second part of this work than to the first, but there was one decision of such importance as to merit special attention. That was "in the case of the Spanish fishing smacks, the *Paquete Habana* and the *Lola.* The particular point decided was that 'coast-fishing vessels, with their implements and supplies, cargoes and crews, unarmed and honestly pursuing their peaceful calling of catching and bringing in fresh fish, are exempt from capture as prize of war.' In reaching this conclusion, however, the court, through Mr. Justice Gray, who delivered the opinion, announced and applied a principle which, though often recognized by publicists, has perhaps never before been so clearly and precisely enunciated by a judicial tribunal—that is, the principle of the progressive development of international law. Referring to a decision of Lord Stowell, in which it was said that the exemption of vessels, such as those in question, was 'a rule of comity only, and not of legal decision,' Mr. Justice Gray said:

"'The word "comity" was apparently used by Lord Stowell as synonymous with courtesy or good will. But the period of a hundred years which has since elapsed is amply sufficient to have enabled what originally may have rested in custom or comity, courtesy or concession, to grow, by the general assent of civilized nations, into a settled rule of international law. As well said by Sir James Mackintosh: "In the present century a slow and silent but very substantial mitigation has taken place in the practice of war; and in proportion as that mitigated practice has re-

36 *Ibid.*, pp. 176–177.

ceived the sanction of time, it is raised from the rank of mere usage and becomes part of the law of nations.' *Discourse on the Law of Nations,* 38; *Miscellaneous Works,* 360."

The progressive character of International Law.—"It may be hoped that this enlightened declaration will lead our courts to abandon the repetition of the unfortunate *dicta* in *Brown v. United States,* based upon the theory that it was the peculiar prerogative of a remote age to fix by its customs, however rude and barbarous they may have been, an immutable law, in comparison with which the customs of modern times are merely 'comity' or 'courtesy,' which may be discarded at will."[37]

The question of the Cuban debt.—In the Peace Negotiations the question was earnestly argued of the obligation of the United States to assume the so-called Cuban debt. The Spanish Commissioners claimed that all outstanding obligations that had been legally contracted for the service of Cuba and Porto Rico, and which were chargeable to their individual treasuries, always distinct and separate from the Treasury of the Peninsula, were Cuban or Porto Rican obligations, that is, local obligations, solely and exclusively affecting the territory of the islands and their inhabitants.[38]

The American Commissioners, in reply, pointed out that while it was true that the "Cuban Treasury" was not a branch of the Spanish Treasury, the finances of the islands were exclusively controlled by the Spanish Government; that the debt creating power, such as commonly belongs to communes or municipal corporations, never was delegated to Cuba, and that such a thing as a Cuban obligation, created by the Island in the exercise of powers either inherent or delegated, was unknown to the markets of the world. They then sketched the history of the debt, showing that most of it had been incurred in suppressing the insurrections in the islands, and that, while the Spanish Government had undertaken to pay the bonds issued as late as 1890, out of the revenues of Cuba, their national character was demonstrated by the fact that on their face their payment was guaranteed by the Spanish nation. From no

[37] *Ibid.*, pp. 165–166.
[38] Sen. Doc. No. 62, Part II, 55th Cong. 3d Sess., p. 43.

point of view, said the American Commissioners, could these debts be considered as local debts of Cuba, or as debts incurred for the benefit of Cuba. In no sense were they obligations properly chargeable to that island. They were debts created by the Government of Spain for its own purposes and through its own agents, and in whose creation Cuba had no voice.[39] To this the Spanish Commissioners replied that, since the bonds in question had been expressly secured by certain and determinate revenues and receipts, Spain had a right to consider that she was only under a subsidiary obligation to pay them in the event of the revenues and receipts primarily hypothecated for the payment thereof proving insufficient.[40] The American Commissioners closed the discussion by quoting the degree of autonomy signed by the Queen Regent on the 25th of November, 1897, in which it was declared that the future payment and guarantee of the debts should be the subject of a law on the termination of the war, as evidence that the so-called Cuban debt was really a national debt, and that the pledge of the revenues of Cuba was considered by the Spanish Government itself as being wholly within its control, so that it could be modified or withdrawn at will without affecting the obligation of the debt.[41]

Were they properly mortgage debts?—Here the Commissioners were clearly at issue. Did the promise of the Spanish Government to pay the bonds out of the revenues of Cuba give the purchasers of those bonds a property right in those revenues, analogous to the right of the ordinary mortgagee, which with other private properties was bound to be respected by the cession or relinquishment of the island? Or did the promise at best create merely a moral obligation on the part of Spain to turn over those revenues to the holders of the bonds as long as she retained her sovereignity over the island? To state the question would appear to answer it. The holders of the bonds had apparently no such means of enforcing the alleged hypothecation in the ordinary courts as the ordinary mortgagee possesses, nor was there apparently any means taken to make it effective by placing someone in the customs house in the

[39] *Ibid.*, pp. 48–50.
[40] *Ibid.*, p. 87.
[41] *Ibid.*, p. 101.

interests of the bondholders. Means of this kind would at least have indicated that the promise of payment from the revenues was regarded as an essential part of the obligation of the bonds; and although the grant of a property right in a governmental function is to be looked on with disfavor, it might thus have been held that the attempt to create a property right was so clear that it should be respected by subsequent sovereigns. But here there was no such clear intention. At most the promise might be interpreted as a promise to pay from the Cuban revenues as long as Spain had them to dispose of.

If not, were they properly local debts?—The controversy is thus narrowed down to the question whether the debts were properly local debts. In that case entirely apart from the question whether they were secured by the Cuban revenues they should have passed with the territory. The Spanish Commissioners no doubt felt that what Spain had done for the colonies she had done for their benefit. It was natural that they should so feel, but to an outsider it would appear that whatever good intentions Spain may have had, her power was misused, and that she could not expect to shift the burden of her own mistakes to those who had suffered so grievously from them already.

Recognition of the continued obligation of certain debts due American citizens by the treaty of February 17, 1834.—A commendable feature of the war was the promptness with which Spain recognized the continuing obligation of the treaty of February 17, 1834, by which she had settled the claims of American citizens growing out of the wars with her colonies. Her acknowledgment of the continuance of this obligation was emphasized by the payment of two overdue instalments of interest, one of which had accrued during the war as well as by the explicit declaration that such payment was to be considered as a proof of "the punctiliousness" with which the Government of Her Catholic Majesty attended to its "international obligations."[42]

[42] Moore, Effect of War on Public Debts and on Treaties, in the Columbia Law Review, Vol. I, pp. 209, *et seq.*

CHAPTER XII.

THE FIRST PEACE CONFERENCE.

The Russian proposal of a Peace Conference.—Twelve days after the signing of the protocol suspending hostilities between the United States and Spain, the Russian Foreign Minister, Count Mouravieff, took the first steps towards The First Peace Conference by communicating to the diplomatic representatives at St. Petersburg the wish of the Czar that a conference be called which should seek for some means of "insuring to all peoples the benefits of a real and durable peace, and, above all, of putting an end to the progressive development of the present armaments."[1] By October 24, 1898, all the invitations to the Conference had been formally accepted.[2]

Subjects for consideration.—In a circular of January 11, 1899 (New Style), Count Mouravieff offered the following subjects for the consideration of the Conference:

"1. An understanding not to increase for a fixed period the present effective of the armed military and naval forces, and at the same time not to increase the Budgets pertaining thereto; and a preliminary examination of the means by which a reduction might even be effected in future in the forces and Budgets above mentioned.

"2. To prohibit the use in the armies and fleets of any new kind of firearms whatever, and of new explosives, or any powders more powerful than those now in use, either for rifles or cannon.

"3. To restrict the use in military warfare of the formidable explosives already existing, and to prohibit the throwing of projectiles or explosives of any kind from balloons or by any similar means.

"4. To prohibit the use, in naval warfare of submarine torpedo boats or plungers, or other similar engines of destruction; to give an undertaking not to construct, in the future, vessels with rams.

[1] Holls, The Peace Conference at The Hague, p. 8.
[2] *Ibid.*, p. 14.

"5. To apply to naval warfare the stipulations of the Geneva Convention of 1864, on the basis of the Additional Articles of 1868.

"6. To neutralize ships and boats employed in saving those overboard during or after an engagement.

"7. To revise the Declaration concerning the laws and customs of war elaborated in 1874 by the Conference of Brussels, which has remained unratified to the present day.

"8. To accept in principle the employment of good offices, of mediation and facultative arbitration in cases lending themselves thereto, with the object of preventing armed conflicts between nations; to come to an understanding with respect to the mode of applying these good offices, and to establish a uniform practice in using them."[3]

The powers represented.—At the request of the Russian Government the Queen of The Netherlands offered The Hague as the seat of the Conference, and its sessions were opened there on May 18, 1899. Twenty-six powers had sent representatives comprising practically all of Europe, and in addition the United States, Mexico, China, Japan, Persia and Siam. "Of the independent Governments of the world, the Central and South American Republics, the Sultanates of Morocco and Muscat, the Orange Free State, the Principality of Monaco, the Republic of San Marino and the Kingdom of Abyssinia, were the only ones not represented in the Peace Conference."[4] The omission of the South American Republics would seem to have been unfortunate.

Organization of the Conference.—The Presidency of the Conference was naturally conferred on the first Russian delegate, Baron de Staal, the representative of the Czar at the court of St. James. At his suggestion it was agreed that the Conference divide itself into three committees; the first of these to consider the first four articles of Count Mouravieff's Circular, the object of which was largely economic; the second, to consider the next three articles, whose object was essentially humanitarian; and the third, to consider the last article, which dealt with arbitration. Every state was to be represented on every committee by a member or members designated by the ranking member of the

[3] *Ibid.*, pp. 25–26.
[4] *Ibid.*, p. 332.

delegation. Members could be appointed on more than one committee, it being possible for diplomatic members to be on every committee. Scientific and technical delegates might participate in the full meetings of the Conference. In both the conference and the committees, each country was to have one vote. Communications to the press of the proceedings of each committee were to be made through a Bureau in conjunction with the President. Otherwise, there was to be absolute secrecy.[5]

Division of the work among the committees.—The committees were divided into subcommittees, in which most of the work was done. Articles 2 and 3, as to arms and explosives, were referred to the military subcommittee of the first committee, while article 4, as to torpedoes and other instruments of marine warfare, was referred to the naval subcommittee. Most of the propositions in the military subcommittee were presented by Colonel Gilinsky, the Russian delegate.

Powders, shells, explosives and field guns.—As to powders, by which was meant the propelling force of projectiles as distinguished from the bursting charge, it was proposed that none should be employed more powerful than those already in use, but Captain Crozier, of the American Delegation, pointed out that perhaps more powerful powders might be produced which would explode at a lower temperature, thus causing less injury to the gun and being more economical than existing powders. The point was so well taken that the proposal was unanimously rejected. It was also proposed to forbid the use of mining shells in field artillery, but the proposal was defeated by eleven votes to ten. The proposition that no new explosives should be used, nor any of that class known as high explosives, was also lost by a vote of twelve to nine. The proposal that no new field guns, superior to the best material already in use in any country, was unanimously rejected, Russia and Bulgaria abstaining from voting.[6]

The throwing of projectiles from balloons.—"The subcommittee first voted a perpetual prohibition of the use of balloons or similar new machines for throwing projectiles or explosives. In the full committee this subject was

[5] *Ibid.*, pp. 63–64.
[6] *Ibid.*, pp. 93–95.

brought up for reconsideration by the United States Delegate and the prohibition was, by unanimous vote, limited to cover a period of five years only. The action taken was for humanitarian reasons alone, and was founded upon the opinion that balloons, as they now exist, form such an uncertain means of injury that they cannot be used with accuracy; that the persons or objects injured by throwing explosives from them may be entirely disconnected from any conflict which may be in process, and such that their injury or destruction would be of no practical advantage to the party making use of the machines. The limitation of the interdiction to five years' operation preserves liberty of action under changed circumstances which may be produced by the progress of invention."[7]

Proposed rule as to muskets.—We have seen that the Conference refused to prohibit field guns superior to any already in use. With regard to muskets, it was proposed that no Power should change its existing type, as the various types in use were considered to be essentially the same, but that this should not prevent improvements in existing types. As no agreement, however, could be reached as to the difference between an improvement within the type and an entire change thereof, no result was reached. One of the questions discussed under this head was the prohibition of automatic muskets. "The states voting in favor of the prohibition were Belgium, Denmark, Spain, Holland, Persia, Russia, Siam, Switzerland and Bulgaria (nine). Those voting against it were Germany, the United States, Austria-Hungary, Great Britain, Italy, Sweden and Norway (six). And those abstaining were France, Japan, Portugal, Roumania, Servia and Turkey (six). From this statement it may be seen that none of the great Powers of the world, except Russia, was willing to accept restrictions with regard to military improvements when the question of increase of efficiency was involved, and that one great Power (France) abstained from expressing an opinion on the subject."[8] In the Full Committee the question was put aside for the consideration of a future conference, as was also "the use of new means of destruction, which might possibly have a tendency to come into vogue, such as those depend-

[7] Captain Crozier's Report, *Ibid.*, p. 509.
[8] Captain Crozier's Report, pp. 509–510.

ing upon electricity or chemistry.''[9] Towards all these questions the United States delegation took the position that it ''did not consider limitations in regard to the use of military inventions to be conducive to the peace of the world.''[10]

Expanding bullets.—The subject of bullets ''gave rise to more active debate and to more decided differences of view than any other considered by the subcommittee. A formula was adopted as follows, 'the use of bullets which expand or flatten easily in the human body, such as jacketed bullets, of which the jacket does not entirely cover the core, or has incisions in it, should be forbidden.'

Position of the British Government.—''When this subject came up in the Full Committee the British representative, Major-General Sir John Ardagh, made a declaration of the position of his Government on the subject, in which he described their Dum-dum bullet as one having a very small portion of the jacket removed from the point, so as to leave uncovered a portion of the core of about the size of a pinhead. He said that this bullet did not expand in such manner as to produce wounds of exceptional cruelty, but that on the contrary the wounds produced by it were in general less severe than those produced by the Snider, Martini-Henry, and other rifles of the period immediately preceding that of the adoption of the present small bore. He ascribed the bad reputation of the Dum-dum bullet to some experiments made at Tübingen in Germany with a bullet from the forward part of which the jacket, to a distance of more than a diameter, was removed. The wounds produced by this bullet were of a frightful character, and the bullets being generally supposed to be similar to the Dum-dum in construction, had probably given rise to the unfounded prejudice against the latter.''

In his declaration Sir John Ardagh had also pointed out that after the battle of Omdurman it was found that the bullets then in use had not been sufficient to put the dervishes *hors de combat,* and that for use against them the Dum-dum bullet had been manufactured.[11]

Position of the United States.—''The United States rep-

9 *Ibid.*, p. 511.
10 *Ibid.*, p. 510.
11 *Ibid.*, p. 99.

resentative here for the first time took part in the discussion, advocating the abandonment of the attempt to cover the principle of prohibition of bullets producing unnecessarily cruel wounds by the specification of details of construction of the bullet, and proposing the following formula:

" 'The use of bullets which inflict wounds of useless cruelty, such as explosive bullets and in general every kind of bullet which exceeds the limit necessary for placing a man immediately *hors de combat* should be forbidden.'

"The Committee, however, adhered to the original proposition, which it voted without acting on the substitute submitted."[12]

Upon the matter coming before the full conference, Captain Crozier presented this formula with the following objections to that adopted by the Committee:

Objections presented by Captain Crozier.—"First, that it forbade the use of expanding bullets, notwithstanding the possibility that they might be made to expand in such regular manner as to assume simply the form of a larger calibre, which property it might be necessary to take advantage of, if it should in the future be found desirable to adopt a musket of very much smaller calibre than any now actually in use. Second, that by thus prohibiting what might be the most humane method of increasing the shocking power of a bullet and limiting the prohibition to expanding and flattening bullets, it might lead to the adoption of one of much more cruel character than that prohibited. Third, that it condemned by designed implication, without even the introduction of any evidence against it, the use of a bullet actually employed by the army of a civilized nation."[13]

Views of Great Britain and the United States overruled.—Notwithstanding these objections the conference adopted the formula of the committee, Great Britain and the United States voting no. It is strange that the position of the United States did not have greater weight with the conference than it did. The reasoning of Captain Crozier in this Committee and of Captain Mahan in the Naval Committee seems eminently sound and convincing.

Work of the naval subcommittee.—The history of the

12 Captain Crozier's Report, *Ibid.*, pp. 511–512.
13 *Ibid.*, p. 513.

naval subcommittee is much the same as that of the military. The proposition to limit the calibre, velocity and length of guns and the thickness of armor plate was almost unanimously rejected. More than a majority of the governments declared their readiness to cease to construct warships armed with rams, on the condition of unanimity, but this was prevented by the adverse votes of Germany, Austria-Hungary, Denmark and Norway and Sweden. The subject of the prohibition of new types of rifles and naval guns was dismissed with the wish that the subject should be the subject of further study on the part of the various governments.[14]

The prohibition of projectiles whose sole purpose is to spread asphyxiating gases.—One subject that received much attention from the naval subcommittee was the prohibition of the use of projectiles, the sole use of which is, on bursting, to spread asphyxiating or deleterious gases. The United States was the only country voting "no" on this proposition, Great Britain's vote, however, being conditioned on unanimity. The reasons which Captain Mahan, the delegate of the United States gave for his action, and in this he was supported by the whole delegation of the United States, were: "1. That no shell emitting such gases is as yet in practical use, or has undergone adequate experiment, consequently a vote taken now would be taken in ignorance of the facts as to whether the results would be of a decisive character, or whether injury in excess of that necessary to attain the end of warfare, the immediate disabling of the enemy, would be inflicted. 2. The reproach of cruelty and perfidy, addressed against these supposed shells, was equally uttered formerly against firearms and torpedoes, both of which are now employed without scruple. Until we knew the effects of such asphyxiating shells there was no saying whether they would be more or less merciful than missiles now permitted. 3. That it was illogical, and not demonstrably humane, to be tender about asphyxiating men with gas, when all were prepared to admit that it was allowable to blow the bottom out of an ironclad at midnight, throwing four or five hundred men into the sea to be choked by water, with scarcely the remotest chance of escape. If, and when, a shell emitting asphyxiating gases

[14] *Ibid.*, pp. 117–118.

alone has been successfully produced, then, and not before, men will be able to vote intelligently on the subject.''[15] This argument would appear to be unanswerable.

Adaptation of the principle of the Geneva Convention to maritime warfare and the adoption of the convention for the regulation of warfare on land.—The second committee, to which were assigned articles 5, 6 and 7 of the Russian Circular, was divided into two subcommittees, the first dealing with the adaptation to naval warfare of the Geneva Convention of 1864, on the basis of the Additional Articles of 1868, and the neutralization of boats or launches employed in the rescue of the shipwrecked during or after naval battles; and the second, dealing with the revision of the Project of Declaration of the Brussels Conference of 1874.

Naval Red Cross Convention.—Of the Convention applying the principles of the Geneva Convention to naval warfare it is perhaps sufficient to say that it was a complete remodeling of the Additional Articles of 1868, and that both in form and substance it evidenced the care and study which had been given to the subject in the interim.

Regulation of the Laws and Customs of War on Land.—Nothing like the same changes had to be made in the Project drawn up at Brussels for the regulation of the Laws and Customs of War on Land. Changes were made, however, in order to guard more surely against any implication of rightful authority on the part of one belligerent over the subjects of the other and articles were added for the increased comfort of prisoners of war and for the recognition of societies formed for their aid. These were largely due to the efforts of the eminent Belgian, M. Romberg-Nisard, who, since the Franco-German War, had devoted much of his energy to securing their adoption. In the main, however, what was done was to adopt the substance of the work of the Brussels Conference, so that the discussions there held are the best commentary we have on The Hague Regulations. But the form of the work was changed. Instead of a Declaration it was put into the form of a Convention by which the Contracting Powers agreed to issue instructions to their armed land forces, which should be in conformity with the Regulations respecting the Laws

[15] *Ibid.*, pp. 494–495.

and Customs of War on Land annexed thereto. The placing of the rules of warfare in the Annex instead of in the Convention did not detract from their obligatory character and it had three advantages. It made the issuance to the armies of regulations conforming thereto obligatory, it allowed the terminology of the regulations to be adapted to the needs of the different armies and finally it satisfied the scruples of the smaller Powers, who felt that it made any implication of an acknowledgment on their part of the rightful authority of a hostile belligerent over their nationals less likely.

Men of special distinction.—Of the many able and distinguished men of the second subcommittee it is difficult to mention some without slighting others, but it may be permissible to refer especially to the President, M. de Martens, of Russia, who enjoyed the unique honor of having also been a delegate to the Conference of Brussels, and to the Secretary, M. Edouard Rolin, of Ghent, son of Rolin-Jaequemyns, and now Editor-in-Chief of the Revue De Droit International, through whose readiness of comprehension and fairness and accuracy of statement many a serious difficulty was avoided.

Declaration of United States as to exemption of private property at sea from capture.—Among the notable declarations made at the Conference was that of Mr. White, on behalf of the United States, in favor of the exemption of private property at sea from capture. The Conference, however, felt that the adoption of such a declaration was beyond its powers, and so referred the matter to a future Conference.

Final Act of the Conference.—The Conventions and Declarations were not, however, the entire work of the Conference. After mentioning them, the Final Act goes on:

"Guided by the same sentiments, the Conference has adopted unanimously the following resolution:

" 'The Conference is of opinion that the restriction of military charges, which are at present a heavy burden on the world, is extremely desirable for the increase of the material and moral welfare of mankind.'

"It has, besides, formulated the following wishes:

Revision of the Geneva Convention.—"1. The Conference, taking into consideration the preliminary steps taken by the Swiss Federal Government for the revision of the Geneva Convention, expresses the wish that steps may be shortly taken for the assembly of a Special Conference having for its object the revision of that Convention.

"This wish was voted unanimously.

Rights and duties of neutrals.—"2. The Conference expresses the wish that the questions of the rights and duties of neutrals may be inserted in the programme of a Conference in the near future.

Changes in rifles and naval guns.—"3. The Conference expresses the wish that the questions with regard to rifles and naval guns, as considered by it, may be studied by the governments with the object of coming to an agreement respecting the employment of new types and calibres.

Limitation of war budgets and of land and naval forces.—"4. The Conference expresses the wish that the governments, taking into consideration the proposals made at the Conference, may examine the possibility of an agreement as to the limitation of armed forces by land and sea, and of war budgets.

Inviolability of private property at sea.—"5. The Conference expresses the wish that the proposal, which contemplates the declaration of the inviolability of private property in Naval Warfare, may be referred to a subsequent Conference for consideration.

Bombardment of towns by naval forces.—"6. The Conference expresses the wish that the proposal to settle the question of the bombardment of ports, towns, and villages by a naval force may be referred to a subsequent Conference for consideration.

"The last five wishes were voted unanimously, saving some abstentions."[16]

Appreciation of the work of the Conference.—The final session of the Conference was held on July 29, 1899, more than two months after it first assembled. Aside from the increased prominence the Conference gave to the principle of arbitration, it will always deserve a high place in the history of the laws of war for its adaptation of the principles of the Geneva Convention to naval warfare, and for the adoption and improvement of the rules concerning the laws and customs of war laid down at Brussels in 1874.

[16] *Ibid.*, pp. 377–379.

CHAPTER XIII.

THE WAR IN SOUTH AFRICA.

Less than the three months after the First Peace Conference adjourned, Great Britain was engaged in a struggle with the South African Republics, which for desperateness rivaled that which the ancestors of the Boers had maintained against Philip II. Into the causes of wars it it not the purpose of this work to go.

The use of expanding bullets.—Among the early charges made was that of the use of expanding bullets. England had not signed the Declaration prohibiting them, and, as we have seen, claimed that those she had used were not unnecessarily cruel. Nevertheless, she did not use them during the war and her reason for not doing so is given in the following extract from the report of the Commission appointed to investigate the conduct of the war:

"Moreover the reserve of 151,000,000 rounds included about 66,000,000 rounds which, as events went, were not available at all for the purposes of this war. This was the ammunition known as Mark IV. It had been found from the experiences of the Chitral campaign that the Mark II ammunition then in use was not deadly enough to stop a rush of religious fanatics, and steps were taken which with their consequences in the summer of 1899, are best described in the words of Sir Henry Brackenbury:

" 'In India they produce the Dum-dum ammunition, in which the head of the bullet is not covered by the nickel envelope. In this country we produced a bullet in which there is a small cylindrical hole in the lead at the top and this is left as an opening, and is not covered over with the nickel. This bullet was an expanding bullet. We had every intention of using this bullet and making it, in fact, the bullet for the British Army all over the world, and, I think about 66,000,000 of it, up to the 31st March, 1899, had been delivered, and formed part of our stock of 172,000,000. It was known as Mark IV. We had an exceptionally hot summer in 1899, and it was found that, especially in the hands of Volunteers, where the rifles had not been kept particularly clean, there were several instances in which this bullet stripped, to use the technical term, that is to say, the lead of the bullet squirted out through this opening in the top of the nickel envelope, and left the envelope behind in the rifle. Then, if there was a second load, you were apt to get an accident, a blow back in the breach. This happened at Bisley, and it happened in several other places with Volunteers. There could be very little doubt of what was the cause of it; it was due to exceptional heat, and it required a rifle which was not clean. We carried out a great number of experiments to try to reproduce this, and we always found it most difficult to reproduce, and the only conditions under which we could reproduce it were the conditions of great heat and a dirty rifle. Those two conditions of great heat and a dirty rifle were exactly the conditions which were likely to occur in war, and, therefore, it seemed to me, and I so advised the Commander-in-Chief and the Secretary of State, that none of this ammunition should be considered serviceable for war, and consequently, 66,000,000, or thereabouts, of our reserve was noneffective for purposes of war. It was about the same time also in that summer that The Hague Convention sat, and passed a resolution against all expanding bullets, but our Government was not a party to that Convention, and they declined to be bound by it, but, nevertheless, it is impossible to avoid a feeling that it had a certain moral effect, and that it was not considered desirable to use an expanding bullet in time of war. The reason why we did not use the expanding bullet in South Africa was not The Hague Convention, however, but because the Mark IV ammunition, our expanding ammunition, had proved unfit to be used in war. Consequently about two-fifths of our reserve of ammunition could not be used. We were driven to great straits at one time, because we had actually got reduced in this country to two or three boxes of Mark II ammunition; so that if we had had to go to war with a European Power we should have had to fight them with expanding bullets.'

"The War Office sent out 4,000,000 rounds of Mark IV ammunition to South Africa in the early summer of 1899, but on the 15th July telegraphed out orders that it was to be used in practice only, and on the 17th October directed that it should all be sent home."[1]

It is quite certain that occasionally on both sides during the war expanding and even explosive bullets used in hunting were made use of, but this was very exceptional and happened in spite of the earnest effort of the authorities to prevent it.

Use of natives as soldiers.—It was early apprehended that the natives would be used as soldiers, and the apprehension was natural in view of the great preponderance of the native population. There seems to be no question, however, that neither belligerent made general use of the Kaffirs as soldiers, although ample opportunity was certainly offered the British from the hostility of the natives towards the Boers. Both armies made use of them for teamsters, servants, guides and scouts, and to this it would seem no serious objection can be made.[2] Kaffirs connected with the British forces were, however, viewed with suspicion by the Boers, and many cases of their harsh treatment by the latter reached the ears of the British authorities. Sir A. Conan Doyle says that "when it was found that they were systematically shot they were given rifles, as it was inhuman to expose them to death without any means of defense."[3] Likewise, on the occasion of Boer raids into Zululand, it was declared by the British Government that if the Boers invaded "native districts" the natives would be encouraged to defend themselves.[4] A more questionable proceeding was the use of armed Kaffirs late in the war for the defense of the railroad lines.[5] If the destruction of the railway lines had always been illegal, the use of the armed natives in their defense might have been justified, but, as we shall see later, this was not the case.

Combatant character of Boers.—In The Hague Regulations are enumerated four conditions which entitle those satisfying them to the privileges of soldiers, two of these being the carrying of some distinctive sign recognizable at a

[1] Report of His Majesty's Commissioners on the War in South Africa, p. 86.

[2] A. Conan Doyle, The War in South Africa, p. 120.

[3] A. Conan Doyle, The War in South Africa, p. 121.

[4] Parl. Debates, Fourth Series, Vol. LXXIX, pp. 58, 558.

[5] Doyle, The War in South Africa, p. 121.

distance and carrying arms openly.[6] It is questionable whether the Boers always complied with these two conditions,[7] but this fact is not in itself conclusive of wrongdoing on their part, as the four conditions enumerated in The Hague Regulations were intended to insure combatant rights to those satisfying them, not necessarily to place others not satisfying them outside the combatant class. Cases not coming within the terms of the provisions were to be left to the unwritten law of nations. Great Britain, at both Brussels and The Hague, had taken a high stand with regard to the right of the population to participate in the defense of its country, and, as might have been expected, seems to have made no objection to the Boer forces on account of their at times informal costume, although in the early stages of the war the Boers invaded British territory and so were not strictly fighting in defense of their own country. The refusal of the British authorities to acknowledge the belligerent character of the Boer forces in the later stages of the war seems to have been caused by their feeling of the uselessness of the guerilla struggle rather than by the noncompliance of the Boer forces with the conditions necessary to entitle them to combatant privileges.

Charges and countercharges.—A practice condemned by the laws of war is fighting in the uniform of the enemy, and of this individual Boers were evidently guilty.[8] Charges of violation of the white flag and of the Geneva Convention were made on both sides, and the charge of not giving quarter was made against a small detachment of British soldiers at Elandslaagte;[9] but most of these charges were either denied or explained. No war, however, can be entirely free from such incidents, and the authorities on both sides seem to have kept them at a minimum. With regard to the treatment of prisoners, and the sick and wounded, there appears to have been little of which to complain, except possibly the unpreparedness of the British authorities for the care of the sick and wounded at the outbreak

6 Article 1.

7 Doyle, The War in South Africa, pp. 112–118; F. Despagnet, La Guerre Sud-Africaine, p. 107.

8 Doyle, p. 118.

9 Despagnet, La Guerre Sud-Africaine, p. 132.

of the war.[10] During the later part of the war the British authorities refused to allow neutral field hospitals to proceed to the relief of the Boers on account of the abuse which had been made of them earlier in the war. Thus, it was reported that the mission sent by the Committee of Antwerp was the means of volunteers joining the Boer army under the protection of the Red Cross, and the Dutch field hospital which left July 5, 1900, was immediately arrested for carrying information to the enemy, and its male contingent retained as prisoners for a considerable time.[11]

Embargo.—An interesting case of embargo was the forced return of a British ship which had left Durban, in Natal, for Lorenzo Marques, and the compulsory disembarkment of all the passengers not of British nationality.[12]

Fears for the gold mines.—It was very much feared that the Boers would seek revenge on the owners of the gold mines, whom they considered largely responsible for their troubles, by wrecking the mining plants. Suggestions to that effect were made to the Boer Government, but they were never carried out, and the British took possession of the mines substantially uninjured.[13] The Boer Government, however, needed the output of the mines in order to carry on the war, and requisitioned in all, it is said, £450,000. But, in consequence of many of the concessionary companies leaving the country, the government was compelled to work the mines itself.[14]

Refusal of the British Government to recognize forfeitures and alienations.—In the London Times of January 16, 1900, it is stated that all mines were threatened with confiscation which did not produce monthly 30 percent of their average yield, taking the three months preceding the war as the basis of the calculation.[15] Possibly this was the occasion of the notice of January 26, 1900, that the British Government would not recognize the validity of forfeitures of property within the Transvaal or The Orange Free State, or of charges, fines, or encumbrances of whatsoever descrip-

[10] Report of Royal Commission on Care and Treatment of Sick and Wounded during the South African Campaign, p. 4.

[11] Despagnet, La Guerre Sud-Africaine, pp. 371–374.

[12] *Ibid.*, p. 139.

[13] Blue Book, South Africa, 1901 (cd. 547), p. 56.

[14] Despagnet, La Guerre Sud–Africaine, p. 142.

[15] *Ibid.*, p. 142.

tion declared, levied or charged upon such property, or of conveyances of the same made subsequently to the beginning of the war by the two governments.[16] On March 19 this was supplemented by a Proclamation refusing to recognize alienations of property, whether of lands, railway mines or mining rights made by the two governments subsequent to the date of the Proclamation.[17] Neither of these measures, it would seem, went beyond the right of the British Government. As it was probable that most of the forfeitures would be made for complicity with the British cause, it would have been most ungrateful for the British Government to have recognized their validity. As to the second measure, the success of the British arms was apparently so certain at the time of its promulgation that the grant of any concession, or the alienation of any public property, must have seemed to the British authorities merely an attempt to deprive them of the fruits of victory and not the exercise of legitimate governmental power.

Commandeering of British subjects.—Complaints were early made to the British authorities that the Orange Free State was compelling British subjects to join its forces, and in a telegram of October 11, 1899, Lord Milner inquired whether it was true that British subjects, who had never taken the oath required by law, had been so treated on the ground of residence or of possessing property in the state.[18] President Steyn replied by telegraph on the same day that "No one is regarded or treated as a burgher who has not been with his knowledge and consent put on the burgher list and exercised in elections or otherwise the privileges of burghers."[19] Nevertheless, complaints continued to be made and with great positiveness by Lord Milner.[20] It is also reported that foreign residents generally were compelled to enter the service of the Free State.[21]

Treatment of British subjects in the Transvaal and of dangerous persons in British Territory.—British subjects in the Transvaal were required to leave the country on

16 Parl. Papers, 1900, Vol. LVI (cd. –53).
17 Parl. Papers, 1900, Vol. LVI (cd. –128).
18 Parl. Papers, 1900, LVI (cd. –43), p. 125.
19 Parl. Papers, 1900, LVI (cd. –43), p. 205.
20 Parl. Papers, 1900, LVI (cd. –261), p. 9.
21 For liability of foreign residents to military service, see *infra*, p. 213.

the outbreak of the war, unless they received special permission to remain. Many, however, whether with special permission or not, did remain, but in certain places were subjected to subsequent expulsion.[22] The British also had to expel from their territory individuals whose presence appeared to be dangerous. Probably in some cases individuals were expelled on insufficient ground. An assurance was given by Great Britain to Germany that reparation would be made where the expulsion of the latter's subjects was unjustified.[23]

The annexation of the Boer Republics.—So far the conduct of the British has not been open to serious criticism. With regard to their annexation of the two republics, there is more room for doubt. It has become too well established in the laws and customs of war to need elaboration, that conquest is not complete until substantial resistance has ceased, and that until then sovereignty remains where it was before the war, so that previous to that time the annexation of territory is improper. It was claimed by the British that the Boers proclaimed the annexation of British territory earlier in the war, but this the Presidents of the two Republics denied; and it does not appear that the British Government justified its action on the ground of reprisals. Leaving that out of account, subsequent events show that the annexations were premature, and that many of the claims to obedience, made in proclamations in consequence, were unjustified. But "hindsight is better than foresight," and it does not appear than the British authorities were altogether unreasonable in thinking the war practically at an end at the time of the annexations. A year later the end of the war seemed much further off than it did then. Of this fact no stronger evidence can be demanded than the letter of President Steyn to Lord Kitchener somewhat more than a year later, in which he said:

Letter of President Steyn to Lord Kitchener on the retrogression in British affairs from the middle of 1900.—"I also note that Your Excellency assumes that our struggle is hopeless. I do not know whereon Your Excellency founds your assumption. Let us, for a moment, compare our respective positions now with those of a year ago.

22 Despagnet, pp. 143, 224, *et seq.*
23 *Ibid.*, p. 225.

"A year ago, after the surrender of General Prinsloo the Cape Colony was altogether peaceful and free from our commandos. The Orange Free State was almost totally in your hands, not alone capital, railway line, and other towns, but also the whole country, except there where Commandant Haasbroek was with his commando, and it was almost the same in the South African Republic. That country was altogether in your hands, excepting where General Delarey was with his commando, and General Botha with his, in the back country—the Boschveld. How do matters stand today? The Cape Colony is, so to speak, filled with our commandos, and they are in reality in possession of the greater portion of that Colony, and trek about as they wish, and we have continually many of our race and others joining us, thereby protesting against the gross injustice done to the Republics.

"In the Orange Free State I freely acknowledge that Your Excellency is in possession of the capital, railways, and a few other towns not lying on the railway, but that is the extent of your possessions.

"The whole Orange Free State, with the above exceptions, is in our possession. In the majority of the chief towns Landdrosts have been appointed by us, and where the chief towns are not in our possession the Landdrosts are appointed in the districts. Law and order in the Orange Free State are maintained by us and not by Your Excellency. In the Transvaal the conditions are similar. There also law and order are maintained by the magistrates appointed by the Government.

"Allow me to remark that your Excellency's jurisdiction extends only as far as your cannon can reach."[24]

This confirmed by Sir Alfred Milner's letter of February 6, 1901.—The general purport of this as to the retrogression in British affairs from the middle of 1900 is confirmed by Sir Alfred Milner's letter to Mr. Chamberlain of February 6, 1901.[25]

The proclamations following annexation.—From the steps taken immediately thereafter, it is evident that the annexation of the Orange Free State, at least, was not intended to be a dead letter. The Proclamation of annexa-

[24] Blue Book, 1902, Vol. 67 (cd. 903), p. 84.
[25] Blue Book, 1901, Vol. 47 (cd. 547), p. 55.

tion was issued May 24, 1900. A week later Lord Roberts declared "that the Orange River Colony is, as a temporary measure, and until further notice, placed under martial law, as such law is understood and administered in British territory and by British officers."[26]

By another Proclamation, of the following day, he warned all inhabitants of the Orange River Colony who should be found in arms fourteen days thereafter, that they would be liable to treatment as rebels and to suffer in person and property accordingly. He also required the surrender of arms and ammunition under penalty.[27]

Injustice of treating those "on commando" as rebels.—While few appear to have been brought before the courts-martial on the mere charge of bearing arms, it is probably only too true that the threats in this proclamation were at times carried out by the burning of farms; for in the list prepared by the British Government of the farms that were burnt, the only cause assigned in many cases was that the owner was "on commando."[28] The punishment thus inflicted was most unfortunate as well as most unjust, and apparently it had much to do with the renewed activity of the Boers and the prolongation of the war. The injustice of treating those "on commando" as rebels was so manifest that by a proclamation of September 1, 1900, Lord Roberts declared that only those burghers resident in the Orange River Colony, who had not been continuously "on commando" since a time prior to the annexation, were considered as subjects of the Queen, and that burghers who had been so on commando, should, if captured, be treated as prisoners of war.[29]

The Oath of Neutrality.—One of the first steps taken by Lord Roberts on entering Bloemfontein, in March, 1900, was to issue a proclamation, the main part of which reads: "All burghers who have not taken a prominent part in the policy which has led to the war between Her Majesty and the Orange Free State, or commanded any forces of the Republic, or commandeered or used violence to any British subjects, and who are willing to lay down their arms at

26 Parl. Papers, 1900, Vol. 56 (cd. -426), p. 6.
27 Parl. Papers, 1900, Vol. 56 (cd. -426), p. 8.
28 Parl. Papers, 1901, Vol. 47 (cd. -524).
29 Parl. Papers, 1900, Vol. 56 (cd. -426), p. 15

once, and to bind themselves by an oath to abstain from further participation in the war, will be given passes to allow them to return to their homes, and will not be made prisoners of war, nor will their property be taken from them.''[30]

Differed from a Prisoner's Parole.—This was evidently something different from the release of prisoners on parole. It was an inducement to lay down arms, which may have looked unobjectionable from the British point of view, but which must have looked to the South African Governments as a bribe offered for desertion from their cause. The so-called Oath of Neutrality must have been regarded as the consummation of the desertion rather than as the parole of a prisoner of war.

It is not surprising that neither of the Republics recognized its validity. Their action in compelling the men who had taken the oath to go again on commando would therefore appear to have been justifiable.

Where this oath was taken voluntarily it was binding on the taker unless he was released by the violation of the conditions of the oath on the part of the British authorities.—But it was not justifiable for the men who had taken the oaths to retake arms voluntarily, unless they had been released from the obligation of their oaths by the failure of the British Government to live up to its part of the contract. This, General De Wet claims, was the case. He claims that the British Government violated its contract in the first place by requiring the inhabitants, both those who had not taken the oath of neutrality and those who had, to furnish information with regard to the presence of Boer forces on or near their land, and in the second place by requisitioning the property of those who had taken the oath.[31] Whether these things were or were not violations of the contract, it is easy to see how the Boers regarded them as such, and therefore felt justified in voluntarily retaking arms. On the other hand, it is easy to see how the British authorities should have felt they were not violations of the contract, and how they accordingly felt justified in punishing the Boers who again took up arms.

The injustice of punishing those who were forced to vio-

30 *Ibid.*, p. 3.

31 De Wet, Three Years' War, p. 159, *et seq.*

late their oath.—If these had been all whom the British authorities punished, there would be little ground for harsh comment, but they were not. A large number of those who resumed fighting were terrorized into doing so by the Boer forces. The hardship of their being punished on that account is evident. On this point, Sir A. Conan Doyle says: "Their promise was in a sense conditional upon effective protection from our troops. We had no right to place a man in so terrible a position that he had to choose between breaking his parole and death at the hands of his own countrymen. If we were not sure that we could protect them we could have retained them in guarded camps, as we eventually did. If we chose to turn them loose on the wide veldt, then it was our fault more than theirs that they were forced into the ranks of the enemy. To their credit be it said that even under such pressure many of them were true to their oaths.

"But, if their guilt is indeed no greater than our own, then how are we justified in burning down their houses?"[32]

The great evil of the war.—This brings us to the great evil of the war—the burning of the farms. From June, 1900, to January, 1901, 634 in all are reported to have been destroyed in this way.[33] In many cases the causes assigned for the burning constituted serious offences against the laws of war, such as irregular shooting and train wrecking; but the causes more often assigned, such as harboring Boers, and laying waste country used as a base by the enemy, were capable of the widest extension, while the burning of farms on account of the involuntary breaking of the neutrality oath, or merely on account of the owner being "on commando," was, as we have seen, absolutely unjustifiable. One of the worst features of such a practice is the rapidity with which it develops when once entered upon. It gives rise to such exasperation that the incidents that call for its exercise are multiplied many fold; its exercise is multiplied in even greater proportion; and so the movement goes on, driving the whole population to desperation, putting new life into the war and making its speedy termination improbable. This is precisely what happened in the Boer War. The buildings

32 A. Conan Doyle, The War in South Africa, p. 79.
33 Parl. Papers, 1901, Vol. 47 (cd. –524).

burnt in October, 1900, reached the number of 189. In November it increased to 226. This was intolerable. It aroused public sentiment everywhere, and the Boers, strengthened by the recruits it brought, regained territory on every hand. The British authorities came to realize this and on November 18, 1900, Lord Roberts issued the following Proclamation: "As there appears to be some misunderstanding with reference to burning of farms and breaking of dams, Commander-in-Chief wishes the following to be lines on which general officers commanding are to act:

The practice practically stopped by a proclamation of Lord Roberts.—"No farm is to be burnt except for act of treachery, or when troops have been fired on from premises, or as punishment for breaking of telegraph or railway lines, or when they have been used as bases of operations for raids, and then only with direct consent of general officer commanding, which is to be given in writing. The mere fact of a burgher being absent on commando is on no account to be used as reason for burning a house. All cattle, wagons, and food stuffs are to be removed from all farms; if that is found to be impossible, they are to be destroyed, whether owner be present or not."[34]

The effect of this proclamation was instantaneous. From 226 farms burnt in November, the number fell in December to six. But the harm was done. From this time on the war was characterized by bitterness seldom witnessed in modern warfare.

The difficulty in maintaining lines of communication.—One of the great difficulties of the war was the maintenance of lines of communication. With that end in view, Lord Roberts issued the following proclamation June 16, 1900:

"Whereas, small parties of raiders have recently been doing wanton damage to public property in the Orange River Colony and the South African Republic by destroying railway bridges and culverts and cutting the telegraph wires, and whereas such damage cannot be done without the knowledge and connivance of the neighboring inhabitants and the principal civil residents in the districts concerned;

"Now, therefore, I, Frederick Sleigh, Baron Roberts, etc., warn the said inhabitants and principal civil residents, that,

[34] Parl. Papers, 1900, Vol. 56 (cd. -426), p. 23.

whenever public property is destroyed or injured in the manner specified above, they will be held responsible for aiding and abetting the offenders. The houses in the vicinity of the place where the damage is done will be burnt and the principal civil residents will be made prisoners of war.''[35]

In another proclamation three days later was added the following:

''1. The principal residents of the towns and districts will be held jointly and severally responsible for the amount of damage done in their districts.

''2. In addition to the payment of the damage above mentioned, a penalty depending upon the circumstances of each case, but which will in no event be less than the sum of 2s. 6d. per morgen on the area of each farm, will be levied and recovered from each burgher of the district in which the damage is done in respect of the land owned or occupied by him in such district. Furthermore, all receipts for goods requisitioned in such district on behalf of the military authorities will be cancelled, and no payment whatsoever will be made in respect of the same.

''3. As a further precautionary measure, the director of military railways has been authorized to order that one or more of the residents, who will be selected by him from each district, shall from time to time personally accompany the trains while traveling through their district.

''4. The houses and farms in the vicinity of the place where the damage is done will be destroyed, and the residents in the neighborhood dealt with under martial law.''[36]

In the first place, it is to be noticed that the destruction of lines of communication is here treated as an offense against the laws of war; and, insofar as it is done by noncombatants, this is correct; but, insofar as it is a part of regular military operations, it is not. In the earlier proclamation, Lord Roberts speaks of ''small parties of raiders,'' but he does not affirm that such parties did not satisfy the conditions of belligerency, and in many cases we have good evidence that they did. In such cases the treatment of the destruction of the railways as an offense against the laws of war was not justifiable.

[35] *Ibid.*, p. 10.
[36] *Ibid.*, p. 11.

The use of notables on trains to protect communications.—The third provision of the second proclamation introduced the practice of placing hostages on railway trains for their protection. If there had been no Boer forces in the field entitled to belligerent rights, this measure might have been justified as a preventative measure; but, while there were such forces in the field having a perfect right to tear up railroads, the measure was one analogous to placing prisoners of war where the enemy is liable to attack, so that, if he does attack, his fellow-countrymen must suffer first. The objections to this practice as to trains have already been noted in treating of the Franco-German War. Evidently the attention of the British forces was called to them, and a little over a month later this section of the proclamation was repealed. It was, however, again resorted to by Lord Kitchener late in the following year.

Destruction of railroads punished by the burning of farms in the vicinity.—The burning of farms for the causes indicated in this proclamation was one of the features of farm burning that the Boers most bitterly complained of. Collective responsibility of any kind for acts of individuals over whom a community has not effective control is harsh enough, even where the penalty is less severe than burning, but it was especially harsh in this case, where the destruction of the railway lines was often a perfectly proper act of war.

Collective responsibility.—Where the destruction was the work of noncombatants, however, it would seem to have been proper to hold the communities to some degree of collective responsibility, if, as Lord Roberts claimed in his proclamation of June 16, it could not have been "done without the knowledge and connivance of the neighboring inhabitants and the principal civil residents in the districts concerned." In such a case it did not come within the provisions of The Hague Regulations as to "individual acts for which they (communities) could not be regarded as collectively responsible."

The Concentration Camps.—This brings us to the consideration of the question of the Concentration Camps, the number of whose inmates increased from 20,000 at the end of the year 1900 to more than 100,000 at the end of 1901.[37]

[37] Doyle, The War in South Africa, p. 82.

The British position with regard to them is best given in the language of Lord Kitchener's letter to Mr. Brodrick, of December 6, 1901. It was, in part, as follows:

Lord Kitchener's justification of them.—"Numerous complaints were made to me in the early part of this year by surrendered burghers, who stated that after they had laid down their arms, their families were ill-treated and their stock and property confiscated by order of the Commandants-General of the Transvaal and Orange Free State. These acts appear to have been taken in consequence of the circular dated Roos, Senekal, 6th November, 1900, in which the Commandant-General says: "Do everything in your power to prevent the burghers laying down their arms. I will be compelled, if they do not listen to this, to confiscate everything movable or immovable, and also to burn their houses.' * * * .

"In addition to the families of surrendered burghers who either came in of their own accord, or were brought in solely to save them from the reprisals of the enemy, there are three other classes represented in our refugee camps:

"(a) Families who were reported to be engaged in a regular system of passing information to the enemy.

"(b) Families from farms which were constantly used by the enemy as places from which to snipe at our troops.

"(c) Families from farms which were used as commissariat depots by the enemy. * * *

"The majority of the women and children in the refugee camps are those of surrendered burghers; but neither they nor the wives of prisoners of war, nor of men on commando, make any serious complaint, although they are constantly being invited by commissions, inspectors, etc., to say something, however little it may be, against the arrangements made for their comfort, recreation and instruction."[38]

Where a whole population engages in warfare the distinction between combatant and noncombatant vanishes.—To the majority in them, as Lord Kitchener states, the camps established by the British authorities were truly camps of refuge. To a minority, however, there can be no question that they were camps of concentration. But it has always been an accepted principle of war that, if those who are ordinarily noncombatants engage in hostili-

[38] Blue Book, 1902, Vol. 68 (cd. 902), p. 119.

ties, they cannot claim the privileges of noncombatants. The Boers felt they were fighting for the sacred cause of liberty. If they were willing to suffer martyrdom in that cause, all honor was due them, but when in order to continue the struggle, they found it necessary to resort to guerilla fighting, thus involving the whole people in the war, they had no right to complain when the British authorities made prisoners of those who had ceased to be noncombatants.

The sufferings of those who were not brought into the camps worse than the suffering of those who were brought in.—Indeed, General Botha, in a letter to Mr. Chamberlain of November 12, 1902, lays special stress on the suffering of those who were not brought into the concentration camps. He said: "My remark at Paris about the sufferings of the women and children, which you quote, has reference more particularly to those remaining outside the camps, who had their dwellings with the furniture, food, and all that they contained, burnt or destroyed by British troops; their herds killed or removed, and they themselves left destitute on the veldt. These were certainly sufferings."[39] It was certainly a mercy to bring women and children such as these, who had had their provisions destroyed as a means of war, within the concentration camps.

The conduct of the Concentration Camps.—The conduct of these camps has, however, been severely criticised. But, after careful investigation, it may be stated that the following extract from the letter of Mr. Chamberlain to General Botha, to which the letter from which the last extract was taken was a reply, sums up accurately the true facts with regard to them: "No one deplores more than the British Government the high mortality in the camps during the epidemic of measles and pneumonia, but nothing was spared that money or science could afford to reduce it, and for the last six months the average total death rates in the camps have been about 21 per 1,000 per annum."[40]

The threat of banishment from South Africa.—One of the last important measures taken by the British authorities was embodied in the proclamation dated August 6, 1901, which, after stating that regular warfare had ceased,

[39] Parl. Papers, 1902, Vol. 69 (cd. 1329), p. 7.
[40] *Ibid.*, p. 4.

declared that all Boers not surrendering before the 15th of next September should be permanently banished from South Africa, and that the cost of the maintenance of the families of all burghers fighting thereafter should be recoverable from them and should be a charge on the movable and immovable property in the colonies.[41]

A most unfortunate one.—This proclamation is very much to be regretted. The attitude taken toward the Boers for their continuing the struggle, and the refusal to recognize them as any longer entitled to belligerent rights, though in many ways the Boers were in a better position than they had been a year earlier, are explained but not justified by the strain which the continuance of the war had caused the British authorities. Especially was the threat of banishment for life reprehensible. As a matter of fact it was never carried out. Its fate was settled by the following telegram of May 27, 1902, from Lord Milner to Mr. Chamberlain, which reflects the unfortunate attitude which the British authorities finally assumed.

Its approval by Lords Milner and Kitchener.—"Referring to your telegram of 26th May, no promises have been made or asked for. The Boers are no doubt aware that legislation is required to give effect to banishment, and feel that we would not introduce such legislation if Article 3 of proposed agreement is accepted. This is obvious, and it follows that if surrender comes off banishment will be passively dropped. I was in favor of banishment proclamation and was prepared to go even further, as I thought, and I still think, that resistance of Boers had ceased to be legitimate at that stage, and that it was our duty to impose special penalties upon those responsible for adoption of guerilla methods by which the country was being ruined and by which alone the struggle could be kept up at all.

"So far from regretting the proclamation, I believe it has had great effect in increasing the number of surrenders, and in inducing the Boers still in the field to desist from further fighting. That has certainly been Kitchener's opinion, as he has always pressed and given the greatest publicity to the lists of banished leaders, but it would be a mistake if the Boers now give in in a body and live as British subjects to continue a proscription which would only

[41] Parl. Papers, 1901, Vol. 47 (cd. 732), p. 6.

keep up bitter feeling and tend to prevent the country from settling down.

"Kitchener agrees entirely."[42]

Boxer uprising in China.—While the South African war was still in its earliest stages, there broke out in China the Boxer uprising, followed by the shooting of the German Ambassador, and the siege of the legations. In bidding farewell to the troops which he sent to avenge the murder of his representative, Emperor William is reported to have bade them give no quarter to their enemies, and make their name a by-word for centuries to come.[43] As this was a measure of reprisal and no very definite limitations have yet been developed with regard to reprisals, this cannot be said to have been a violation of the laws of war; but it takes us back to the stern measures of Cromwell, which many had supposed were relegated to the memories of a less humane age. Other measures taken during the campaign in China can likewise be justified only as part of the scheme of reprisals, and cannot serve as precedents for the conduct of ordinary warfare.

The war in the Philippines.—The principal feature of the war in the Philippines was the establishment of zones of refuge, outside of which supplies of every kind were either removed or destroyed. The condition of affairs much resembled that in South Africa, although in many respects they were much worse. An irregular guerilla warfare was carried on, friendly populations were terrorized, and outrages of every kind were frequent. The only apparent remedy for this state of things was to draw a sharp line between territory which could be effectively policed and that which could not be, and then to destroy the provisions in that which could not and thus reach the enemy through their stomachs. Accordingly, the inhabitants were invited within the protected area, and cared for there while the territory outside was ravaged. There were no concentration camps in the sense that inhabitants were forced to come into them. The results were almost instantaneous. In a few months order was restored and the inhabitants were able to return to their homes.[44]

42 Parl. Papers, 1902, Vol. 69 (cd. 1096), p. 9.

43 Annual Register, 1900, p. 300.

44 House Doc. No. 2, 57th Cong., 2d Session, pp. 231–234.

CHAPTER XIV.

THE RUSSO-JAPANESE WAR.[1]

Outbreak of hostilities.—The world was watching with ever-increasing interest the apparently inevitable approach of the conflict between Russia and Japan over Manchuria and Korea when it was electrified by the news that about midnight of the 8th of February, 1904, the Japanese had made a torpedo boat attack on the Russian fleet in the outer harbor of Port Arthur with a probable loss to the Russians of a first-class protected cruiser and the two most powerful battleships of the fleet. But no formal declaration of war had yet been made by Japan, nor was any made until the tenth and the admiration for the brilliancy and dash of the Japanese was even exceeded by the indignant clamor of Russian partisans who claimed that the attack had been a violation of international law in that it had been treacherous and that it had been made prior to the formal declaration.

A declaration not a prerequisite.—There was nothing in the second charge as the law with regard to formal declarations at the beginning of the century[2] had not changed, and this was conceded by F. de Martens, the ablest of Japan's critics.[3] France had been especially punctilious in declaring war in 1870, and it was urged by some writers, principally French, that the practice of the preceding fifty years had made a declaration a prerequisite to hostilities, but this is disproved by the careful study of M. Dupuis of the wars of that period.[4] In view of the facts he brings out, the contention that modern practice required a prior declaration must have been based on a conception of declaration other than that generally accepted. The Institute

[1] It is a matter of regret that notice of the publication of La Guerre Russo-Japonaise au Point de Vue Continental et le Droit International, by Nagao Ariga, reached the writer too late to allow him to make use of it.

[2] See *supra*, p. 41.

[3] 11 R. G. D. I. P., 148.

[4] 13 R. G. D. I. P., 725.

of International Law subsequently expressed the opinion that war ought not to be commenced without a declaration or an ultimatum, with conditional declaration, and the Second Peace Conference embodied that opinion in a Convention,[5] but neither the one nor the other was acting as an exponent of the positive law.

But treachery unlawful.—However, even such writers as Bynkershoek and Ward, who had done more than any other two men to incorporate into legal literature the doctrine that a previous declaration was unnecessary, believed that before recourse could be had to arms demand of satisfaction for the injury complained of was necessary and a denial or delay thereof. It is requisite, therefore, to determine whether Japan lived up to these conditions.

Diplomatic events leading up to the war.—Russia had deprived Japan of what the latter felt to be the fruits of her war with China, and instead of evacuating Manchuria seemed to be strengthening her hold there and to be attempting to get a foothold in Korea. This Japan felt to be in violation of what she considered her special rights in the former and her preponderating rights in the latter, but apparently she hoped to protect her interests without resorting to arms and so commenced negotiations by the delivery of a note August 12, 1903. To this note Russia replied October 3. It is sufficient to say that Russia wished Japan to recognize Manchuria as outside her sphere of influence and to engage not to take advantage of her privileged position in Korea to gain a strategical foothold there. A second note of October 30 was answered on December 11 with no indication of any concessions on Russia's part, and a third *note verbale* of December 23, on January 6. A last effort was made on January 13, 1904, when Mr. Kurino, the Japanese representative at St. Petersburg, was instructed to deliver a fourth note to Count Lamsdorff, with a request for an early reply. From January 23 on, Mr. Kurino made at least four attempts to get a reply or at least an assurance as to the date by which a reply might be expected, but, although the dates given out by the Japanese and Russian authorities respectively are somewhat conflicting, it seems clear that towards the end of January the Japanese came to understand that they might hope for a

[5] See *infra*, p. 198.

reply by February 2,[6] but on pressing for a more definite assurance, were told that the reply would be sent as soon as possible, but that no exact date could be given.[7] This was the diplomatic situation on the first of February. There was certainly strong ground for contention on the part of the Japanese that the satisfaction of their claims had been delayed, but whether these facts in themselves would have justified the Japanese in commencing hostilities it is unnecessary to decide as the importance of the diplomatic events was soon overshadowed by the steps taken by the Russian military authorities on land and sea.

Military and naval events.—On the 21st of January two battalions of infantry and some of the artillery were sent from Port Arthur and Talien to the northern frontier of Korea; on the 28th, Viceroy Alexieff ordered the Russian troops next the Yalu to be placed on a war footing and on February 1, the Governor of Vladivostock asked the Japanese Commercial Agent at that port to prepare to withdraw the Japanese residents to Habarofsk, as he was ready at any time to proclaim martial law under the instructions of his government.[8] About the same time the Russian Mediterranean fleet under the command of Admiral Wirenius left Suez for the far east.[9] But the deciding factor seems to have been the sailing of the Russian fleet from Port Arthur. For three days from the 31st of January to the 3d of February, the Russian ships were being towed from the inner to the outer harbor of Port Arthur, and on the latter date, with the possible exception of one vessel, all the best of the Russian ships put to sea.[10]

War. Port Arthur.—On the same day the members of the Japanese Cabinet and of the Privy Council held a conference. No reply had as yet been received from St. Petersburg, although there had been reason to expect one by the 2d and the sailing of the fleet from Port Arthur under the circumstances could only be looked upon as a hostile measure. On the following day the Russian fleet, twenty-six ships in all, was seen off the Shantung promontory

[6] Kurino to Komura, Jan. 28, 1904, 42 Memorial Diplomatique, 306.

[7] Kurino to Komura, Feb. 1, 1904, *Ibid.*

[8] Reply of the Japanese Government, Asakawa, The Russo-Japanese Conflict, p. 353.

[9] Lawrence, p. 22.

[10] Times History, p. 42.

between Port Arthur and the Japanese coast.[11] This was the 4th of February. The same day another conference was held between the members of the Cabinet and Privy Council, this time before the throne, and the result was war. On the following afternoon, the 5th, at 2 p. m. two notes were telegraphed to Mr. Kurino, the one breaking off diplomatic relations, the other terminating the negotiations and declaring that "the Imperial Government reserve to themselves the right to take such independent action as they may deem best to consolidate and defend their menaced position, as well as to protect the acquired rights and legitimate interests of the Empire."[12] Shortly afterwards orders were sent to Vice-Admiral Togo at Sasebo to go in search of the Russian fleet, and he sailed from that port on the following morning, the 6th, at 7 o'clock.[13] Two hours later he seized the *Ekaterinoslau,* a ship belonging to the Volunteer Fleet Company, of Russia.[14] This was the first hostile act of war. He then proceeded to Port Arthur and about midnight of the 8th and 9th surprised the Russian fleet in the outer harbor. The Japanese torpedo boats succeeded in holing the two most powerful battleships of the Russian fleet, besides a first-class protected cruiser, thus inflicting incalculable damage to the fleet.[15]

Attack at Chemulpo.—Earlier on the same day a detachment of the Japanese navy under Admiral Uriu, accompanied by transports, had arrived off Chemulpo, and, it is reported, had been fired on by the old unarmoured gunboat *Korietz,* which had then run for the harbor to join her consort, the *Variag,* a first-class protected cruiser.[16] Early the following morning the neutral warships in the harbor received notice from the Japanese commander that unless the senior Russian naval officer complied with his demand to leave port before 12 o'clock to keep away from the scene of the action, which would inevitably follow within the port, but which he would not commence before 4 o'clock. The commanders of the French, British and

[11] The war in the Far East—By the Military Correspondent of the Times, p. 42.

[12] Asakawa, p. 343.

[13] Rey, XIV R. G. D. I P., 314; Takahashi, 591.

[14] Takahashi, p. 583.

[15] Times History, p. 49.

[16] *Ibid.*, p. 52.

Italian warships protested against the violation of Korean neutrality, but warned the Russian commander that if he should not comply with the Japanese demand, they would be compelled to leave.[17] Accordingly the Russian ships sailed out of port about noon, but after an engagement of thirty-five minutes at from 5,250 to 9,800 yards returned to the harbor.[18] It was decided by the Russian commander that it was useless to renew the engagement, and so the crews of the vessels, including the wounded, were removed to the British, French and Italian warships, the *Korietz* was blown up and the *Variag* set on fire and sunk.[19] Formal Declaration of War was made on the following day, the 10th. Besides the acts of hostility prior to the Declaration mentioned above, there were four other merchant ships seized in addition to the one, the seizure of which had marked the opening of hostilities.[20]

Comment.—Extended comment on the above facts is not necessary. Whether the delay in the reply to the last Japanese note would in itself have justified the commencement of hostilities or not it is clear that when considered in connection with the military measures taken by the Russian authorities, and especially the sailing of the Russian fleet, it not only justified them, but in the case of a high-spirited and powerful nation as Japan proved herself to be, rendered any other course almost out of the question. It was not to be expected that Japan would wait for a reply to her note until her shipping had been seized or some strategical advantage gained. Russia made a hostile demonstration, and she had nothing to complain of when Japan took it at its face value.

Charges made by the Russian Government.—It were unnecessary to continue the subject further if it were not for the direct charges of bad faith made by the Russian Government, the reply by the Japanese Government and the rejoinder. These constitute the only serious indictment of the Japanese, and if substantiated would have reflected materially on the Japanese irrespective of the question of the commencement of hostilities prior to a declaration.

17 For. Rel. (1904), pp. 781, 783.
18 Times History, p. 52.
19 For. Rel. (1904), p. 781.
20 Rey, 14 R. G. D. I. P., 340; Takahashi, p. 761.

To understand them, it will be necessary to take up the thread of the negotiations where we dropped them, with the refusal of the Russian authorities to fix the date for the reply to the Japanese note.

The breaking off of diplomatic relations.—About 8 o'clock on the evening of the 4th of February, Mr. Kurino was requested to see Count Lamsdorff, and was told that the reply to the Japanese note had just been sent to Viceroy Alexieff to be transmitted by him to Baron Rosen at Tokio, after making such local changes as he felt to be desirable. To save time it had also been sent direct to Baron Rosen. The general nature of the reply was not indicated, but from the expressions Count Lamsdorff gave of his personal opinion it does not seem likely that it differed vitally from the previous replies.[21] At 5:05 o'clock the following morning Mr. Kurino telegraphed the substance of his interview to Baron Komura and the telegram reached Tokio at 5:15 that afternoon.[22] As we have already seen, three hours earlier notes had been telegraphed to Mr. Kurino breaking off diplomatic relations and reserving to the Japanese "the right to take such independent action as they may deem best to consolidate and defend their menaced position, as well as to protect the acquired rights and legitimate interests of the Empire." Mr. Kurino communicated them to Count Lamsdorff at 4 o'clock on the afternoon of the 6th.

Japan did not consider the war to have commenced with the breaking of diplomatic relations.—The above reservation has a special importance from the fact that when the claim was made that Japan had violated international law by commencing hostilities prior to a declaration, it was used as an argument *ad hominem* to confound these critics as amounting in itself to a declaration. And this has even been urged in support of the contention that the practice of the last fifty years has made a prior declaration obligatory. But whatever strength there may be in such an argument, it seems clear that it was but an after thought on the part of the Japanese Government and that she justified her conduct mainly on the grounds already given. The seizure of at least two merchant ships

[21] 42 Memorial Diplomatique, 306.
[22] *Ibid.*

had occurred prior to the handing of the note to Count Lamsdorff and the Higher Prize Court in the case of the *Ekatineroslau* held that the war had commenced when the intention to make war was carried into action, that is, with the sailing of Admiral Togo's fleet.[23]

The Japanese note, however, was delivered more than two days prior to the attack at Port Arthur.—This note was, however, a complete answer to the Russian charge that "without previously notifying us that the rupture of such relations implied the beginning of warlike action, the Japanese Government ordered its torpedo boats to make a sudden attack on our squadron in the outer roadstead of the fortress of Port Arthur,"[24] and the Japanese Government contented itself with replying that the independent action she had reserved to herself in breaking off diplomatic relations implied "all, including, as a matter of course, the opening of hostile acts. Even if Russia were unable to understand it, Japan had no reason to hold herself responsible for the misunderstandings of Russia."[25] As the note was delivered to Count Lamsdorff during the afternoon of the 6th and the attack at Port Arthur did not occur till the midnight of the 8th, there was an interval of more than forty-eight hours, even subtracting the difference in time of seven hours, between the warning and the attack. Even the convention drawn up at The Hague Conference requires no such delay. That Russia did not consider the note a warning seems explicable only on the ground that the strength and spirit of Japan were greatly underrated. This brings us to the charges of treacherous interference with the telegraph service.

Charges of treacherous interference with telegraph service.—In the circular of February 22, addressed by Count Lamsdorff to Russia's representatives abroad, he charges that the Japanese Government "with a division of its fleet made a sudden attack on February 8, that is, three days prior to the declaration of war, on two Russian warships in the neutral port of Chemulpo. The commanders of these ships had not been notified of the severance of diplomatic

23 Takahashi, p. 591.
24 Asakawa, p. 345.
25 *Ibid.*, p. 354.

relations, as the Japanese maliciously stopped the delivery of Russian telegrams by the Danish cable and destroyed the telegraphic communication of the Korean Government.''[26]

On March 9 the Japanese Government made the following reply: ''The Imperial Government declare that the Russian allegation that they stopped the delivery of Russian telegrams by the Danish cable and destroyed the Korean Government's telegraphic communication is wholly untrue. No such acts were done by the Imperial Government.''[27]

Russia rejoined on the 12th as follows : ''Japan's denial of malicious interference with the transmission of Russian telegrams over the Danish cable cannot be sustained. A telegram to Baron Rosen (then Russian Minister to Japan), at Tokio, sent from St. Petersburg, February 4, was not delivered till the morning of February 7. That delay did not occur on the Siberian line, as was shown by the fact that a reply to a telegram from Viceroy Alexieff, sent at the same time, was received the same day. Therefore it is conclusive that the Rosen telegram was held by the Japanese and not delivered for two days. Communication with M. Pavloff (then Russian Minister to Korea) by the Korean telegraph ceased in the middle of January. As the Koreans were enjoying friendly relations with Russia, there is good ground for believing that the interruption was due to the Japanese. Thereafter M. Pavloff used a mail steamer or a special warship to communicate with Port Arthur. The Minister of Russia at Seoul, February 8, therefore, knew nothing of the diplomatic rupture.''[28]

The communication by the Korean cable had ceased three weeks before hostilities commenced.—With regard to the interference with the telegraphic communications of the Korean Government we have the positive denial of the Japanese Government against the ''good ground for believing'' of the Russian. But if the charge had been at all substantiated it would not have involved Japan in a treacherous opening of hostilities as communication by telegraph had ceased three weeks before they commenced.

[26] Asakawa, p. 356.

[27] Asakawa, p. 358; Takahashi gives the date of this reply as March 2, p. 12.

[28] Asakawa, p. 361.

As to the charge that the attack was made in a neutral port, that in itself could not have surprised Russia, as the use of Korea for strategic purposes was one of the very things that Japan was insisting upon in the negotiations that led up to the war. It was one of the objects of the war, and like most causes of wars and assumptions of power over weaker peoples, must be judged of by other standards than those of international law.

The nondelivery of the Rosen telegram and the charge in the purported extracts from a Red Book.—The nondelivery of the Rosen telegram, therefore, remains the only basis for the contention that the Japanese Government was guilty of malicious interference with the telegraph service at the opening of hostilities, but from the fact that this telegram was sent two days *before* the breach of diplomatic relations it is clear that it gives no support to the charge made in Count Lamsdorff's circular of February 22, that it was in part responsible for the fact that the commanders of the ships in Chemulpo harbor were not notified of the breach itself. No further attention to the nondelivery of this telegram would be necessary if it were not that it has an apparent connection with the charge made in what purported to be extracts from a Russian Red Book, that the Japanese Government had held up the reply to their last note until after they had broken off diplomatic relations.[29] These extracts were denied all authority by the Russian Government and the Red Book, if ever issued, suppressed.[30] But as this charge is the only thing that gives any importance to the nondelivery of the Rosen telegram, and as it throws light on the conflicting statements as to the date of the reply of the Russian authorities to the last Japanese note, it deserves passing notice.

Versions of the same story.—That the nondelivery of the Rosen telegram and the charge in the purported extracts are versions of the same story can hardly be questioned. They agree in their main points, and there would be little or no chance for difference of opinion were it not that it is not stated in the rejoinder of March 12 that the delayed telegram was the reply to the Japanese note and that the date of the telegram is given as the 4th of February,

[29] 43 Memorial Diplomatique, 396.
[30] Rey, 13 R. G. D. I. P., 336.

whereas in the official Russian statement of February 20 the date of the reply is given as the 3d.[31] Very little importance, however, is to be attached to this discrepancy in dates, as it is stated in the purported extracts that the telegram containing the reply was the only one of all the documents that was undated, while a general inaccuracy as to dates is shown by the fact that the Russian statements of February 20 and 22 gave the date of the Japanese Declaration as the 11th, whereas the correct date was the 10th. That the reply was sent on the 4th is further borne out by the fact that Mr. Kurino reported to his superiors in Tokio that Count Lamsdorff told him on the evening of the 4th that the telegrams containing the reply had just been sent.[32]

It will be taken then, as established beyond reasonable doubt, that the charges in the rejoinder of March 12 of the nondelivery of the Rosen telegram and in the supposed extracts, of the holding up of the Russian reply are versions of the same story and that the reply was sent on the 4th instead of the 3d. It remains then to consider whether there is any foundation for the charge that the Japanese held up the note until after the breaking off of diplomatic relations in order to justify their conduct by a claim of delay.

Any delay in delivering the Rosen telegram must have been at most only a few hours prior to the sending of the note to Mr. Kurino.—There seems no reason to question the Japanese statement that their note breaking off diplomatic relations was sent early on the afternoon of the 5th. If there was any hold up, then it must have been prior to that time and subsequent to the sending of the telegram the day before. This time must be still further reduced by the difference in time of seven hours between St. Petersburg and Tokio and the time necessary for the transmission of the message. This may be calculated at twelve hours as that was the time taken by the telegram of Mr. Kurino from St. Petersburg to Tokio sent the morning of the 5th. But if this twelve hours is added to the time of the sending of the reply it makes it extremely improbable that it could have reached Tokio before the morning of the 5th. At most

31 Asakawa, p. 350.
32 42 Memorial Diplomatique, 306.

there could have been but a delay of a few hours in the delivery of the telegram before the sending of the telegram breaking off diplomatic relations. But even this delay would have been evidence of bad faith on the part of Japan if she had given the delay in receiving the Russian answer as one of her reasons for going to war when she herself was preventing its delivery.

Most probable that any such delay would have occurred at Port Arthur.—The statement of the Russian case is that "the delay did not occur on the Siberian line, as was shown by the fact that a reply to a telegram from Viceroy Alexieff sent at the same time was received the same day. Therefore, it is conclusive that the Rosen telegram was held by the Japanese and not delivered for two days."[33] The reasoning is not very convincing at best, but in the light of the fact that Viceroy Alexieff was to make such local changes as he saw fit in the reply, it seems, with M. Rey, that it is far more probable that the delay occurred at Port Arthur than that it did at Tokio.[34] As the only official charge with regard to the nondelivery of the Rosen telegram is the rather innocuous one in the rejoinder of March 12, it might have been better to have allowed it to go unconsidered until the Russian Government itself had fathered the more serious charge, but the purported extracts from the Red Book have had a certain authority and that must be the apology for the consideration of this charge at all.

Days of grace.—Mention has already been made of the capture of certain Russian merchant vessels at the outbreak of the war. On the 9th of February the Japanese Emperor issued an ordinance decreeing that Russian merchant vessels in Japanese ports at the time might discharge or load their cargoes and leave the country not later than February 16, that such vessels, if provided with the proper certificate, should not be seized on their way back to the nearest Russian port or to a leased port or to their original destination and that Russian vessels leaving for a Japanese port before February 16 might enter and discharge their cargo at once and leave the country. All Russian vessels carrying contraband of war or analogues of contraband were excluded from the benefits of the ordinance. This or-

[33] Asakawa, p. 361.
[34] 13 R. G. D. I. P., 624.

dinance was strictly construed by the prize courts and held not to apply to ships leaving Japanese ports prior to February 9,[35] and the latter part of the ordinance only to "ships of commerce" going into a Japanese port to take on or discharge a cargo. Accordingly it was held not to apply to ships fitted out for deep-sea fishing and most of the early captures were of ships of this character, nor to boats which had been sent out to watch the fishing boats, but which otherwise retained their private character, nor to ships having no cargo to discharge, nor to ships nominally the property of the East China Railroad Company, but liable to be incorporated into the Russian navy in time of war. Nor was the ordinance applied to Russian vessels going from one enemy port to another nor from one neutral port to another.[36] The time allowed in this ordinance, seven days, will be seen to be much shorter than has become customary in the wars of the last half-century. The Imperial Order of the Russian Government dealing with this as well as other questions was not issued until February 28. It allowed Japanese merchant vessels in Russian ports at the declaration of war to remain and load their cargoes provided these did not consist of contraband of war and provided also that this period should in no case exceed forty-eight hours from the publication of the order of the local authorities. As the declaration of war had been made on the 10th, this gave Japanese vessels in Russian ports at that time twenty days from the declaration of war and somewhat more than that from the opening of hostilities plus the time taken by the local authorities to post the Czar's order. In length of time allowed the Russian action was therefore more liberal than the Japanese, although when it came it was very sudden.

Russians resident in Japan.—On the 10th of February the Japanese Minister of the Interior issued instructions allowing Russian subjects to remain in Japan during the war subject of course to such precautionary measures as might be necessary on the part of the Japanese authorities. On the same day the Minister of Public Instruction addressed a note to the school teachers instructing them that

[35] The Mukden, Takahashi, p. 603.

[36] Rey, XIV R. G. D. I. P., p. 338, *et seq.;* for the decisions of the Japanese Prize Courts, see Takahashi.

students should be careful not to manifest hostility towards Russian subjects. A little over a week later the Minister of the Interior likewise warned the heads of the various Shinto and Buddhist sects that the war should make no difference in the freedom of the exercise of their religion by the Russians and that they should call the particular attention of their clergy to these instructions.[37] During the course of the war several important localities had to be subjected to martial law, namely, Nagasaki, the island of Tsushima and the surrounding waters, Hakodaté and Sasebo, but Mr. Akiyama says that to his personal knowledge there was not a single case of expulsion or embargo or even of restriction of residence or travel of Russian subjects even in these localities.[38]

Japanese resident in Russian territory.—The continued residence of Japanese subjects in Russian territory was regulated by Article I of the Czar's order of February 28. It authorized all Japanese to remain except those in the Imperial Lieutenancy of the Far East.[39] As most of the Japanese lived in that district, however, the exception puts the rule to a very severe test and there were serious complaints of the indignities suffered by the Japanese in Manchuria and Siberia,[40] but Lawrence states that much of the cruelty was due to mob violence and to lawless subordinate officials, and that Alexieff exerted himself to secure better treatment for the refugees so that those who returned later spoke of the kindness which they had received.[41] In considering this order of the Czar we must remember that it was the Lieutenancy of the Far East that was the theatre of military operations and not Japan and that the Japanese subjects in Manchuria and Siberia were much more of a menace than the Russian subjects in Japan.

Sinking of Japanese merchantmen.—The sinking of a Japanese merchant vessel on February 11, and of a Japanese trading steamer and of a transport on April 25 by the Vladivostock Squadron, excited unfavorable comment, but each case was within one of the generally-recognized rules

37 Nagaoka, R. D. I., p. 480.
38 P. 5.
39 Hershey, p. 269.
40 Hershey, p. 298.
41 Lawrence, p. 39.

where the destruction of the ship is allowable. In the first case the sea was very rough; in the second a superior Japanese squadron was in close proximity and in the third resistance was made by part of the crew and the vessel was finally sunk by a torpedo. In the first case the crew were taken to Vladivostock and eventually sent back to Japan; in the second they were ordered ashore, and in the third that part of the troops which surrendered were taken on board the Russian ships as prisoners of war.[42] In all there appear to have been 21 Japanese vessels sunk and 5 bombarded but not sunk,[43] but the above cases are typical.[44]

Threat to treat wireless operators as spies.—Early in the war there arose an incident somewhat similar to that in the Franco-German war when Prince Bismarck threatened to treat balloonists as spies. On the 15th of April the Russian ambassador notified the State Department that: "In case neutral vessels, having on board correspondents who may communicate war news to the enemy by means of improved apparatus not yet provided for by existing conventions, should be arrested off the coast of Kwantung or within the zone of operations of the Russian fleet, such correspondents shall be regarded as spies and the vessels provided with wireless telegraph apparatus shall be seized as lawful prize."[45]

Validity of threat.—The occasion of this incident was the presence of the Chinese despatch boat *Haimun* in the service of the London and New York Times as near Port Arthur as was practicable whence it was sending messages in cipher to the British port of Wei-hai-wei.[46] There was apparently no claim that the war correspondents were giving information directly to the Japanese. The United States Government in taking note of the Russian declaration expressly refused to waive any right it might have in case of the arrest of an American citizen or the seizure of an American vessel,[47] but happily no such case arose. Un-

42 Lawrence, pp. 40–42.

43 Takahashi, p. 275.

44 For a detailed account of the sinking of merchantmen, see Takahashi, Part III, Chap. I.

45 For. Rel. (1904), p. 729.

46 Hershey, p. 117.

47 For. Rel. (1904), p. 729.

doubtedly if the correspondents had been guilty of communicating with the enemy they could have been treated as in the enemy service and the vessels seized as lawful prize and it is also clear that the Russian authorities had a right to police the seas in the neighborhood of the fleet in order to prevent the obtaining of information, but it is equally clear that as the war correspondents were not "acting clandestinely or under false pretences" they were not spies.[48]

Floating mines.—During the civil war General Sherman made his famous protest against the planting of explosives along the roads in rear of the retreating armies as unjustified by the laws of war. An analogous situation at sea arose during the Russo-Japanese war. A Japanese warship, the *Hatsuse*, was sunk by what is supposed to have been a marine mine on May 15, while cruising ten miles southeast of Port Arthur and hence on the high seas. It is also stated in the Report of the United States Delegation to the Second Peace Conference that enormous loss of life and property was caused by floating mines in the China Sea in the vicinity of Port Arthur after the close of hostilities.[49] Public interest was aroused and the demand that anchored mines which may break loose from their moorings, shall, by the fact of going adrift, become harmless and that non-anchored mines shall become inoffensive within a very short time, one or two hours at the longest, after they have passed out of the control of the party who planted them[50] has been embodied in one of The Hague Conventions.[51]

Conversion of merchant ships—The Peterburg and the Smolensk.—An interesting point was raised during the war as to the conversion of merchant ships into warships. By the Treaty of Paris of 1856, Turkey, when at peace, must close the passage of the straits to ships of war of all foreign states unless it may be deemed necessary to open them to secure the observance of the treaty itself. In the Black Sea, however, Russia has what is known as the Volunteer Fleet, nominally owned by an Association, but always at

[48] See 21 Annuaire, pp. 76, 293.
[49] P. 41.
[50] *Ibid.*
[51] See *infra*, p. 280.

the disposal of the Minister of Marine, the funds of the Association being derived in most part from the Government. The officers belong to the Imperial navy, the crews are under military discipline and one-third of them must have served in the Active Fleet. In times of peace they are used for the transportation of troops and criminals from the Black Sea to the Far East and the tea and passenger trade between those points is in their hands. They are always in the service of the government. Prior to the war they had been allowed to pass the straits with occasional protests by the British Government. At the outbreak of the war they commenced to carry guns and ammunition in their holds and thus were ready to assume a warlike character at any moment. Early in July two vessels of this fleet, the *Peterburg* and the *Smolensk* passed the Dardanelles under the merchant flag. After passing through the Suez Canal the *Peterburg* raised the Russian naval ensign, completed her armament and on July 13 captured the British steamer *Malacca* bound for Yokohama, via Hong-Kong. This created the greatest excitement, but the affair was finally closed by the release of the *Malacca* after a purely formal examination with the understanding that the *Peterburg* and the *Smolensk* should no longer act as cruisers.[52] There could be little question that these ships satisfied the requirements for warships if it were not for the fact that they had assumed that character on the high seas, and as to whether that made any difference the Second Peace Conference was unable to come to an agreement. Great Britain's strongest ground for protest would seem to have been that by ships of war the treaty of Paris intended to include ships capable of being converted into ships of war on the high seas, but it is not surprising that Russia gave an opposite construction to a treaty which has always been exceedingly irksome to her.

Proclamation of Viceroy Alexieff.—In a proclamation of February 3 (old style) Viceroy Alexieff informed the peoples and officials in the vicinity of the Chinese Eastern Railway that they would be held responsible for injuries to the railroad and to the telegraph and telephone wires in their districts and concluded with the remarkable provision that "should any of the Chinese officials or people look upon

[52] For this whole question see Lawrence, pp. 202–218.

the Russian troops with enmity the Russian Government will surely take measures to exterminate such persons; on no account will any leniency be shown them.''[53] This would have been an extraordinary exercise of authority on the part of sovereignty over its own subjects whereas Russia was not sovereign where this proclamation was to be published nor was it her subjects to whom the proclamation was addressed.

Comparatively few recriminations.—The recriminations which were so marked a characteristic of the South African and Franco-German Wars were not altogether lacking and instances of them are given by Mr. Takahashi and by Mr. Hershey, but fortunately they were not numerous. Military operations were conducted on soil foreign to both belligerents, except on the island of Sakhalin, and so the regrettable incidents which are almost inevitable where an invading army occupies enemy soil inhabited by a patriotic population did not arise.

Care of the sick and wounded.—Both belligerents were parties to the Geneva and Hague Conventions. While it is stated that the feelings between the besiegers and the besieged at Port Arthur became so bitter that flags of truce for the burial of the dead were ignored and that in consequence so many unburied Japanese dead lay on the ground as to make the stench unendurable,[54] yet in general the treatment of the dead and the care of the sick and wounded on both sides seems to have been excellent. In his work entitled The Real Triumph of Japan, Dr. Seaman testifies to the wonderful efficiency of the Japanese sanitary service and in the chapter devoted to the Red Cross Society in his From Tokio through Manchuria shows the thorough preparation the society had made for the war.[55] He states that it has the distinction of being not only the richest but probably the largest of the national Red Cross Societies.[56] Supplementary to the Red Cross Society was the Volunteer Nurses Association.[57] An unusual function of the Red

[53] For. Rel. (1904), p. 128.

[54] Hershey, p. 303.

[55] P. 217.

[56] P. 216.

[57] For the history and organization of these remarkable societies see Ariga, La Croix-rouge en extreme Orient. To the author of that work much of the credit for their efficiency is due.

Cross Society in this war was the care taken of Chinese refugees who had been engaged on the Russian works at Port Arthur before the war, but who had been discharged when war commenced. They were largely from the south of China and without the aid of the society would have been subject to fearful privations.[58] The Russians seem to have had fewer field hospitals than the Japanese, but a notable feature of their sanitary service were twenty hospital trains fitted out with the latest improvements, each capable of carrying four hundred men to the base hospitals at Mukden, Harbin and even Moscow.[59] Twenty was also the number of the hospital ships fitted out by the Japanese.[60]

The Russian regulations.—In his order of February 28, 1904, the Czar directed the military authorities to conform their conduct to the St. Petersburg Declaration and to the Geneva and Hague Conventions. Copies of these were distributed to the troops and in addition a set of instructions was issued on July 14, 1904, embodying the main provisions of The Hague Regulations applicable to troops in the field. These were divided into two parts, the first being directed to officers and the second to noncommissioned officers and soldiers. They formed a valuable supplement to the convention as they conformed more closely to the needs of the national army than an international convention could. The latter part was especially commendable. It put in short and popular form those provisions of the convention which it was especially desirable to bring home to the common soldier.[61]

Specific regulations of the Japanese.—In Japan, The Hague Convention had been proclaimed by an imperial decree in 1900. No such general instructions based on the convention were issued, but detailed instructions covering special points of the convention were and these have been made the subject of a most enlightening commentary by Masanosuké Akiyama, formerly Professor of Law at the University of Tokio, Counsellor to the Minister of War and to the Bureau of Legislation of the Imperial Cabinet

58 Seaman, p. 224.
59 Seaman, p. 226.
60 Takahashi, p. 375.
61 See 94 Archives Diplomatiques, p. 500, and Hershey, p. 271.

and Secretary during the war to the Bureau of Information for Prisoners of War. His work constitutes a valuable contribution to the laws of war, and, with his permission, it will be followed in considerable detail. Due proportion, however, prevents its inclusion here. A summary of his article is given as Appendix I.[62]

62 See *infra*, p. 332.

CHAPTER XV.

THE REVISION OF THE GENEVA CONVENTION AND THE SECOND PEACE CONFERENCE.

The Geneva Convention of 1864 and the Additional Articles of 1868.—The Geneva Convention of 1864 had many imperfections. It was an important step in the right direction, but it was not based on the experience and discussion that are necessary to the best legislation. Its imperfections soon became apparent and as we have seen the attempt was made to remedy them in the Additional Articles of 1868, and to suggest a remedy at the Brussels Conference of 1874. However great the authority of the Additional Articles became, and unquestionably their authority became very great, they never became more than a *modus vivendi* for particular wars or an interpretation of great scientific value of the articles of the convention itself. They were not free themselves from the objection of not taking sufficiently into account military necessities, and when combined with the convention formed a patchwork which was even more confusing than the convention itself.

Steps towards revision.—About the time of the Brussels Conference there appeared two works on the Convention of great value, Das Princip der Genser Convention und der freiwilligen nationalen Hülfsorganization für den Krieg, 1874, by Schmidt-Ernsthausen and Die Genser Convention, Historisch und kritischdogmatisch mit Vorschlägen zu ihrer Verbesserung, unter Darlegung und Prüsung der mit ihr gemachten Erfahrungen und unter Benutzung der amtlichen, theilweise ungedruckten Quellen bearbeitet, gekrönte Preisschrift, 1876, by Lueder, but despite the suggestions made by the Brussels Conference, little was seriously done towards the revision of the Convention until 1892, when two meetings were held by the sanitary staff of the Swiss army at Olten, at which the convention was discussed with great ability and care and a text adopted embodying the work of the assembly. Colonel Ziegler, chief of the sanitary staff of the Swiss army, was charged with the work of getting the Federal Council, if possible, to call an International Conference, and with this end in view he drew up a project of convention based largely on the deliberations at Olten, and submitted this to the Federal Council, with the prayer that they examine it and take some action in the matter.[1]

Initiative of Swiss Federal Council.—The Federal Council consulted the International Committee of the Red Cross which approved the conclusions of Ziegler, but insisted on the extention of the convention to naval war. Independently of this the Italian Government had been thinking of calling a Conference to consider the extension of the Convention to naval war, but when it learned of the steps already taken by the Swiss Government,. it courteously yielded the initiative to the latter which soon after prepared a provisional program on which it sought the advise of those competent in the matter.[2] One of the results of this initiative was a work by M. Moynier entitled, La Revision de la Convention de Genève, published in 1898.

But before any final action had been taken in the matter there appeared the famous circular of Count Mouravieff of the 24th of August, suggesting the First Peace Conference. In his second circular of January 11, 1899, the Count included in the program of the Conference the extension of the Geneva Convention to naval war. This resulted in the naval convention of 1899, but it left untouched the revision of the Geneva Convention itself, although the Conference expressed the hope that the Swiss Government would take the initiative in calling another Conference to bring that about.[3]

The Geneva Conference of 1906.—Accordingly in the month of May, 1901, a note of the Swiss Government was made public inviting the powers signatory of the Geneva Convention to a conference to discuss the advisability of a revision of the Convention and the modifications to be introduced.[4] This finally resulted in the Conference, the opening session of which was held in the Assembly Hall

[1] Gillot, p. 126.
[2] Gillot, p. 127, *et seq.*
[3] Gillot. p. 130, *et seq.*
[4] *Ibid.*, p. 136.

of the University of Geneva, at 4 P. M., on June 11, 1906.[5] But before taking up the work of the Conference, it may be well to touch for a moment on the work the Red Cross Societies and the Institute of International Law had been doing to make the convention more effective.

Preliminary work of the Red Cross Societies and of the Institute of International Law.—The favor with which the Red Cross had been received all over the world, early led to its use as a trademark and tradename, and for purposes which though charitable were in no way connected with the Red Cross Societies or the official sanitary service. The German Red Cross Society took up this matter at its meeting at Frankfort on the Main in 1880, but the Imperial authorities considered that little could be done in the matter without international action. Accordingly this was made the subject of discussion at the International conferences of the Red Cross societies at Geneva in 1884, Carlsruhe in 1887, and Rome in 1892, and the wish expressed at each of these conferences that the Governments would take effective steps to check this abuse of the Red Cross. In 1888 the International Committee of Geneva made inquiry to find out what steps had been taken by the various Governments, and was able to report that action had been taken, notably in the case of Austria, but in order to clarify ideas and get concerted action it offered a prize for the best paper on the subject, which was awarded to M. Buzzati, who came to the conclusion that an international agreement on this subject was necessary.[6] The question of a penal sanction for violations of the convention was also earnestly discussed at the different conferences of the Red Cross societies, and the Institute of International Law at its Cambridge meeting in 1895, expressed hope that the powers signatory of the Geneva Convention would enter into an agreement to pass military penal legislation covering all possible infractions of the Convention. Both the Red Cross societies and the Institute of International Law also considered the establishment of an international commission charged with the examination of alleged infractions of the convention, but this was rejected by both. Other suggestions of the Red Cross societies were the taking of meas-

[5] Report of the United States Delegation, p. 2.
[6] Gillot, p. 104.

ures for the identification of the dead and for bringing the knowledge of the convention to the troops.[7] It would be unfair before passing to the work of the Conference not to mention the very able work of M. Gillot, entitled La Revision de la Convention de Genève au point de vue historique et dogmatique, published in Paris in 1902.

Organization of the Conference.—The Conference was called to order by the President of the Swiss Confederation and proceeded to the election of the Hon. Edouard Odier, the first Swiss delegate, as president, who named M. Gustave Moynier, Honorary President of the Conference. There were thirty-seven powers represented, including all those powers, except Turkey, which had participated in the first conference of The Hague, together with the Central and South American Republics, and Korea and the Congo. Nearly all of the independent powers of the world were represented.

Membership.—"It is interesting to observe that the membership of the conference comprised fifteen ambassadors and ministers, including chargés d'affaires; eighteen officers of the diplomatic or consular service; thirty-eight officers of the army, of whom twenty were members of the medical or sanitary departments of the states which they represented; two officers of the navy; eight professors and publicists, and four officers of volunteer Red Cross societies. Although but few of the delegates directly represented the volunteer associations which have been organized in nearly all states of the civilized world, many of the representatives have been officially associated with these societies in various capacities, and most of the delegates were entirely familiar with the work which has been accomplished by them during the past forty years."[8]

Committees.—As a basis for the deliberations of the Conference, fourteen questions had been submitted to the Powers by the Swiss Government some months in advance and to facilitate its work these were apportioned among four committees, (1) on the sick, wounded and dead; (2) personnel of sanitary formation; (3) sanitary material, medical stores and supplies; (4) emblem of the convention, with the measures necessary to prevent its abuse, together

[7] Gillot, p. 100–107.

[8] Report of United States Delegation, p. 7.

with questions which were not especially assigned to other committees.[9]

Rules.—"In the deliberations of the committees the widest freedom of discussion was not only permitted, but encouraged. Members of one committee were permitted to attend the meetings of the other committees, to take part in their discussions, and submit projects for consideration or adoption. In all votes, however, whether in committee or in full conference, each state was entitled to a single voice. In each committee votes were taken upon subjects submitted in the form of questions or statements of principle, leaving to the subcommittees appointed for that purpose the duty of recasting them in the form of articles, with a view to their consideration by the several committees prior to their submission to the conference in plenary session.

The signing of the Convention.—"Triweekly sessions were held by each of the committees into which the general membership of the conference was divided, and the discussion of the questions referred to them was prosecuted with such diligence and industry, during the morning and the afternoon sessions of each day, that their work was completed, ready for submission to the conference, on June 27. At two plenary sessions, which were held on June 27 and 28 the drafts of the several paragraphs assigned to them for preparation were approved and referred to a committee for editorial revision and arrangement, with a view to their incorporation in the final draft of the convention. The treaty in the form proposed by its editing committee was formally adopted at a plenary session of the conference which was held in the Hall of the Grand Council of State on July 5, 1906. The convention was signed on July 6, 1906, by the plenipotentiaries, whose full powers had been examined and verified at a plenary session of the conference on the preceding day."[10]

Reservations.—In signing the Convention Japan, Korea, China and Great Britain made reservations as to the engagement to elaborate a military penal code against infractions of the Convention, as to the obligation to spread the knowledge of it among the troops and population and as

[9] Report of United States Delegation, p. 9.
[10] *Ibid.*, p. 13.

to the international regulation of the distinctive sign and name of the Red Cross.[11]

Formal articles.—It is expressly stipulated in the convention that it shall only be obligatory on the contracting parties in case of war between two or more of them, that it shall supersede the Convention of August 22, 1864, in the relations between the Contracting Powers, but that that convention remains in force between parties who signed it but who are not signatories of this convention; that Powers not represented at the conference and not signatories of the old convention may accede to it if within a year from its notification to the Swiss Federal Council, such Council has not been advised of any opposition on the part of any of the contracting parties, and finally that although it may be denounced, such denunciation shall take effect only one year after notification to the Swiss Federal Council.

Incorporated in the final Protocol, although not a part of the Convention itself, was the following:

"In addition and in conformity with article 16 of the convention for the pacific regulation of international conflicts of July 29, 1899, * * * the conference has expressed the following wish:

Wish expressed by the Conference.—"The Conference expresses the wish that in order to reach an interpretation and an application of the Geneva Convention as exact as possible, the contracting parties submit to the Permanent Court of The Hague, if the case and the circumstances allow of it, the differences which, in time of peace, arise between them relative to the interpretation of the said convention."[12]

Merits of the Convention—Terminology.—Of the very great merits of the new convention too much can hardly be said. The old convention had "neutralized" ambulances, military hospitals and the sanitary personnel, but this gave a very misleading impression of the protection intended. The ambulances and hospitals were not to be treated as so much neutral territory and as such free from military operations. They were not even free from seizure, and the equipment of military hospitals as distinguished from ambulances remained subject to the laws of war. Equally objectionable

11 Delpech, 13 R. G. D. I. P., 653.
12 Delpech, 13 R. G. D. I. P., 666.

was the term as applied to the sanitary personnel. It must have been galling to the patriotic surgeon to have been considered a "neuter" and not as fully in the service of his country as his military brother, and on the other hand, the term would have seemed to imply a freedom from control by the belligerent holding him in its power incompatible with military necessity. As M. Moynier had written it was "a neutrality relative, conditional and temporary."[13] It was possible to express the idea sought to be expressed in much simpler language and in its desire for clearness the Conference even avoided the use of the word inviolability which many had suggested in the place of neutrality. Hence in the new convention "neutrality" is used in its ordinary acceptation and in no sense peculiar to the Convention. The Conference took advantage of the technical and juristic study and discussion which the old Convention had undergone, and is a monument to the value of such work in clarifying and crystallizing international conventions.

Substantive matter.—But the Conference did not content itself with questions of form, important as these were. It embodied the experience of the wars during which the old Convention had been in force, made better provision for military necessity, and at the same time provided for the policing of the field of battle, the examination and identification of the dead, the recognition of the Red Cross societies, the protection of the name and sign of the Red Cross and for the spread of the knowledge of the Convention and its effective execution through military penal codes. The work was effectively and ably done and the Conference may well challenge comparison with any of its kind.

THE SECOND PEACE CONFERENCE.

The Second Peace Conference.—"The Second International Peace Conference, proposed in the first instance by the President of the United States of America, having been convoked on the invitation of His Majesty, the Emperor of All the Russias, by Her Majesty, the Queen of the Netherlands, assembled on the 15th of June, 1907, at The Hague, in the Hall of the Knights, for the purpose of giving a fresh

[13] La Convention de Genève, p. 141.

development to the humanitarian principles which served as a basis for the work of the First Conference of 1899.''[14] The delegates represented practically the civilized world. An important addition to the Powers represented at the First Conference were the South and Central American Republics. Forty-seven nations in all received invitations and these were responded to and representatives sent by all but three.

Organization and rules.—The practice of the First Conference in bestowing the Presidency on the first Russian delegate was followed by the selection of M. Nelidow. At the second meeting of the conference he proposed that the Conference follow the procedure of the First Conference, adapting it, however, to the new conditions. Accordingly a series of twelve rules was adopted. These provided that commissions should be appointed, that the plenipotentiaries should be free to register on these commissions at their convenience and to appoint technical delegates to take part therein, that the Conference should appoint the presidents and vice-presidents of each commission, and the commissions their secretaries and their reporter, and that each commission should have the power to divide itself into subcommissions which should organize their own bureaus. An editing committee for the purpose of coordinating the acts adopted by the Conference and preparing them in their final form was to be appointed by the Conference at the beginning of its labors. The members of the delegations were all authorized to take part in the deliberations at the plenary sessions of the conference as well as in the commissions of which they formed part, it being possible for the members of the same delegation to replace each other. Those members of the Conference attending commissions of which they were not members were not authorized to take part in the deliberations without the special authorization of the president of the commission. Each delegation was given one vote which was taken by roll call, in the alphabetical order of the Powers represented. The proposal that the delegation of one Power might be represented by the delegation of another Power was supressed. Proposed resolutions or desires to be discussed by the Conference had, as a general rule to be delivered in writing to the president

[14] Final Act.

and to be printed and distributed before being taken up for discussion. There were similar provisions with regard to the reports of the commissions and subcommissions. Succinct résumés of the deliberations of the plenary sessions and of the commissions were to be delivered to the members and not read at the beginning of the sessions. Each delegate was to have the right to request the insertion in full of his official declarations and to make observations regarding the minutes. The public was to be admitted to the plenary sessions by ticket, except where the bureau might decide that certain sessions should not be public. Finally, the French language was recognized as the official language of the deliberations and of the acts of the Conference, and the Secretary General was directed, with the consent of the speaker himself, to see that the speeches delivered in any other language should be summarized orally in French.

Division of the work among four commissions.—Four commissions were appointed, and the subjects outlined in the program of the Conference were divided among them as follows:

FIRST COMMISSION.

Arbitration.

International commissions of inquiry and questions connected therewith.

SECOND COMMISSION.

Improvements in the system of the laws and customs of land warfare.

Opening of hostilities.

Declarations of 1899 relating thereto.

Rights and obligations of neutrals on land.

THIRD COMMISSION.

Bombardment of ports, cities and villages by a naval force.

Laying of torpedoes, etc.

The rules to which the vessels of belligerents in neutral ports would be subjected.

Additions to be made to the convention of 1899 in order to adapt to maritime warfare the principles of the Geneva Convention of 1864, revised in 1906.

FOURTH COMMISSION.

Transformation of merchant vessels into war vessels.

Private property at sea.

Delay allowed for the departure of enemy merchant vessels in enemy ports.

Contraband of war. Blockades.

Destruction of neutral prizes by *force majeure.*

Provisions regarding land warfare which would also be applicable to naval warfare.

Organization of the commissions.—M. Leon Bourgeois, of France, was selected as the President of the first commission, M. Beernaert, of Belgium, as the president of the second, and M. T. M. C. Asser, of The Netherlands, as assistant president, Count Tornielli, of Italy, as the president of the third commission, and M. de Martens, of Russia, as the president of the fourth. The recommendation that the deliberations of the commissions be kept secret, or at least not communicated to the press was unanimously adopted, but was not universally adhered to by the delegates.

Signing of the Final Act.—The first, second and third commissions were subsequently divided into subcommissions, and at various times committees were appointed to still further expedite work of the Conference. Most of the work of the editing committee, provided for in the rules of the Conference, was done by a subcommittee of eight. The results, so far as the several commissions desired, were reported to the full Conference, and after approval were put into proper form by the subediting committee. The results thus reached were included in the Final Act and signed by the plenipotentiaries on the 18th day of October, 1907, upon which date the Conference adjourned.[15]

Work of the Conference coming within the scope of this work.—The work of the first commission, arbitration and international commissions of inquiry, lies outside of the scope of this work. The same may be said with regard to

[15] The above account is taken from the Report of the American Delegation.

the rights and obligations of neutrals on land, the rules to which the vessels of belligerents in neutral parts would be subjected, contraband of war, blockades and the destruction of neutral prizes by *force majeure.* Two other matters which were made the subject of convention, but which were not included in the original program, the use of force in the collection of contract debts and the establishment of an international prize court are omitted for the same reason. Although the British plan restricting the International Court to matters affecting neutrals was rejected, the interest of neutrals in the Court is so preponderating as to preclude its consideration in a work on the laws of war as between belligerents. Of the thirteen Conventions and one Declaration drawn up by the Conference, nine in all, including the Declaration, come with the scope of this work. These will be considered in the order in which they were divided among the commissions.

Convention respecting the Laws and Customs of War on Land.—The Convention respecting the Laws and Customs of War on Land of 1899 was found to need little amendment. Its provisions had been the subject of so much expert discussion ever since they were first drawn up at Brussels that even the South African and Russo-Japanese Wars offered little occasion for change. Two changes which may possibly be charged to the latter are the requirement of greater detail in the card kept for prisoners of war in Article XIV, and the requirement of Article XVII that the scale of pay for officers who are prisoners of war shall be that of the captor's army and not that of their own. On the proposition of Germany, clause XXIII (h) was added which forbids declaring abolished, suspended or inadmissible in a Court of law the rights and actions of the nationals of the hostile party. This, apparently, works an important change in Anglo-American law in allowing an alien enemy to sue.[16] It had always been recognized as harsh that a belligerent could compel the nationals of the hostile party to serve him as guides. The worst features of this practice, if not the practice itself, is forbidden by the new article XLIV.[17]

Article LII was amended so as to give the receipts for

[16] See *infra,* p. 210.
[17] See *infra,* p. 310.

articles which have been requisitioned somewhat more of the character of indemnities[18] and, strange as it may seem, submarine cables connecting an occupied territory with a neutral territory were placed within the protection of the Convention in Article LIV. Former Articles LIV, LVII, LVIII, LIX and LX became, respectively, Articles XIX, XI, XII, XIV and XV of the Convention respecting the Rights and Duties of Neutral Powers and Persons in case of War on Land. In the Convention proper there was added as Article III, a provision, penal in its nature, making a belligerent party responsible in damages for acts committed by persons in its service in violation of the Regulations.

This important statement is made in the preamble:

Statement of general principles in the Preamble.—"According to the views of the High Contracting Parties, these provisions, the wording of which has been inspired by the desire to diminish the evils of war, as far as military requirements permit, are intended to serve as a general rule of conduct for the belligerents in their mutual relations and in their relations with the inhabitants. * * *

"Until a more complete code of the laws of war has been issued, the High Contracting Parties deem it expedient to declare that, in cases not included in the Regulations adopted by them, the inhabitants and the belligerents remain under the protection and the rule of the principles of the law of nations, as they result from the usages established among civilized peoples, from the laws of humanity and the dictates of the public conscience.

"They declare that it is in this sense especially that Articles I and II of the Regulations adopted must be understood."

Opening of Hostilities.—The Convention relative to the Opening of Hostilities was a result of the Russo-Japanese War. Although one of its express purposes is "that hostilities should not commence without previous warning," the Conference failed to agree on even a delay of twenty-four hours between the declaration and the commencement of hostilities, so that it will in no degree lessen the necessity of preparedness for action, to obviate which a warning might have been desirable. On the other hand it is likely to give rise to the controversies which characterized

[18] See *infra*, p. 319.

the former period when a previous declaration of war was considered necessary.[19] As was said in the Report of the American Delegation, its importance "to prospective belligerents may be open to doubt." The American Delegation, however, felt that it safeguarded the rights of neutrals and so gave it their approval.

Declaration concerning the discharge of projectiles from balloons.—Of the Declarations of 1899, the only one considered was that with regard to discharging projectiles from balloons which had expired by its five-year limitation. This was renewed for a period extending to the close of the Third Peace Conference.

Bombardment by naval forces.—The Convention respecting Bombardment by Naval Forces in Time of War, marked the fulfillment of the wish of the First Conference. In many respects it is an adaptation of the principle of the Land Convention with regard to bombardments to naval warfare, but in others it is an improvement on that convention and it gave concrete form to principles of independent value. It provides that undefended towns shall not be bombarded on account of failure to pay money contributions, and that military establishments in undefended towns shall ordinarily not be subject of bombardment, unless all other means be impossible and a reasonable time given to the inhabitants to destroy them themselves, and in that case the commander shall take all due measures in order that the town may suffer as little damage as possible. The improvements over the Land Convention were in requiring a warning "if the military situation permits" instead of excepting only cases of assault and in specifying the sign to indicate monuments, etc., as "large, stiff, rectangular panels divided diagonally into two colored triangular portions, the upper portion black, the lower portion white."

Automatic submarine contact mines.—The Convention relative to the Laying of Automatic Submarine Contact Mines leaves to the unwritten law the anchoring of such mines in the high seas beyond the territorial waters of the belligerents, but as far as it goes[20] it regulates a subject with regard to which little law has grown up and which

19 See *infra*, p. 200.
20 See *infra*, p. 280.

the events of the Russo-Japanese War showed needed regulation.[21] It is limited to seven years, but if not denounced continues in force after the termination of this period.

Naval Red Cross Convention.—The Convention for the Adaptation to Naval War of the Principles of the Geneva Convention was an admirable piece of work rendered less difficult by the labors of the Geneva Conference of 1906. Perhaps the most notable improvements over the naval convention of 1899 are the placing of neutral hospital ships under the control of one of the belligerents, and the specification of the right of the belligerents to demand that the sick, wounded or shipwrecked on board military hospital ships, hospital ships belonging to relief societies or to private individuals, merchant ships, yachts or boats, whether enemy or neutral, shall be handed over.[22]

The Convention relative to the Conversion of Merchant Ships into Warships leaves untouched the question whether such conversion may take place on the high seas, but it forms a valuable supplement to the Declaration of Paris in defining the conditions under which private owned ships may engage in hostilities. The United States did not sign or adhere to this Convention, because it is not a party to the Declaration of Paris.

Effort to exempt private property at sea from capture.—The Convention relative to Certain Restrictions with regard to the Exercise of the Right of Capture in Naval War is what is left of the effort of the United States for the general exemption of private property at sea. In accordance with the action of the United States at the First Peace Conference, Mr. Choate proposed the exemption from capture at sea of all property, except under the laws of contraband and blockade. Other proposals were made by Belgium, Brazil and France. The Belgium proposal provided that merchantmen and their cargoes, in certain cases the value of the property destroyed, and in cases where the cargoes are perishable, "the sales moneys, were to be restored to the owners by the captors' state, without any indemnity, for deprivation of enjoyment, or for deterioration not caused by grave fault; but that the state might shift the

[21] See *supra*, p. 170.
[22] See *infra*, p. 272.

burden to the enemy state by the treaty of peace."[23] This is somewhat like the treatment to which private munitions of war, seized on land, will probably be subjected under H LIII. The Brazilian proposal provided for the giving of receipts as in cases of requisition on land. The French proposal was based on the idea that the right of prize should appear solely as a means of bringing pressure to bear on the hostile state, that, accordingly, all profit to the individual captor should be excluded, and that, furthermore, losses incurred by individuals should fall in last resort on their state. Accordingly the French Delegation proposed that the commission should express the wish that shares of prize money should be suppressed and that states should take some measures to reimburse those suffering by capture. On a vote being taken in the fourth commission on the proposal of the United States, there were 21 votes in favor of it and 11 against, with some abstentions. Among those who voted in favor of it were Austria-Hungary, Belgium, Brazil, Germany (with reservations), Italy, The Netherlands, Switzerland and the United States. Among those who voted against it were France, Great Britain, Japan, Russia and Spain. This made four of the great naval powers against it as opposed to possibly three, Germany, Italy and the United States, in favor of it. The vote on a test clause of the Brazilian proposal was 13 to 12 against it and it was withdrawn. The vote on the first clause of the Belgian proposal was 14 to 9 in its favor, but as the opposition to it was also strong it was withdrawn. Later the French proposal was modified so as to convey an invitation to the Powers to abolish prize money, rather than to express a wish to that effect, and this was carried by a vote of 16 to 4 with 14 abstentions. The second part of the French proposal, looking to the indemnification of the owners of captured property was lost by a vote of 13 to 7, with 14 abstentions. All this had occurred in the Fourth Commission.[24] It evidently considered that no satisfactory report could be made to the full Conference, so that the Final Act is without an expression of opinion on the general subject,

23 Westlake, II International Law, 312.

24 For this whole matter, see Westlake, II International Law, 311–314.

except insofar as that is involved in its fourth wish which is as follows:

Wish of the Conference.—"The Conference expresses the opinion (*voeu*) that the preparation of regulations relative to the laws and customs of naval war should figure in the programme of the next Conference, and that in any case the Powers may apply, as far as possible, to war by sea the principles of the Convention relative to the Laws and Customs of War on Land."[25]

Special restrictions on the right of capture.—The special restrictions on the right of capture in naval war that did find their way into the Convention, however, were not unimportant, and the statement in the preamble that it is expedient to commence codifying in regulations of general application the guarantees due to peaceful commerce and legitimate business, may give a glimpse of hope to those who wish for wider restrictions in the future. The restrictions exempting coast fishing vessels, and vessels charged with religious, scientific or philanthropic missions embody the customary law, but the exemption of small boats employed in local trade is new, and the provision exempting postal correspondence from capture is an innovation of great value. The provisions in regard to the treatment of the captain, officers and crews of captured merchant ships allow their release on parole. Neutral members of crews are to be released without condition.

Status of enemy ships at outbreak of hostilities.—The Convention relative to the Status of Enemy Merchant Ships at the Outbreak of Hostilities innovated on the existing practice by conditioning the right of a ship, leaving its last port of departure before the commencement of the war, to enter the hostile port, on its ignorance of hostilities. Even in case of ignorance it may be detained subject to be restored or requisitioned, or even destroyed on payment of compensation. The American Delegation felt that this was reactionary, so that the United States neither signed nor adhered to it.[26]

Formal parts of the Conventions.—For the formal parts of the above Conventions common to all or most of them, the reader is referred to the text of the Convention respect-

25 The Second International Peace Conference, p. 198.

26 See *infra*, p. 205.

ing the Laws and Customs of War on Land, given as Appendix II. The preamble, with the exception of the reasons on which the Conventions are based, is common to all. Article II providing that the provisions of the Convention do not apply except between Contracting Powers, and then only if all the belligerents are parties to the Convention, is common to all except the Convention relative to the Opening of Hostilities. Its language is hardly applicable to that convention because it would be anomalous for that Convention to speak of *belligerents* prior to a declaration. Article III of that Convention, however, is open to a similar construction.

Article IV of the Land Convention is similar to G N XXV, and provides that the Convention, duly ratified, shall as between the contracting Powers, be substituted for the old Convention of July 29, 1899, but that the Convention of 1899 remains in force between the Powers which signed it, and which do not also ratify the new Convention.

Article V is common to all the conventions. It provides that the Convention shall be ratified as soon as possible; that the ratifications shall be deposited at The Hague, and makes provision for the sending by The Netherlands Government of duly certified copies of the *procès-verbal* relative to the first deposit of ratifications, of the notification of the subsequent ratifications and the instruments of ratification accompanying them, together with notice of the date at which the latter were received, to the Powers invited to the Second Peace Conference and the other adhering Powers. Article VI is common to all the conventions, except the Geneva Naval Convention. It provides for the adhesion of nonsignatory Powers by notice to The Netherlands Government, which shall make this known to the other Powers as in the preceding Article. The corresponding article of the Geneva Naval Convention restricts the adhesion of nonsignatory Powers to those who have accepted the Geneva Convention of July 6, 1906. Article VII is common to all, and provides that the Convention shall go into effect sixty days after the date of the *procès-verbal* of the first deposit or a similar period after the receipt of the notification of ratification by The Netherlands Government.

Article VIII deals with denunciations and is common to all except the Convention relative to Automatic Submarine

Contact Mines. It provides that in the event of one of the Contracting Powers wishing to denounce the Convention, it may do so by notice to the Netherlands Government, which shall notify the other Powers, and that this shall only have effect in regard to the notifying Power, and one year after the notification has reached The Netherlands Government. The corresponding article in the Mines Convention varies because of its limitation to seven years and fixes six months as the period in which the denunciation shall go into effect instead of one year.

Article IX is common to all the Conventions and provides that a registry be kept by The Netherlands Ministry for Foreign Affairs of ratifications, notifications and denunciations, to which each of the Contracting Powers is entitled to access, and to be supplied with a certified copy. The original Convention is deposited in the archives of The Netherlands Government, and duly certified copies sent to the Powers invited to the Second Conference.

Difference in form between Conventions and Declaration.—For the difference in form between the Conventions and the Declaration the reader is likewise referred to the text of the Declaration Prohibiting the Discharge of Projectiles from Balloons, given as Appendix III. It will be seen that the Declaration is in the name of the Plenipotentiaries, instead of in the name of the Chief Executives, as is the case with the Conventions, and that the requirements for ratification are less formal, but that otherwise there is little difference.

The Final Act.—The Conventions and Declaration form so many separate acts. In addition the Conference drew up its Final Act. This is not a Convention, but rather a statement of the work and opinions of the Conference itself. Some of the views expressed by the Conference have been given elsewhere in this work.[27] Its last recommendation is as follows:

Wish for a Third Peace Conference.—"Finally, the Conference recommends to the Powers the assembly of a Third Peace Conference, which might be held within a period corresponding to that which has elapsed since the preceding Conference, at a date to be fixed by common agreement between the Powers, and it calls their attention to the neces-

[27] See pp. 190, 214.

sity of preparing the programme of this Third Conference a sufficient time in advance to ensure its deliberations being conducted with the necessary authority and expedition.

"In order to attain this object the Conference considers that it would be very desirable that, some two years before the probable date of the meeting, a preparatory Committee should be charged by the Governments with the task of collecting the various proposals to be submitted to the Conference, of ascertaining what subjects are ripe for embodiment in an International Regulation, and of preparing a programme which the Governments should decide upon in sufficient time to enable it to be carefully examined by the countries interested. This Committee should further be intrusted with the task of proposing a system of organization and procedure for the Conference itself."

Signatories.—The Final Act was signed by the Plenipotentiaries of all the Powers, except Paraguay and Turkey, with a reservation on the part of Switzerland to wish No. 1 concerning a Judicial Arbitration Court which was not acceptable to the Federal Council. The Powers which signed none but the Final Act were Germany, Austria, Hungary, China, Ecuador, Great Britain, Italy, Japan, Nicaragua and Switzerland, but it is thought that ultimately at least there will be practical unanimity on most of the Conventions and the Declaration which come within the scope of the work.

M. Renault.—Before closing the account of the Conference it is fitting to allude to the preeminent work of one man, M. Renault. It has been said that "from the 15th day of June to the 18th day of October, he dominated the Second Hague Conference, not as a Frenchman or as a member of the French Delegation, but as a citizen of the world, the trusted friend and adviser of his colleagues."[28]

The work of the Conference.—The great work of the Conference lay elsewhere, but in codifying the law on which there was a consensus of opinion, in introducing into the law such beneficent provisions as those protecting mails, and finally in showing the progressive nature of the conventional law of war, it accomplished results of permanent value.

[28] 2 American Journal of International Law, 153.

PART II.

COMMENTARY.

CHAPTER I.

COMMENCEMENT OF WAR.

Measures of force falling short of war.—All measures of force infringing the rights of another state are, strictly speaking, acts of war, but in the past, especially, it has been felt desirable that there should be measures of force which should not involve all the serious consequences of war, but which could yet be resorted to for the purpose of bringing a refractory state to terms. Down to the end of the eighteenth century the two most common measures of this kind were embargo and reprisals. Embargo generally consisted of the detention of the ships of the offending state until satisfaction was secured, while reprisals consisted of almost any other hostile seizure of persons or property not intended to constitute formal war. Property thus seized was not usually applied immediately to the satisfaction of the injury complained of, but was set aside for some time in hope of satisfaction being granted by the other party.[1] General Reprisals were national acts, and must be distinguished from the practice of Special Reprisals, which flourished during the Middle Ages, and which were merely means of private redress. Since the Napoleonic period both the Embargo and General Reprisals have fallen very generally into disuse.

Pacific blockades.—Towards the more backward powers, however, those which have shown an inability or a disinclination to live up to their international obligations, measures of force falling short of war are still quite frequently used. They usually take the form of Pacific Blockades. These are directed at the shipping of the offending power, and do not affect neutrals; for the power which is seeking to enforce its claim can have no authority on the high seas or in the territory of the other power over the vessels of a third power except through the belligerent rights which war gives.[2] This principle is well established.[3] The in-

[1] Halleck, Inter. Law, p. 471.

[2] Annuaire de Institut de Droit International, 1887–8, p. 300.

[3] But see Westlake, II International Law, 17.

efficacy of blockades which do not affect neutral shipping, however, often leads to its inclusion in blockades which are intended as the only hostile measures against the refractory power, and which thus bear a close resemblance to blockades that are pacific. They are, however, unequivocal acts of war, and involve all the legal consequences of war. In Pacific Blockades property may be sequestered but not confiscated unless war ensues.[4]

The opening of hostilities.—The opening of hostilities is regulated by the following Convention drawn up at the Second Peace Conference.

Considering that it is important, in order to ensure the maintenance of pacific relations, that hostilities should not commence without previous warning.

That it is equally important that the existence of a state of war should be notified without delay to neutral Powers [the Plenipotentiaries of the Contracting Powers] have agreed upon the following provisions:

ART. I. *The Contracting Powers recognize that hostilities between themselves must not commence without previous and explicit warning, in the form either of a reasoned declaration of war, or of an ultimatum with conditional declaration of war.*

ART. II. *The existence of a state of war must be notified to the neutral Powers without delay, and shall not take effect in regard to them until after the receipt of a notification, which may, however, be given by telegraph. Neutral Powers, nevertheless, cannot rely on the absence of notification if it is clearly established that they were in fact aware of the existence of a state of war.*

ART. III. *Article I of the present Convention shall take effect in case of war between two or more of the Contracting Powers.*

Article II is binding as between a belligerent Power which is a party to the Convention and neutral Powers which are also parties to the Convention.

Comment of the American delegation.—"The convention is very short and is based upon the principle that neither belligerent should be taken by surprise, and that the neutral shall not be bound to the performance of neutral duties until it has received notification, even if only by telegram, of the outbreak of the war. The means of notifica-

[4] *Ibid.*

tion is considered unimportant, for if the neutral knows, through whatever means or whatever channels, of the existence of war, it cannot claim a formal notification from the belligerents before being taxed with neutral obligations. While the importance to prospective belligerents may be open to doubt, it is clear that it does safeguard in a very high degree the rights of neutrals and specifies authoritatively the exact moment when the duty of neutrality begins. It is for this reason that the American delegation supported the project and signed the convention.''[5]

Of doubtful utility to belligerents.—The doubt expressed by the American Delegation as to the utility of the convention to belligerents, is well founded. Although the delegation reecho the sentiment of the preamble that the convention is based upon the principle that neither belligerent should be taken by surprise, its real effect, as Westlake says, has been to confirm rather than to weaken ''the necessity that, in order not to be taken unprepared, every nation must rely on its own vigilance, and on no formal rule.''[6] If some provision had been inserted, like the resolution of the Institute of International Law, that hostilities should only be commenced after the expiration of a delay sufficient to prevent the requirement of a previous and nonequivocal delay being elusive,[7] it might have been contended that the convention would have had a tendency to prevent war by postponing the active military preparations which immediately precede operations, and which at present have a tendency to precipitate war, until after the formal declaration or the ultimatum. But not only was no such provision inserted, but even the proposal of a delay of twenty-four hours made by the delegation of The Netherlands was rejected.[8] It may justly be contended that such a delay is implied, but it is clear that no government would be justified in foregoing military preparations in reliance on such an implication.

Treachery in the initiation of war illegal.—It is true now, just as it has been for centuries, that where one nation has a grievance against another, it is bound to de-

[5] Report of the American Delegation, p. 34.
[6] Westlake, II International Law, 267.
[7] 21 Annuaire, 293.
[8] Westlake, II International Law, 267.

mand redress, and not to resort to force until there has been a denial or delay in satisfying its claim, except, for instance, where it is attacked. And there has been little cause for complaint on this ground during the last hundred years. But this principle, that treachery in the initiation of hostilities is illegal, is quite remote from the question whether a formal declaration in the nature of a warning should be required.

Advantages and disadvantages of convention.—As between belligerents, the convention has this advantage, if it be such, that it will more sharply differentiate measures falling short of war from war itself, but on the other hand, it has the distinct disadvantage that it is liable to give rise to endless controversy and recrimination. One of the most mooted questions with the old publicists was as to when a declaration of war was not necessary. Many held that it was not necessary in a defensive war, but it is often difficult to say when a war is defensive. Take, for instance, a conflict over a boundary. Each claimant is liable to say that the other committed the first overt act. Numerous other instances might also be given where controversy is likely to arise. Where an ally has joined one of the belligerents, is it necessary to declare war against him? Would it have been necessary in the South African War, where Great Britain claimed a sort of suzerainty, and which accordingly was somewhat in the nature of a civil war? All these things are what render the utility of the convention as between belligerents doubtful.

The expression "reasoned declaration of war" in the first article is not a very happy one. The translation given in the American Journal of International Law, "a declaration of war with the reasons therefor"[9] better expresses the sense of the original. Nor should the article read that hostilities "*must* not commence without, etc." A more correct rendering is that they "*should* not begin without, etc.,"[10] or that they "*ought* not to commence without, etc."[11]

Effect of the breaking out of war on the general legal relations of the belligerents and their citizens.—War works

9 Vol. 2, p. 86.
10 *Ibid.*
11 II Westlake, 267.

a profound change in the legal relations between the belligerents and between those private persons who are affected with the enemy character. The treaties between the two powers are perhaps for the most part abrogated; contracts between private persons are suspended[12] or dissolved, and new contracts entered into are null and void, unless they arise from the war, as for instance ransom bills, or are excepted from the usual prohibition of commercial intercourse. Furthermore, commercial intercourse of every kind is usually prohibited, although there is a growing tendency to make the prohibition less general.

Effect on treaties.—Just what treaties or provisions of treaties are not abrogated has been a matter of controversy. As to the continued obligation of stipulations whose only operation is in time of war, which acknowledge indebtedness, or by which a "status is permanently established or a right permanently vested," there is no question.[13] A stipulation that the citizens of each belligerent found in the territory of the other at the outbreak of war may have a reasonable time in which to wind up their affairs and leave the country, obviously can have no application except in time of war. It is also well settled, on the foundation of the good faith and credit of governments, that the obligation of national debts, and of treaties acknowledging such debts, remain unimpaired by war. As to treaties by which a "status is permanently established or a right permanently vested," it would have been intolerable if the breaking out of the War of 1812 had broken the force of the acknowledgment of our independence by Great Britain in 1783, or if a subsequent war had broken the force of the treaties settling boundary disputes and left all those disputes to be settled over again. Another exception is that of "treaties establishing arrangements to which third powers are parties, such as guarantees and postal and other unions."[14] Beyond these lines, the law has been little developed. Continental writers incline to the view against abrogation, except in the case of treaties of alliance, and there may be a tendency in that direction; but it cannot

12 But see *infra*, p. 210.

13 Moore, The Effect of War on Public Debts, Columbia Law Review, Vol. I, p. 216.

14 Westlake, II International Law, 31.

be said to have yet attained the dignity of law; and, except as to treaties whose continuing obligation is clear, it is advisable to deal with the subject in the treaty of peace.

Effect on commercial intercourse.—It is usual to state that war itself renders all intercourse between private persons invested with the enemy character illegal. While this may in a strict sense be true, there exists a tendency to assume that intercourse not unequivocally forbidden is allowed, which practically amounts to the doctrine of the continental publicists, that it is not the war itself that renders such intercourse illegal, but its prohibition by the political authorities. This tendency was shown in the opinion of the Supreme Court of the United States, in the case of *Matthews v. McStea,*[15] decided in 1875. The question involved was whether a partnership existing between residents of New York and Louisiana, at the outbreak of the Civil War was still in existence on April 23, 1861, the court having already held that the President had recognized a state of war as existing by his blockade proclamation of April 19, while the proclamation of nonintercourse, which Congress had authorized on July 13, was not issued till August 16. If the war itself broke all legal relations between enemies, then the partnership was dissolved by April 19; but the court held that the partnership was still in existence four days later. What makes the case the more important is, that early in the opinion Justice Strong says "it is undeniable that civil war brings with it all the consequences in this regard (as to the cessation of commercial intercourse) which attend upon and follow a state of foreign war." Further on he says: "No declaration of war was ever made. The President recognized its existence by proclaiming a blockade on the 19th of April; and it then became his duty as well as his right to direct how it should be carried on. In the exercise of this right he was at liberty to allow or license intercourse, and his proclamations, if they did not license it expressly, did, in our opinion, license it by very cogent implications. It is impossible to read them without a conviction that no interdiction of commercial intercourse except through the ports of the designated states was intended. But in a

[15] 91 United States, 7.

civil more than in a foreign war or in a war declared, it is important that unequivocal notice should be given of the illegality of traffic or commercial intercourse; for, in a civil war only the government can know when the insurrection has assumed the character of war.''[16]

Interdiction of commercial intercourse.—It is desirable that the view that war itself does not put an end to commercial intercourse, but that its illegality depends on its interdiction by the political authorities, should find even wider recognition that it has; for, when once the stoppage of traffic requires positive action on the part of the authorities, a long step ahead has been taken in securing the continuance of the ordinary conditions of peace between those parts of the territories of the belligerents not the scene of active military operations. Where commerce is allowed, the rule that an alien enemy has no standing in court does not apply, and contracts can be made and enforced as in time of peace.[17] Since the beginning of the Crimean War, a very large indulgence in commerce between belligerents has been allowed. Thus, in the Spanish-American War, neutral vessels laden with American-owned cargoes other than contraband of war were cleared for Spanish ports.[18]

Treatment of the citizens of the other belligerent in the country at the outbreak of war.—Even where commerce is generally interdicted, it may now be said to have become a rule of law that a belligerent must allow a reasonable time for the nationals of the enemy to close up their affairs and withdraw from the country. An exception was made to this principle with regard to those nationals called home for service in the active army, by the French in the Franco-German War, and its reasonableness has commended itself to Calvo and others. It has even become customary to allow the nationals of the enemy to remain in the country throughout the war, on condition of good behavior, but they are often subject to regulations, such as registration, and cases may easily arise where expulsion is justifiable, although it has generally been considered that the expul-

[16] 91 United States, pp. 12–13.
[17] Phillimore, Inter. Law, III, pp. 134–136.
[18] Moore, Inter. Law Situations, pp. 176–177.

sion of the Germans by the French in 1870 was extreme and carried out with unnecessary harshness.

Right to withdraw goods in the territory of the other belligerent at the outbreak of war.—Withdrawal of goods from the enemy's country within a reasonable time after the outbreak of war, does not render them liable to confiscation on the ground that the owner has been engaged in commerce with the enemy. So the Supreme Court of New York held in 1818,[19] in an opinion delivered by Chief Justice Thompson, afterwards a member of the Supreme Court of the United States and one of the ablest judges that ever sat on that bench. The effect of this decision is somewhat restricted by the previous decision of the Supreme Court of the United States in the case of *The Rapid*,[20] in which it was held that, where a person went after the outbreak of war to withdraw goods from the enemy's territory, even though they had been purchased in time of peace, he was guilty of trading with the enemy and his property subject to confiscation. But this decision is contrary to the tendencies of today and would probably not be followed. The right to withdraw goods would probably be held to include the right to dispose of them, or the right to put them into such shape as to be easily transported, provided this was done in good faith and without the intention of engaging in forbidden traffic.[21]

No right to confiscate private debts.—Again, although in the past, the right to confiscate the property of subjects of the enemy, including debts due to them by private persons, has been asserted, and although *dicta* to that effect are to be found in the case of *United States against Brown*,[22] such a position would be clearly untenable today,[23] and a government attempting to exercise such a power would be severely condemned[24] even without the express prohibition drawn up at the Second Peace Conference.[25]

19 Amory et al. v. McGregor, 15 Johnson, 24.

20 8 Cranch, 155.

21 Forty-two bales of cotton, Blatchford's Prize Cases, 664; *Sarah Starr* and cargo, Blatchford's Prize Cases, 650.

22 8 Cranch, 110.

23 See H XLVI.

24 As to the action of the United States and Confederate Governments, during the Civil War, see *supra*, p. 75.

25 H XXIII (h).

Enemy merchant ships at outbreak of hostilities.—The status of an enemy merchant ship at the outbreak of hostilities was made the subject of the following convention at the Second Peace Conference, although it was not signed or ratified by the United States.

Anxious to ensure the security of international commerce against the surprises of war, and wishing, in accordance with modern practice, to protect as far as possible operations undertaken in good faith and in process of being carried out before the outbreak of hostilities; [the Plenipotentiaries of the Contracting Powers] have agreed upon the following provisions:

ART. I. *When a merchant ship belonging to one of the belligerent Powers is at the commencement of hostilities in an enemy port, it is desirable that it should be allowed to depart freely, either immediately, or after a reasonable number of days of grace, and to proceed, after being furnished with a pass, direct to its port of destination or any other port indicated.*

The same rule should apply in the case of a ship which has left its port of departure before the commencement of the war and entered a port belonging to the enemy, while still ignorant that hostilities had broken out.

ART. II. *A merchant ship, unable, owing to circumstances of force majeure, to leave the enemy port within the period contemplated in the above Article, or which was not allowed to leave, can not be confiscated.*

The belligerent may only detain it, without payment of compensation, but subject to the obligation of restoring it after the war, or requisition it on payment of compensation.

ART. III. *Enemy merchant ships which left their last port of departure before the commencement of the war, and are encountered on the high seas while still ignorant of the outbreak of hostilities can not be confiscated. They are only liable to detention on the understanding that they shall be restored after the war without compensation, or to be requisitioned, or even destroyed, on payment of compensation, but in such case provision must be made for the safety of the persons on board as well as the security of the ship's papers.*

After touching at a port in their own country or at a neutral port, these ships are subject to the laws and customs of maritime war.

ART. IV. *Enemy cargo on board the vessels referred to in*

Articles I and II is likewise liable to be detained and restored after the termination of the war without payment of compensation, or to be requisitioned on payment of compensation, with or without the ship.

The same rule applies in the case of cargo on board the vessels referred to in Article III.

ART. V. *The present Convention does not affect merchant ships whose build shows that they are intended for conversion into warships.*

Disapproval of American delegation.—"The uninterrupted practice of belligerent Powers since the outbreak of the Crimean War has been to allow enemy merchant vessels *in their ports at the outbreak of hostilities,* to depart on their return voyages. The same privilege has been accorded to enemy merchant vessels which sailed before the outbreak of hostilities, to enter and depart from a belligerent port without molestation on the homeward voyage. It was therefore the view of the American delegation that the privilege had acquired such international force as to place it in the category of obligations. Such, indeed, was the view of a majority of the Conference, but as the delegation of Great Britain adhered to the opinion that such free entry and departure was a matter of grace, or favor, and not one of strict right, the articles regard it as a delay by way of favor and refer to the practice as *desirable.* * * * But all these immunities are conditioned upon ignorance of the existence of hostilities on the part of the ship. This condition forms no part of the existing practice, and it was the opinion of the delegation that it substantially neutralized the apparent benefits of the treaty and puts merchant shipping in a much less favorable situation than is accorded to it by the international practice of the last fifty years."[26]

The law independent of convention.—The legal position taken by the American delegation is supported by strong authority. Such an able British publicist as Westlake, writing just before the Conference, was of opinion that the liberal practice of the last fifty years had ripened into law,[27] and probably few who believe with the Supreme

26 Report of the American Delegation, pp. 38–39.

27 II International Law, 40.

Court in the case of the *Paquete Habana*[28] that the customary law of nations is subject to growth, would differ from him. It was matter for argument, however, and probably little importance would have been attached to the word "desirable" if the existing practice had been embodied in the convention in the form it has usually appeared in the prize regulations. The rule of the convention does not differ as to the most usual case, where the ship arrives at the hostile port without any such information as to charge it with knowledge of the hostilities, but the provision with regard to knowledge is new, and may be of considerable importance if the enemy cruisers choose to lie off the hostile ports for the purpose of notifying incoming merchant ships. It is also of importance to ships equipped with wireless telegraphy apparatus. The idea seems to be that it would be unfair to capture a hostile vessel in port at the time war breaks out, or even one coming in afterwards in ignorance of the hostilities, but that if an enemy vessel becomes aware of hostilities before entering an enemy port, it is only natural that she should return home or seek a neutral port. This seems somewhat less liberal than practice has been, but it is more rational unless one sees in the practice the entering wedge for the exemption of private property at sea altogether.

Apparent misconception in American report.—In criticising the Convention, the American report goes on to say that "an enemy merchant vessel approaching a hostile port which is notified by an armed cruiser, or which obtains the information under circumstances calculated to charge it with knowledge of the fact that hostilities exist, forfeits the immunities conferred by the treaty and becomes *eo instante* liable to capture."[29] If this is intended to mean that a ship which has been warned and changes its course for a home or neutral port, is liable to capture, it is submitted that this is error. The second paragraph of Article III would then have no signification. That paragraph must be taken to mean that if after receiving notice of hostilities, the ship makes for a neutral or home port, it is not liable to *capture* until it has touched at one or the other. Although not liable to capture, however, it is liable

[28] 175 U. S., 694.
[29] P. 39.

to detention without compensation, or to requisition or even destruction, with compensation.

On the whole it is not perhaps unnatural that the American delegation took the attitude they did towards this Convention, in view of their stand for the exemption of private property at sea from capture altogether, and even on the narrower ground that it was less liberal than the existing practice, but it might well be urged that it was not so much a change from existing practice as a more careful and matured expression of it, and that it substituted for a practice of doubtful obligation and uncertain tenor an agreement that was clear cut and rational, if not so liberal.

Contracts made during the general suspension of intercourse are in general void.—Contracts made with the enemy from the time that the general interdiction of commerce goes into effect until the interdiction is raised, are in general void. This, however, does not apply to contracts entered into by nationals of the opposing belligerents both residing in the territory of one of them, where it is clear that the contract was not entered into with any design of violating the policy of nonintercourse. So a lease made during the Civil War in Mississippi, by a citizen of Mississippi to a citizen of Massachusetts, whose residence was in Mississippi, where the continued residence of the lessee upon the demised premises throughout the term seemed to be contemplated and where there was no evidence of intention that the crop or the rent should be sent across the hostile lines, was held to be valid.[30] So, also, contracts for the relief of the necessities of prisoners of war in a hostile country have been held valid.

Contracts rendered void.—Conversely, contracts which necessitate intercourse between the two countries are rendered void. Thus, partnerships are dissolved as well as agencies to collect and transmit money; but an agency to collect and hold money if such agency was created before the war is not annulled.[31] And where, by the terms of a policy of insurance, the contract was avoided by the nonpayment of premiums, it was held that although the ex-

30 Kershaw v. Kelsey, 100 Mass., 561.

31 Matthews v. McStea, 91 United States, 7; Insurance Company v. Davis, 95 U. S., 425.

istence of war, and the consequent legal inability to pay the premiums, which had fallen into arrears, had annulled the contract, yet the insured was entitled to recover back the equitable value of the policy at the time the war broke out.[32]

Insurance against the acts of the government of the insurer.—Insurance against the action of the government of the insurer is held to be void. It seems eminently reasonable that the government should not allow its nationals to nullify its own acts by giving insurance against them. In a case arising during the South African War, insurance was allowed against the act of the Transvaal Government in commandeering the property of a corporation, originally incorporated in Natal but also incorporated in the Transvaal.[33] Whether the corporation be viewed as a British or as a Boer[34] corporation, this decision was eminently sound, for the rule is that an insurance company shall not nullify the act of its own government, not that it shall not nullify the act of the enemy. Insuring a British corporation against loss by acts of the enemy would certainly be proper, and there seems no sound reason why an enemy corporation should not receive like protection, as forced levies during war are more likely to be caused by the fact that the incorporators are members of the state hostile to the one that has incorporated them than by any other.

Right of alien enemy to sue.—It has been the general rule in Anglo-American courts that an alien enemy has no right to sue during the cessation of commercial intercourse; but, even before Justice Story's time, the plea of alien enemy was not favorably received,[35] and it was held to be necessary to set forth in the plea every fact that would negative the plaintiff's right to sue. The Supreme Court of the United States has also held that, "whatever may be that extent of the disability of an alien enemy to sue in the courts of a hostile country, it is clear that he is liable to be sued, and this carries with it the right to use all the means and appliances of defense."[36]

32 New York Life Ins. Co. v. Stathem, 93 U. S., 24.
33 Nigel Gold Mining Co., Ltd., v. Hoade, 2 K. B. (1901), 849.
34 Driefontein, etc., Mines, Ltd., v. Janson (1901), 2 K. B., 419.
35 The Society, etc., v. Wheeler, 2 Gallison, 127.
36 McVeigh v. United States, 11 Wallace, 267.

The effect of the disability to sue has been that the alien's remedy has been for the time suspended, not that his right has been extinguished. There are cases in the United States that hold that interest accruing during war cannot be collected afterwards,[37] but the better opinion, even before The Hague Convention, would appear to have been that of Lord Erskine, in a bankruptcy proceeding in 1806, in which he held that the dividend due an alien enemy should be reserved for him, as it was only the right to recover which had been suspended.[38] Judgments gained before the war, but not executed can be enforced afterwards; and, as a general rule, the running of statutes of limitation has been suspended during war.[39]

Apparent change in law.—The law on this subject, however, appears to have been vitally changed by H XXIII (h). A fair interpretation of that provision seems to do away with the plea of alien enemy. If it does, and aliens are allowed to sue during war, then there is no longer reason for the general suspension of the statutes of limitations.

Where commercial intercourse is allowed.—The disability to sue and make contracts must be understood to exist only when commerce is not allowed. So far as commerce is allowed, contracts may be made and enforced.

Miscellaneous rules.—In prize proceedings, even more than in ordinary proceedings, the rule that ignorance of the law excuses no one prevails. It is the ulterior destination of goods that counts at least in trading with the enemy, even if the route be through a neutral country. The liability to confiscation for illegal trading lasts till the end of the voyage and then terminates.[40] Military Occupation in itself does not legalize intercourse with territory, traffic with which has been prohibited.[41]

Licenses now generally obsolete or local.—Exceptions to the interdiction of trade have in recent times usually been general in their application; but, in the peculiar circumstances of the Napoleonic Wars, Great Britain made extensive use of special licenses, 16,000 of them being is-

[37] See note in Scott's Cases on International Law, p. 500.
[38] *Ex parte* Boussmaker, 13 Vesey Jun., 71.
[39] Hanger v. Abbott, 6 Wall., 532.
[40] Halleck's International Law, Vol. II, pp. 132–133.
[41] Hamilton v. Dillin, 21 Wallace, 95.

sued in the years 1808 and 1809, and 8,000 in 1811.[42] A great body of law was developed with regard to them.

Rules as to licenses.—"A license is a kind of safe-conduct, granted by a belligerent State to its own subjects, to those of its enemy, or to neutrals, to carry on a trade which is interdicted by the laws of war and it operates as a dispensation from the penalties of those laws, with respect to the State granting it, and so far as its terms can be fairly construed to extend. The officers and tribunals of the State under whose authority they are issued are bound to respect such documents as lawful relaxations of the ordinary state of war; but the adverse belligerent may justly consider them as *per se* a ground of capture and confiscation. Licenses are necessarily *stricti juris*, and cannot be carried beyond the evident intention of those by whom they are granted; nevertheless, they are not construed with pedantic accuracy, nor will their fair effect be vitiated by every slight deviation from their terms and conditions. Much, however, will depend upon the nature of the terms which are not complied with. Thus a variation in the *quality* or *character* of the goods will often lead to more dangerous consequences than an excess of *quantity*. Again, a license to trade, though safe in the hands of one person, might become dangerous in those of another; so also with respect to the limitations of *time* and *place* specified in a license. Such restrictions are often of material importance, and cannot be deviated from with safety. A license may be qualified, in which the party seeking to protect himself under it must conform exactly to its requisitions."[43]

This passage from Halleck indicates the nature of the questions which arose in connection with licenses, but into which it would be useless to enter in detail now.

42 Calvo, Le Droit International, 4, 91.
43 Halleck, Inter. Law, II, 343–344.

CHAPTER II.

ENEMY CHARACTER AND PROPERTY.

Neutral property identified with the country is subject to the same liabilities as that belonging to citizens of the country.—In providing for the needs of an army in a foreign country, it makes little difference whether the supplies taken are owned by persons owing allegiance to the enemy or to a neutral power. As Féraud-Giraud says, a commander under the necessity of providing for his army cannot stop to argue the question as to whether provisions which he chances to need belong to enemies or neutrals.[1] Where the provisions are in course of transportation, and the neutral character of their owner is apparent on the face of it, only extreme necessity can warrant their seizure; but when such indications do not exist the commander is justified in treating those who have identified themselves with the country in the same way in this respect as those who have entered into the closer relation of political allegiance. Requisitions and Contributions are assessed to the former to the same extent as to the latter, and so long as the belligerent does not exceed the rights which the laws of war give him with regard to the latter and treats both alike, the neutral government has no grounds for complaint.

Treatment of neutral railway material.—The treatment of neutral railway material is provided for by Article XIX of the Convention respecting the rights and duties of neutral powers and persons in case of war on land, as follows:

Railway material coming from the territory of neutral Powers, whether it be the property of the said Powers or of Companies or private persons, and recognizable as such, shall not be requisitioned or utilized by a belligerent, except where and to the extent that it is absolutely necessary. It shall be sent back as soon as possible to the country of origin.

A neutral Power may likewise, in case of necessity, retain and

[1] Féraud-Giraud, Recours à Raison des Dommages, Causés par la Guerre, p. 278.

utilize to an equal extent material coming from the territory of the belligerent Power.

Compensation shall be paid by one party or the other in proportion to the material used, and to the period of usage.

Right of angary.—The second paragraph giving the neutral power a right similar to that of the belligerents is new. The rest of the article is a combination of Article LIV of the original Hague Regulations, and of the principle identified with the right of angary that the invader can seize neutral property distinguishable as such, and not identified with the country, only under pressing necessity, and that then compensation must be made.

Liability of neutrals domiciled in a belligerent country to military service.—In the same way the country in which the neutral has settled may require of him all the pecuniary support which it may exact of its own citizens, and may also require of him aid in suppressing local disorder, as no more than a fair return for the protection he has enjoyed. That the belligerent may go beyond this, and may require aid of domiciled foreigners in repelling invasion, was claimed by the Confederate Government during the Civil War and was not denied by the British Government, although the latter claimed that this principle was not to be applied to the case of a civil war, the participants in which were liable to be treated as rebels, and that in any event time should be allowed, after the passage of the act, for those who desired to do so, to leave the country. The drafting of domiciled aliens for service in foreign wars would certainly seem harsh; but it does not appear to be unreasonable to hold that those who have permanently taken up their abode in a country should bear their part in repelling invasion or in preserving the integrity of the nation, at least after due notice has been given and especially after those who have come merely for purposes of foreign trade have had a chance to leave.[2]

Attempt to place the neutral in a more favored position at the Second Peace Conference.—The attempt was made at the Second Peace Conference to place the neutral residing in the territory of one of the belligerents, in a

[2] See correspondence as to drafting British subjects domiciled in the South during the Civil War, Parl. Papers, 1864, Vol. 62, North Amer. No. 13, p. 24.

more favored position than above indicated, but the only result of that attempt was the adoption of Article XVI of the Convention with regard to the rights and duties of neutrals on land to the effect "that the nationals of a State which is not taking part in the war are considered as neutrals." Without the articles to which it was to serve as an introduction, it leaves the law unchanged.[3] The attitude of the United States in this matter can be seen from the following, extracted from the report of General Davis, and included in the report of the American Delegation:

"It has been seen that both the committee and the Conference finally rejected a proposition which had been prepared with a view to minimize the effects of war upon neutral commerce and in conformity with the tendencies of modern industry and trade, which demand for their development and maintenance the widest markets, and which are in the highest degree sensitive to the disturbing effects of war.

"The German proposition, by protecting stocks of goods in the hands of neutral agents in belligerent territory from seizure or requisition, was calculated to give to neutral undertakings the broadest immunity from belligerent interference by restricting the burdens and operations of war to the belligerent States and their subjects. But the proposition so conceived and submitted was dismissed with the following expression of desire, which may be accepted as showing the importance which is attached to the development of modern industry and commerce by a majority of the Governments of the civilized world:

"The Conference expresses the hope:

"I. That in case of war the competent authorities, civil and military, should make it their special duty to assure and protect the commercial and industrial relations between the belligerent Powers and neutral States.

"II. That the high (signatory) Powers should seek to establish in agreements with each other uniform contractural undertakings determining in respect to military burdens, the relations of each State in respect to the strangers established in its territory."[4]

[3] See Westlake, II International Law, 286.

[4] Report of the American Delegation, p. 58.

Enemy character.—Private property at sea belonging to the enemy or invested with enemy character is still confiscable. In determining who are enemies, France, and the continent of Europe in general, has followed the simple rule of considering as enemies all those who owe allegiance to the enemy power. At first blush this would seem to be the natural rule, but as it is the enemy's commerce that is to be struck at, and not his person, the more practical rule for this purpose would appear to be to treat as enemies all those who carry on enemy commerce, or, in other words, all those whose commercial domicil is in the enemy's country. This is the rule followed by the courts of Great Britain and the United States.

Commercial domicil.—Commercial domicil is acquired by taking up residence in a country with the intention of engaging in business there permanently. In determining whether it has been acquired, a great variety of circumstances must be considered, such as the presence of the family, the ownership of real estate, the payment of taxes and the enjoyment of political rights; but the most important are the nature of the business and the time during which it has been carried on. Entering on a business permanent in its nature, is sufficient to constitute domicil immediately; and although the original purpose of the residence be to collect debts or to manage a particular undertaking, a long continued stay is sufficient to outweigh the original purpose. But the domicil of origin easily reverts. Whenever the intention to remain is changed and is shown by facts which amount in good faith to a putting in motion to return to the country of origin, the domicil of origin revives even before departure from the country.

Property of citizens domiciled in the enemy's country at the outbreak of war.—In the case of *The Venus*[5] it was held by the United States Supreme Court, by a vote of three to two, that the property of an American citizen, domiciled in Great Britain before the outbreak of war, which was shipped before the beginning of hostilities, was subject to confiscation, notwithstanding that previous to the decision, and within a reasonable time after the outbreak of war, although after the capture, the owner put himself in motion to return to his country. Chief Justice

[5] 8 Cranch, 253.

Marshall, however, in a vigorous dissenting opinion, maintained that a person in such a situation should not be presumed to have intended to continue in the enemy's country, and that his property should not be confiscated until he had had a fair opportunity to leave the country. This opinion, which seems not only to have been the more reasonable one, but the one with the greater weight of authority behind it, was expressly approved in a decision of the King's Beach, in 1901, in a case growing out of the South African War, in which it was held that the property of a Transvaal corporation, seized at the outbreak of the war by the Transvaal Government, should not be considered enemy property, as the corporation, which had originated in Natal and was still incorporated there and essentially British, was not to be presumed to intend to continue its operations in the Transvaal during the war.[6]

Houses of trade.—Commerce carried on through houses of trade established in the enemy's country, or by means of special privileges, such as monopoly and incorporation, is affected with the hostile character, although, as just noticed, the British courts have shown a tendency to look behind the corporation, to the nationality of its members, when it has suffered from the hostile action of the government under which it is incorporated. The establishment of a mere agency in the enemy's country, however, has not this effect. On the other hand, the commerce carried on by a person domiciled in the enemy country, no matter where it may be, is affected with his enemy character, as is also the interest he may hold in a partnership established in a neutral country. Where a man's time is so divided between different countries that none of them can be said to be his commercial domicil rather than another, only the commerce carried on by the house in the enemy country is considered hostile.

Enemy character of the products of the enemy's soil and of the ships flying his flag.—The soil of the country is so intimately r ated to the country itself that its produce, while in the hands of the original owner, is affected with its hostile character, although the owner of the soil may himself be neutral. Military or civil service in a foreign country, or habitual employment in its merchant marine,

[6] Nigel Gold Mining Co., Ltd., v. Hoade, 2 K. B. (1901), 849.

also imparts the national character of that country during the service or employment. The enemy character of the owner is imparted to ships as to other property, and the use of the flag or the pass of the enemy, or the engaging in his trade, also affects them with that character, although in France the presumption that a ship sailing under the flag and pass of an enemy is an enemy ship may be overcome by proof of its neutral ownership.[7]

Transfer of property in transitu.—In general, commerce between a belligerent and a neutral may be carried on in time of war as in time of peace, but the likelihood of the belligerent endeavoring to protect his commerce under the guise of neutrality has given rise to certain rules in the British and American courts as to the ownership of property *in transitu* not applicable in time of peace. One of these is that transfers of property *in transitu* during war are invalid. In the *Sorensen* cases the Privy Council declared the reason of this to be that mere paper transfers of property *in transitu*, without delivery, were too liable to be colorable in time of war to be recognized. Where, however, delivery is possible before the termination of the voyage, the Privy Council held that the rule did not apply, and that the transfer might be perfected on delivery.[8] The rule as to the nontransferability of property *in transitu* in time of war does not extend to transfers made immediately before the outbreak of war, without the intent to avoid belligerent capture.

Ownership of consigned goods and nonrecognition of liens.—It is also held that, although in time of peace there may be a special agreement that goods sent in fulfillment of an order, which ordinarily vest in the consignee on delivery to the common carrier, shall become the property of the consignee only on delivery to him, no such agreement can be set up in time of war as to goods sent by a neutral consignor to an enemy consignee since such agreements would be used to exempt large amounts of property otherwise liable to capture. On the other hand, if an enemy consignor retains any right in goods sent to a neutral consignee beyond that of stopping them in case of the insolvency of the consignee, the goods are still considered

[7] Rivier, Principes du Droit des Gens, II, 343.

[8] 11 Moore's Privy Council Caaes, 146.

enemy goods. So, liens on ships or cargoes, such as mortgages, factors' liens, and bottomry loans, which do not attach, as freight does, from the fact of carriage itself, are necessarily overriden by the capture of the goods since otherwise condemnation proceedings would be so complicated and open to fraud as to be almost hopeless.

Transfers of ships during war.—The transfer of enemy ships to neutrals in time of war is allowed, but as such transfers may be only colorable, they are viewed with suspicion, and the reservation of any enemy interest invalidates them. By the old French rule, all transfers *durante bello* were invalid, but this rule was abandoned during the Franco-German War and is apparently no longer the law.[9]

Conquest by the enemy confers enemy character on the inhabitants of the conquered territory.—In the case of *Thirty Hogsheads of Sugar v. Boyle,* Chief Justice Marshall held that, "although acquisitions made during war are not considered as permanent until confirmed by treaty, yet to every commercial and belligerent purpose they are considered as a part of the domain of the conqueror, so long as he retains the possession and government of them. The island of Santa Cruz, after its capitulation, remained a British island until it was restored to Denmark."[10] In other words, he held that for belligerent purposes, Santa Cruz had the national character of the conqueror. Conquest by the British had made the inhabitants enemies, and the soil enemy soil. It must not be lost sight of, however, that the *conquest* which effects such a change can *now* only take place on the conclusion of hostilities, and that consequently the decision in the case would probably be different today. Just how the inhabitants of occupied territory shall be regarded is for the determination of the political authorities. That enemy character, even for purposes of maritime capture, does not result from military occupation, as distinguished from conquest, was early laid down by Lord Stowell,[11] was affirmed by the Privy Council in the case of *The Gerasimo,*[12] growing out of the Crimean War, and is

9 Rivier, Principes du Droit des Gens, II, 415.
10 9 Cranch, 195.
11 The Santa Anna, 1 Edwards, 182.
12 11 Moore's Privy Council Cases, 88.

so completely in line with modern theory as to be apparently beyond serious attack.

Character of territory in de facto possession of other belligerent.—Where one of the belligerents holds *de facto* possession of territory, without having the legal title to it, it is for the political authorities of the other belligerent to decide whether such territory shall be included in hostile measures, and whether the inhabitants shall be treated as enemies. This situation arises not only in cases of military occupation proper, but also in cases of practically permanent occupation, such as that of Bosnia and Herzigovina by Austria and that of Egypt by England. In such cases it is fact, not fiction, that should be regarded, and, if the titular sovereign is only nominally such, his neutrality should be respected, while against the *de facto* power it is permissible to take any such action as would be justified against a sovereign who is sovereign in name as well as in fact.[13]

Personal unions.—A war undertaken by one of the states connected by a personal union does not involve the other state. Where, however, the common ruler is not subject to constitutional limitations, or exercises a predominating influence in the government in the country not engaged in the war, his actions are liable to be viewed with suspicion, and may be considered a justifiable cause of war against that country when similar action on the part of the ruler of an ordinary neutral country would not be. The neutrality of states in a personal union has generally been respected, although Napoleon seems to have violated it in his conduct towards Hanover, which was then in personal union with Great Britain.[14]

Allies.—At the outbreak of war, an ally of the enemy may be so closely associated with him that it will be justifiable to treat them as one. Usually, however, the alliance is more or less restricted, so that the ally must judge whether the case in hand comes within the terms of the treaty. In such a case fairness as well as policy would ordinarily dictate that the ally should not be attacked before he has had opportunity for decision. Thus, in the case of purely defensive alliances the mere fact that one of the

[13] Hall's Inter. Law, pp. 530–532.
[14] Hall's Inter. Law, pp. 532–534.

belligerents is attacked first does not necessarily indicate that the war on his part is defensive, for the offensive operations may have been in reality merely the most efficient means of defense. The ally must judge for himself in each case whether there is really a *casus foederis.* It has been sometimes said that the party to an alliance is not bound thereby, if the war on which his ally enters is not a just one; but modern opinion generally considers that third parties are not in a position to judge of the justice of the wars of others, and the refusal to carry out the terms of an alliance on that account would be regarded as a mere attempt to evade the obligations of the treaty. In both personal unions and alliances, then, the question of the enemy character of the state is one for the political authorities and not for the courts. It is not for the latter to say that, by the mere fact of war, the subjects of either have become enemies, or that their property is liable to confiscation as enemy property.

Importance of old prize rules lessened by modern conditions of transportation, business and law.—These rules as to enemy character have not the importance they once had, as conditions of transportation, of business and of law have vitally changed since the time when most of them were elaborated at the beginning of the last century. The steamship has largely taken the place of the sailing vessel, business is coming more and more into the hands of corporations, and, what is still more important, enemy goods in neutral bottoms are no longer subject to confiscation. The tendency is to drive the commerce of belligerents into neutral ships and to drive the merchant marine of belligerents off the sea entirely. Accordingly, there will be much less use for these rules in the future than there has been in the past, even though private property at sea continues to be subject to capture.

Exemptions from right of capture on high seas.—Certain restrictions with regard to the exercise of the right of capture in naval war, were embodied in the following convention at the Second Peace Conference.

Recognizing the necessity of more effectively ensuring than hitherto the equitable application of law to the international relations of maritime Powers in time of war;

Considering that, for this purpose, it is expedient, in

giving up or, if necessary, in harmonizing for the common interest certain conflicting practices of long standing, to commence codifying in regulations of general application the guarantees due to peaceful commerce and legitimate business, as well as the conduct of hostilities by sea; that it is expedient to lay down in written mutual engagements the principles which have hitherto remained in the uncertain domain of controversy, or have been left to the discretion of Governments;

That, from henceforth, a certain number of rules may be made, without affecting the common law now in force with regard to matters which that law has left unsettled; [the Plenipotentiaries of the Contracting Powers] have agreed upon the following provisions:

POSTAL CORRESPONDENCE.

ART. I. *The postal correspondence of neutrals or belligerents, whatever its official or private character may be, found on the high seas on board a neutral or enemy ship is inviolable. If the ship is detained, the correspondence is forwarded by the captor with the least possible delay.*

The provisions of the preceding paragraph do not apply, in case of violation of blockade, to correspondence destined for or proceeding from a blockaded port.

ART. II. *The inviolability of postal correspondence does not exempt a neutral mail ship from the laws and customs of maritime war as to neutral merchant ships in general. The ship, however, may not be searched except when absolutely necessary, and then only with as much consideration and expedition as possible.*

Mails.—This was the practice followed with regard to neutral mail during the Civil War. It is here extended to the correspondence of belligerents as well.

THE EXEMPTION FROM CAPTURE OF CERTAIN VESSELS.

ART. III. *Vessels used exclusively for fishing along the coast or small boats employed in local trade are exempt from capture, as well as their appliances, rigging, tackle and cargo.*

They cease to be exempt as soon as they take any part whatever in hostilities.

The Contracting Powers agree not to take advantage of the harmless character of the said vessels in order to use them for military purposes while preserving their peaceful appearance.

ART. IV. *Vessels charged with religious, scientific or philanthropic missions are likewise exempt from capture.*

Vessels in the habit of bringing in fresh fish.—It was evidently the intention to embody in the convention the rule of law laid down in the cases of *The Paquete Habana* and *The Lola.*[15] The criterion for the exemption there laid down that the vessels should be in the habit of bringing in *fresh* fish is doubtless applicable here also. *The Lola* had proceeded to Yucatan, fished there eight days and started back with a cargo of about 10,000 pounds of live fish, but was held by the Supreme Court to come within the exemption.[16] The provision with regard to small boats employed in local trade is new. The exemption specified in both these articles is exemption from capture because of enemy character, and is conditioned not only on abstention from hostilities, but on compliance with such military measures as blockades, when the latter are applicable.

REGULATIONS REGARDING THE CREWS OF ENEMY MERCHANT SHIPS CAPTURED BY A BELLIGERENT.

ART. V. *When an enemy merchant ship is captured by a belligerent, such of its crew as are nationals of a neutral State are not made prisoners of war.*

The same rule applies in the case of the captain and officers likewise nationals of a neutral State, if they promise formally in writing not to serve on an enemy ship while the war lasts.

ART. VI. *The captain, officers and members of the crew, when nationals of the enemy State, are not made prisoners of war, on condition that they make a formal promise in writing not to undertake, while hostilities last, any service connected with the operations of the war.*

ART. VII. *The names of the persons retaining their liberty under the conditions laid down in Article V, paragraph 2, and in Article VI, are notified by the belligerent captor to the other belligerent. The latter is forbidden knowingly to employ the said persons.*

ART. VIII. *The provisions of the three preceding Articles do not apply to ships taking part in the hostilities.*

The mere fact of taking service on board an enemy ship

15 175 U. S., 677.

16 See also Westlake, II International Law, 133.

affects the neutral to some degree with the nationality of the ship, and so in the past has made him liable to capture along with the nationals of the enemy on board, but there has been considerable controversy in the past as to the rights of a belligerent over the crew of a merchantman, and this Convention puts an end to that controversy.

Exemption of personal effects.—One case of exemption of enemy property at sea not included in the convention, but referred to by Westlake is that of the personal effects of the captain and crew of a captured vessel, and possibly of the passengers as well. He says that the same favor has also been extended to the small adventures which it has been customary to allow captains to make on their own account.[17] Ship-wrecked vessels are sometimes considered to be exempt from capture, but the rule is one of chivalry or courtesy rather than of law.

Old rules as to when the title to captured property was lost.—It has always been a much-mooted question as to just what is necessary to divest the title of the old owner of a captured vessel so effectually that on its recapture it does not return to him, but becomes the property of the recaptor. The old rule here, as with territory, was that firm possession was necessary to give good title, and the technical test of firm possession was the bringing of the captured vessel within a place of safety, such as a port or the vicinity of a fleet, or possession for twenty-four hours. The former rule was embodied in the *Consolato del Mare* and prevailed until in the seventeenth century, the latter rule threatened to displace it. Both are now practically obsolete, although the rule of *intra praesidia* is embodied in the Prussian Code.[18]

The new rule requiring the condemnation of a prize court.—The definite incorporation of a new doctrine into the English law dates from 1758, when Lord Mansfield embodied in a decision[19] the principle that to perfect the title of the captor not only firm possession is necessary, but condemnation by a prize court. This doctrine was approved

17 II International Law, 133.

18 Rivier, Principes du Droit des Gens, II, 358.

19 Goss et al. v. Withers, 2 Burrows, 683.

by Lord Stowell,[20] and was incorporated in American legislation and taken up by the courts of the United States and by American writers until it has come to be known as an American doctrine.[21] In the United States the rights of the old owners on recapture are cut off by condemnation proceedings.

These rules of domestic prize law have come to have international significance.—These questions as to when the title of the individual captor becomes vested, and as to when the title of the old owner is so cut off as not to revive on recapture, are evidently questions of domestic prize law, but they have been bound up with the international question as to when a neutral gets good title to a prize as against the original owner, and have been influential in establishing as law the proposition that the title of the capturing nation itself is not complete until condemnation by a prize court. This is not as yet universally accepted, but it appears to have the weight of authority. Its influence is apparent in the practice, which has sometimes been followed, of restoring vessels which, at the conclusion of peace, have not yet been condemned. France followed this practice with Austria, in 1859, and with Prussia, in 1871. Here, however, as in the case of territory, the rule of *uti possidetis* is applied, and if nothing is said in the treaty of peace as to the return of vessels, that fact in itself perfects the title of the capturing belligerent.

Much of the confusion upon the question as to when the title to the captured ship vests in the captor has arisen from the confusion of the doctrine of *recapture* with that of *postliminium.* At the time when the latter doctrine was much more important than it is today, and consequently the subject of far more study, the generally accepted doctrine was that it did not apply to ships at all, that, while perfect title to territory could not be acquired during hostilities, this was not true of captured ships, but that until the bringing of the ship *intra praesidia,* or its possession for twenty-four hours or the condemnation of a prize court, the right of the captor was possessory merely, but that it then became an absolute title. If the ship were recaptured before that time, the title did not *revest* in the old owner

20 The *Hendrick* and *Maria,* 4 Robinson Admiralty Reports, 55.
21 Heffter, Le Droit Inter. de L'Europe, 460.

as it would under the doctrine of postliminium, but it was his because it had never passed from him. Recent practice has tended to allow the old owner to recover the ship as long as it is recovered before the termination of hostilities. If countries following this practice still hold to the old rule that title passes and only passes on the fulfillment of one of the old conditions, then we have an instance of postliminium, or revested title, if the ship is recaptured after the fulfillment of the conditions, but before the end of the war. In cases of recapture the rule of reciprocity is generally applied to allies and neutrals, unless their practice is less liberal.

What is necessary to constitute capture.—Capture takes effect on a vessel's lowering her colors, or on being brought within the effective control of the enemy without having done so. The sending aboard of a prize crew is not necessary at least in the United States and Great Britain. Evidence of intention to retain possession, however, must be given to prevent subsequent captors from regarding the prize as abandoned; but such evidence may be afforded by the presence of a single prize-master who in no way controls the navigation of the vessel, provided the circumstances are such as to warrant the belief that the vessel will be conducted safely to port.

Captured vessels should be brought in for adjudication if possible.—Where circumstances permit, all nations require that vessels should be brought into port for adjudication. This is essential to a proper control over naval forces, as well as to protect the interests of neutrals and to some degree those of the enemy. Where a captured vessel cannot be brought into a domestic port or the port of an ally, three principal courses are open to a captor (1), to take it into a neutral port (2), to burn or scuttle it, and (3) to ransom it.

Prizes in neutral ports.—The first course is proper according to Article XXI of the convention on the rights and duties of neutral powers in naval war in case of unseaworthiness, stress of weather, or want of fuel or provisions, but the prize "must leave as soon as the circumstances which justified its entry are at an end." Article XXIII of that convention also allows prizes to enter neutral ports "when they are brought there to be sequestered

15

pending the decision of a Prize Court." This is "to prevent the destruction of prizes or render it less frequent."[22] But it was criticised by the American Delegation as the "revival of an ancient abuse"[23] in allowing the title to property captured in war to be perfected through the protection afforded by neutral territory, and it was not adhered to by the United States.

Destruction of captured ship.—The second course involves a terrible destruction of valuable property and has been severely condemned, but if a belligerent can be effectively struck at through his commerce, as those who uphold the capture of private property at sea must contend, it is hard to say that he may not be struck at through the destruction of his ships as well as through their confiscation. It must always remain an extreme measure to be avoided where possible, but under pressing circumstances its legality is unquestionable. In such a case, neutral property on board the enemy ship would appear to share the fate of the ship. Such was the decision of a French appellate tribunal in the case of the *Ludwig* and *Vorwärts* during the Franco-German War. While the Declaration of Paris does not allow the confiscation of neutral goods in enemy ships, it does not forbid the destruction of the vessel because of their presence. If this were the case, enemy ships could free themselves altogether from this right of the belligerent by carrying small amounts of neutral goods.

Rules of the Institute of International Law.—The destruction of a ship is permissible under the model Regulation for Maritime Prizes of the Institute of International Law:

"1. When it is not possible to hold the ship to the fleet on account of its poor condition, there being a rough sea;

"2. When the ship sails so poorly that she is not able to follow the ship of war and would be recaptured by the enemy;

"3. When the approach of a superior enemy force makes the recapture of the ship apprehended;

"4. When the ship of war is not able to place in the

22 Westlake, II International Law, 331.

23 Report of Delegation, p. 53.

ship seized a sufficient crew without diminishing that which is necessary to its own safety.

"5. When the port where it will be possible to conduct the vessel is too far distant."[24]

At the Second Peace Conference a proposition absolutely forbidding the destruction of neutral prizes was vigorously supported by Great Britain and the United States but failed of adoption.

Ransom.—The third course open to the captor is to sell his interest in the prize to the original owner. This is done by means of a ransom bill, which serves as a free-conduct for the captured vessel to return to its own country, as long as it keeps within the course marked out by the bill. On the Continent suit can be brought on the bill directly by the holder, even though he be an alien enemy, and judging by the opinion of American jurists a similar procedure would probably be followed in the United States, in spite of the English practice of requiring the bill to be enforced by means of a suit for his liberty by the hostage who was retained at the time of the capture. If the bill is captured before arrival at a place of safety, it is rendered invalid. The subsequent wrecking of a ransomed vessel does not invalidate the ransom bill. As ransoming is a less severe measure than confiscation, it has often been prohibited by governments except under grave circumstances. The sum secured is liable to be small compared with the value of the vessel and the crew are not made prisoners of war. Ransoming has never been forbidden, however, by the United States.

As prize law and the proceedings of prize courts are mainly of municipal or neutral concern, the attempt will not be made here to discuss them further.

[24] 6 Annuaire, 221.

CHAPTER III.

THE QUALIFICATIONS OF BELLIGERENTS.

The present and subsequent chapters are, mainly, a commentary on The Hague and Geneva Conventions.

H I. THE *laws, rights and duties of war apply not only to armies, but also to militia and volunteer corps fulfilling the following conditions:*

1. *To be commanded by a person responsible for his subordinates;*
2. *To have a fixed distinctive emblem recognizable at a distance;*
3. *To carry arms openly; and*
4. *To conduct their operations in accordance with the laws and customs of war.*

In countries where militia or volunteer corps constitute the army, or form part of it, they are included under the denomination "army."

Where militia are considered part of the army.—Just what the force of this last paragraph is it is hard to say. It was introduced by Colonel Hammer, the Swiss delegate, at Brussels, for the reason that in Switzerland the militia forms a part of the regular army, but it was not discussed and was apparently considered merely a question of nomenclature. The whole article, however, is open to the construction that, if militia or volunteer corps constitute the army or form part of it, they are entitled to the privileges of combatants, irrespective of satisfying the four preceding requirements. It is hardly possible that any country would treat as an army an organization that failed to meet any of the four requirements, except the second, which exacts a distinctive mark, fixed and recognizable at a distance. At Brussels, Colonel Staaf, the delegate of Sweden and Norway, said that the militia which formed part of the army of the countries he represented, was without such a distinctive mark; and, in the war in South Africa the Boer forces were similarly situated. Where men act in large bodies, after the manner of armies, it would seem that the lack of a uniform, or of something approaching it, would not subject them to penal measures, and it did not do so in South Africa. Where such forces are detailed on detached service, however, all the reasons for some fixed sign to distinguish combatants from noncombatants come into play, and the fact that such forces are considered part of the "army" would appear to be immaterial.

The Evil and the Inspiration of irregular fighting.—One of the greatest evils in warfare has been irregular fighting. Individuals, moved no doubt often by patriotic sentiments, have taken the fighting into their own hands, and the enemy, unable to distinguish between them and the worst breakers of the peace, has been compelled to resort to measures of punishment which have embittered the struggle and sown the seeds of national distrust and hate. Governments have organized partisan corps to act on the flank and rear of armies, and, as in our Civil War and the Franco-German War, these have been such a scourge to friend and foe alike that their organization has been regretted and even put an end to by those who were responsible for it. Again, conflicts have eventually degenerated into guerilla warfare and extreme measures, such as those of reconcentration, have been the consequence. The evils and general ineffectiveness of guerilla fighting are not likely to be exaggerated. On the other hand, many of the brightest pages in history are accounts of the heroic struggles carried on by the burgher and peasant populations of Holland and Switzerland, and the incidents which we love longest to linger over in the birth of our own nation, are the impromptu fights such as those at Lexington and Concord, and the daring exploits and privations of bands such as those of Marion and Sumter. And in wars so recent as those of Napoleon, the possible effectiveness of such fighting was shown by the part the Spanish people played in driving him from the Peninsula.

Division between the large and small powers at Brussels and The Hague.—Both of these things, the horrors of irregular warfare and the inspiration of its heroic sacrifices, were present in the minds of the delegates at Brussels and at The Hague; but it was the horrors that predominated in the minds of the delegates of the great military powers while it was the memory of their childhood heroes that appealed most strongly to the representatives of the others.

The Original Project at Brussels limited those entitled to

the rights of regular combatants to a definite class.—The original Russian Project at Brussels contained an affirmative article, corresponding to this article of The Hague Convention; but it was supplemented, as we have seen,[1] by a negative clause which proposed to hand over to military justice all who should engage in hostilities without complying with its terms. The affirmative stipulation deprived no one of combatant rights, but left the question of who is *not* entitled to such rights to the unwritten law of nations. The addition of the negative clause would have avoided resort to the unwritten law, and would have substituted certainty in this regard for uncertainty; but the representatives of the smaller powers felt that that would be the certainty of injustice, as was shown by their indignant protest that they could consent to no provision having "a tendency either to weaken national defense or to detach citizens from their duty towards their country."[2]

The Russian delegates considered that this article would not restrict rights of defense, but would merely impose a duty on governments to give some organization to the defense in times of peace.—The Russian delegates on the other hand urged that the articles of their project could have no such tendency, but that they would, on the contrary, by making it the duty of governments to organize their defense, tend to strengthen, rather than weaken, the national defense. The argument was made in vain.

Refusal of the smaller powers to agree to the negative article of the original Project.—There were two possible forms of warfare which the negative clause condemned, but in the condemnation of which the delegates of the smaller powers absolutely refused to concur. These were (1) the *levee en masse* in occupied territory, and (2) individual acts of hostility in unoccupied territory, such as the blowing up of bridges in face of the invader by persons not satisfying the conditions of the affirmative stipulation.[3] The second of these is not likely to be of much importance, but the first is, and it gave rise to a bitter debate which will be considered under the next article. The firm attitude of the delegates of the smaller powers rendered the adoption of

1 *Supra*, p. 104.
2 Protocol 1 of the Committee.
3 Protocol 18 of the Committee.

the negative clause impossible and it was dropped early in the Conference and was not again taken up. The article as finally adopted at Brussels therefore, had no negative supplement, and in this form was included in The Hague Regulations as Article I.

The article finally adopted, which is embodied in The Hague Convention, is not restrictive.—The fact that this article, the negative supplement having been dropped, can convey no negative implication, can not be too clearly brought out. It was repeatedly emphasized at Brussels and at The Hague,[4] and was the only basis on which agreement was possible. When reading this article, therefore, we are constantly to bear the fact in mind, that, while it assures recognition as soldiers to those who satisfy its conditions, it neither by assertion nor by implication denies such recognition to anyone. If anyone engaging in hostilities is denied such recognition, it must be because he has acted contrary to the unwritten law of nations. Just what acts are so proscribed is more or less uncertain, but it is probable that none but those brought out by the delegates of the smaller powers at Brussels will cause much difficulty. Others may possibly arise, however, and it is well they were not prejudged by the adoption of a hard and fast rule.

Orders from headquarters not necessary to give a volunteer corps the character of regular combatants.—The original draft of this article, at Brussels, required that militia and volunteer corps should be subject to orders from headquarters, but the Austrian delegate pointed out the difficulty a detached corps often would encounter in communicating with the commander-in-chief, and the clause was dropped. It would almost wholly have prevented the organization of such corps in occupied territory. Any person commanding the respect of his community through his personality, his property or his official position, and conversant with the laws of war, is a responsible person in the sense of Clause I.[5]

Necessity of a fixed emblem.—A fixed distinctive emblem is necessary in order to draw a sharp line between combatants and noncombatants. Without such an emblem, it

[4] Conference Internationale de la Paix, p. 50; see also preamble to Convention drawn up at second Conference, *supra*, p. 186.

[5] Protocol 12 of the Committee.

is impossible to distinguish combatants from noncombatants when the former are acting in detached bodies, and the whole population is apt to be drawn into the struggle. The emblem need not be a uniform, but it must be something recognizable at a distance and which cannot be put on and off at pleasure. That combatants must carry arms openly and observe the laws and customs of wars might have been taken for granted, but it was thought best to give to these requirements the emphasis of express statement.

Employment of savage troops.—Possibly the fourth requirement was aimed at the employment of savage or semicivilized troops. Ever since Lord Chatham uttered his famous protest against the employment of Indians in the war with the colonies, it has been recognized as improper to employ troops whose accustomed manner of warfare gives evidence that they will not live up to the standards of civilized life.

H I applicable in occupied as well as unoccupied territory.—Article 1, which has just been discussed, unlike Article II, which will next be taken up, applies to corps acting either in unoccupied territory, or in occupied territory, or in the territory of the enemy.

H II. *The inhabitants of a territory which has not been occupied, who, on the approach of the enemy, spontaneously take up arms to resist the invading troops without having had time to organize themselves in accordance with Article* 1, *shall be regarded as belligerents if they carry arms openly and if they respect the laws and customs of war.*

Levees en masse in unoccupied territory.—This article was the result of a compromise. The delegates of the smaller powers wished a general recognition of *levees en masse* —spontaneous risings of the population—in occupied and unoccupied territory alike, irrespective of any compliance with the conditions of Article I. On the other hand, the German delegate in particular contended that *levees en masse* should be required to comply with the terms of Article I, no matter where they should take place. After an acrimonious debate, the question of risings in occupied territory was left to the unwritten law of nations; while it was decided that in unoccupied territory, if there has been no

6 See also Westlake, II International Law, 90.

opportunity to organize in conformity with Article I, those engaged in popular risings may enjoy the privileges of combatants irrespective of their compliance with requirements 1 and 2 of Article I. The requirement of carrying arms openly was added at the Conference of 1907.

Levees en masse in occupied territory complying with the conditions of Article I are entitled to regular combatant rights.—Beyond this there is much uncertainty. It seems beyond question, however, that, where a population in occupied territory has complied with the conditions of Article I, it is entitled to combatant privileges. Possibly the occupant may be entitled, by virtue of his rights as such, to punish individual members of the population for joining the military organizations of their country after the occupation; but, once having joined, they are entitled to the privileges of combatants. Not only are penal measures against them for what they have done improper, but the communities from which they come cannot properly be held collectively responsible therefor, since the act of joining the military organizations of their country, though it may be contrary to the orders of the military occupant, is not contrary to the law of nations. Where penalties have been imposed on individuals in occupied territory for such acts they have been much less severe than the penalties inflicted for popular uprisings.

Unsuccessful uprisings in occupied territory may entitle the occupier to use repressive measures.—A second point in relation to the action of populations in occupied territory also seems clear. This is, that, where the population has not been organized in accordance with Article I, and the uprising is not even temporarily successful, the occupant is entitled to use severe repressive measures. Not only do many of the privileges of noncombatants cease from the wiping out of the distinction between combatants and noncombatants, but in addition to this it has been customary for the belligerent to go farther and punish with severity the attempt made to overthrow his authority. The position of the occupant in the occupied territory is to a certain degree analogous to that of a sovereign. Some authority is necessary wherever highly civilized life is to exist and as in the occupied territory the only territorial authority for the time being is the occupant, he is entitled to punish all attempts made against him there by any other than the properly qualified forces of the enemy. Attempts made to overturn a sovereign can alone be justified by success, and so it is of attempts made against an occupant.

Uprisings which are temporarily successful do not give occasion for repressive measures.—If the success in displacing the occupant's authority is final, no question can arise as to the punishment of the population which has participated in the uprising. But the case was suggested at Brussels, although not authoritatively discussed, where the uprising is temporarily successful, but the occupant ultimately regains his authority. It was suggested that, as the test of occupation is the ability to suppress insurrection, the fact of the uprisings being even temporarily successful shows that the occupation was not effective, and that the self-styled occupant, being such in name and not in fact, has no right to resort to repressive measures available to a real occupant. This position would appear to be unanswerable, and was not authoritatively questioned by any of the delegates. Nice questions are liable to arise as to just when an insurrection is temporarily successful, but, if the test of success is the effective displacement of the power of the belligerent for the time being, it would seem that there should be no greater difficulty about the application of this rule than of many others.

H III. *The armed forces of the belligerent parties may consist of combatants and noncombatants. In the case of capture by the enemy, both have a right to be treated as prisoners of war.*

This article, almost superfluous, it was deemed advisable to add in order to ensure to the noncombatant part of the army equal treatment with the combatant.[7]

PRIVATEERING.

Abolition of privateering.—The Declaration of Paris of 1856 contains the following provision: "Privateering is and remains abolished." Although the United States has never adhered to the Declaration, Spain and Mexico, the most notable of the other nonadhering powers, took occa-

[7] Protocol 13 of the Committee.

sion of the Second Hague Conference to do so and it is probable that the above statement is the expression of an historic fact. Privateering has stood for much that was patriotic and gallant, but it has also stood for all that was worst in visit and search and in the capture of private property on the high seas, and if revived, its former evils would hardly be tolerated now.

Conversion of merchantmen.—The Declaration of Paris has been supplemented by the following convention drawn up at the late Peace Conference, but not signed or adhered to by the United States because of its nonadherence to the Paris Declaration. It is not likely, however, that any of the rules it lays down will be repudiated.

Whereas, it is desirable, in view of the incorporation in time of war of merchant ships in the fighting fleet, to define the conditions subject to which this operation may be effected;

Whereas, however, the Contracting Powers have been unable to come to an agreement on the question whether the conversion of a merchant ship into a warship may take place on the high seas, it is understood that the question of the place where such conversion is effected remains outside the scope of this Agreement and is in no way effected by the following rules;

[the Plenipotentiaries of the Contracting Powers] have agreed upon the following provisions:

ART. I. *A merchant ship converted into a warship cannot have the rights and duties accruing to such vessels unless it is placed under the direct authority, immediate control and responsibility of the Power whose flag it flies.*

ART. II. *Merchant ships converted into warships must bear the external marks which distinguish the warships of their nationality.*

ART. III. *The commander must be in the service of the State and duly commissioned by the competent authorities. His name must figure on the list of the officers of the fighting fleet.*

ART. IV. *The crew must be subject to military discipline.*

ART. V. *Every merchant ship converted into a warship must observe in its operations the laws and customs of war.*

ART. VI. *A belligerent who converts a merchant ship into a warship must, as soon as possible, announce such conversion in the list of warships.*

As to the place of conversion, "the American Delegation wishing to obviate controversies in the future insisted that the transformation should take place either within the home port or territorial waters of the transforming country. Other delegations insisted that the transformation might take place not only within the home ports and territorial waters, but upon the high seas. As the difference of opinion was radical and irreconcilable, it was agreed to eliminate the question from the Convention."[8] On general principles it is hard to see why the conversion should not take place on the high seas as well as in territorial waters, unless it is an attempt to evade treaty obligations or general international obligations such as those of neutrality.

Noncommissioned vessels may resist when attacked, and may make good prize of the attacking vessel. Otherwise they have no combatant rights.

[8] Report of American Delegation, p. 40.

CHAPTER IV.

PRISONERS OF WAR.

H IV. *Prisoners of war are in the power of the hostile Government, but not of the individuals or corps who capture them.*

They must be humanely treated.

All their personal belongings, except arms, horses and military papers, remain their property.

Prisoners are prisoners of the opposing government and not of the individuals or corps which make the capture.—The principle underlying this article may seem to be almost too obvious today for utterance, but it was much debated among the earlier writers on the law of nations. In the Middle Ages the feeling of the knights was strong that prisoners captured were their prisoners and that booty captured was their booty, and the feeling was not unnatural when the capture of prisoners and booty was so much a matter of personal prowess. But the lessening of personal contact between combatants with the introduction of firearms, and the change of warfare from an aggregation of personal combats to a highly organized contest of armies, caused the importance of the individual to decline, and with the growth of the powerful modern state the principle that prisoners and booty pertain to the government and not to individuals came to have unquestioned authority.

Under no circumstances can prisoners be put to death except for crime or offenses against martial law.—The question was also long discussed whether in cases of extreme necessity it might not be permissible to put prisoners to death, but it is hardly conceivable that circumstances warranting such action could arise today.

The use of violence towards prisoners of war only warranted in special cases.—It was provided in the original draft of the Declaration of Brussels that prisoners should not be subjected to any violence. This provision, from the spirit of which there was no dissent, would have made corporal punishment impossible, besides putting under the ban many of the gravest abuses in the treatment of prisoners of war in the past; but it was shown that there were cases where the use of force is absolutely necessary, as where a prisoner obstinately refuses to march; and it was therefore decided only to require that prisoners be "humanely treated."[1]

Private property of prisoners.—The exclusion of arms, horses and military papers from the general exemption of the private property of prisoners from confiscation, is in line with the tendency to regard property which at sea would be contraband of war as still subject to capture.[2] The exemption of the private property of the prisoner from capture, however, does not prevent its sequestration during the period of captivity, especially where, as in the case of the retention of considerable sums of money, its retention by the prisoner would be likely to enable him to escape. As Professor Holland says: "It may be a question whether large sums of money found upon prisoners, or in their baggage are in fact their private property."[3] The American Articles even went so far as to lay down that large sums found in the private luggage of prisoners should not be treated as private property at all.[4]

H V. *Prisoners of war may be interned in a town, fortress, camp or other place, and bound not to go beyond certain fixed limits; but they cannot be confined except as an indispensable measure of safety and only while the circumstances which necessitate the measure continue to exist.*

No ignominy attaching to the condition of a prisoner of war.—The terms of this article were chosen with especial care, in order to negative any possible implication of ignominy attaching to the condition of a prisoner of war. The humane treatment of prisoners of war during and since the Franco-German War is one of the most commendable things in modern military history. The last clause providing that prisoners shall be confined "only while the circumstances which necessitate the measure continue to exist," was added in 1907. Those confined in so-called concentration camps are clearly entitled to as liberal treatment as regular prisoners of war, but it would seem with

1 Protocol 5 of the Committee.
2 But see *infra*, p. 326.
3 T. E. Holland, The Laws and Customs of War on Land, p. 11.
4 Article 72.

Westlake that H III and V have no direct bearing on concentration.[5]

H VI. *The State may utilize the labor of prisoners of war according to their rank and aptitude, officers excepted. The tasks shall not be excessive and shall have no connection with the operations of the war.*

Prisoners may be authorized to work for the public service, for private persons, or on their own account.

Work done for the State is paid at the rates in force for work of a similar kind done by soldiers of the national army, or, if there are none in force, at a rate according to the work executed.

When the work is for other branches of the public service or for private persons, the conditions are settled in agreement with the military authorities.

The wages of the prisoners shall go towards improving their position, and the balance shall be paid them on their release, after deducting the cost of their maintenance.

The condition of the prisoner of war not that of slavery or penal servitude.—This article strikingly demonstrates how radically the condition of a prisoner of war differs from slavery and other forms of involuntary servitude, and especially from that of punishment for crime. The prisoner of war is subject to such restraints as will prevent him from rejoining the forces of his country, but he is not a criminal, nor is he the slave for the time being of the state which has captured him. But, as the belligerent is entitled to requisition the services of the inhabitants of the country through which his army passes so long as these services are not connected with military operations, it is eminently reasonable that he should be entitled to claim the same services of prisoners of war for whose maintenance he is primarily liable. It has been claimed that inhabitants whose services have been requisitioned have a right to be compensated for them, but, if they have not, that is no reason why prisoners should have no such right, as the services of the inhabitants are occasional, while those of prisoners are apt to extend over a considerable period, so that, if they should be uncompensated, their condition would truly bear a close resemblance to penal servitude if not slavery itself.

Democracy the rule in the military service.—In the orig-

[5] II International Law, 268.

inal draft of the Brussels Declaration, the first paragraph of this article reads that certain labour might be required of prisoners of war, "provided such employment be not excessive or humiliating to the rank and social position which they occupy in their own country." At the suggestion of General Voigts-Rhetz, the German delegate, the reference to social position was suppressed. His words are memorable:

"The man of the most noble birth and the peasant of the lowest class, the scholar and the artisan, the rich and the poor, are equals in the military service; they should equally remain so if taken prisoners; they should work on the same footing."[6]

Labor of prisoners not to involve participation in military operations against their country.—The provision that the labor required of prisoners of war shall have nothing to do with the operations of war is liable to be fruitful of interpretations. It unquestionably forbids forced participation in military operations having an *immediate* connection with the war, but whether it goes further than this and forbids work on fortifications not in the theatre of war, seems to be an open question. The better opinion would appear to be that it does not forbid the requirement of such work.[7] For further treatment of this subject, see Articles XXIII and XLIV.

That the terms of agreement for working should be settled with the military authorities seems unavoidable. Prisoners would be in no position to enforce their claims, and constant bickering between the prisoners and the inhabitants would be inevitable. Besides, prisoners might be enabled to escape through the help of secret sympathizers, or by the use of money if it were paid directly to them.

British and French practice not to deduct cost of maintenance from earnings.—In neither the British nor the French army, is it the practice to deduct the cost of their maintenance from the earnings of prisoners of war, but Professor Holland says that the British government expects reciprocity of treatment from the other belligerent.[8]

6 Protocol 5 of the Committee.

7 Holland, The Laws and Customs of War on Land, p. 11. But see Westlake, II International Law, 64.

8 *Ibid.*, p. 12; Guelle, Prècis des Lois de la Guerre, I, 202.

The phrase "officers excepted" in the first paragraph is new as is also the provision in the third paragraph that "if there are none in force, at a rate according to the work executed." The latter change was made upon the representation of several delegates that the laws and regulations of the states which they represented made no provision for the compensation of prisoners of war for service rendered to the captor state, or to individuals or corporations with the consent of that government.[9]

H VII. *The Government into whose hands prisoners of war have fallen is charged with their maintenance.*

In the absence of a special agreement between the belligerents, prisoners of war shall be treated as regards board, lodging and clothing on the same footing as the troops of the Government who captured them.

Duty to care for prisoners especially in resorting to such extreme measures as reconcentration.—The principle of this article is especially important where extreme measures such as reconcentration camps, are resorted to. No government is justified in enforcing such measures which is unwilling or unprepared to take proper care of its prisoners.

H VIII. *Prisoners of war shall be subject to the laws, regulations and orders in force in the army of the State in whose power they are. Any act of insubordination justifies the adoption towards them of such measures of severity as may be considered necessary.*

Escaped prisoners who are retaken before being able to rejoin their own army or before leaving the territory occupied by the army which captured them are liable to disciplinary punishment.

Prisoners who, after succeeding in escaping, are again taken prisoners, are not liable to any punishment on account of their previous flight.

One of the few instances of the sanctioning of penal power in this Convention.—This is one of the few articles sanctioning the exercise of penal power by a belligerent.

Summons necessary before shooting at escaping prisoners.—The Brussels Declaration provided that "arms may be used, after summoning, against a person attempting to escape;" and this is substantially included in the second paragraph of the present article, allowing such measures

[9] General Davis, II American Journal of International Law, 68.

of severity as are necessary in cases of insubordination. A mere attempt to escape is not an act of insubordination, until the prisoner has been summoned to stop; so that the old provision is clearly included in the new. It may well be wished, however, that the express requirement of a summons before firing had been retained.

Prisoner who has succeeded in escaping not liable to subsequent punishment.—The escape of a prisoner is not an offense against the laws of war; consequently, if, after making his escape, he is recaptured, he is not liable to punishment, although he may be placed under stricter surveillance. But, if there were no liability to punishment for attempting to escape, such attempts would be unceasing, while the belligerent, except by keeping a close guard, would have to look on with hands folded. A distinction is therefore made between successful and unsuccessful attempts, the latter being subject to disciplinary punishment such as confinement, while the former are not. The prisoner, however, is not justified in using violence in attempting to escape; and, if he resorts to such methods, may be punished under the first paragraph of this article, according to the laws, regulations and orders in force in the army of the State into whose hands he has fallen.

Conspiracy and revolt.—Conspiracy and revolt are also punishable under the first paragraph. Conspiracy to escape is a less serious offense than revolt.[10]

H IX. *Every prisoner of war is bound to give, if he is questioned on the subject, his true name and rank, and if he infringes this rule, he is liable to have the advantages given to prisoners of his class curtailed.*

Unfairness of misrepresentation of rank in case of exchange.—The unfairness of a prisoner's misrepresenting his rank in a matter such as that of exchange is evident.

H X. *Prisoners of war may be set at liberty on parole if the laws of their country allow, and, in such cases, they are bound, on their personal honour, scrupulously to fulfil, both towards their own Government and the Government by whom they were made prisoners, the engagements they have contracted.*

In such cases their own Government is bound neither to require of nor accept from them any service incompatible with the parole given.

10 Protocol 5, 6, of the Committee.

Where there is not express allowance of parole by the prisoner's government or where it is forbidden.—Two cases are likely to arise not dealt with in this article; the first, where the law of the country of the prisoner is silent as to whether he may parole himself; the second, where the law expressly forbids him to do so. In the first case, it would seem that, if his government subsequently disapproves his parole, it is bound to give him the opportunity to preserve his good faith by returning to captivity. If the other belligerent refuses to receive him, he is released from his parole. In the second case, the prisoner's government would not appear to be bound by the parole, even if it had not communicated to the other government the law or order forbidding parole, since governments are supposed to know each other's rules in such matters. The American Instructions, however, indicate that it is the practice for belligerents to communicate to each other their regulations concerning paroles,[11] and this is more in harmony with good faith. In either case, however, the parole is personal and subjects the person who has broken it to punishment by the other side on recapture.

What the parole includes.—Article 130 of the American Instructions states the general law as to what is meant by the usual pledge, given in the parole, not to serve against the paroling power or its allies during the existing war unless exchanged. "This pledge," so reads the article, "refers only to the active service in the field, against the paroling belligerent or his allies actively engaged in the same war. These cases of breaking the parole are patent acts, and can be visited with the punishment of death; but the pledge does not refer to internal service, such as recruiting or drilling the troops, fortifying places not besieged, quelling civil commotions, fighting against belligerents unconnected with the paroling belligerents, or to civil or diplomatic service for which the paroled officer may be employed."

Should the parole be confined to officers.—It has been customary in the American and in the British army to allow paroles to be given only through an officer unless in cases of extreme hardship. This rule seems to have survived the times when "the honor of a gentleman" was sup-

[11] Order No. 100, Instructions, etc., Sec. 132.

posed to be confined to a much smaller class than it is today, and no reason appears now to exist why soldiers other than officers should not be permitted freely to give their parole, at least when no officers are imprisoned with them. In France, no such distinction between the officers and the men seems to be made.[12]

H XI. *A prisoner of war can not be compelled to accept his liberty on parole; similarly the hostile Government is not obliged to accede to the request of the prisoner's to be set at liberty on parole.*

Parole not compulsory.—Parole is a contract entered into between the prisoner and the government which has him in its power. Like other contracts, it is a voluntary agreement. Persons can not be compelled to agree to abstain from fighting for their country, nor can a belligerent be under any duty to run the risk of such a promise being broken. Article 128 of the American Instructions declares the general law when it says:

"No paroling on the battlefield, no paroling of entire bodies of troops after a battle, and no dismissal of large numbers of prisoners, with a general declaration that they are paroled, is permitted or of any value."

H XII. *Prisoners of war, liberated on parole and recaptured bearing arms against the Government to whom they had pledged their honour, or against the allies of that Government forfeit their right to be treated as prisoners of war, and can be brought before the Courts.*

Desirability of a trial for all violations of the law of war.—Probably a negative can be implied so that a prisoner charged with breach of his parole cannot be punished without a trial by the military courts, a principle which, it may be hoped, will become universal in dealing with offenses against the laws of war.

H XIII. *Individuals who follow an army without directly belonging to it, such as newspaper correspondents and reporters, sutlers and contractors, who fall into the enemy's hands and whom the latter thinks fit to detain, are entitled to be treated as prisoners of war, provided they are in possession of a certificate from the military authorities of the army which they were accompanying.*

Usual course towards those who follow the army, but are

12 Guelle, Prècis des Lois de la Guerre, I, p. 208.

not a part of it.—As a general rule it is not likely that such persons will be detained, unless, as in the case of reporters, their conduct has been such as to incur the indignation of the capturing belligerent. Military reasons may, however, often render immediate release inconvenient, or make their immediate return to the camp of the enemy unwise. The necessity of obtaining protection against the noxious characters who infest armies, and the possibility of combatants escaping in the guise of noncombatants, make the certificate of identification necessary.

H XIV. *An inquiry office for prisoners of war is instituted on the commencement of hostilities in each of the belligerent States, and, when necessary, in neutral countries which have received belligerents in their territory. It is the function of this office to reply to all inquiries about the prisoners. It receives from the various services concerned full information respecting internments and transfers, releases on parole, exchanges, escapes, admissions into hospitals, deaths, as well as other information necessary to enable it to make out and keep up to date an individual return for each prisoner of war. The office must state in this return the regimental number, name and surname, age, place of origin, rank, unit, wounds, date and place of capture, internment, wounding and death, as well as any observations of a special character. The individual return shall be sent to the Government of the other belligerent after the conclusion of peace.*

It is likewise the function of the inquiry office to receive and collect all objects of personal use, valuable letters, etc., found on the field of battle or left by prisoners who have been released on parole, or exchanged, or who have escaped, or died in hospitals or ambulances, and to forward them to those concerned.

Articles XIV-XX, the work of M. Romberg, not a part of the Brussels Declaration.—The adoption of Articles XIV-XX was largely due to the unremitting efforts of M. Romberg, who, as head of the Brussels committee for the care of prisoners of war during the Franco-German War, had seen the need of stipulations of this kind. They were brought before the Brussels Conference, but were there regarded as innovations and so beyond the scope of the Conference. The Conference, however, recommended them to the attention of the various governments, and when they were presented by the Belgian delegate at The Hague, they were adopted with comparatively little discussion. The last two sentences of the first paragraph detailing the particulars to be kept on each card and requiring the card to be delivered to the other belligerent at the end of the war are new. They embody the practice followed by the Japanese in their war with Russia. The inclusion of "releases on parole, exchanges, escapes" in the information to be obtained by the bureau and of prisoners who have been "released on parole, or exchanged, or who have escaped" among those whose valuables are to be received, collected and forwarded, is also the work of the Second Conference.

H XV. *Relief societies for prisoners of war, which are properly constituted in accordance with the laws of their country and with the object of serving as the channel for charitable effort shall receive from the belligerents, for themselves and their duly accredited agents every facility for the efficient performance of their humane task within the bounds imposed by military necessities and administrative regulations. Agents of these societies may be admitted to the places of internment for the purpose of distributing relief, as also to the halting places of repatriated prisoners, if furnished with a personal permit by the military authorities, and on giving an undertaking in writing to comply with all measures of order and police which the latter may issue.*

H XVI. *Inquiry offices enjoy the privilege of free postage. Letters, money orders and valuables, as well as parcels by post, intended for prisoners of war, or dispatched by them, shall be exempt from all postal duties in the countries of origin and destination, as well as in the countries they pass through.*

Presents and relief in kind for prisoners of war shall be admitted free of all import or other duties, as well as of payments for carriage by the State railways.

Relaxation of charges on letters and parcels sent to prisoners of war.—During the Franco-German War, many of the things sent to relieve the condition of prisoners never reached them on account of the charges imposed. The representatives of the powers at The Hague felt that the relaxation of these charges would be insignificant as compared with the general expenses of the war, and that the governments could well afford it in view of the great good likely to result.

H XVII. *Officers taken prisoners shall receive the same rate of pay as officers of corresponding rank in the country where they are detained, the amount to be ultimately refunded by their own Government.*

Officers to receive pay in force in captor's army.—The rule laid down in the old convention was that officers taken prisoners should be paid their full salaries by the captor, but the consensus of opinion for some time has been in favor of the rule laid down in this article.

H XVIII. *Prisoners of war shall enjoy complete liberty in the exercise of their religion, including attendance at the services of whatever Church they may belong to, on the sole condition that they comply with the measures of order and police issued by the military authorities.*

H XIX. *The wills of prisoners of war are received or drawn up in the same way as for soldiers of the national army.*

The same rules shall be observed regarding death certificates as well as for the burial of prisoners of war, due regard being paid to their grade and rank.

H XX. *After the conclusion of peace, the repatriation of prisoners of war shall be carried out as quickly as possible.*

To what extent peace is an amnesty.—Prisoners may be detained after the conclusion of peace to serve out imprisonment imposed for common law crimes and possibly even for disciplinary offenses imposed when the war is "plainly nearing its end" although the latter is doubtful,[13] and ordinarily not likely to be practiced. Offenses which may be properly said to arise out of the war are wiped out by the peace and especially offenses against the orders of the occupant, but not in themselves violations of the laws of war. But the fact that an offense has been committed with a patriotic motive does not necessarily remove it from the category of common law crimes.

Exchange.—The exchange of prisoners of war is a subject not dealt with in The Hague Regulations. Although not obligatory, it has become a usage of modern wars. Cartels, or agreements, are entered into for carrying it out, and commissaries are permitted to reside in the respective countries to facilitate exchanges and to see that the terms of the cartels are observed. The general rule is that of equality, "rank for rank, wounded for wounded." Where it is desirable to exchange prisoners of different rank, those

13 Westlake, II International Law, 67.

of superior rank are exchanged for a greater number of inferior rank. As it is claimed that exchanged prisoners should not fight again during the same war unless it is expressly stipulated to the contrary, it is best to make express stipulations in this regard in the cartel.[14]

[14] Hall, International Law, p. 430.

CHAPTER V.

THE SICK, WOUNDED AND SHIPWRECKED.*

H XXI. *The obligations of belligerents with regard to the sick and wounded are governed by the Geneva Convention.*

THE SICK AND WOUNDED.

G I. *Officers, soldiers and other persons officially attached to armies who are sick or wounded shall be respected and cared for, without distinction of nationality, by the belligerent in whose power they are.*

However, a belligerent, when compelled to leave his wounded in the hands of the enemy, shall leave with them, so far as military conditions permit, a portion of the personnel and matériel of his sanitary service to assist in caring for them.

The Geneva Convention.—Paragraph 1 entitles to the privileges of this convention all the combatant and noncombatant members of the military forces enumerated in H I-III, as well as all other members of the military forces not enumerated there, if such there be, who are entitled to the treatment of prisoners of war by the unwritten law,[1] and also those individuals not directly belonging to the military force mentioned in H XIII.

"These clauses are very broadly stated, and are intended to apply not only to the case where a successful belligerent occupies the battlefield, but also to a case in which both of the opposing armies occupy new positions at some distance from the field in which the losses were incurred."[2]

Unsuccessful belligerent to leave material behind.—Paragraph 2 is new and of vital importance. It would clearly be the height of injustice to require the occupant of the battlefield to strip itself in caring for the sick and wounded of its adversary without the obligation on the part of the

* It is a matter of regret that notice of the publication of the Manuel de la Croix-Rouge, by Fauchille and Politis, Paris, 1908, did not reach the writer in time to make it available for this work.

[1] See *supra*, p. 231.

[2] Report of the United States Delegation, p. 16.

latter "to make reasonable provision for the care and treatment of the wounded who are left behind."[3]

G II. *Subject to the care that must be taken of them under the preceding article, the sick and wounded of an army who fall into the power of the other belligerent become prisoners of war, and the general rules of international law in respect to prisoners become applicable to them.*

The belligerents remain free, however, to enter into such mutual stipulations in regard to sick and wounded prisoners as they may deem appropriate. They shall have special authority to agree:

1. *To mutually restore the sick and wounded left on the field of battle after an engagement.*
2. *To send back to their own country the sick and wounded who have recovered, or who are in a condition to be transported, and whom they have no desire to retain as prisoners.*
3. *To send the sick and wounded of the enemy to a neutral state, with its consent and on condition that they shall be interned until the close of hostilities.*

Sick and wounded falling into the power of the enemy are prisoners of war.—The old convention left to the unwritten law the status of the sick and wounded who fall into the hands of the enemy. This was undesirable. It left open to argument the contention that they were "neutral," and thus inspired hopes of release and of freedom from military supervision unwarrantable in prisoners of war and at the same time rendered it doubtful whether or not as prisoners of war they were entitled to the privileges of that class. But whereas the old convention had left the question an open one, Article V of the Additional Articles of 1868 gave positive support to the view of the exceptional position of the sick and wounded by requiring the sending back of all soldiers, whether incurably wounded or not, with the exception of officers whose detention might be important to the fate of arms, on condition of their not again bearing arms during the continuance of the war.

Special authority to enter into stipulations.—Article VI of the old convention had provided that commanders-in-chief should have the power to deliver immediately, to the outposts of the enemy, soldiers who had been wounded in an engagement, when circumstances permitted this to be

[3] *Ibid.*

done, and with the consent of both parties, that those who were recognized after their wounds had healed, as incapable of serving, should be sent back to their own country, and that others might also be sent back, on condition of not again bearing arms during the continuance of the war. Clause 1 of paragraph 2 of the present article, it will be seen, follows closely the first of the above provisions, but says nothing of agreeing in the cartels that the sick and wounded shall be delivered "immediately" or "to the outposts of the enemy." The second of the above provisions of the old convention that those recognizable as incapable of serving shall be sent back, was omitted, because of the difficulty of determining whether a wounded officer or soldier is incapable of serving or not. An officer incapable of active service may be of the greatest assistance in direction and advice. Accordingly clause 2 of the paragraph 2 of the present article was substituted. As a belligerent will generally wish to send back those who can be of no use to its adversary, clause 2 will serve much the same end as the old provision without giving chance of recriminations when an officer no longer capable of active service is retained as a prisoner because of superior ability along other lines. The third provision of the old convention that the sick and wounded in general may be sent back on parole is now covered for all prisoners by H X and was omitted altogether.

Clause 3 of paragraph 2 supplements Article XIV of the Convention respecting the Rights and Duties of Neutral Powers and Persons in case of War on Land and like it is favorable to the sick and wounded in that it allows the neutral power to relieve a belligerent of his sick and wounded prisoners without being guilty of unneutral conduct.

It is to be noticed that in the present article it is the "belligerents" to whom power is given to enter into these agreements while in Article VI of the old convention it was the "commander-in-chief" to whom it was entrusted. The change must be taken to suggest that it may be desirable that the power to enter into these cartels be not confined to commanders-in-chief. The United States Delegation use the broader term "commanding generals."*

* Report of United States Delegation, p. 17.

G III. *After every engagement the belligerent who remains in possession of the field of battle shall take measures to search for the wounded and to protect the wounded and dead from spoliation and ill treatment.*

He will see that a careful examination is made of the bodies of the dead prior to their interment or incineration.

Policing of the field of battle.—Neither of the provisions of this article is to be found in the old convention. Nothing is said there of policing the field of battle or of taking measures for the protection of the dead, and it was feared at the late conference that the first paragraph might be interpreted as a guarantee against all unlawful acts on the field of battle. It was clearly, however, not the purpose of this article to make the occupant an insurer against all crime on the battlefield, but merely to indicate his duty to take all steps in his power to minimize it as far as possible. This is imposing no new duty, but the stories familiar to all of the ghouls of battlefield show how inadequate the policing of this kind has been in the past.

Examination of the dead.—As to the examination of the dead it was felt by some that a doctor's certificate of the fact of death as provided for in France should be required, but it was felt best to leave the details of the examination to each belligerent. It was also urged that the soldiers should be identified in some way as by a number, button or medallion in accordance with actual practice in more armies than one, but this was rejected.[4] Its advantage as a means of identifying the dead is evident, but to require it by international agreement would be likely to result practically in adding as a requisite for belligerent character the very requirement which was so bitterly rejected at Brussels and The Hague.[5]

G IV. *As soon as possible each belligerent shall forward to the authorities of their country or army the military tokens, or badges of identification, found upon the bodies of the dead, together with a list of the sick and wounded taken in charge by him.*

Belligerents will keep each other mutually advised of internments and transfers, together with admissions to hospitals and

[4] Delpech, La Conference de Revision de la Convention de Geneve, 13 R. G. D. I. P., 673.

[5] See *supra*, pp. 104, 231.

deaths which occur among the sick and wounded in their hands. They will collect all valuable personal belongings, letters, etc., which are found upon the field of battle, or have been left by the wounded, or by those who have died in sanitary formations or other establishments, for transmission to interested persons through the authorities of their own country.

The provisions of this article, supplement H XIV and H XVI[6] although they go somewhat further in specifying that the property and information shall be forwarded "as soon as possible."

G V. *Military authority may make an appeal to the charitable zeal of the inhabitants to receive, and under his supervision, to care for the sick and wounded of the armies, by granting to persons responding to such appeals special protection and certain immunities.*

Appeal to the charity of the inhabitants.—This article corresponds to Article V of the old convention, and Additional Article IV. Article V of the old convention had provided that any inhabitant who should have entertained wounded troops in his house should be exempted from the quartering of troops as well as from part of the contributions of war which might be imposed. This granted more than military necessity would admit, and so in Additional Article IV of 1868 it was provided that in the quartering of troops and imposition of contributions account should be taken of the zeal of the inhabitants in an equitable manner only. It will be noticed that the present article is merely an authority to the commander to make appeals to the inhabitants by granting "special protection and certain immunities" without specifying what those immunities are.

The United States Delegation in their report say: "It was also recognized that the methods which now prevail in the treatment of the sick and wounded no longer permit their isolation in scattered dwellings and outbuildings, which are difficult of access and in which sanitary conditions cannot be controlled. For that reason the collection of patients in tents and suitable hospital buildings under the most advanced conditions in respect to sanitation and antiseptic treatment was strongly favored by the conference."[7]

[6] See *supra*, pp. 245, 246.
[7] P. 17.

SANITARY FORMATIONS AND ESTABLISHMENTS.

G VI. *Movable sanitary formations (i. e., those which are intended to accompany armies in the field) and the fixed establishments belonging to the sanitary service shall be protected and respected by belligerents.*

Civil hospitals.—By H LVI[8] all property devoted to charitable purposes, even though belonging to the state is treated as private property. This made it unnecessary to provide for such permanent hospitals as are intended for the needs of the civil population and operate in peace as well as in war. The protection accorded them is even greater than that accorded to the fixed establishments belonging to the sanitary service for the latter remain subject to the laws of war, as modified by G XV, as public property devoted to military purposes while civil hospitals are subject only to the right of requisition to which all private property is subject and which in their case should be made use of only under pressing necessity.

Respect due to movable sanitary formations.—This article settles the question so much debated at the Brussels Conference as to what are meant by movable sanitary formations as contrasted with the fixed establishments which are still subject in large part to the unwritten laws of war. The old convention used the term "ambulance" and in Additional Article III this term was interpreted to mean "field hospitals and other temporary establishments, which follow the troops on the field of battle to receive the sick and wounded." It was urged by the German delegate at Brussels that this enlarged the meaning of the term whereas it was desirable to restrict it or do away with the exemption of the material altogether. But he was apparently alone in his contention, and as will be seen by a comparison of the two articles the idea of Additional Article III was embodied in the present article.

Not entitled to protection merely "so long as sick or wounded may be therein."—A significant change from Article I of the old convention is that the qualification that the sanitary formations will be protected and respected "so long as any sick or wounded may be therein" has been dropped. This made it possible to subject to capture am-

[8] See *infra*, p. 330.

bulances which had completed their duty and were returning to their army merely because they happened to have no sick and wounded in them at the time. Practice, however, seems to have been more liberal than the strict language of the convention required[9] and the present article was drafted in accordance with the practice. M. Moynier is of the opinion that the practice of the Franco-German War went even further than this and exempted depots of sanitary supplies. Accordingly in his Project of Revision he proposed to assimilate depots of sanitary material to movable sanitary formations.[10] Insofar as such depots are movable sanitary formations following the army in its operations in order to keep the ambulances and field hospitals properly supplied it would seem that his suggestion is a valuable one,[11] but the Geneva Conference did not follow him in assimilating depots of sanitary supplies as such to movable sanitary formations, so that it would appear that when fixed they are subject to the laws of war, at any rate to the same extent as other fixed sanitary establishments.

G VII. *The protection due to sanitary formations and establishments ceases if they are used to commit acts injurious to the enemy.*

Protection conditioned on nonbelligerent action.—This article states more clearly than Article I of the old convention that the protection of the convention is conditioned on abstention from belligerent action. If the sanitary formation is used to quarter troops, as a storehouse for military supplies or employed as a base of operations or for any other military purpose, its privileged character ceases and if this is done treacherously it subjects the offenders to the military penal laws.

G VIII. *A sanitary formation or establishment shall not be deprived of the protection accorded by article VI by the fact that:*

1. *The personnel of a formation or establishment is armed and uses its arms in self-defense or in defense of its sick and wounded.*

2. *In the absence of armed hospital attendants, the forma-*

9 Moynier, La Convention de Genève Pendant la Guerre Franco Allemande, p. 26.

10 Article 17, Gillot, p. 362.

11 Gillot, p. 271; Delpech, 13 R. G. D. I. P., 702.

tion is guarded by an armed detachment or by sentinels regularly established.

3. *Arms or cartridges, taken from the wounded and not yet turned over to the proper authorities, are found in the formation or establishment.*

Sanitary formation may be defended.—This article is the necessary complement of the preceding. Sanitary formations must not be used to commit acts injurious to the enemy, but it would be intolerable if the personnel of a formation should be compelled to go unarmed or without the protection of a picket in order to be entitled to the protection of the convention. The unsettled condition of affairs following every battle makes it imperative that the personnel of sanitary formations should be so armed or guarded as to ensure the safety of themselves and of those entrusted to their care. The last paragraph was added as a result of the experience of the South African War.[12]

PERSONNEL.

G IX. *The personnel exclusively charged with the removal, transportation and treatment of the sick and wounded, as well as with the administration of sanitary formations and establishments, and the chaplains attached to armies shall be respected and protected under all circumstances. If they fall into the hands of the enemy they shall not be regarded as prisoners of war.*

Detail of personnel left to the Governments.—It was thought best by some to be more specific in the enumeration of the sanitary personnel, but the varying organization of the armies of different countries rendered this undesirable so that the detailed application of this article must be worked out by the governments for themselves. It would seem that the domestics of the sanitary personnel should receive the same treatment as themselves, but this is subject to some doubt.[13] In according the protection of this article to the personnel of the guard of sanitary formations, the Geneva Conference made what would seem to be a very notable advance over the Brussels Conference. It would

[12] Delpech, 13 R. G. D. I. P., 706.
[13] Gillot, p. 207.

seem the only adequate way of safeguarding the sick and wounded in the troublous times of retreat and pursuit.[14]

Distinction between sanitary personnel and those temporarily aiding the sick and wounded.—The provision that the sanitary personnel proper shall include only those who are "exclusively" charged with the care of the sick and wounded was added to exclude from the sanitary personnel the litter-bearers (*brancardiers*), etc., who are generally taken for the time being from the active military service. When they form a distinct and fixed branch of the sanitary service, as in Switzerland and Austria, they of course meet the requirements of the article.[15] It is to be observed, however, although these temporary litter-bearers do not form part of the sanitary personnel any more than the guard of sanitary formations does, that like the latter, they are not to be retained as prisoners, but are to be sent back under G XIV and XVII.

G X. *The personnel of volunteer aid societies, duly recognized and authorized by their respective governments, who are employed in the sanitary formations and establishments of armies, are assimilated to the personnel described in the preceding article, upon condition that the said personnel shall be subject to military laws and regulations.*

Each state shall make known to the other, either in time of peace or at the opening, or during the progress of hostilities—in any case, before actual employment—the names of the societies which it has authorized to render assistance, under its responsibility, in the official sanitary service of its armies.

Volunteer aid societies.—This article is a notable advance over the old convention, which did not recognize volunteer societies at all. The possible interference with military affairs which was feared from the recognition of these societies is avoided by the provisions that they must be duly authorized by their respective governments and be subject to military law and regulations, and by making the governments authorizing them responsible for their conduct in the same way that it is for its official personnel.

Function in case of floods, fires, earthquakes, etc.—"The details of organization of these societies together with the preparation of regulations governing their activity in the

14 Gillot, p. 207.
15 Delpech, 13 R. G. D. I. P., 684.

field and fixing their relations with the sanitary department of the army, were wisely left to the discretion of the individual powers. It is proper to observe, however, that the furnishing of relief by such associations to communities suffering in time of peace from pestilence or famine, or from the visitation of floods, fires or earthquakes, will always constitute a proper subject for their humanitarian endeavor; and the use or display of the insignia of the convention upon such occasions does not come within the prohibitory requirements which are embodied in articles XXVII and XXVIII of the new convention.

Field of activity generally confined to second line.—"It was the sense of the committee that the field of activity of these societies should be restricted to the second line of sanitary formations and to the fixed hospitals established at the bases of supply in which the sick and wounded are habitually collected for permanent treatment; but, as the control and supervision of their philanthropic activity is vested by the terms of the convention in the state which authorizes them, it was not deemed best to insert such a stipulation in the text of an international agreement."[16]

G XI. *A recognized society of a neutral state cannot lend the services of its sanitary personnel and formations to a belligerent except with the prior consent of its own government and the authority of such belligerent. The belligerent who has accepted such assistance is required to notify the enemy before making any use thereof.*

Neutral societies.—The remarks under Article X apply to this article also. It would seem beyond question that the belligerent state in authorizing the neutral ambulance to come to its assistance assumes responsibility for its conduct and that the neutral ambulance is subject to its laws and regulations in the same way as if it were organized by its own citizens.

G XII. *Persons described in articles IX, X and XI will continue in the exercise of their functions after they have fallen into the power of the enemy and under his direction.*

When their cooperation is no longer indispensable they will be sent back to their army or country, within such period and by such route as may accord with military necessity.

[16] Report of the United States Delegation, p. 16.

They will carry with them such effects, instruments, arms and horses as are their private property.

Duty of personnel to remain.—Paragraph 1 of this article is in accord with Additional Article I in making it a positive duty on the part of the personnel engaged in tending the sick and wounded to remain with them. Article III of the old convention was merely permissive.

Personnel to be sent back when no longer indispensable.—Paragraph 2 treats of one of the most delicate questions in the entire convention. On the one hand the retiring belligerent is apt to be tempted not to leave a portion of his sanitary personnel with the sick and wounded if he is going to be deprived of their services for a considerable time. On the other hand the belligerent into whose hands the personnel may fall is apt to be under the temptation to retain it in order to avoid all danger of spying, and even in order to weaken his enemy by keeping from him his sanitary staff. The old convention provided that the staff might withdraw and that they should be delivered to the outposts of the enemy. This was clearly incompatible with military necessity and was modified by Additional Article I. The present article seems to present the wisest possible solution of the vexed question. In the first place it makes it an absolute duty to send the staff back and allows their retention not during the entire period when they can be of service to their sick and wounded, but only so long as their services are indispensable. This will generally confine their labors, it would seem, to the first line of sanitary formations, and enable them to be sent back as soon as the emergency work following a battle is over.[17] In the second place the commanding general "is permitted to exercise a reasonable discretion in respect to the time when and the method and route by which the restoration shall be accomplished."[18] This, no doubt, leaves a great responsibility in the hands of the commanding general. It is in his power to render this most important provision of the convention so much blank paper on the plea of military necessity, but the high character of the modern military service renders this possibility little to be feared.

G XIII. *While they remain in his power, the enemy will se-*

[17] Gillot, p. 228.

[18] Report of the United States Delegation, p. 14.

cure to the personnel mentioned in article IX the same pay and allowances to which persons of the same grade in his own army are entitled.

To receive pay in force in captor's army.—Experience has proved that pay in the army of the captor is a better criterion for the pay of the prisoner than the pay to which he has been accustomed. The conventions are now uniform on this point.

MATERIEL.

G XIV. *Mobile sanitary formations that have fallen into the power of the enemy shall retain their matériel and means of transportation of whatever kind, including teams and the personnel charged with their management.*

Competent military authority, however, shall have the right to employ them in caring for the sick and wounded. The restoration of the matériel shall take place in accordance with the conditions prescribed for the sanitary personnel, and, as far as possible, at the same time.

Composition of movable sanitary formation.—"To each of the movable sanitary formations a surgical and administrative personnel is attached; tents, bedding, ambulances and other means of transportation are provided, together with a sufficient equipment of surgical instruments, and medical and hospital supplies. To the personnel and material constituting such a movable sanitary formation the quality of inviolability is attached by the terms of the convention, and in the event of its falling into the hands of the enemy, the entire establishment, when its sick and wounded have been evacuated or transferred to fixed or base hospitals, is required to be returned to the lines of its own army with the least possible delay."[19]

Just as the personnel is under the direction of the enemy into whose power it falls, so the material is subject to competent military authority to employ it in the care of the sick and wounded as long as it is indispensable.

G XV. *Buildings and matériel pertaining to fixed establishments shall remain subject to the laws of war, but cannot be diverted from their use so long as they are necessary for the sick and wounded. Commanders of troops engaged in opera-*

[19] Report of United States Delegation, p. 14.

tions, however, may use them, in case of important military necessity, if, before such use, the sick and wounded found in them have been provided for.

Fixed establishments.—That public fixed hospitals and the material therein shall not be turned from their charitable purpose so long as they are necessary for the sick and wounded, is an important modification of the long standing rule that they remain subject to the laws of war, that is, to the right of the occupant to the enjoyment of the usufruct of the buildings and to the capture of the material. It is to be noticed that the first provision of this article is not confined, as the second is, to the sick and wounded contained in the hospital itself. As long as the buildings or their material are necessary for any sick and wounded they cannot be diverted from their purpose, except insofar as this is modified by the second provision of the article. The respect and protection guaranteed by the article, does not mean, of course, that hospitals may not be the scene of military operations. If a hospital occupies a strategic point, consideration for its occupants may have to give way to military necessity, however much it is to be regretted.

G XVI. *The matériel of aid societies, admitted to the benefits of this convention in conformity to the conditions herein prescribed, is regarded as private property and, as such, will be respected under all circumstances, save that it is subject to the right of requisition by belligerents in conformity to the laws and usages of war.*

Matériel of aid societies.—The material of aid societies found in fixed hospitals, like that belonging to the state, it is to be presumed, cannot be diverted from its use so long as it is necessary for the sick and wounded. The only question at the Conference seems to have been as to whether it was entitled to better treatment than similar public property and the Conference resolved this doubt by assimilating it to private property, which, at least on land, is not subject to capture, but merely to requisition. It was desired to do away with the right of requisition, or at least, to restrict its application, when taken by the way of requisition, to the use of the sick and wounded; "but there were decided differences of view in this regard among the delegates, and the clause as adopted represents a compromise of widely divergent opinions."[20] It clearly should not be requisitioned, however, unless the necessity is pressing.

CONVOYS OF EVACUATION.

G XVII. *Convoys of evacuation shall be treated as movable sanitary formations with the following exceptions:*

1. *A belligerent intercepting a convoy may, if required by military necessity, vacate such convoy by charging himself with the care of the sick and wounded whom it contains.*

2. *In this case the obligation to restore the sanitary personnel, as provided for in article XII, shall be extended to include the entire military personnel employed, under proper authority, in the transportation and protection of the convoy.*

The obligation to return the sanitary matériel as provided for in article XIV shall apply to railway trains and vessels intended for interior navigation which have been especially equipped for evacuation purposes, together with the equipment of such vehicles, trains and vessels which belong to the sanitary service.

Military vehicles, with their teams, other than those belonging to the sanitary service, may be captured.

Civilians and means of transportation obtained by requisition, including railway matériel and vessels utilized for convoys, are subject to the general rules of international law.

Convoys.—The translation of the French *"dispositions"* in the first sentence of this article into "exceptions" is unfortunate. If it had been translated to read: "Convoys of evacuation shall be treated as movable sanitary formations subject to the following provisions," it would seem that the sense of the original would have been more accurately preserved as subparagraphs 1 and 2 amplify the first sentence rather than form exceptions to it.

Subparagraph 1 corresponds to the second provision of G XV. Not only may the course of the convoy be changed in order to retain the sick and wounded therein as prisoners of war or for some other reason, but the convoy may be broken up entirely in case of military necessity, provided those contained therein are cared for.

In subparagraph 2 the distinction between the military personnel temporarily employed in aiding the sick and

[20] Report of the United States Delegation, p. 15.

wounded and the sanitary personnel proper is more clearly brought out than in G XIV, or even than in paragraph 2 of G IX, which provides for the sending back of the guard of sanitary formations. This distinction is particularly important in connection with G XX, which confines the wearing of the arm badge to the sanitary personnel proper.

Military vehicles temporarily used fcr sick and wounded.—Paragraph 3 provides that a different rule shall be applied to military vehicles temporarily used for the sick and wounded from that applied by subparagraph 2 to the military personnel temporarily employed in aiding them. The personnel is returned while the material is not. This is because a provision for the return of such material would have been liable to grave abuse. It would have been too great a temptation to a retreating belligerent to save its transportation by using it for the sick and wounded.

DISTINCTIVE EMBLEM.

G XVIII. *In homage to Switzerland the heraldic sign of the red cross on a white ground, formed by the reversal of the federal colors, is continued as the emblem and distinctive sign of the sanitary service of armies.*

"Heraldic" sign of the Red Cross in honor of Switzerland.—The use of the term 'heraldic' in describing the insignia of the convention excludes the view that any religious association attaches to the distinctive emblem of the convention's philanthropic and humanitarium activity. Turkey was not represented in the conference, and it is worthy of note that the representatives of Japan, China. Persia and Siam expressed a willingness on the part of their Governments to accept the Red Cross as the official insignia of the convention."[21] Persia, however, took a different attitude at the second Peace Conference.[22]

G XIX. *This emblem appears on flags and brassards as well as upon all matériel appertaining to the sanitary service, with the permission of competent military authority.*

Sign for means of transportation.—It was urged by Colonel MacPherson, of the British delegation, that the means of transportation intended exclusively for sanitary service

[21] Report of the United States Delegation, p. 18.

[22] See *infra*, p. 270.

should be painted white on each side with a red cross as large as the dimensions of the vehicle would allow, in partial analogy to hospital ships, but it was felt best to leave questions of detail to the respective governments, and also that such a regulation might interfere with military operations by attracting the attention of the enemy.[23]

G XX. *The personnel protected by the provisions of paragraph 1, article IX, and articles X and XI will wear attached to the left arm a red cross on a white ground, which will be issued and stamped by competent military authority, and accompanied by a certificate of identity in the case of persons attached to the sanitary service of armies who do not have military uniform.*

Personnel entitled to arm badges.—As already pointed out the arm badges are for the sanitary personnel proper, not for those temporarily in the service of the sick and wounded, such as the pickets guarding sanitary formations, litter-bearers and the military personnel engaged generally in the transportation of the sick and wounded, so that it is clear that the arm badge is not always a prerequisite to the protection of the convention.[24]

Certificates of identity.—The provision that those not in military uniform shall be provided with a certificate of identity is an application of the general principle of H XIII that individuals accompanying an army, but not forming an integral part of it, such as war correspondents, sutlers and contractors, are entitled to be treated as prisoners of war on condition that they are provided with proper certificates of authority.

It is to be noticed that the arm badge is to be attached to, not merely slipped over the left arm. It is essential that the character of medical personnel shall not be put on and off at pleasure.

G XXI. *The distinctive flag of the convention can only be displayed, with the consent of the military authorities, over sanitary formations and establishments whose protection it secures. It shall be accompanied by the national flag of the belligerent to whose service the formation or establishment is attached.*

Sanitary formations which have fallen into the power of the

23 Delpech, 13 R. G. D. I. P., 715.
24 Gillot, p 276.

enemy, however, shall fly no other flag than that of the Red Cross so long as they continue in that situation.

Importance of national flag for movable formations.—Even if no national flag were required over fixed establishments, there would generally be little difficulty in determining its nationality, but the same thing cannot be said of movable formations. They are located near the ever varying line between the two armies, and it is important to know whether their occupants are enemies to be captured on the one hand, or on the other to be held responsible for acts violative of the laws of war.

Those in the power of the enemy to fly only the Red Cross flag.—It would perhaps have been desirable in the interest of the captured ambulance for it to have retained the double flag after falling into the power of the enemy, as the anomaly of a hostile flag in camp would have been a constant reminder that its retention was to be temporary,[25] but the fact that it would have been such an anomaly was fatal to it, and the rule that the Red Cross flag shall be flown, is in line with the general thought of the convention that prisoners who are sick and wounded are, nevertheless, prisoners, and that the ambulance including the personnel is subject to the direction of the enemy while in his power.

G XXII. *Neutral sanitary formations, which, under the conditions set forth in article XI, have been authorized to render their services shall fly, with the flag of the convention, the national flag of the belligerent to which they are attached. The provisions of the second paragraph of the preceding article are applicable to them.*

Flags for neutral formations.—This article does not expressly provide that the neutral sanitary formation shall not fly its own national flag, and from the fact that neutral hospital ships may, it may be contended that there is nothing to prevent the neutral sanitary formation from doing so also. But in the case of the neutral hospital ship there is express permission to fly its national flag, while in this article the intent seems to be that the use of the flag of the convention and of the belligerent to which the formation shall be attached shall be exclusive. The anomaly of

[25] Delpech, 13 R. G. D. I. P., 719.

the flag of a neutral power in an enemy camp is not to be encouraged.

G XXIII. *The emblem of the red cross on a white ground and the words RED CROSS or GENEVA CROSS can only be used, whether in time of peace or war, to protect or designate sanitary formations and establishments, the personnel and matériel protected by the convention.*

APPLICATION AND EXECUTION OF THE CONVENTION.

G XXIV. *The provisions of the present convention are obligatory on the contracting powers only, in case of war between two or more of them. The said provisions shall cease to be obligatory from the time when one of the belligerent powers shall not be signatory to the convention.*

G XXV. *The commanders-in-chief of the belligerent armies shall have to provide for the details of execution of the foregoing article, as well as for unforseen cases, in accordance with the instructions of their respective governments, and conformably to the general principles of this convention.*

G XXVI. *The signatory governments shall take the necessary steps to acquaint their troops, and particularly the protected personnel, with the provisions of this convention and to make them known to the people at large.*

REPRESSION OF ABUSES AND INFRACTIONS.

G XXVII. *The signatory powers whose legislation should not now be adequate engage to take or recommend to their legislatures such measures as may be necessary to prevent the use, by private persons or by societies other than those upon which this convention confers the right thereto, of the emblem or name of the Red Cross or Geneva Cross, particularly for commercial purposes by means of trade-marks.*

The prohibition of the use of the emblem or name as above shall be enforced at and from the time set by each legislation and not later than five years after the convention goes into effect. Upon the said going into effect, it shall be unlawful to use a trade-mark or commercial label contrary to such prohibition.

American act protecting the Red Cross.—By section 4 of the Act incorporating the American National Red Cross,

33 Statutes at Large, 600, it is provided among other things that it shall not be lawful "for any person or corporation, other than the Red Cross of America, not now lawfully entitled to use the sign of the Red Cross, hereafter to use such sign or any insignia colored in imitation thereof for the purpose of trade or as an advertisement to induce the sale of any article whatever" under penalty of not less than $100 and not more than $500, or not more than a year's imprisonment, or both, for each offense. Under this law the Commissioner of Patents has refused to register the Red Cross as a trademark.

G XXVIII. *In the event of their military penal laws being insufficient, the signatory governments also engage to take, or to recommend to their legislatures, the necessary measures to repress, in time of war, individual acts of pillage and ill treatment of the sick and wounded of the armies, as well as to punish, as usurpations of military insignia, the wrongful use of the flag and brassard of the Red Cross by military persons or private individuals not protected by the present convention.*

They will communicate to each other through the Swiss Federal Council the measures taken with a view to such repression, not later than five years from the ratification of the present convention.

NAVAL WAR.

G N I. *Military hospital ships, that is to say, ships constructed or assigned by States specially and solely with a view to assisting the wounded, sick and shipwrecked, the names of which have been communicated to the belligerent Powers at the commencement or during the course of hostilities, and in any case before they are employed, shall be respected, and cannot be captured while hostilities last.*

These ships, moreover, are not on the same footing as warships as regards their stay in a neutral port.

Military hospital ships. Communication of names.—The communication of the names of hospital ships to the other belligerent at the beginning of the war, or, if that is not possible, before the ship is placed in service, is especially desirable in order to prevent ships from claiming exemption from capture, which may have been turned into hospital ships at the last moment only with a view to secure such immunity. The names of the hospital ships may also well be sent to neutral as well as to belligerent powers, in view of the exemption secured to them by this article from the rules applicable to warships in neutral ports.

G N II. *Hospital ships, equipped wholly or in part at the expense of private individuals or officially recognized relief societies, shall be likewise respected and exempt from capture, if the belligerent power to whom they belong has given them an official commission and has notified their names to the hostile Power at the commencement of or during hostilities, and in any case before they are employed.*

These ships must be provided with a certificate from the competent authorities declaring that the vessels have been under their control while fitting out and on final departure.

Private hospital ships.—The privileges of this article were extended to ships equipped by individuals as well as to those equipped by officially recognized societies, in order to encourage the placing of craft, such as private yachts, in the medical service.

G N III. *Hospital ships, equipped wholly or in part at the expense of private individuals or officially recognized societies of neutral countries, shall be respected and exempt from capture, on condition that they are placed under the control of one of the belligerents, with the previous consent of their own Government and with the authorization of the belligerent himself, and that the latter has notified their name to his adversary at the commencement of or during hostilities, and in any case, before they are employed.*

Neutral hospital ships under the control of one of the belligerents.—G N III marks a distinct advance over Article III of the Naval Convention, drawn up at the first Peace Conference. That article made no provision for placing the neutral hospital ship under the control of one of the belligerents, and accordingly the use that would have been made of them was problematical, as their apparent independence would, unavoidably, have given rise to much friction, and they would constantly have given rise to suspicions of unneutral service.

G N IV. *The ships mentioned in Articles I, II and III shall afford relief and assistance to the wounded, sick and shipwrecked of the belligerents without distinction of nationality.*

The Governments undertake not to use these ships for any military purpose.

These vessels must in no wise hamper the movement of the combatants.

During and after an engagement they will act at their own risk and peril.

The belligerents shall have the right to control and search them; they can refuse to help them, order them off, make them take a certain course, and put a Commissioner on board; they can even detain them, if important circumstances require it.

As far as possible the belligerents shall enter in the log of hospital ships the orders which they give them.

Hospital ships subject to control analogous to that over movable sanitary formations.—These provisions were not so necessary in this convention as in the old, because of the change in the preceding article placing neutral hospital ships under the control of one of the belligerents, but they are wise as emphasizing the conduct the hospital ship is expected to follow, and in placing beyond cavil the fact that while the hospital ships of the enemy are not subject to capture, nevertheless they are subject to a control analogous to that of ambulances and convoys.

Not to be used for military purposes.—The provision that they shall not be used for any military purpose is exemplified in the instructions issued to the United States hospital ship *Relief* during the Spanish-American War: "No guns, ammunition or articles contraband of war, except coal or stores necessary for the movement of the vessel shall be placed on board nor shall the vessel be used as a transport for the carrying of dispatches, officers or men not sick or disabled, other than those belonging to the medical department."[26] As to arms for maintaining or for defending the sick, see G N VIII.

G N V. *Military hospital ships shall be distinguished by being painted white outside with a horizontal band of green about a metre and a half in breadth.*

The ships mentioned in Articles II and III shall be distinguished by being painted white outside with a horizontal band of red about a metre and a half in breadth.

The boats of the ships above mentioned, as also small craft which may be used for hospital work, shall be distinguished by similar painting.

All hospital ships shall make themselves known by hoisting,

26 Davis, International Law, p. 535.

with their national flag, the white flag with a red cross provided by the Geneva Convention, and further, if they belong to a neutral State, by flying at the mainmast the national flag of the belligerent under whose control they are placed.

Hospital ships which, in the terms of Article IV, are detained by the enemy, must haul down the national flag of the belligerent to whom they belong.

The ships and boats above mentioned which wish to ensure by night the freedom from interference to which they are entitled, must, subject to the assent of the belligerent they are accompanying, take the necessary measures to render their special painting sufficiently plain.

Emblem.—That the neutral hospital ship shall fly the flag of the belligerent to which it is attached accords with the suggestion of Captain Mahan at the first Peace Conference. It is unfortunate that the second Conference did not go still further and refuse to sanction the use of the national flag of the neutral hospital ship at all. Its presence in a hostile fleet is too likely to engender hostile feeling towards the neutral. Persia reserved the right and this was recognized by the Conference to use the Lion and Red Sun instead of and in place of the Red Cross.[27]

G N VI. *The distinguishing signs referred to in Article V can only be used, whether in time of peace or war, for protecting or indicating the ships therein mentioned.*

Exclusive use.—This article is supplemented by G N XXI, providing that suitable legislation shall be enacted, or at least proposed, punishing the unjustifiable use of these marks.

G N VII. *In the case of a fight on board a warship, the sick wards shall be respected and spared as far as possible.*

The said sick wards and the matériel belonging to them remain subject to the laws of war; they cannot, however, be used for any purpose other than that for which they were originally intended, so long as they are required for the sick and wounded.

The commander, however, into whose power they have fallen may apply them to other purposes, if the military situation requires it, after seeing that the sick and wounded on board are properly provided for.

Sick wards.—The treatment of hospital ships is similar to that of movable sanitary formations on land. The treat-

27 The Second International Peace Conference, p. 215.

ment of sick wards, it will be seen, is similar to that of fixed sanitary formations, this article being in the main a reproduction of G XV, the remarks on which article apply to this also.

G N VIII. *Hospital ships and sick wards of vessels are no longer entitled to protection if they are employed for the purpose of injuring the enemy.*

The fact of the staff of the said ships and sick wards being armed for maintaining order and for defending the sick and wounded, and the presence of wireless telegraphy apparatus on board, is not a sufficient reason for withdrawing protection.

Sick and wounded may be defended.—This article corresponds to G VII and VIII. The presence of wireless telegraphy apparatus *per se* is not objectionable, but it must not be employed for the purpose of injuring the enemy.

G N IX. *Belligerents may appeal to the charity of the commanders of neutral merchant ships, yachts, or boats to take on board and tend the sick and wounded.*

Vessels responding to this appeal, and also vessels which have of their own accord rescued sick, wounded or shipwrecked men, shall enjoy special protection and certain immunities. In no case can they be captured for having such persons on board, but, apart from special undertakings that have been made to them, they remain liable to capture for any violations of neutrality they may have committed.

Appeal to charity of merchant ships, etc.—G N IX corresponds to G V. Special immunity for violations of neutrality may be granted, but no general immunity results from the mere rescue of the sick, wounded or shipwrecked. This article is supplemented by G N XII.

G N X. *The religious, medical and hospital staff of any captured ship is inviolable, and its members cannot be made prisoners of war. On leaving the ship they take away with them the objects and surgical instruments which are their own private property.*

This staff shall continue to discharge its duties while necessary, and can afterwards leave, when the Commander-in-Chief considers it possible.

The belligerents must guarantee to the said staff, when it has fallen into their hands, the same allowances and pay which are given to the staff of corresponding rank in their own navy.

Personnel not prisoners of war.—This ground is covered for war on land by G IX, XII and XIII.

G N XI. *Sailors and soldiers on board, when sick or wounded, as well as other persons officially attached to fleets or armies, whatever their nationality, shall be respected and tended by the captors.*

Compare with this, G I.

G N XII. *Any warship belonging to a belligerent may demand that sick, wounded or shipwrecked men on board military hospital ships, hospital ships belong to relief societies or to private individuals, merchant ships, yachts or boats, whatever the nationality of these vessels, should be handed over.*

Right to demand sick and wounded rescued by merchantmen.—The situation met by this article was not provided for in the old convention. Captain Mahan had noticed this. In his report he said: "The omission was one likely to occur to an American old enough to remember the very concrete and pertinent instance of the British yacht *"Deerhound"* saving the men of the Alabama, including her captain, who were then held to be under the protection of the neutral flag."[28] His attention had been attracted to this omission too late to effect the final result, however, and this was possibly the cause of the ultimate exclusion of Article X of the old Convention, now G N XV. G N XII, which covers much the same ground as the second of the articles proposed by Captain Mahan at the first conference, was proposed by the German delegation and supported by the reporter, M. Renault, who argued that in absence of an international convention, not only could a belligerent do all that is allowed by this article, but that except for international convention, the neutral ships would be liable to confiscation on the ground of unneutral service. It is to be noticed that the article does not mention neutral warships.

Position taken at first by British Government.—The British Government at first refused to acquiesce in the position that the belligerent warship would have the right to demand the surrender of the rescued on board a neutral merchant ship, but later withdrew this reservation. The position was one somewhat similar to that taken by the British Government in the Trent Affair, although the cases are clearly dis-

28 Holls, p. 500.

tinguishable, as in the latter case, Mason and Slidell, though military agents also, were in a somewhat quasi diplomatic position. That the original British position was not correct is admitted by Westlake[29] and few will disagree with him. The analogy between the deck of a merchant ship on the high seas and the soil of its country has never been carried so far as to protect those in the military service of an enemy from capture when on board such a ship.

Liability of neutral to capture for rescue work independent of convention.—On the second point the liability of the neutral to capture, except for international convention, Westlake disagrees with the position taken by Renault. He says: "There would be no ground for presuming that he intended to restore them to the military service of their own side. If he had the correct intention to see to their safe internment, it is not clear what benefit the enemy would derive from internment being substituted for capture, and there would be no room for suggesting the existence of an improper arrangement between him and the enemy."[30] Such a presumption would be a reasonable one, but it is doubtful whether a Court inclined to the condemnation of prizes would sanction it. The old statements of the liability of neutral ships to confiscation for carrying those in the enemy's service are so sweeping that it seems likely that any but liberally inclined courts would place on the neutral a burden of overcoming the suspicion raised by the transportation of hostile troops.

G N XIII. *If sick, wounded or shipwrecked persons are taken on board a neutral warship, every possible precaution must be taken that they do not again take part in the operations of the war.*

Can such a demand be made of warships?—To Westlake it apparently seems clear that no such demand can be made of neutral warships rescuing the sick, wounded and shipwrecked, as is allowed in the preceding article of merchant ships. The analogy in this respect between the deck of the warship and the soil of its country seems to him complete. There is much to be said for this. Warships lying in territorial waters enjoy a very wide immunity from the control of the territorial authorities, and notwithstanding the fact

29 II International Law, 278.
30 *Ibid.*

that the sovereignty of the territorial authorities is of a higher degree than the authority exercised by the successful belligerent over the scene of the engagement on the high seas. Then, too, as has just been seen, it has been seriously questioned whether there is any such right even over neutral merchant ships.

To be avoided.—That the neutral warship is not to be treated precisely as neutral soil, however, is evident from a comparison of this article with G N XV. That article reads that the rescued "must * * * be guarded by the neutral State so as to prevent them again taking part in the war." This article on the other hand merely provides that "every possible precaution must be taken that they do not again take part in the operation of the war." The difference in phraseology may be due to the greater difficulty of guarding men on shipboard or to the possible necessity of landing the rescued in a belligerent port or of turning them over to a merchant ship, but it leaves open to the unwritten law the possibility of the successful belligerent demanding of the neutral warship those of the enemy whom it has rescued and has on board. No greater precaution could be taken that they should not again take part in the operations of the war than by handing them over. Such a demand would be one to be avoided, as it would be likely to result in serious controversy, but as a matter of strict right it is a grave question whether it might not be made. The successful belligerent is entitled to reap the reward of his victory, and to that end has very wide authority over the scene of the engagement, and there seems no decisive reason why, if it chooses to run the chance of the exercise of that authority by entering on the theatre of operations, it should not be just as liable to turn over those whom it has prevented the victor capturing as it would be to turn over a fugitive from the process of the courts in whose territory it was lying.

G N XIV. *The shipwrecked, wounded or sick of one of the belligerents who fall into the power of the other belligerent are prisoners of war. The captor must decide, according to circumstances, whether to keep them, send them to a port of his own country, to a neutral port, or even to an enemy port. In this last case, prisoners thus repatriated cannot serve again while the war lasts.*

The shipwrecked, etc., falling into the power of the enemy are prisoners of war.—The last paragraph of this article might well have been omitted. It was thought that it would be applied in the main to prisoners incapable of further service, whom the captor no longer cared to retain. But as to them there would be no need of providing that they should not serve again, while the war lasts. As to others it is objectionable on the ground that it amounts to compulsory parole. There is danger that a belligerent, notwithstanding the fact that he may be compelled to land the prisoners at an enemy's port, may, nevertheless, be able to prevent their serving again by means of this provision. Probably the enemy could refuse to receive them absolutely, or make a condition of receiving them that the parole be waived, but even such a conditional refusal might seem harsh, and it is unfortunate that the provision was not omitted as was suggested by M. Rolin at the First Peace Conference.

G N XV. *The shipwrecked, sick or wounded, who are landed at a neutral port with the consent of the local authorities, must, unless an arrangement is made to the contrary between the neutral State and the belligerent States, be guarded by the neutral State so as to prevent them again taking part in the operations of the war.*

The expenses of tending them in hospital and interning them shall be borne by the State to which the shipwrecked, sick or wounded persons belong.

Shipwrecked, etc., landed at a neutral port.—This article was excluded from the old convention as finally ratified, largely because it enabled the neutral state to become a prison-keeper for the belligerents, thus relieving one or both belligerents of much of the care of the sick and wounded, and allowing a more complete attention to purely military affairs. It is easy to see how this might turn to the decided advantage of a belligerent engaged at some distance from his home territory. By landing his sick and wounded at a nearby neutral port, he might overcome much of the advantage which his enemy had from fighting nearer home. Again the chance of capturing the sick, wounded or shipwrecked is much less where they may be left with a convenient neutral. Added to this it was feared that the sick, wounded and shipwrecked on board neutral vessels might be held immune from capture, thus greatly augmenting the number that would be landed at neutral ports and lessening the possible number of prisoners. This last objection has been obviated by G N XII, and possibly on this account those powers which had objected to the old Article X acquiesced in this article at the Second Conference. Possibly, however, it was because they felt that the benefit to the sick, wounded and shipwrecked would outweigh the possible disadvantage from a military point of view.

G N XVI. *After every engagement, the two belligerents, so far as military interests permit, shall take steps to look for the shipwrecked, sick and wounded, and to protect them as well as the dead, against pillage and ill treatment.*

They shall see that the burial, whether by land or sea, or cremation of the dead shall be preceded by a careful examination of the corpse.

Compare G III.

G N XVII. *Each belligerent shall send, as early as possible, to the authorities of their country, navy or army the military marks or documents of identity found on the dead and the description of the sick and wounded picked up by him.*

The belligerents shall keep each other informed as to internments and transfers as well as to the admissions into hospital and deaths which have occurred among the sick and wounded in their hands. They shall collect all the objects of personal use, valuables, letters, etc., which are found in the captured ships, or which have been left by the sick or wounded who died in hospital, in order to have them forwarded to the persons concerned by the authorities of their own country.

Compare G IV.

G N XVIII. *The provisions of the present Convention do not apply except between Contracting Powers, and then only if all the belligerents are parties to the Convention.*

G N XIX. *The Commanders-in-Chief of the belligerent fleets must see that the above Articles are properly carried out; they will have also to see to cases not covered thereby, in accordance with the instructions of their respective Governments and in conformity with the general principles of the present Convention.*

Compare G XXV.

G N XX. *The Signatory Powers shall take the necessary measures for bringing the provisions of the present Convention to the knowledge of their naval forces, and especially of the members entitled thereunder to immunity, and for making them known to the public.*

Compare G XXVI.

G N XXI. *The Signatory Powers likewise undertake to enact or to propose to their Legislatures, if their criminal laws are inadequate, the measures necessary for checking in time of war individual acts of pillage and ill-treatment in respect to the sick and wounded in the fleet, as well as for punishing, as an unjustifiable adoption of naval or military marks, the unauthorized use of the distinctive marks mentioned in Article V by vessels not protected by the present Convention.*

They will communicate to each other, through the Netherland Government, the enactments for preventing such acts at the latest within five years of the ratification of the present Convention.

Compare G XXI.

G N XXII. *In the case of operations of war between the land and sea forces of belligerents, the provisions of the present Convention do not apply except between the forces actually on board ship.*

Parties that have already made landings are subject to the Geneva Convention.

CHAPTER VI.

MEANS OF OFFENSE AND DEFENSE.

H XXII. *The right of belligerents to adopt means of injuring the enemy is not unlimited.*

Special Conventions and Declarations restricting the means of injuring the enemy.—The most notable special Conventions limiting the means of injuring the enemy are the Declaration of St. Petersburg, the two Declarations drawn up at the First Peace Conference against the use of projectiles diffusing asphyxiating gases, and expanding bullets, the Declaration of the Second Peace Conference against discharging projectiles from balloons and the Convention of the same Conference relative to automatic submarine contact mines. They will be taken up in order.

The St. Petersburg Declaration.—The St. Petersburg Declaration reads as follows:

Considering that the progress of civilization should have the effect of alleviating as much as possible the calamities of war;

That the only legitimate objects which states should endeavor to accomplish during war is to weaken the military force of the enemy;

That for this purpose it is sufficient to disable the greatest possible number of men;

That this object would be exceeded by the employment of arms which uselessly aggravate the sufferings of disabled men, or render their death inevitable;

That the employment of such arms would, therefore, be contrary to the laws of humanity;

The contracting parties engage mutually to renounce, in case of war among themselves, the employment, by their military or naval forces, of any projectile of less weight than four hundred grammes,[1] *which is explosive, or is charged with fulminating or inflammable substances.*

The limitation of the weight of the projectiles was to

[1] Fourteen ounces avoirdupois.

confine the prohibition to bullets. It is obvious that the use of shells is a legitimate means of warfare.

Misinterpretation of the preamble of the St. Petersburg Declaration.—The second clause of the preamble is to be interpreted in the light of the body of the Declaration and of the other clauses of the preamble to mean that the only legitimate object which states should endeavor to accomplish during war is *to weaken* the military forces of the enemy, that is, not to cause them useless injury. There was no occasion for laying down any such proposition that the weakening of the *military forces* should be the only way of bringing pressure to bear on the hostile state, thus condemning commercial blockades and the capture of private property at sea. This has often been lost sight of in citing this clause. The United States is not a party to this Declaration.

Expanding bullets—Projectiles for diffusing asphyxiating gases.—The two declarations of the First Hague Conference still in force are as follows:

The contracting Powers agree to forbid the employment of projectiles which have for their sole purpose the diffusion of asphyxiating or deleterious gases.

The contracting Powers agree to forbid the employment of bullets which expand or flatten easily in the human body, such as bullets the jackets of which do not entirely cover the core or are provided with incisions.

The United States has never become a party to these Declarations.[2] If the question ever becomes a practical one, however, both of these means of injuring the enemy are forbidden to the United States in case they are "calculated to cause unnecessary suffering," by H XXIII (e). The question is not likely to become a practical one, as there were no such projectiles as those described in the first Declaration in existence at the time the Declaration was drawn up and no such bullets as those described in the second Declaration are now manufactured.[3]

Discharge of projectiles from balloons.—The Declaration drawn up at the Second Peace Conference is as follows:

The Contracting Powers agree to prohibit, for a period extending to the close of the Third Peace Conference, the discharge

[2] See *supra*, pp. 132, 134.

[3] 2 Am. Jour. of Inter. Law, 75.

of projectiles and explosives from balloons or by other new methods of a similar nature.

This is the renewal of the Declaration drawn up at the First Peace Conference, which had expired by reason of its five-year limitation. The change in the limitation prevents another lapse before the next Conference. It was thought that some limitation was necessary, as with improved methods of aerial navigation this may become an effective and not unnecessarily cruel means of warfare.

Automatic submarine contact mines.—The Convention relative to the laying of automatic submarine contact mines is as follows:

Inspired by the principle of the freedom of sea routes, the common highways of all nations;

Seeing that, although the existing position of affairs makes it impossible to forbid the employment of automatic submarine contact mines, it is nevertheless desirable to restrict and regulate their employment in order to mitigate the severity of war and to ensure, as far as possible, to peaceful navigation the security to which it is entitled, despite the existence of war;

Until such time as it is found possible to formulate rules on the subject which shall ensure to the interests involved all the guarantees desirable; [the Plenipotentiaries of the Contracting Powers] have agreed upon the following provisions:

ART. I. *It is forbidden:*

1. *To lay unanchored automatic contact mines, except when they are so constructed as to become harmless one hour at most after the person who laid them ceases to control them;*

2. *To lay anchored automatic contact mines which do not become harmless as soon as they have broken loose from their moorings;*

3. *To use torpedoes which do not become harmless when they have missed their mark.*

ART. II. *It is forbidden to lay automatic contact mines off the coast and ports of the enemy, with the sole object of intercepting commercial shipping.*

ART. III. *When anchored automatic contact mines are employed, every possible precaution must be taken for the security of peaceful shipping.*

The belligerents undertake to do their utmost to render these mines harmless within a limited time, and, should they cease to be under surveillance, to notify the danger zones as soon as military exigencies permit, by a notice addressed to ship owners, which must also be communicated to the Governments through the diplomatic channel.

ART. IV. *Neutral Powers which lay automatic contact mines off their coasts must observe the same rules and take the same precautions as are imposed on belligerents.*

The neutral Power must inform ship owners, by a notice issued in advance, where automatic contact mines have been laid. This notice must be communicated at once to the Governments through the diplomatic channel.

ART. V. *At the close of the war, the Contracting Powers undertake to do their utmost to remove the mines which they had laid, each Power removing its own mines.*

As regards anchored automatic contact mines laid by one of the belligerents off the coast of the other, their position must be notified to the other party by the Power which laid them, and each Power must proceed with the least possible delay to remove the mines in its own waters.

ART. VI. *The Contracting Powers which do not at present own perfected mines of the pattern contemplated in the present Convention, and which, consequently, could not at present carry out the rules laid down in Articles I and III, undertake to convert the matériel of their mines as soon as possible, so as to bring it into conformity with the foregoing requirements.*

Convention incomplete.—This Convention is to remain in force for seven years, but unless denounced it is to continue in force after the expiration of that period. In the event of the question not having been already reopened and settled by the Third Peace Conference the Contracting Powers also undertake to reopen the question six months before the expiration of the seven year period. It was evidently thought at the time this period was fixed that the Second Conference would meet within seven years instead of eight, as finally decided on. It is to be noticed that the placing of anchored mines on the high seas is not prohibited. This was bitterly objected to on the part of Great Britain which desired to restrict the placing of these mines at least to a distance of ten miles from the position of the guns on land and to make more effective the prohibition against commercial blockades by mines. She insisted that her position in attempting to confine the use of these mines to the territorial waters of the belligerents and for strategic purposes was supported by international law independent of convention,[4] and in this could claim the support of the provisional action of the Institute of International Law in 1906.[5] That the Convention did not go further was a concession to belligerent rights.

H XXIII. *In addition to the prohibitions provided by special Conventions, it is especially forbidden:*

(a) *To employ poison or poisoned weapons;*

(b) *To kill or wound treacherously individuals belonging to the hostile nation or army;*

Article 148 of the American Instruction reads as follows:

American Article against assassination.—"Assassination. The law of war does not allow proclaiming either an individual belonging to the hostile army or a citizen, or a subject of the hostile government, an outlaw, who may be slain without trial by any captor, any more than the modern law of peace allows such international outlawry; on the contrary, it abhors such outrage. The sternest retaliation should follow the murder committed in consequence of such proclamation, made by whatever authority. Civilized nations look with horror upon offers of rewards for the assassination of enemies, as relapses into barbarism."

(c) *To wound or kill an enemy who, having laid down his arms, or having no longer means of defense, has surrendered at discretion;*

Quarter even to those who have violated the laws of war.—The term "surrender at discretion" was objected to on the ground that it implied a right of life and death over the prisoner, and it was urged that the qualifying phrase "at discretion" should be dropped; but, on the other hand, it was urged that those who have been guilty of violations of the laws of war are still liable to suffer death at the hands of their captors, so that, instead of the qualifying phrase making the provision harsh, it rendered it more

4 Westlake, II International Law, 322–326.

5 See 21 Annuarie, 88, *et seq.*, 330, *et seq.*

humane by extending even to these the privilege of quarter.[6]

When not practicable.—Westlake says: "The admitted case in which it is not practicable is that which occurs during the continuance of fighting, when the achievement of victory would be hindered and even endangered by stopping to give quarter instead of cutting down the enemy and rushing on."[7]

(d) *To declare that no quarter will be given;*

Prohibition of declaration of "no quarter."—The need of this provision against the declaration of no quarter is even greater than that against the refusal of quarter, as instances of threats to give no quarter have been more numerous than the actual refusal to give it.

(e) *To employ arms, projectiles or material calculated to cause unnecessary suffering;*

Prohibition of unnecessarily cruel arms and projectiles.—This principle is applied in the declarations against explosive and expanding bullets, so that, if those bullets are unnecessarily cruel, the signatories of this article are just as much bound not to use them as are the powers which have adhered to the express declarations against them. The declaration which Capt. Crozier wished to substitute for the declaration against expanding bullets was along these lines,[8] although in forbidding the use of bullets exceeding the limit necessary to place a man immediately *hors de combat* it was more specific and so of independent value.

(f) *To make improper use of a flag of truce, of the national flag or the military insignia and uniform of the enemy, as well as the distinctive signs of the Geneva Convention.*

Uniform of the enemy may be used for approach but not for fighting.—The use of the national flag and of the uniform of the enemy is allowed for purposes of approach, but before fighting is begun, the true character of the ship or of the soldiers must be disclosed. This right of approach is well settled, although made little if any use of in recent

[6] Protocols 1 of the Committee and 4 of the full Conference, Parl. Papers, 1875, Vol. 82, Misc. No. 1.

[7] II International Law, 75.

[8] See *supra*, p. 132.

[9] See also, H, XXIV.

times, especially on land. Complaints of fighting in the uniform of the enemy, however, have been numerous.

The American Instructions, Article 64, provide:

"If American troops capture a train containing uniforms of the enemy and the commander considers it advisable to distribute them for use among his men, some striking mark or sign must be adopted to distinguish the American soldier from the enemy."

(g) *To destroy or seize the enemy's property, unless such destruction or seizure be imperatively demanded by the necessities of war;*

Use of devastation.—This provision was considered superfluous by some, as the treatment of enemy property is treated in much greater detail in the subsequent articles, but the later articles refer especially to the treatment of property by an occupying army, while the provisions of the present article especially refer to its treatment in connection with active military operations. In other words, it refers particularly to devastation as a means of injuring the enemy. Devastation was formerly considered a legitimate means of bringing an enemy to terms or of diverting him from his intended plan of operations, but it is no longer considered proper as an independent military operation, and is now allowed only as incidental to other military measures, as where the destruction of houses is necessary to clear the field of battle or where whole districts are swept of supplies in order to prevent their use by the enemy.

Principles of H XXIII applicable to maritime warfare also.—The principles of the above prohibitions apply to naval forces equally with land forces, although their application to naval forces has not yet been made the subject of international agreement.

(h) *To declare abolished, suspended or inadmissible in a Court of law the rights and actions of the nationals of the hostile party;*

Interpretation.—This clause was introduced at the Second Peace Conference by the German delegation and has received little or no comment. The prohibition against the extinguishment of private choses in action is merely declaratory of what has probably been the law for many years, but the prohibition against the suspension of choses in action apparently works a decided change, at least in Anglo-

American law. A literal interpretation of the clause would not work a change, as it is directed at declarations of the political authorities, whereas in the United States and England it has not been customary to make such declarations, but the suspension of the choses of action of the enemy has been considered by the courts to arise from the war itself. The intention of the provision is clear, however, that these choses in action shall not be suspended by the political authorities even as a war measure, much less that they shall be suspended as a matter of course. It will, however, be a question for the courts to decide. In England the plea of alien enemy has been enforced with a good deal of strictness. In the United States, on the other hand, it has not been favorably received, so that the courts are liable to interpret this clause with the liberality which is its due.

A belligerent is likewise forbidden to compel the nationals of the hostile party to take part in the operations of war directed against their own country, even if they were in the belligerent's service before the commencement of the war.

This corresponds to Article XLIV of the old convention. The universal character of the prohibition is probably brought out better here than under the head of Occupation. There are similar prohibitions in H VI and H LII. In H LII the Government translation reads "military operations" for the same expression that is here translated "operations of war." The latter is the better expression, but the difference seems not to have the significance given it by Westlake.[10] It would seem that the latter merely expresses more adequately what was intended to be expressed by the former.

Services not to be required of nationals of the enemy.—This provision forbids forcing the nationals of one belligerent into the hostile army or compelling them to labor on works of offense or defense in the theatre of war. Beyond this it is difficult to say how far it goes. Count Lanza declared at Brussels that "no Government would engage not to press guides into the service, not to employ the laborers of the country on lines of communication, not to compel carriers to transport the means of subsistence, and to per-

[10] II International Law, 269.

form other services.''[11] Compulsion to serve as guides has now been regulated by H XLIV, but otherwise his statement seems to be still accurate. The last clause specifying that this prohibition holds ''even if they were in the belligerent's service before the commencement of the war'' was added at the Second Conference.

Inciting to treason or desertion unlawful.—Westlake adds that ''it is considered unlawful to incite the enemy's troops to treason or desertion, a rule which was probably introduced for the mutual convenience of commanders and by a kind of chivalry between them and which should carry with it the unlawfulness of enrolling deserters as recruits * * * but it is not considered unlawful to stir up insurrection in the enemy's country.''[12]

H XXIV. *Ruses of war and the employment of measures necessary for obtaining information about the enemy and the country are considered permissible.*

Ruses of war.—This article must be read subject to the numerous exceptions contained in the other articles of the Regulations. While strategems are a perfectly lawful means of warfare, they do not warrant breaches of faith, treachery or the use of the Red Cross or of flags of truce for other than their acknowledged purposes.

H XXV. *The attack or bombardment, by whatever means, of towns, villages, dwellings or buildings, which are undefended is prohibited.*

Undefended towns not to be bombarded.—This is an application of the principle of H XXIII (g) that property of the enemy shall not be seized or destroyed except where this may be imperatively demanded by the necessities of war. The necessities of war cannot demand the bombardment of an undefended town as a military measure. This article, however, does not deny the use of bombardment as a penal measure where a legitimate demand for contributions or requisitions has been refused or where the population has been guilty of violating the laws of war, or as a measure of retorsion; but its use even in these cases would be extreme and only justified by imperative necessity. The phrase ''by whatever means'' was added by the second conference so as to include bombardments by airships or

11 Protocol 4 of the Committee.

12 II International Law, 76.

other means which the ingenuity of man may devise. At the present time, however, the bombardment of even defended towns by airships is prohibited by the special Declaration.[13]

It is to be noticed that this article speaks of undefended, not of unfortified, towns. Only where there are no fortifications, no troops, and no open resistance by the population, does this article apply.

Bombardment of the resident portions of towns.—It has been questioned whether towns separated somewhat from the fortifications which defend them are liable to bombardment. This is a part of the larger question as to whether the portions of towns not used for military purposes are exempt from bombardment. It must be admitted, however, that this is one of the rigors of war which belligerents have held to be so useful as not to be given up. Of its hardship there can be no question, though it cannot compare with that of a siege.

H XXVI. *The officer in command of an attacking force must, before commencing a bombardment, except in cases of assault, do all in his power to warn the authorities.*

Necessity of giving warning of bombardment except in cases of assault.—Notice is not required in case of assault, because it would often defeat the object of the assault by putting the enemy on guard against it. The exception is more specific than that in the naval convention, which only requires notice "if the military situation permits."[14] If the more general exception is desirable for naval warfare it is hard to see why it should not be equally desirable in land warfare. The original Brussels article was broader. It made an exception of cases of "surprise." Notice in case of bombardment is ordinarily required, in order that precautions may be taken for the safety of works of art, etc., mentioned in the following article, as well as that those who wish to withdraw from the town may do so. Such withdrawal is often allowed at the commencement of a bombardment or siege even when it is refused later. At neither time may the withdrawal be regarded as a strict right.

[13] See *supra*, p. 279; For bombardments by naval forces see *infra*, pp. 288-291.

[14] See *infra*, p. 291.

H XXVII. *In sieges and bombardments all necessary steps must be taken to spare, as far as possible, buildings dedicated to religion, art, science or charitable purposes, historic monuments, hospitals and places where the sick and wounded are collected, provided they are not being used at the time for military purposes.*

It is the duty of the besieged to indicate the presence of such buildings or places by distinctive and visible signs, which shall be notified to the enemy beforehand.

"Historic monuments" were included within the protection of this article by the Second Conference at the suggestion of Greece.

Sign for protection of churches, etc.—As the Red Cross is designed to protect hospitals and ambulances, etc., it should be used only in connection with them. Some other sign is necessary in the case of churches, museums, schools, etc. It would have seemed desirable to have brought this article into conformity with the naval Convention by requiring the signs which are there specified in similar cases[15] instead of leaving the matter to the local authorities, but as a matter of fact it is likely that the practice will conform.

Bombardments by naval forces.—Bombardments by naval forces were made the subject of the following convention by the Second Conference:

Animated by the desire to realize the wish expressed by the First Peace Conference respecting the bombardment by naval forces of undefended ports, towns and villages;

Whereas, it is expedient that bombardments by naval forces should be subject to rules of general application, which would safeguard the rights of the inhabitants and assure the preservation of the more important buildings, by applying as far as possible to this operation of war the principles of the Regulation of 1899 respecting the Laws and Customs of Land War;

Actuated, accordingly, by the desire to serve the interests of humanity and to diminish the severity and distress of war;

[the Plenipotentiaries of the Contracting Powers] have agreed upon the following provisions:

15 See *infra*, p. 290.

ART. I. *The bombardment by naval forces of undefended ports, towns, villages, dwellings or buildings is forbidden.*

A place cannot be bombarded solely because automatic submarine contact mines are anchored off the harbour.

Reservations.—Compare H XXV. Several of the Powers made reservations as to the last paragraph. It hardly seems logical that the particular kind of defense should make a difference as to whether a town may be bombarded, but it is conceived that if a fleet wished to occupy a town and was prevented from doing so by automatic contact mines that it would be at liberty to effect its purpose by means of bombardment. The evident idea of the drafters was that a fleet might wish to bombard a town protected by fortifications merely for the purpose of destroying the fortifications, but that automatic contact mines could not be destroyed in that way, so that it would be fruitless to bombard a town *solely* because they happened to be in front of it.

ART. II. *Military works, military or naval establishments, depôts of arms or war matériel, workshops or plant which could be utilized for the needs of the hostile fleet or army, and the ships of war in the harbour, are not, however, included in this prohibition. The commander of a naval force may destroy them with artillery, after a summons followed by a reasonable time of waiting, if all other means are impossible, and when the local authorities have not themselves destroyed them within the time fixed.*

He incurs no responsibility for any unavoidable damage which may be caused by a bombardment under such circumstances.

If for military reasons immediate action is necessary, and no delay can be allowed the enemy, it is understood that the prohibition to bombard the undefended town holds good, as in the case given in paragraph 1, *and that the commander shall take all due measures in order that the town may suffer as little harm as possible.*

Art. II peculiar to naval convention.—There is no similar provision in the convention for war on land. It was probably felt that the army would have no such difficulty as the navy in destroying war material in an undefended town. The provision that the other parts of the town shall be damaged as little as possible is notable.

ART. III. *After due notice has been given, the bombardment of undefended ports, towns, villages, dwellings, or buildings may be commenced, if the local authorities, after a formal summons has been made to them, decline to comply with requisitions for provisions or supplies necessary for the immediate use of the naval force before the place in question.*

These requisitions shall be in proportion to the resources of the place. They shall only be demanded in the name of the commander of the said naval force, and they shall, as far as possible, be paid for in cash; if not, they shall be evidenced by receipts.

Requisitions. Military execution.—As is the case with the land forces, so with the naval forces it is proper to resort to bombardment as a penalty for not furnishing requisitions. This article should be carefully compared with H LII. The form of the second paragraph is in accord with Article LII of the old convention and does not prescribe as H LII does, that the "payment of the amount due shall be made as soon as possible."

ART. IV. *Undefended ports, towns, villages, dwellings or buildings may not be bombarded on account of failure to pay money contributions.*

Money contributions by naval forces forbidden.—Here naval warfare differs from that on land. In certain cases money contributions may be exacted by military forces,[16] and in those cases they may be enforced by the bombardment of undefended towns, but the reasons for allowing contributions by land forces do not apply to naval forces. The latter would be too much of the nature of ransoms from pillage.

ART. V. *In bombardments by naval forces all the necessary measures must be taken by the commander to spare as far as possible sacred edifices, buildings used for artistic, scientific or charitable purposes, historic monuments, hospitals and places where the sick or wounded are collected, on the understanding that they are not used at the same time for military purposes.*

It is the duty of the inhabitants to indicate such monuments, edifices or places by visible signs, which shall consist of large stiff rectangular panels divided diagonally into two coloured triangular portions, the upper portion black, the lower portion white.

16 See *infra*, p. 314.

Improvement over land convention.—Compare H XXVII. The specification of the kind of sign to be used is a great improvement.

ART. VI. *If the military situation permits, the commander of the attacking naval force, before commencing the bombardment must do his utmost to warn the authorities.*

Compare H XXVI. As already pointed out, the proviso, "if the military situation permits," might well be substituted in H XXVI for "except in cases of assault."

ART. VII. *A town or place, even when taken by storm, may not be pillaged.*

Compare H XXVIII.

H XXVIII. *The pillage of a town or place, even when taken by assault, is prohibited.*

Towns taken by assault not to be pillaged.—The pillage of a town taken by assault and the refusal of quarter to its defenders, especially where there had been an obstinate resistance, had seemed to be so unavoidable as to have been recognized in times past as legitimate, even when it was regretted. So well established was the old rule that it was deemed necessary to have this special article in addition to the later article prohibiting pillage in general.

H XXIX. *A person can only be considered a spy when, acting clandestinely or on false pretenses, he obtains or endeavors to obtain information in the zone of operations of a belligerent, with the intention of communicating it to the hostile party.*

Thus, soldiers not wearing a disguise who have penetrated into the zone of operations of the hostile army, for the purpose of obtaining information, are not considered spies. Similarly, the following are not considered spies: Soldiers and civilians, carrying out their mission openly, intrusted with the delivery of despatches intended either for their own army or for the enemy's army. To this class belong likewise persons sent in balloons for the purpose of carrying despatches and, generally, of maintaining communications between the different parts of an army or a territory.

Seeking information within the lines of the enemy clandestinely the essence of spying.—By a soldier not in disguise is meant a soldier in uniform. It was urged at Brussels that, so long as a soldier is capable of identification as such, he should be entitled to the benefit of the second paragraph since it is to be presumed that he is acting with honorable motives, and therefore should not be subject to the same treatment as the professional spy. But it was the opinion of the Conference that the act should be looked to and not the motive.[17] The Conference appeared to regard spies generally as scamps, who deserve the treatment they get.

Balloonists not spies.—As acting secretly is, by the first paragraph, made one of the essentials of spying, balloonists cannot be considered as spies, even if they do not come within the terms of the example given in the second paragraph and are not carrying despatches, but are engaged in observing the positions and movements of the enemy.

H XXX. *A spy taken in the act shall not be punished without previous trial.*

A spy has a right to trial.—This principle should be applied in every case where penalties are inflicted under the laws of war.

H XXXI. *A spy who, after rejoining the army to which he belongs, is subsequently captured by the enemy, is treated as a prisoner of war, and incurs no responsibility for his previous acts of espionage.*

Spying wiped out by successful termination.—Spying is one of those acts which are not contrary to the laws of war, but which may be of great injury to a belligerent, and which he may therefore punish if he can catch the offender in the act. The principle is, "Catch me if you can; but if you can't, you have no right to punish me."

[17] Protocol 4 of the Full Conference.

CHAPTER VII.

NONHOSTILE INTERCOURSE OF BELLIGERENTS.

H XXXII. *A person is regarded as bearing a flag of truce who has been authorized by one of the belligerents to enter into communication with the other, and who advances bearing a white flag. He has a right to inviolability, as well as the trumpeter, bugler or drummer, the flag-bearer and interpreter who may accompany him.*

H XXXIII. *The commander to whom a flag of truce is sent is not in all cases obliged to receive it.*

He may take all the necessary steps to prevent the envoy taking advantage of his mission to obtain information.

In case of abuse, he has the right to detain the envoy temporarily.

The flag of truce not to be misused.—The provisions of this article are necessary to prevent the flag of truce from being used either to gain time, or to deprive the enemy of an advantage, or to discover his movements. If the bearer of a flag of truce presents himself during an engagement, the enemy is not obliged to forego an advantage which he is about to gain and instantly to cease firing, and if the bearer of the flag of truce is accidentally injured no blame is incurred by the other belligerent.

"If the flag proceeds from the enemy's lines during a battle, the ranks which it leaves must halt and cease their fire. When the bearer displays his flag, he will be signalled by the opposing force, either to advance or to retire; if the former, the forces he approaches will cease firing; if the latter, he must instantly retire, for, if he should not, he may be fired upon."[1]

Declaration not to receive flag of truce for fixed period disapproved of.—The Brussels Declaration contained a provision recognizing the right of a commander to refuse to receive the bearer of flags of truce for a fixed period, but at The Hague it was thought that this was a practice to be regarded with disfavor and the provision was dropped.

[1] Halleck, International Law, II, p. 334.

The bearer of a flag of truce may be blindfolded.—The bearer of a flag of truce may be blindfolded and prevented from holding communication with persons other than those designated to conduct negotiations, in order to prevent his obtaining information.

H XXXIV. *The envoy loses his rights of inviolability if it is proved in a clear and incontestable manner that he has taken advantage of his privileged position to provoke or commit an act of treachery.*

H XXXV. *Capitulations agreed upon between the contracting parties must take into account the rules of military honour.*

Once settled, they must be scrupulously observed by both parties.

Powers of a commander with respect to capitulations.—The terms of a capitulation may vary from the absolute surrender of a place or of a body of troops to the grant of "all the honors of war," including the right to march out with colors flying and drums beating. Where there has been no express delegation of powers, the grant of more favorable terms than these is beyond the powers of a commander, and if his government refuses to ratify the capitulation there can be no occasion for charges of bad faith or double-dealing.[2] There is less likelihood of a commander's acting in excess of his powers today, however, than there was formerly, as he is likely to keep in close touch with his government by telegraph.

Property not to be destroyed between the signing and execution of capitulations.—The American Instructions, Article 144, provide: "So soon as a capitulation is signed, the capitulator has no right to demolish, destroy, or injure the works, arms, stores or ammunition in his possession, during the time which elapses between the signing and the execution of the capitulation, unless otherwise stipulated in the same."

H XXXVI. *An armistice suspends military operations by mutual agreement between the belligerent parties. If its duration is not defined, the belligerent parties may resume operations at any time, provided always that the enemy is warned within the time agreed upon, in accordance with the terms of the armistice.*

Use of the terms, suspension of arms, truce and armistice.

[2] Halleck, International Law, II, pp. 319–320.

—International jurists, including British and American, usually make a distinction between "suspensions of arms," temporary and local agreements, and "armistices," of a more general nature. This distinction is also a matter of Continental usage, but it is not found in American and British practice, in which the terms truce and armistice denote loosely almost any suspension of hostilities. On the Continent, the armistice is marked by the fixing of a neutral zone between the hostile armies, which does not exist in the suspension of arms.

H XXXVII. *An armistice may be general or local. The first suspends the military operations of the belligerent States everywhere; the second only between certain fractions of the belligerent armies and within a fixed radius.*

What is permitted during an armistice should be expressly stipulated.—To avoid recriminations it is desirable that just what is and what is not permitted during an armistice should be the subject of express stipulation as the rule that advantage cannot be taken of an armistice to do acts which the enemy could prevent but for the armistice, is difficult of application and not universally recognized.[3]

The American Instructions, Article 143, provide: "When an armistice is concluded between a fortified place and the army besieging it, it is agreed by all the authorities on this subject that the besieger must cease all extension, perfection, or advance of his attacking works, as much as from attacks by main force.

"But as there is a difference of opinion among martial jurists whether the besieged have the right to repair breaches or to erect new works of defense within the place during an armistice, this point should be determined by express agreement between the parties."

Especially as to the supply of provisions in case of a siege.—The introduction of provisions into a besieged place during an armistice cannot be demanded of strict right. It is a question above all others that should be made the matter of express stipulation.

H XXXVIII. *An armistice must be notified officially and in good time to the competent authorities and to the troops. Hos-*

[3] French Manual, p. 62.

tilities are suspended immediately after the notification, or on the date fixed.

Notification of armistice to be made to proper parties.—Unofficial notification is not binding on those to whom it is made, but it puts them on their guard according to the reliability of its source. Where the commencement of an armistice is set for a certain date, and acts are done after that date in contravention of it through excusable lack of notice, no liability to the other belligerent is incurred for them, though restitution must be made.

H XXXIX. *It rests with the contracting parties to settle, in the terms of the armistice, what communications may be held in the theatre of war with the inhabitants and between the inhabitants of one belligerent State and those of the other.*

Neutral zone frequently established in armistices.—As already noticed, the establishment of a neutral zone between the hostile armies is an incident of armistices as distinguished from suspensions of arms in Continental Europe. Where there is no such established practice, it is frequently stipulated in the armistice.

H XL. *Any serious violation of the armistice by one of the parties gives the other party the right of denouncing it, and even, in cases of urgency, of recommencing hostilities immediately.*

H XLI. *A violation of the terms of the armistice by private persons acting on their own initiative only entitles the injured party to demand the punishment of the offenders or, if necessary, compensation for the losses sustained.*

CHAPTER VIII.

MILITARY OCCUPATION—RIGHTS AND DUTIES AS TO PERSONS.

H XLII. *Territory is considered occupied when it is actually placed under the authority of the hostile army.*

The occupation extends only to the territory where such authority has been established and can be exercised.

Occupation must be effective.—The general principle is clear. Occupation exists only where the authority of the invading belligerent can be effectively exercised. There is no such thing as occupation by proclamation. On this there is no disagreement.

How far occupation is analogous to blockade.—To what extent, however, occupation need be evidenced by visible signs is a harder question and one that has given rise to much discussion. At Brussels, Gen. Voigts-Rhetz, the German delegate, while agreeing with the rest of the Conference on the necessity of the effectiveness of occupation, expressed, as has been seen, a strong disapproval of an analogy being drawn between occupation and blockade.[1] There must be large areas where, although the occupying army may make itself felt in case of need, it does not keep troops permanently stationed. Such is the result of all military experience. Col. Hammer, the Swiss delegate, replied that in each district occupied, there should be some fact which can be seized upon by the inhabitants to indicate the authority claimed by the enemy. "One man, provided he be respected, a post or telegraph office, a Commission of any kind established in the district and performing its functions without opposition, would suffice."[2]

Application of rule that occupation must be effective a matter for each belligerent.—This suggestion was not really antagonistic to the views of Gen. Voigts-Rhetz, who was evidently defending flying columns from the attacks which had been made on them, but he did not see fit to adopt it, and the Conference finally avoided the point by adopting

[1] Protocol 10 of the Committee, *supra*, p. 106.

[2] *Ibid.* .

a different phraseology. The force of Col. Hammer's suggestion can not be questioned, but it would seem best to deal with the matter by national laws rather than to incorporate it in an international code. The necessity of effectiveness being established in principle, it is fortunate that the details of its execution have been left to the belligerents themselves.

Beginning and end of occupation. Temporarily successful uprisings.—The accepted criterion of the commencement of occupation exists in the cessation of local resistance. The criterion of its termination, however, is subject to more doubt. Rolin-Jaequemyns has suggested, and his suggestion is embodied in the French Manual, that occupation may be said to exist so long as the belligerent to which the territory belongs is unable to exercise his authority there publicly.[3] The conclusion drawn from this in the Manual is that a rebellion momentarily triumphant is not sufficient to interrupt occupation and to free the inhabitants from the obedience due the occupant.[*] While this is true to the extent that a reasonable time must be given to suppress insurrection, before the occupation can be said to have ceased, still the general principle would seem directly contrary to the principle adopted at The Hague, that occupation must be effective. The authority of the enemy is based on his actual power. If that ceases, it would seem that his authority also ceases and that that of sovereign reverts. In other words, if the power of the occupant is effectively displaced for the time being, that fact in itself shows that his occupation has ceased, and that the displaced occupant has henceforth over the inhabitants only the rights he would have in unoccupied territory.

H XLIII. *The authority of the legitimate power having in fact passed into the hands of the occupant, the latter shall take all the measures in his power to restore and ensure, as far as possible, public order and safety, while respecting unless absolutely prevented, the laws in force in the country.*

Authority to govern occupied territory passes temporarily to the occupant.—The principle of this article is that there cannot be two governing authorities in the same territory at the same time. There should be some authority, for with-

[3] Revue de Droit International, 7, p. 99.
[*] Pp. 87–88.

out it law would be disregarded and the complex social and business life of today paralyzed. But territorial authority can amount to little without the power to make itself respected, and this power for the time being exists only in the occupant. Therefore, this authority, that is, the authority to execute the law and to enact such laws as are necessary for the temporary needs of the occupied territory, passes to the occupant and the authority of the legitimate sovereign to do these things is for the time suspended. This authority to govern, however, is not sovereignty. That exists still in the legitimate power till it is transferred by treaty or lost by conquest, and till then the nationality of the inhabitants and of the territory remains unchanged.

Personal authority over its citizens still continues in the legitimate power.—But, while the territorial authority of the legitimate power is for the time suspended, its personal authority over its subjects still continues. Its territorial legislation, such as tariff laws or administrative regulations, may be suspended in the occupied territory, but this does not deprive it of its authority over its subjects, which exists the world over. As long as its personal legislation does not amount to an attempt to govern the occupied territory, but is really directed at the personal actions of its subjects, it is within the authority of the sovereign and binding on the subjects. The legitimate power may call on its subjects to enlist in its armies; it may forbid them to serve under the enemy; and it may even incite them to insurrection.

Duty to preserve public life and social order falls on occupant.—The substitution of the occupant for the legitimate power as the territorial authority, throws on it the duty of insuring to the inhabitants as far as possible freedom from disorder and protection to their persons and property. Some continental writers are inclined to imply from this duty on the part of the occupant a reciprocal obligation on the part of the inhabitants so broad as to render them practically prisoners on parole. Certain English writers, on the other hand, see in it an obligation incurred in the pursuit of the occupant's own ends, an obligation which the inhabitants would only too gladly have avoided and which does not deprive them of any rights of resistance against the enemy which they had previous to the occupation.

Conflicting views as to the duty of the inhabitants towards the occupant.—There would appear to be a large measure of truth in both these views, contradictory as they are at some points. Insofar as the occupant acts as the territorial authority for the purpose of insuring order and executing the laws, and not for his own immediate belligerent purposes, it would appear to be incontestable that the inhabitant does owe him obedience. It would be a hard rule placing on him the burden of punishing ordinary crime or of carrying out such measures as those of sanitation, if the inhabitants were not to be under any obligation to assist him in them or to render him the obedience due with regard to such things from every inhabitant to the government under which he lives.

Duty of obedience owed him only while he is trying to preserve public life and social order.—So long, then, as the occupant is acting as the territorial authority in carrying out the ordinary purposes of government, and not for his own belligerent purposes, the inhabitants owe him obedience; but, when he goes further and takes measures which are for his own belligerent purposes, it would seem that the inhabitants far from owing him obedience, may still look upon him as the enemy of the government to which they owe allegiance, and, so far as his orders are hostile to that government, may disregard them as far as they can reasonably do so. Where certain acts are in themselves offenses against the laws of war, the inhabitants are bound to abstain from them, but this is not because of obedience due to the occupant but of respect due to the laws of war.

Civil and penal laws not to be changed.—Unless absolutely prevented, the occupant must respect the laws in force in the country. Civil and penal laws should remain untouched, while political and administrative laws should be modified only so far as changes are imperative. Laws of recruitment are necessarily suspended, as part of the law of the territory occupied, and fiscal laws, such as those of taxation and of administrative organization, are liable to be suspended as a matter of fact by the flight of the officials, who alone are familiar with them. Constitutional privileges, such as the freedom of the press, the right of assembly, the right to bear arms, and the right of suffrage, are usually suspended, as ordinarily in case of martial law.

Occupant may make provisional regulations for benefit of occupied territory.—The occupant may enact such provisional regulations as the suspension of the legitimate authority, his own welfare and the good of the territory render necessary. He may even go so far as to establish provisional governments, based on new rules of suffrage, if such a measure will aid him in the settlement of the war. But he must not attempt to change the Constitution of the country, nor do any act implying a change in the nationality of the people or of the territory.

Martial law. Notice to the inhabitants.—One of the most important of the rights of the occupant is the enforcement of martial law. This right springs from the occupation itself, without notice; but "it is the duty of the occupying military authority to inform the inhabitants at the earliest practicable moment of the powers that he exercises as well as to define the limits of the occupied territory."[4] During the Franco-Prussian War these notices were affixed in each canton, about 72 square miles in extent, and took effect immediately throughout the canton.[5]

Offenses arising from noncombatant character of offenders.—Perhaps the most important class of offenses under martial law is that arising from the nonbelligerent character of the offenders. The smaller powers at Brussels were unwilling to admit that there might not be acts of individual hostility, such as the blowing up of a bridge, which would be legal if done in unoccupied territory in the face of an advancing army,[6] although those members of the Institute of International Law who afterwards considered this point, were of opinion that there were not;[7] but even the smaller powers seemed to feel no hesitancy in recognizing the illegality of such acts in occupied territory. Such acts in unoccupied territory have been of such rare occurrence, however, that no usage has grown up with regard to them. In occupied territory, on the other hand,

[4] Rule 32 of the Oxford Manual.
[5] Hall, Inter. Law, p. 500.
[6] Protocol 14 of the Committee.
[7] Revue de Droit Inter., 7, pp. 109, 484–489.

they have been so frequent that their illegality has been so firmly established as not to be questioned. If a distinction should be drawn in favor of such acts in unoccupied territory, it might be made on the ground that there the national law is still in full vigor, so that its restraining force is sufficient, without making an act of this kind an offense against the law of war. In occupied territory, respect for the ordinary law is so apt to be shaken that, unless acts of this kind are made absolutely condemnable by the law of war itself, there is likely to be no sufficient guarantee against them.

Duty to respect the law of war.—The duty to abstain from such acts does not arise therefore from a duty of obedience to the occupant, but from the obligation to respect the law of war, which is not only a part of International Law, but a part of the national law of the country whose territory is occupied, provided that country is itself within the pale of International Law. The laws of war forbid it, because of the useless disorder and loss of life and property which disobedience entails.

Acts of violence.—Notable among the acts of violence thus prohibited are the killing, wounding or robbing of troops of the enemy or their suite; destroying bridges, canals, telegraph lines and railroads; rendering routes impassable, and burning the munitions of war or the provisions of the enemy or the quarters of his troops. The commission of such acts by nonbelligerents is much more likely to result in the injury of the inhabitants than in that of the enemy. If they become prevalent, the orderly life of the community is at an end, and brigandage and lawlessness ensue.

Unsuccessful uprisings in occupied territory.—Unsuccessful uprisings of the populations of occupied territory should, it would seem, be placed in the same category. Success justifies such uprisings and shows that the alleged occupation was not real; but the miseries likely to be visited on all the inhabitants in the attempt to put down the uprisings make them measures to be shunned, unless the chances of success are good.

Acts, not violations of the law of war, but prohibited by the belligerent because injurious to him.—Besides acts of violence which are contrary to the laws of war irrespective of the military regulations of the occupant, there are others which may be prohibited by him because of the assistance they render the enemy or because of their danger to himself. Such measures, taken for his own security, the inhabitants are under no duty to obey, but he may enforce them by such penalties as are not contrary to the laws of war. Acts of this kind are spying against the occupant, giving information to the legitimate power obtained in other ways than by spying, the misguiding of the occupant's troops, the refusal to deliver up arms or other munitions of war, leaving the country without the authority of the occupant, and enrolling in the armed forces of the legitimate power.

Delivery up of arms.—During the Franco-German War the inhabitants of occupied territory were required to deliver up arms, at first under penalty of five years' imprisonment in Germany, or an equivalent fine, but later the mere possession of arms or munitions, without special circumstances to overcome the presumption of a hostile purpose, was declared to render the possessor guilty of treason against the German troops, the penalty for which was death.[8]

German action to prevent the inhabitants of territory occupied by them joining the French army.—The early efforts of the German authorities to stop recruiting were directed merely against the civl functionaries engaged in it. Later, the mayors were required to prepare lists of those liable to serve in the French army, and the families of those whose absence could not be explained were fined fifty francs for each absent individual and for each day of absence. Still later, in Alsace and Lorraine, it was declared that eight days' absence from home without the previous permission of the prefect should give rise to the legal presumption of having joined the French army, and that the offender should be punished by the confiscation of all his goods present and future and banishment for ten years.[9] This declaration, however, was made late in the war, and is said to have been applied, in Alsace at least, only five times.[10] Its provisions warrant detailed examination.

No right to punish those who had succeeded in doing so.—The right to punish the inhabitants of occupied territory

[8] Bray, Occupation Militaire, pp. 184–188.

[9] *Ibid.*, pp. 282–287.

[10] Loening, Revue de Droit International. 5, p. 85.

for leaving the territory and joining the forces of the legitimate power is undoubted, but it was with great force claimed by Rolin-Jaequemyns that the principle applied to blockade runners, namely, that if the attempt to run the blockade is successful, the offense is wiped out, should be applied here also.[11] The inhabitants of the occupied territory are under no duty not to leave the occupied territory and join the forces of their country, but rather to the contrary, and if they are willing to run the chances of being caught in the act and suffering therefor, it would seem only proper that, as in the case of the prisoner of war who has made his escape, they should be relieved from further liability to punishment. The right to punish is based on the power to prevent the doing of the act, and if that power proves to be lacking the right to punish ceases. This being so, the punishment of the families of those who have escaped is especially improper.

Assistance of local officials should not be required to prevent such acts.—Another criticism of the proclamation of the German authorities is that they went beyond their legal powers in requiring the local officials to make lists of those liable to military service in France. They had a right to require the cooperation of the local authorities in suppressing offenses against the laws of war such as the acts of violence which have heretofore been noticed, but when they went further and required the cooperation of the officials in measures hostile to their own goverment, they were doing violence to the most laudable feelings of patriotism, and it is conceived that like action in the future will be prevented by the spirit if not letter of H XLIV.

Penalties of martial law.—The penalties of martial law to be effective must be prompt and severe. Passions run high, respect for law is impaired and the fate of the nation, perhaps, is at stake. Example should be made of offenders sufficient to deter others from becoming offenders also. But in doing this it is extremely necessary to take care that the measures do not defeat the very ends for which they are designed. The confiscation and burning of property is a case in point. There may be times when such measures are justifiable and expedient, but they are very rare. If the Franco-German War and the War in South Africa have

11 Revue de Droit Inter., 3, pp. 317–318.

shown anything, they have shown this. Inflicted, as such punishments generally are, because the offender himself cannot be gotten at, they strike at persons often entirely free from blame and turn into frenzied apostles of hate and revenge those who have been driven to desperation by the loss of everything they possess.

The use of hostages on trains.—A preventative measure that has much to commend it when properly used is that of placing notable citizens on trains to prevent injury to them. As a protection against the acts of belligerent forces this would, of course, be improper, as such acts would be perfectly lawful acts of war; but, as a protection against purely lawless acts in occupied territory, the measure is one to be commended for the slight suffering it entails and for its effectiveness.

Importance of the careful study of the penalties of martial law.—At the Brussels Conference it was urged that an international agreement be entered into fixing penalties for infractions of the laws of war. This is not likely to be brought about, as the smaller powers have shown themselves opposed to recognizing the legality of the exercise of penal power by a belligerent; but it is very desirable that a more careful study should be made of penalties in order that a maximum of prevention be secured with a minimum of suffering. The German military penal code of June 22, 1872, was a step in the right direction. One of its beneficent provisions was the requirement of trial before punishment in every case dealt with by it.[12]

Innocent parties should not be held for the acts of others where it is possible to punish the offender himself.—In every case of infraction of the laws of war the utmost effort should be made to confine the punishment therefor to the actual offender. The punishment of an innocent person for the offense of another is so diametrically opposed to every principle of justice that serious indeed must be the occasion that warrants it.

Reprisals.—The most noxious form of this injustice is the practice of reprisals. At times states are so swayed by the desire of success and the passions of conflict as deliberately to violate the law of war or to refuse to punish those who have committed such violations. This in no way

[12] Revue de Droit International, 5, p. 83.

releases the other belligerent from its obligation to respect the laws of war, and if the offense is slight, it is better to suffer it to pass than run the risk of embittering the struggle; but if the offense is not slight, it may be thought necessary to prevent its recurrence by resorting to measures not ordinarily authorized by the law of war. Where the offense is an individual act, every effort should first be made to punish the offender, and in case that is not possible to secure his punishment by the other belligerent. Where these efforts have failed, the offended belligerent may, if he thinks the facts warrant it, take measures of a nature similar to the acts complained of, provided they be of a less or equal degree. Measures of a greater degree of severity will almost inevitably lead to further measures of retaliation, and once started on this road the war almost certainly becomes a succession of outrages and recriminations.

Article of the Brussels Declaration on the continuance of old officials in office during the occupation.—Article XLIII was followed in the Brussels Declaration by the following article:

"The functionaries and officials of every class who, at the instance of the occupier consent to continue to perform their duties, shall be under his protection. They shall not be dismissed or be liable to summary punishment unless they fail in fulfilling the obligations they have undertaken, and shall be handed over to justice only if they violate those obligations by unfaithfulness."

Position of the Belgian and Dutch delegates at The Hague.—This clause was dropped at The Hague because of the opposition of the delegates from Belgium and The Netherlands, who feared it might be held to imply an authorization to the officials in the occupied territory to enter the service of the enemy.[13] This would be especially important in The Netherlands, where those in charge of the dikes have a special technical knowledge which would be of great value to an enemy, if placed at his service. It is hard to see, however, that any such implication could be made from this provision, and, as it contains important principles, it is unfortunate that it was abandoned.

With territorial authority goes authority over territorial officials.—Authority to govern territory must include au-

[13] See the report of M. Rolin.

thority over the officials through whom it is governed, and as the general authority passes to the occupant for the period of the occupation, so the authority over the officials passes to him, and as long as they hold their positions it is their duty to perform the functions of their office under the direction of the occupant with the same degree of faithfulness as under their own government.

Officials may resign.—But it is not necessary for them to continue to hold their positions. They are entitled to resign, and are under obligation to do so if they feel that the continuance of their functions is inconsistent with their duty to their own country, or if it is forbidden by the government of their own country. As subjects of that government, they still owe obedience to its commands, although as officials they are no longer under its immediate direction.

Political officials necessarily discontinue their functions.—Whether continuance in office is permissible depends largely on the nature of the office. Continental writers make a distinction between political and civil officers, confining the former to the representatives of the central government in the various districts and the latter to the representatives of the various administrative departments. The actions of political officers are largely influenced by the political party which happens to be in power, and they are largely entrusted with carrying out the political measures of the administration; while the civil officers are concerned mainly with affairs which are not the subjects of political controversy and continue in office from administration to administration. The former have large military and police powers, and it would obviously be equivalent to entering into the service of the enemy to remain in such office under his direction. In the United States such officers would include governors of states and all officials under them exercising any military authority. Such officers, as well as those directly in the military, naval or diplomatic service, holding office in the occupied territory, are under obligations to withdraw from their positions for the period of the occupation.

Local officials under a duty not to.—On the other hand, it is generally considered that local officials are under an obligation to remain at their posts. Especially in the large cities the functions of the local government enter so vitally into everyday affairs that their cessation even for a day would seriously cripple the life of the community and result in crime and disorder. It is in the interest of the inhabitants that these officials remain, so that in no sense can it be said that they enter the service of the enemy. It is true that in the collection of contributions and requisitions they are of aid to the enemy, but the aid to the enemy is slight as compared with the suffering and loss that is spared the inhabitants.

Tax officials.—Many of the reasons for local officials remaining in office are fully applicable to tax officials. The local officials serve as a buffer between the occupying army and the inhabitants in the imposition of contributions and requisitions, and it is possible for the tax officials to discharge a similar function in the collection of the regular taxes. The occupant is entitled to these, but if the tax officials leave their posts it is impossible for him to collect them from sheer ignorance of the tax laws, if nothing else, so that he will be compelled to collect their equivalent through contributions, whose burden is sure to be much heavier than that of the regular taxes. Nevertheless, as the proceeds of the taxes go to the occupant for his own purposes, after payment of the expenses of administration, tax officials are likely to feel that by remaining in office they will contribute too directly to filling the coffers of the enemy and thus do something inconsistent with their duty to their country. Experience has shown this to be usually the case, since, as a matter of fact, tax officials appear to have almost invariably left their posts on occupation by the enemy.

Forest officials.—Officials in charge of the private domains of the state, such as the forests, are in somewhat the same position as the tax officials, as the private domains are usually sources of revenue; but the reasons for their remaining at their posts are greater, since, no matter how careful the occupant may be in the administration of the forests, they are liable to suffer some damage from the change in administration.

Postal, railroad and telegraph officials.—Postal officials and officials in the railroad or telegraph service, and it would appear to be immaterial whether these are under the government or not, are almost necessarily called upon to discontinue their functions, since, if they remain, the chances are that they will be required to take an active part in transmitting the correspondence, supplies and forces of the enemy.

Those in charge of museums, etc., should remain.—Political, tax, postal and railroad officials will therefore usually quit their positions, while local officials and those in other departments should retain theirs unless ordered to the contrary. Especially is this true of those in charge of museums, art galleries, palaces, archives and scientific works. Their remaining will be of no special service to the enemy, while their leaving may mean the destruction of the treasures committed to their care. Wherever the courts of justice can readily continue their functions, it is their duty to do so also, and police magistrates and officials are under special obligations to remain at a time when lawlessness is likely to be rampant.

An oath of fidelity may be required of officials.—Functionaries who remain in office may be required to take an oath to perform their duties faithfully and to refrain from using their official powers in hostility to the occupant. Great care must be taken in the wording of this oath not to include in it anything inconsistent with the allegiance of the officials or implying that they have entered into the service of the enemy. Even when no oath has been given, faithfulness in the performance of duties and neutrality of official conduct are a condition of the retention of office. It is to be noticed that in the Brussels Article, failure to perform duty subjects the official only to disciplinary punishment while betrayal of trust renders him liable to punishment under the penal code.

Occupant must not demand of the officials who remain duties contrary to their allegiance.—Over those who remain in office the occupant has the right of direction, suspension and dismissal. He may make such orders as he deems necessary for the temporary administration of the territory, and may impose new duties on the officials, provided such duties be not hostile to their government. Thus he may require of the local officials the collection of contributions and requisitions, and the punishment of offenses against the laws of war; but he has no right to demand that they cooperate in measures such as the punishment of those leaving the occupied territory to join the forces of their country, since acts of this kind are not contrary to the laws of war, and the measures taken for their prevention are measures directly hostile to the country to which the officials still owe their allegiance.

H XLIV. *A belligerent is forbidden to force the inhabitants of territory occupied by it to furnish information about the army of the other belligerent, or about its means of defence.*

Compelling the nationals of the enemy to serve as guides.—Prior to the adoption of this article, the right to compel a national of the hostile belligerent to serve as guide was a much debated one in juristic circles, but it was one that governments seemed loath to forego. The guide was in an exceedingly difficult position, but it was generally held that if he acted under compulsion he was not guilty of treason to his own country. This article forbids compelling inhabitants to act as guides when to do so would be most dangerous to the inhabitant's country and consequently most revolting to his sense of patriotism. By a liberal construction it may be held to forbid every compulsion to act as guide for any ignorance of the country on the part of one belligerent may be considered a "means of defense" to the hostile belligerent. The spirit of the article may also be held to forbid requiring of local officials the names of the inhabitants of occupied territory capable of service in the army with a view to their punishment if they leave the occupied territory to enlist in their country's service.

H XLV. *It is forbidden to compel the inhabitants of occupied territory to swear allegiance to the hostile Power.*

No oath of allegiance to the occupant is to be required.—As we have seen, this does not prevent the requirement of an oath of fidelity from those who continue in office.

H XLVI. *Family honour and rights, the lives of persons, and private property, as well as religious convictions and practice must be respected.*

Private property cannot be confiscated.

Family life should be interfered with as little as possible.—Family honor and rights are not considered to be violated by requiring the quartering or feeding of troops; nor by the search for requisitioned articles, where forced military execution has become necessary; nor by the use of a house for military operations, where such use is necessary. But such incidents are among the most annoying of war on account of their interference with family life. Accordingly they are to be avoided, if possible, and where they cannot be avoided are to be rendered as little irksome as possible.

Churches not necessarily free from right of requisition.—Liberty of public worship does not mean that churches or other ecclesiastical establishments are necessarily exempt from the right of requisition. Gen. Voigts-Rhetz at the Brussels Conference, declared that quartering troops in churches, and the taking of what may be necessary for the subsistence of the army from ecclesiastical establishments, could neither in winter or in case of scarcity of provisions, be given up.[14]

H XLVII. *Pillage is formally forbidden.*

Absence of proprietors not to be considered abandonment of property.—Pillage has generally been forbidden except where towns have been taken by assault, ever since the practice of contributions went into effect. Dwellings from which the inhabitants are absent cannot be considered as abandoned, so that there is no greater right against the property found in them than against that found in other dwellings. The owners, however, are liable to suffer more heavily than others, since, by reason of their absence, the requisition must be executed militarily, and their presence is wanting to restrain unlawful acts on the part of the soldiery.

[14] Protocol 18 of the Committee.

CHAPTER IX.

MILITARY OCCUPATION—RIGHTS AND DUTIES AS TO PROPERTY.

H XLVIII. *If, in the territory occupied, the occupant collects the taxes, dues and tolls imposed for the benefit of the State, he shall do so, as far as is possible, in accordance with the rules of assessment and incidence in force, and shall in consequence be bound to defray the expenses of the administration of the occupied territory to the same extent as the legitimate Government was so bound.*

The occupant has no right to local and provincial taxes. —The limitation that only those taxes may be collected by the occupant which are for the benefit of the State was suggested by Count Lamza, the Italian delegate, in order to exempt local and provincial taxes from the power of the occupant.[1] This exemption is based on the assumption that military affairs are entirely the concern of the central government, and that accordingly only those taxes which would have gone to the central government can be collected by the occupant. In federal governments like the United States, where the States make large military expenditures, it is probable that the State taxes would be assimilated to taxes due the central government rather than to local and provincial taxes.

Rules of incidence and collection of taxes in force, to be followed, if possible.—The rule that the existing tax laws shall be followed as far as possible in the assessment and collection of taxes is an instance of the more general rule that the laws in force in the country shall be respected unless the occupant is absolutely prevented from doing so. It is the duty which he is under to provide for the administration of the territory that entitles him to the taxes. Otherwise he would be entitled only to the surplus after the administration had been provided for.

This generally prevented by withdrawal of tax officials.— As has heretofore been pointed out, however, the desertion of their posts by the tax officials is likely to render the ex-

[1] Protocol 10 of the Committee.

isting laws unenforceable and in that case resort will be had to contributions, which can be only a rough equivalent to the taxes.

Practice in the Franco-German War.—Such was the course of events in the Franco-German War. At first the Germans attempted to collect the taxes according to the French Law, but this proved to be impossible even in the case of the indirect tax, which they sometimes approximated by taking as a basis the indirect taxes for the two preceding years, sometimes by exacting from 100 percent to 200 percent of the direct tax, and in other cases by exacting a lump sum of from twenty-five to fifty francs per head.[2]

Methods of enforcing collection.—In few cases, if any, were the taxes levied directly on individuals. The mayor of the chief city of a department, arrondissement, or canton, was required to reapportion the tax among the communes and inhabitants. An ordinance of the Governor-General of Rheims of February 5, is typical of the means used to secure the prompt payment of the tax. Dilatory communes were threatened with a fine of 5 percent of the amount due for each day of delay, and told that at the end of eight days troops would be quartered on them, which they would be required to lodge and nourish without pay, besides paying six francs daily to each officer and two francs to each soldier, till the amount due had been entirely discharged. Prominent citizens had already been taken as hostages for the payment of these debts, and six days later the Governor-General issued another ordinance warning the inhabitants that, if the taxes were not paid in eight days, the hostages would be sent to Germany and further measures taken against the dilatory communes.[3]

Importance of contributions imposed in lieu of taxes.—The importance of these contributions imposed in lieu of taxes is shown by the fact that comparative estimates of those imposed during the Franco-German War, placed them at from 49 to 62 millions of francs, as against from 30 to 39 millions of francs exacted as war contributions and fines.[4]

Credit given by the French Government for payment of taxes to German authorities.—After peace was established,

[2] Bray, p. 300.
[3] Bray, p. 301.
[4] Bray, p. 302, Feraud-Giraud, **Sec. 32.**

the French Government declared that communes which had been compelled to turn over money in their treasuries to the German authorities should be reimbursed, and that individuals who could show proper evidence of having been compelled to pay taxes to the Germans should be allowed to deduct the amount paid from the contributions for 1870-1871, a reduction being allowed of the amount of the direct tax, to the extent actually paid, and of double the amount of the direct tax on account of what the Germans had exacted as the equivalent of the indirect tax. Everything beyond these amounts was to be considered as war contributions and ruled by different principles.[5]

H XLIX. *If, in addition to the taxes mentioned in the above Article, the occupant levies other money contributions in the occupied territory, this shall only be for the needs of the army or of the administration of the territory in question.*

War contributions.—Contributions levied in lieu of taxes may not be adequate for the needs of administration, and in such a case war contributions proper may be imposed to make up what is lacking. The principal occasion for war contributions, however, will always be, the needs of the army. How these are to be met without imposing too great a burden on the inhabitants was the subject of earnest debate at Brussels and The Hague.

Limitation of War contributions in original Russian Project at Brussels.—The original Russian Project at Brussels was in line with the general principle eventually laid down in Article XLIII that the laws in force in the occupied territory shall be respected by the occupant. It provided that the army of occupation should have the same rights in levying war contributions as the army of the country whose territory was occupied, would have had. It was objected that there might be no laws providing for contributions and requisitions in the country whose territory was occupied; or that the country might be one liable to invasion and have laws that would render the right of the occupant, to contributions nugatory; and finally, that this rule left out of consideration the needs of the army on which the right was chiefly based.

Proposition to confine them to what the occupying army would have a right to in its own country.—On the other

[5] Bray, pp. 302–303.

hand, it was proposed that the laws in force in the country of the occupying belligerent should be the ones to be applied in the occupied territory, but here again, it was argued that there might be no such laws; that constitutional restrictions might prevent them from being enacted; that a country likely to take the offensive might enact a law of the most extreme character, and finally that the logical basis of war contributions, the needs of the army would be ignored by this rule also. The truth was that both these propositions were artificial and impracticable.[6]

Attempt to limit them by requiring the receipts to be indemnities.—A further attempt to limit contributions was involved in the proposal to require that the receipt given for them should be in the nature of a promise of repayment. This proposal was rejected, and the only limitation finally adopted was that the contributions should be imposed either for the needs of the army or the administration of the territory. While this may seem to be almost no restriction, since in modern wars contributions have not nearly reached this limit, still it prevents contributions from being made use of to enrich the coffers of the successful belligerent a practice familiar in ancient history and not unknown in more modern times.

Advantages of paying for provisions.—The desirableness of buying provisions in the open market at a fair price or of paying for them when requisitioned is evident at a glance. Concealment of property is largely avoided, provisions are secured with much less friction, business conditions are not so violently disturbed and the inhabitants are not left penniless. But armies cannot carry sufficient cash with them to pay for what they need, so that, if they pay at all, they must very often raise the money by contributions. The burden of the money payment is likely to be distributed over a wide area or fall on those best able to stand it, while the burden of requisitions in kind is liable to fall on agricultural communities who have what is directly needed for the wants of the army, but are much less able to stand the burden of supporting the army than their rich neighbours in the cities.

Advantages of contributions.—As General Voigts-Rhetz said at Brussels: "An army arrives at a rich town and

6 Protocols 15, 16 of the Committee.

demands a certain number of oxen for its subsistence. The town replies that it has none. The army would in that case be compelled to apply to villages which are frequently poor, where it would seize what it is in want of. This would be a flagrant injustice. The poor would pay for the rich. There is, therefore, no other expedient but to admit an equivalent in cash. This is likewise the mode which the inhabitants prefer. Moreover, it cannot be admitted that a town which is unable to pay in kind shall be exempted from paying in money.'' And again: ''An army arrives at night and is to leave the next day. It must be fed; the town cannot do this; the occupier, with the money which he levies on the spot, will therefore go into the neighboring country and procure what it is in want of by means of the money supplied by the town.''[7]

Contributions of far less importance than Requisitions.—In these cases, contributions certainly appear to be an alleviation of, rather than an addition to, the burdens of war. But after all, their importance is slight as compared with that of requisitions. It has been estimated that during the Franco-German War, the war contributions, outside of the city of Paris amounted to thirty-nine millions of francs, while the requisitions reached the sum of three hundred and twenty-seven millions.[8]

H L. *No general penalty, pecuniary or otherwise, shall be inflicted upon the population on account of the acts of individuals for which they cannot be regarded as jointly and severally responsible.*

No general penalty for acts for which a community cannot be regarded as collectively responsible.—The principle of this article has been observed in the past more in its letter than in its spirit. Almost invariably, when communities have been held liable for acts committed within their bounds, it has been upon the ground that they could and should have prevented them and were thus implicated in their commission. Both these elements should enter into an act before the community is held liable for it. If the acts are individual acts, necessitating little cooperation with the rest of the community, the laying down of any presumption

[7] Protocol 16 of the Committee.
[8] Feraud-Giraud, Sec. 32.

of collective responsibility would appear to be directly opposed to the spirit of this article.

Aid of community may be required in preventing and punishing acts of violence against the law of war.—Even where a community may be able to prevent an act, it should not be held responsible for its commission, unless it is under a duty to prevent it. Acts of violence in occupied territory are likely to be of such a public nature that the intention to commit them may be well known to the community at large, and, if they are contrary to the laws of war, a belligerent is justified in requiring the aid of the community in suppressing them and even in holding the community responsible if they are not prevented. But this liability should not be extended to acts not themselves contrary to the laws of war, but which the occupant opposes for his own safety and in order to prevent aid from reaching the enemy, such as spying, leaving the occupied territory to join the national army, and refusing to give up arms.

The innocent should not suffer for the guilty.—As in the case of reprisals, every effort should first be made to punish the actual offenders. Collective responsibility is so easy of enforcement that there is the temptation to resort to it on the least occasion; but the principle that the innocent should not suffer for the guilty applies here as well as in the case of reprisals so that only as a last resort should collective responsibility be enforced. The same care in placing such responsibility should be taken as is taken in determining and enforcing the liability of the individual. An investigation in the nature of a judicial proceeding is the least that can be demanded.

Fines.—The article under consideration appears to be somewhat out of place in the scheme of the convention, but it was probably inserted here because war contributions and fines are both money exactions, and because collective responsibility is usually exacted in the form of fines.

H LI. *No contribution shall be collected except under a written order, and on the responsibility of a Commander-in-chief.*

The collection of the said contribution shall only be effected as far as possible in accordance with the rules of assessment and incidence of the taxes in force.

For every contribution a receipt shall be given to the contributors.

Receipts for Contributions need not have the character of indemnities.—These receipts need not have the character of promises to pay. As has been seen, attempts to give them that character, both at Brussels and at The Hague, failed, although made by many of the most able and influential men in the conferences. It was earnestly desired to limit the levying of contributions by making the receipts for them indemnities, thus avoiding the impositions of the burdens of the war on individuals; but the general feeling at the Conferences seems to have been that the reimbursement of the individual is a matter of national rather than of international concern.[9] There was no feeling that the individual ought to bear the whole burden of the contribution himself; but it was felt that the reimbursement could best be managed by each government within its own territory.

H LII. *Requisitions in kind and services shall not be demanded from municipalities or inhabitants except for the needs of the army of occupation. They shall be in proportion to the resources of the country, and of such a nature as not to involve the inhabitants in the obligation of taking part in military operations against their country.*

Such requisitions and services shall only be demanded on the authority of the commander in the locality occupied.

Contributions in kind shall as far as possible be paid for in cash; if not, a receipt shall be given and the payment of the amount due shall be made as soon as possible.

Regulations as to the orders authorizing Requisitions.—It will be noticed that while contributions can only be levied by the commander-in-chief and on written order, requisitions may be demanded by the commander in the locality occupied and orally. Requisitions are often made of property of little value, such as forage for the horses, for which it would be incongruous to require the order of the commander-in-chief or even a written order; and often the need for such supplies is so pressing that either would be impracticable. Where it is possible, however, it is desirable that the levying of requisitions should also be on the written authority of the commander-in-chief. Not only is this a great safeguard against the abuse of authority, but the written

[9] *Supra*, p. 107.

order also avoids misunderstanding on the part of those who execute it. Ferrand says that such orders should be "written and signed mentioning clearly the nature and quantity of the payments to be furnished, the length of the service and the day, the hour and the place of delivery."[10]

Expression of the desirability of paying for requisitions in cash.—The last paragraph is the work of the two Peace Conferences. The Brussels Declaration expressed no preference for cash payments. The part the second Conference played was in giving the receipts somewhat the character of indemnities by providing that "the payment of the amount due shall be made as soon as possible." The implication intended by those who would free the individual as far as possible from the burden of the war probably is that the amount is due from the belligerent giving the receipt, but the fact that the provision is not worded more definitely than it is shows that the Governments were unwilling to agree to any absolute obligation in this regard and it is likely that whether the amounts indicated in these receipts are paid or not will be left to the Treaty of Peace or to the action of the country in which the receiver was domiciled, as in the case of receipts given for war contributions.

The French Manual enjoins that the receipt shall contain words and figures which will make it possible to verify its authenticity afterwards and to establish the value of the things exacted; that the officer who gives the receipt shall write the text legibly, note specifically the essential elements which determine the market value of the articles, give the date, indicate in connection with his signature his grade and the corps to which he belongs, and note, if there be occasion for it, that he acts by delegation of superior authority.[11]

Services must not involve military service under the enemy.—Services which cannot be required, because they involve participation in the operations of war against one's country, have already been discussed under H VI, XXIII and XLIV.

Requisitions must be in proportion to the resources of the country.—The limitation that the requisitions be in propor-

10 Ferrand, Requisitions Militaires, p. 96.
11 French Manual, p. 127.

tion to the resources of the country is important, as suggesting to the mind of the commander that account must be taken of requisitions previously made on the community, and a careful investigation made of the resources of the country, so that the burden of the requisitions may be distributed as equitably as possible.

The personal services that may be required.—Personal services that may be required are those of clergymen, physicians, surgeons, pharmacists, etc.; of workmen, such as drivers, farriers, smiths, carpenters, bakers, butchers, etc.; and finally of laborers, provided always that they are for the needs of the army and do not amount to participating in military operations against their country.[12] Others likely to have their services requisitioned are railroad, telegraph and postal employees. Mayors and other notables may be required to aid in levying contributions and requisitions in communicating official decrees to the inhabitants and in performing other functions of a similar nature not inconsistent with loyalty to their own country. It would seem, however, that requisitions cannot be levied to aid in carrying on the administration of the occupied territory, as contributions can, as they are limited strictly to the needs of the army, so that the occupant is not authorized to compel postal employees to continue their functions for the sake of giving a better administration, but can do so only for the needs of his own army.

Articles that may be requisitioned.—Requisitions in kind extend to all objects incidental to the shelter of troops, to the subsistence of the army in campaign, to transportation and communication, to the care of the sick and wounded, to objects of clothing and camp equipment, and finally to all materials, tools, apparatus, etc., suitable for the use of the army.[13]

Sheltering of troops.—Sheltering of troops may be by cantonment, by camp or by bivouac. Bivouacing involves the use of improvised shelter or small tents, or even a stay in the open air. It is inevitable in the presence of an enemy or when the march of troop is concentrated, but is extremely unsanitary and is never resorted to except from neces-

12 Ferrand, p. 32.
13 Ferrand, p. 33.

sity.[14] Camps are places where troops live for a considerable time in large tents or barracks. Camping is the only alternative to quartering, for the purpose of sheltering troops for any considerable period, so that each varies inversely as the other. As French military writers seem to think camps mainly of use in special cases, such as investments,[15] quartering is likely to be largely used by the French army and the practice seems to be the same generally on the Continent. But in England and the United States there has always been a strong feeling against quartering on account of its interference with family life, so that it will probably never be so general in American as it is in Continental armies. Its advantages are its restfulness, its healthfulness and the small degree of preparation it requires on the part of the troops.

Quartering of troops in churches, etc.—At the Brussels Conference, Baron Lambermont tried to have the right to quarter troops in ecclesiastical, charitable and educational establishments limited to the sick and wounded, but General Voigts-Rhetz would not entertain the proposal, at least as applied to churches; and it is probable that in pressing cases any of these institutions may be so used. The quartering of troops in museums, libraries and art galleries would seem to be absolutely forbidden.[16] The inhabitants can be required to keep the streets lighted, to keep lights in their windows and to keep their doors open. Soldiers have a right to light in their quarters, and if circumstances warrant it to fire and straw.[17]

Requisition of food supplies.—Requisitions of food supplies are important even where an army subsists mainly on its convoys; and where the army is engaged in rapid strategical operations, they are its mainstay. Where purchases in the open market are out of the question, requisitions must be resorted to. These take two forms—that of requiring nourishment from the inhabitants with whom the soldiers are quartered, and that of requiring the supplies themselves. The former method does not exact any previous preparation, gives the soldiers a varied food without

14 Ferrand, p. 39.
15 *Ibid.*, p. 40.
16 Protocol 18 of the Committee.
17 Ferrand, p. 36.

delay, causes less fatigue to the soldier, permits convoys of provisions to march separately, utilizes best the provisions of all sorts in the country, and is more economical since it gives rise to less waste and does away, to a great degree, with the necessity for transports.[18] On the other hand, as already mentioned, there is a pronounced sentiment against it both in the United States and Great Britain, on account of its interference with family life.

Local conditions.—In fixing requisitions, it is necessary to have regard to local conditions, to the manner of living, locality itself, etc. Thus, in industrial centers and the great cities, it will be necessary to take into account the working population. They do not produce food products, they do not have provisions with them as country people have, and they often lack the credit and money to procure provisions in advance of their needs.[19]

Regulations as to boarding.—Where the requisition takes the form of boarding, the inhabitants ought to furnish the regulation ration or its equivalent; and, to avoid difficulties, the commandant ordering the requisition should determine the composition of the repast to be furnished. When the nourishment furnished is insufficient, the soldiers should not take matters into their own hands, but should complain to their officers who, if unable to obtain satisfaction from the offending parties, will take the matter to the commandant, who will see that the municipal authorities live up to the obligation imposed upon them of providing suitable quarters.[20] Provisions for the horses may be required in the same way as for the men.

Importance of requisitions.—The possibilities of the abuse of this system are evidently very great; but on the other hand, it was used by Napoleon and by the Germans in 1866 and 1870 with great success, and Ferrand, following Beratier, says that if the exaggerated fear of causing too heavy a burden on the populations should cause this manner of feeding an army to be put aside, or if the temperament of the army should not be strong enough to stand the test of discipline which this method makes necessary, it would

18 Ferrand, p. 47.
19 Ferrand, p. 48.
20 Ferrand, pp. 52–54.

be better to renounce war altogether; an adversary better advised would have from this alone a marked superiority.[21]

Under the head of requisitions of supplies, are classed coal or other combustibles, provisions of all kinds, and even wine and tobacco, which, as the men may be accustomed to them, are likely to add to their comfort and efficiency.[22] In utilizing these supplies, the mills, ovens, etc., of the locality may be made use of.

Land transportation.—Land transportation other than by railroads is of great importance in the conveyance of supplies and of the sick and wounded. For this purpose all sorts of carts, wagons, etc., and their drivers, are needed, but it is the use of the conveyances that is requisitioned and not the conveyances themselves. The period for which they are taken should be short, and the return sure, as they often represent all their owner's working capital.[23] The right to the use of railroads and other like means of communication is treated in H LIII, and so will not be discussed here.

Military execution.—A requisition is usually addressed to the authorities of the community requisitioned, or in default of such authorities to notables of the district, who are held liable for its apportionment among the inhabitants, since they are in a better position than the officers of the hostile army to apportion it equitably. In cases where those to whom the requisition would ordinarily be addressed cannot be found or refuse to act, or where there is great urgency for the requisition at a point so far distant that the municipality can not be regularly notified, the occupant may be compelled to resort to military execution and take the articles desired himself, and if necessary, by force. Military execution involves domiciliary visits and is apt to be marked by the infliction of severe penalties as the occasion for it is perhaps most often the refusal of the inhabitants to furnish the supplies demanded. The resort to it is therefore even more to be shunned by the inhabitants than by the army.[24]

H LIII. *An army of occupation can only take possession of*

21 Ferrand, p. 54.
22 Ferrand, pp. 55–56.
23 Ferrand, pp. 58–63.
24 Ferrand, pp. 95–102.

cash, funds, and realizable securities which are strictly the property of the State, depots of arms, means of transport, stores and supplies, and, generally, all movable property belonging to the State which may be used for military operations.

All appliances, whether on land, at sea, or in the air, adapted for the transmission of news, or for the transport of persons or things, exclusive of cases governed by naval law, depots of arms, and, generally, all kinds of ammunition of war, may be seized, even if they belong to private individuals, but must be restored and compensation fixed when peace is made.

Rights over movable public property of enemy.—The first paragraph deals with rights over the movable public property of the enemy. The right to all such property useful in war springs (1) from the right to prevent its use by the enemy, and (2) from the right of the occupant to indemnify himself for the expenses of the war. The occupant does not become the owner of the property by the fact of succeeding temporarily to the authority of the legitimate power. Title remains where it was before the occupation, until the occupant takes advantage of his position and appropriates the property to himself. In the case of tangible personal property, this appropriation is by means of physical seizure, and some writers have endeavored to make this a general rule, so that without physical seizure there can be no valid appropriation which the legitimate power need recognize when restored to authority. If this be so, the right to appropriate debts owing to the legitimate authority falls of itself, for debts being intangible can not be taken hold of and carried off as tangible property can be.

Right to collect debts due the legitimate power.—The practice of appropriating debts due the legitimate power is too well established, however, to be questioned as a rule of law, and on principle it has the weight of authority in its favor. It is to be assimilated to the rule allowing the occupant to collect the taxes and other obligations due the legitimate power rather than to that for the appropriation of tangible property. It springs from the authority the occupant has over the persons of the inhabitants rather than from that over property itself. If the occupant is entitled to collect the public obligations due the legitimate power, there seems no valid reason why he should not be entitled to the private obligations due the legitimate power also. In both cases, the right of appropriation is purely a *de facto* right. As far as either claim has been actually paid under compulsion, such payment binds the legitimate power, but only so far. The release of an obligation beyond the amount actually collected is in no wise valid against the restored sovereign.

Property held in trust by the State not to be appropriated.—It must always be borne in mind that the movable property liable to seizure is property belonging to the State, not to local communities, and that it must belong to the State in its own right and not as trustee for others, as where savings banks and insurance companies are carried on by it.[25]

Disposition of rolling stock owned by the State.—A point over which there has been much discussion is the proper disposition to be made of the rolling stock of railroads owned by the State. The importance of such rolling stock to a modern community led the Institute of International Law to assimilate it to private property, which must be returned at the end of the war, but this view did not prevail at The Hague, the sentiment of the Committee in charge of the subject being that the disposition of the rolling stock should be settled at the conclusion of peace. This prevents the alienation of the property in the meantime, and so secures some of the advantage that would have been derived from the rule favored by the Institute, and allows all the circumstances of each case to be taken into consideration.

Rights over private property.—The second paragraph deals with private property. Almost necessarily the means of transportation and communication are seized by the occupant and kept under his control during the period of the occupation. They are of the utmost importance to him, and besides may be of the greatest use to the legitimate power if not taken into the occupant's hands. Receipts would be inapplicable to the taking over of properties of this kind and therefore are not mentioned. It was desired, especially at The Hague, that the seizure of these instrumentalities should be regarded as a mere sequestration. This would have entitled the owners to an accounting of rents and profits, when their property was handed back at the conclusion of peace; but violent opposition to this view

[25] Protocol 11 of the Committee.

manifested itself, and it was agreed that the compensation should be arranged at the peace. The idea was not so much that the owners should not be fully compensated, as that it was not a matter of international right. As in the case of contributions, it was thought best to leave the matter of compensating its citizens for losses sustained in the war to the unsuccessful party, and not to compel her to pay part of them in full, when she might feel that she could distribute the burdens of the war more equitably on some other basis.

Difference between means of transportation and communication and munitions of war.—It is to be noticed that means of transportation and communication are here classed with munitions of war but that the provision that they shall be restored and compensation fixed when peace is made is much more suitable for the former than for the latter. If munitions of war are restored why should any compensation be made? In the case of the means of transportation and communication on the other hand it is only fair that some compensation should be made for the loss of profits in the meantime. As a matter of fact, the two classes of property were sharply distinguished at Brussels. It was felt by many to be illogical at least to allow contraband at sea, even though belonging to neutrals, to be captured and confiscated and yet to respect the same kind of property on land when belonging to enemies. The feeling that such property should be subject to capture was so strong that careful provision was made that the requirements about restoration and compensation should not apply to it. The Brussels form of the article was adopted at the first reading at the First Peace Conference, but it was afterwards changed. It seems clear from M. Rolin's report that it was desired to retain the Brussels article intact, except for one clause that might have been construed to uphold the sequestration theory, but that, after the omission of that clause, it was thought desirable to condense the whole paragraph. There was no declared intention of doing away with the distinction between the modes of treatment of the two classes of property mentioned, and any such attempt would certainly have given rise to serious opposition just as it did at Brussels. It is now difficult to see, however, how the article can so be construed as to distinguish between the two classes.[26]

Ships not coming under the rules of naval law.—The limitation that the vessels to which this article applies shall be only those not governed by naval law was added as a result of the suggestion of the Spanish delegate at the Brussels Conference that the provisions of the article should be limited to vessels "appertaining to the navigation of inland waters, of unnavigable rivers and streams, in communication with the sea." Baron Lambermont proposed the phrase "ships apart from cases governed by maritime law," as the equivalent of this, and it was accepted.[27] In the United States the jurisdiction of the courts of admiralty extends to all waters navigable from the sea by vessels of ten tons burden and it seems likely that the Duke de Tetuan had some rule of this kind in mind, but it was evidently not what the Conference, as a whole, intended, for on the final reading of the Project in full conference, Baron Baude, the French delegate said that his government feared the article might not be interpreted to give the protection the Conference intended it to give to "the maritime commerce of sea ports situated on large streams," but that his government would interpret the phrase in its broadest and most absolute manner. Baron Lambermont, who had proposed the phrase, said he would interpret it in the same way, and no objection was made to either of these declarations.[28] The meaning of the Conference would appear to be that, where vessels are captured in the interior of a country by land forces, even though naval forces may have cooperated in the seizure, such seizure will be subject to the rules applicable to seizures by the land forces and not to those applicable to captures by the navy. In the case of *The Thalia* arising during the Russo-Japanese War it was held that a ship lying on the land alongside a dock did not come within the exception.[29]

The phrasing "all appliances, whether on land, at sea, or in the air, adapted for the transmission of news, or for the transport of persons or things," is the work of the

[26] Conference Internationale de la Paix, Part I, p. 62.

[27] Protocol 11 of the Committee.

[28] Protocol 4 of the Full Conference.

[29] See Takahashi, p. 605, *et seq.*

second Conference and is more inclusive than the old phraseology.

H LIV. *Submarine cables connecting an occupied territory with a neutral territory shall not be seized or destroyed except in the case of absolute necessity. They must likewise be restored and compensation fixed when peace is made.*

Submarine cables.—At the Brussels Conference it was proposed by the Danish delegate that landing cables should be included in the protection of the preceding article, but the subject was one on which the Conference had received no instruction and the matter was left to a future conference. The Danish proposal was adopted at the first Peace Conference in subcommittee, but was dropped at the last minute in full conference for the sake of harmony, the British delegate having received instructions from his government that it feared the proposed amendment touched on maritime law.[30] So this article is new, taking the place of the old Article LIV which dealt with the railway plant coming from neutral States and which is now Article XIX of the Convention respecting the Rights and Duties of Neutrals in case of War on land. The seizure or destruction may take place within the territorial waters of the occupied territory; whether beyond this is a question of grave doubt.[31]

H LV. *The occupying State shall be regarded only as administrator and usufructuary of public buildings, real estate, forests and agricultural estates belonging to the hostile State, and situated in the occupied country. It must safeguard the capital of these properties, and administer them in accordance with the rules of usufruct.*

Contracts of exploitation are rendered void by the conclusion of peace.—An occupant has the right to the use and the revenues of immovable property of the hostile State within the occupied territory. In pursuance of this right, he may, for instance, farm out the public railroads, agricultural lands and forests. Any contracts he may make for this purpose, however, become inoperative with the cessation of the occupation since a belligerent cannot be allowed to exploit the territory of another after his occupation has ceased; and, if he has no such right himself, he cannot impart it to another by means of a contract. The contract

30 Conference Internationale de la Paix, Part I, p. 94–95.
31 Westlake, II International Law, 280–283.

must be construed as subject to termination by the cessation of the occupation. Where acts of appropriation under the contract are completed before the cessation of hostilities, they will be recognized as binding by the legitimate power when its authority is restored, but when the acts are not completed as where wood has been cut, but good title to it has not yet been given at the cessation of the occupation, the legitimate authority will not recognize the right of the contractors to go ahead and perfect the title.

Rights over forests.—It was desired at Brussels that the rights of the occupant in the forests for instance should be less than those of usufruct, and that he should not be allowed to touch the trees of larger growth. This being clearly contrary to the sentiment of the committee, it was proposed that it should at least be required that the forests should be worked according to the laws of the occupied country; but, as this would often be impossible through the refusal of forest officials to cooperate with the occupant, the proposal was rejected and the prevailing sentiment was that the occupant does not exceed his rights so long as he works the forests according to some recognized method of forest administration.[32]

Contracts entered into by the occupant as administrator of the occupied territory.—A distinction must be made between contracts of exploitation which the occupant makes for his own advantage, and those which he makes in his capacity of administrator for the benefit of the community. Measures for the permanent benefit of the community should be left, when it is possible, to the legitimate power, but there may be cases where the needs of the community are so pressing as to admit of no delay, and if in such a case a contract is let for the work which extends beyond the period of occupation, such contract is valid even then, if it was reasonably within the scope of the occupant's essentially provisional power. Such was the decision of the Supreme Court of the United States in a case rising out of the Civil War. During the military occupation of New Orleans by the United States forces, it became necessary to make certain repairs along the water fronts involving the expenditure of large sums of money. Accordingly a contract was entered into by the occupant for the making of the needed

32 *Supra*, p. 96.

repairs, a part of the contract being a lease for ten years of that portion of the water front to which the repairs were to be made. It was held that this lease was valid, as coming within the reasonable scope of the occupant's administrative powers, although the war ended less than a year later.[33]

H LVI. *The property of municipalities, that of institutions dedicated to religion, charity and education, the arts and sciences, even when State property, shall be treated as private property.*

All seizure of, destruction or wilful damage done to institutions of this character, historic monuments, works of art and science, is forbidden and should be made the subject of legal proceedings.

Property of localities, churches, etc., to be treated as private property.—It may be that in some cases such property will be subject to the right of requisition as has been seen. General Voigts-Rhetz, at Brussels, expressly refused to agree to a proposal absolutely forbidding the quartering of troops in religious, charitable and educational institutions, and in hospitals, but if such quartering is ever allowable, it should be confined to cases where the necessity for it is imperative.

A belligerent party which violates the provisions of the said Regulations shall, if the case demands, be liable to pay compensation. It shall be responsible for all acts committed by persons forming part of its armed forces.

This article was originally intended as H LXI, but it now forms Article III of the Convention as distinguished from the Regulations.

Sanction.—"Its operation will be to require those charged by their Governments with the exercise of high military command to maintain such a constant supervision over the acts of their subordinates as will be calculated to secure the exact and rigorous enforcement of the several requirements of the convention. If the circumstances of a particular war are such as to suggest the application of a rule of limitation to cases arising under the article, such mutual stipulations in that regard as are warranted by the facts may properly find a place in the treaty of peace."[34]

[33] 20 Wallace, 387.

[34] Extract from the report of Gen. Davis, included in the Report of the American Delegation, p. 37.

TERMINATION OF WAR.

Termination of war.—Hostilities generally cease, if a general armistice is not already in existence, on the signing of the preliminaries of peace, or of the treaty of peace itself, notwithstanding that in either case ratification may be necessary to make these agreements fully binding. The state of war is usually terminated by the ratification of a treaty of peace, or by the absorption of one of the belligerents by the other. In either case, the controversies that gave rise to the war are deemed to be settled by it, and although amnesty for all offenses connected with the conduct of the war is usually stipulated in the treaty of peace, if it is not so stipulated, it is implied from the Peace itself. Prisoners are repatriated as soon as possible, and normal relations between the two countries and the inhabitants thereof are resumed. Where no stipulation is made to the contrary in the Treaty of Peace, territory in the possession of each belligerent at the conclusion of the treaty is retained by him. This is a convenient rule, as it saves the unsuccessful belligerent from the necessity of acknowledging a cession of territory he may be compelled to make. Private rights in either ceded or conquered territory remain unaffected by the transfer.

APPENDIX I.

REGULATIONS AND INSTRUCTIONS OF THE JAPANESE GOVERNMENT ON THE TREATMENT OF RUSSIAN SUBJECTS DURING THE RUSSO-JAPANESE WAR.

Being a summary of an article, extracted from the Revue de Droit International, by Masanosuké Akiyama, Professor-doctor in law, former professor in the University of Tokio, Counsellor to the Minister of War, Counsellor to the Bureau of Legislation of the Imperial Cabinet, and Secretary of the former Information Bureau for Prisoners of War.

Information Bureau.—The Bureau of Information was constituted by imperial decrees of February 21 and September 12, 1904. Its functions were carefully worked out to conform to H XIV, XVI and XIX. At its head was to be placed a director of the rank of either general or colonel, who was to be responsible to the Minister of War and who was to have authority to demand the necessary information from the different military and naval authorities and from the hospitals and ambulances. Beginning with March 30, 1904, the Bureau sent the information required by The Hague Regulations every ten days to the French Minister at Tokio, but an agreement was reached in August between the Japanese and the Russian Bureau, whereby the former was to send its information to the Russian legation at Pekin and the latter to the Japanese legation at Berlin. From this time to the end of the war the Japanese Bureau forwarded its information the 5th, 15th and 25th of each month. Special effort was made to obtain the desired information concerning Russian officers who had been made prisoners of war, by telegraph. The work of the Bureau increased greatly as the war progressed. At its close its personnel consisted of the director, General Hongo, four secretaries, a financial officer, three translators, five clerks and twenty employees.

Regulation of service in detail.—By decrees of the Minister of War of February 27, and September 12, 1904, the service was regulated in detail. Individual cards were to be made giving the information with regard to prisoners of war now specified in H XIV. They were also to indicate crimes or infractions committed by prisoners. Similar cards were also to be made for the sick and wounded and those found dead upon the field of battle. After the reestablishment of peace this card was to be returned to the other belligerent, a provision now incorporated in H XIV, and a copy kept by the Minister of War. The Bureau was also, if occasion offered, to give its views to the Minister of War on the regulations for the surveillance of stations of prisoners brought to its attention, and under the same circumstances, on the confiscation or prohibition of communications or parcels sent to or by the prisoners. Finally it was required to present a report to the Minister of War each month relative to the execution of the service and to the information concerning the prisoners both in Japan and Russia.

Statistics of the Bureau.—Until May 1, 1904, the number of prisoners was very small, but from then on it increased until at the end of 1904 there were 136 officers and 4,469 petty officers and soldiers held as prisoners, while at the end of the war there were 1,436 officers and 70,784 petty officers and men interned in the various stations in Japan. In the following statistics of the Bureau the figures for 1905 include those for 1906 until the liberation of all the prisoners in February.

	1904.	*1905.*
Bureaucratic communications sent	659	5,211
" " rec'd	1,728	11,601
Information, number of times sent	246	1,824
" " " " rec'd	778	4,090
Postal messages sent	855	10,217
" " rec'd	1,170	16,684
Telegrams sent	75	961
" rec'd	270	2,226
Individual cards made (prisoners)	3,838	68,482
" " " (enemies killed in battle)	370	1,101

Letters and postal cards from prisoners..........	1,318	145,537
" " " " to prisoners...........	508	67,750
Gifts in money to prisoners....................	1,439.36 yen	89,768.45 yen
Gifts in kind to prisoners.....................	12,641	61,637
Remittances of objects left by deceased prisoners..	15	193
" " " " " enemies killed in battle....................................	53	26
Remittances of wills of prisoners of war.........	3	14

The number of times information was sent does not indicate the number of individuals with regard to whom it was sent. Often the names of 6,000 prisoners figured on a single list. These figures as to letters and postal cards refer only to those which passed through the Bureau. Correspondence between the prisoners and between other persons and prisoners was free, subject to the censorship of the officials at each station. The smallness of the number of cards made out for those fallen on the field of battle and of the number of objects left by them is explained by the fact that the Russian officers and soldiers did not carry about them cards or other marks necessary to establish their identity.[1] The Bureau also verified the information received from the Russian bureau as to Japanese prisoners in Russia, and published the same in the official gazette.

General regulations as to prisoners of war.—The treatment of prisoners of war was regulated by orders of the Minister of War and of the Marine. The order of the Minister of War was issued February 14, 1907. That of the Minister of Marine was issued three days later and was along the same lines, although not as detailed. What made it notable was that it applied to prisoners taken by naval forces, the rules laid down in The Hague Regulations for prisoners taken by the army, although there was no international convention applicable to the former. Both orders were based on a careful study of the Regulations and breathe their humanitarian spirit. The order of the Minister of War consisted of thirty-four articles, but they require little comment. Article 8 applied the ordinance on disciplinary punishments for the army on land, to the prisoners of war, except where special provision was made. Article 23 provided that the prisoners should be divided

[1] For table of objects belonging to Russians dead on the field of battle or dying afterwards, see Takahashi, p. 121.

among different rooms according to rank, etc., and that in each room a chief should be appointed who should represent the prisoners and be responsible for discipline. Article 25, among other things, prohibited the use of ciphers in letters and telegrams. Article 27 required that the regulations drawn up by the commandants for the surveillance of prisoners of war be communicated to the Minister of War, and to the Bureau of Information. Finally, Article 28 provided that the sick and wounded considered incapable of further military service should be sent back to their country on condition of not retaking arms, although this was not to be applicable to those who might be of importance in the war.

Statistics as to prisoners.—The total number of prisoners during the war was 84,445. Of these 10,442 were freed on the scene of operations, 1,704 died before their arrival in the interior, 379 died in the stations and a number escaped after the establishment of peace. Besides the 1,271 officers captured at Port Arthur, 77 out of the 257 officers captured in the naval battle of the Sea of Japan received permission to retain their swords. There was no exchange of prisoners, although negotiations had been commenced a little before the end of the war, but in the course of the campaign the Government permitted the sick and the wounded recognized as incapable of further military service to return to their country; 4,039 went from Port Arthur, 95 from Kobé. The Empress displayed the same humanity towards the prisoners as towards the Japanese soldiers in supplying them with artificial eyes and limbs; 154 prisoners received glass eyes and 133 artificial limbs.

More detailed regulations as to prisoners of war—Of even more interest and value than these general regulations were the special ones which the exigencies of the war called forth. The capture of 604 prisoners at Chiu-lien-Cheng gave occasion for the more detailed regulation as to the treatment of prisoners of war of May 15, 1904. Article 4 provided that prisoners of war who were officers or adjutants should be entitled to choose orderlies from among the prisoners, ordinarily at the rate of one orderly to two officers. Articles 9 and 10 guarded against the improper use of any right of visiting given to foreigners and at the same time shielded the prisoners from the curiosity of the inhabitants by requiring express permission of the commandant of the garrison to enter the stations. In giving permission to visit to those who had relatives among the prisoners, the authorities were very liberal, and many subordinates of Bishop Nicolais of the Russian Church, as well as Catholic priests and ministers of other religions received authority to celebrate their offices in the stations, while the prisoners were allowed to confess and were otherwise left alone with the priests, notwithstanding the provision of Article 10 that interviews with foreigners should only be allowed under surveillance.

Nourishment of prisoners of war.—The nourishment of prisoners of war was to be furnished in kind at the rate of 60 sen per day for officers and adjutants, and 30 sen per day for petty officers and soldiers. These sums were nearly twice those allowed Japanese soldiers. For the officers and adjutants the cooking was to be done by the orderlies, or if necessary by hired men, while the petty officers and soldiers were to be divided into small groups and to cook for themselves. Provision was also made that the above sums might be employed to provide tea, biscuits, cakes and fruits between meals. Sutlers were to be admitted to the stations, but the prices and the quality of the objects sold were regulated by the commandants of the garrisons.

Bedding and clothing.—By Article 19, suitable bedding and toilet facilities were to be provided for the officers and men and they were to be allowed to retain their clothing. When this was worn out new clothing was to be provided for officers and adjutants, and, if necessary, for the petty officers and soldiers. Ordinarily, however, the latter were to receive second-hand clothing. The maximum to be spent in this way for generals was 30 yen[2] in winter and 12 yen in summer, for hats, coats and trousers; 5 yen in winter and 2.50 yen in summer, for underwear; while the amount paid for shoes was to be determined by their cost at the time. From these maxima the tariff ranged down to those for petty officers and men which amounted to 8 yen in winter and 3 yen in summer for hats, coats and pants, .83 yen both winter and summer for underwear, while the amount to be paid for shoes was determined in the same way as with the

[2] A gold yen corresponds roughly to our dollar. A sen is the one-hundredth part of a yen.

officers. These sums were in accord with those allowed in the national army. Clothing given in this way was to remain the property of the prisoners after their liberation.

Amounts allowed for keeping clothes in repair and for objects of consumption.—In addition to the above provisions made for lodging, clothing and food, the prisoners were to be allowed certain amounts for keeping their clothes in order and for objects of consumption. Officers and adjutants were to receive definite sums ranging from 25 yen per month for the generals to 5 yen a month for the adjutants. Those below adjutants were to receive the actual amounts spent, not to exceed 1 yen per month for the petty officers and .50 yen per month for the soldiers. In considering these sums it is necessary to bear in mind that the cost of living in Japan is hardly half of that in Europe, as shown by the comparative pay in the French and Russian and Japanese armies.[3] Deceased prisoners of war as a general rule were to be buried, the expense thereof not to exceed 20 yen for officers and adjutants, 15 yen for petty officers and 10 yen for the soldiers.

Places of Internment. Interpreters.—The prisoners were interned in barracks, public buildings, temples and large private dwellings, and in some localities many temporary barracks were erected. Stations for the officers and adjutants were established separate from those for the petty officers and soldiers. The Government took care to attach a certain number of interpreters to each station, besides choosing the officials of the station from those versed in French, English or German, and although there was much difficulty in doing this on account of the number needed at the front, 182 interpreters in all were attached to the different stations. They helped the prisoners in their work and even went with them in their walks outside the stations.

Reading matter.—Because of the difficulty of obtaining a sufficient number of interpreters to read all the journals of the world, the journals in a foreign tongue to which the prisoners were allowed access, were limited to the Japan Times, Japan Mail, Daily Advertiser and Japan Gazette of

[3] The question as to the pay to be given the prisoners did not arise, as Russia made a remittance to the French consul each month for that purpose. The pay ranged from 150 yen per month for the generals to 50 sens for the soldiers. Takahashi, p. 124.

Japan, the London Times, Standard and Daily Telegraph of England, le Temps, le Radical and la Lanterne of France, The Sun, The Tribune and Washington Post of the United States, Norddeutsche Allgemeine Zeitung and Berliner Lokal-Anzeiger of Germany, and the Neue Freie Presse of Austria. In addition they were allowed to read all the Japanese journals and books, pamphlets or journals which were sent them, with the exception of two kinds of pamphlets entitled Osbovozgenie and Revolutionia Russia which had been sent to the Bureau of Information, but were not allowed to be distributed on account of their hostility to the Russian Government. The printed matter donated to the prisoners was as follows:

	1904.	*1905.*
Journals	777	50,495
" parcels	2	157
Books and pamphlets	10,198	341,939
" " parcels	10,198	334
Illustrated pamphlets and portraits	1,344	10,178
" " " parcels	1,344	6

Postal service.—The postal service, including the parcels-post and the money order service, were regulated by orders of the minister of communications of March 3, 1904. In accordance with The Hague Regulations postal communication was made free. The controllers of the various stations were given wide powers in receiving and delivering receipts for parcels and letters of declared value, and in cashing money orders without special procuration. All letters and telegrams were examined by the officers of the stations, but few letters were not allowed to pass. Those messages which were sent to or received by the prisoners on the field of operations and those which it was difficult to examine in the stations were sent for examination to the Bureau of Information. As at times the correspondence was written in Hebrew, Finnish, Lithuanian, etc., it was required of the prisoners that they write either in Russian, Japanese, French, German or English. The number of communications of the prisoners of war to the end of 1905 is as follows:

LETTERS, CARDS AND PARCELS FREE OF TAXES.

	Sent.	Interdicted.	Received.	Confiscated.
1904.				
Interior mail.....	1,049	0	1,071	2
Foreign mail.....	8,337	7	2,237	0
1905.				
Interior mail.....	32,294	25	51,851	48
Foreign mail.....	444,296	174	183,975	1

MONEY ORDERS FREE OF TAXES.

	Sent.	Received.
1904—Interior mail	13	28
Foreign mail	0	18
1905—Interior mail	545	328
Foreign mail	30	3,324

TELEGRAMS.

	Sent.	Received.
1904—Interior service	35	14
Foreign service	27	18
1905—Interior service	1,164	949
Foreign service	1,043	806

Regulations as to punishment of prisoners of war.—As the number of prisoners increased cases of resistance against the authorities multiplied. In October an imperial decree was issued regulating the punishment of prisoners of war, and this was changed to a law in February, 1905. By Article 7 of the law the imperial penal code was made applicable by analogy to offenses committed by prisoners in absence of more specific provisions. According to the code, deportation and detention are applied in the case of crimes, imprisonment in the case of delicts. Deportation to an island prison is inflicted for crimes whose penalty is from 12 to 15 years, detention in an interior prison for crimes whose penalty is from 5 to 11 years, and major or minor imprisonment in a house of imprisonment for delicts whose penalty is from 11 days to 5 years. Prisoners of war culpable of resistance or violence to the authorities were to be punished by a detention major, or in case of extenuating circumstances by a minor imprisonment of from 6 months to 5 years, but when either of these acts should have been committed as a result of conspiracy, the leaders were to be punishable with death, the others to deportation, and under extenuating circumstances, to major detention. Whenever there should be a collective escape resulting from conspiracy, the principal authors were to be condemned to deportation, and in case of aggravating circumstances to death, while the others were to suffer major detention, or under extenuating circumstances minor imprisonment from 6 months to 5 years. Breach of parole was to be punished by a major detention; if accompanied by an act of hostility with arms in hand, by death. Breach of promise not to attempt to escape was also to be punished by major detention; the violation of all other engagements by minor imprisonment. The penalties for acts of resistance and violence, and plots to escape were to be applicable only during a first imprisonment, and were to be wiped out by a successful escape.

Infractions.—During the war there were in all 23 cases of infractions of the regulation, but no one was executed, the most severe penalty being the deportation of a Cossack officer for twice having attempted a collective escape as principal. At the end of the war, 95 prisoners, comprising 11 officers, were detained for crimes or delicts in virtue of the regulation, or of the penal code. They were all put at liberty with permission to return to their country, by a special amnesty of the Emperor on the day of the publication of the treaty of peace.

Employment of prisoners.—There was no great demand for workers during the war either for public works or for the great corporations, and the most part of the prisoners did no work even on their own account, although on certain occasions individual prisoners were voluntarily hired by private persons. In these cases the Government allowed them to dispose of their entire earnings. The result of this lack of work was that there was little occasion for the application of the order of the minister of war of September 10, 1904, regulating the work of prisoners of war. It was based on a careful study of The Hague Regulations, however, and is of value as an interpretation of them.

Regulations as to free promenade and living in private houses.—Despite the decree of October for punishment of prisoners of war, an officer and five soldiers made a new attempt to escape the following January. Notwithstanding this, however, the long promised regulation for giving officers the privilege of free promenade and of living in private houses was proclaimed by an order of the minister of war of March 18, 1905. Under it officers who would give their parole not to escape and to submit to the discipline and good manners of the imperial army, might be permitted by the commandant of the garrison to promenade freely, or to live in private houses, in case they should wish to live with their wives, or under other special circumstances. The permission to live in private houses, however, had to be approved by the minister of war. The time for the promenade was generally fixed at from eight o'clock in the morning to midday, and from one to four in the afternoon. Nearly all the officers were enabled to take advantage of this privilege.

Prisoners of war receiving either of the above privileges were not to carry arms, nor were those who had the privilege of free promenade to send or receive correspondence during the promenade, while those dwelling in private houses, and their cohabitants, were to subject letters sent by them to the supervision of the authorities of the station, and were to receive correspondence only after it had undergone like censorship. Those on promenade were not to visit those dwelling outside the station without the authority of the commandant of the station. The officers dwelling in private houses were not to go beyond certain limits, were to be subject to the orders of the various authorities, and were to be formed into groups of about ten under the authority of their senior, who was to represent and be responsible for them. Each day they and their cohabitants were to indicate their presence by signing the roll book kept for that purpose. A special book and a special journal were to be kept for them, giving their statistics, physical description and photographs. Instead of the allowances made to prisoners within the stations, generals were to receive 800 yens per year, superior officers 600 yens and inferior officers 500 yens. Not many of the officers took advantage of this opportunity of living outside the stations.[4]

[4] Mr. Takahashi says that many applications were made, but that as it was impossible to grant all the applications without hazarding the maintenance of order, it was decided to grant but a few. The number reached 39 in all. Takahashi, pp. 108–109.

Treatment of Russian sanitary personnel.—At the beginning of the war a number of the Russian sanitary personnel were detained for some time at Matsuyama, possibly with a view to assuring the secrecy of military operations, but from the battle of Liao-Yang in August, 1904, those who fell into the power of the Japanese army were sent regularly to the advance-posts of the enemy or to the French consul of the nearest Chinese port. The Russian sanitary personnel at Port Arthur, consisting of 2,790 persons, remained from the date of the capitulation, January 5, 1905, until March of the same year, concurring with the Japanese sanitary personnel in the care of the 15,138 sick and wounded Russians.

Gifts and relief in kind.—The second paragraph of H XVI providing that gifts and relief in kind for prisoners of war shall be free from imposts and other duties as well as from charges for carriage by Government railways, was carefully observed. Many of the private railroad and navigation companies voluntarily adopted a like rule.

Care for the dead.—In the course of this war as in the Chinese-Japanese war, the sick, the wounded and the dead of both armies were searched and cared for immediately after each action without distinction. The bodies of the dead Japanese were burned, and those of the enemy buried, only after proof of death, and after the attempt had been made to identify the bodies by all available means. In the order of the minister of war of May 30, 1904, there were carefully elaborated provisions to ensure proper sanitary arrangements for the collection, burning and burial of the dead, not only of the two armies, but of the bodies of the inhabitants found on the field of battle. Objects left by dead Russians, except arms, horses and military documents, were to be sent with the information obtained, to the Bureau of Information. Those left by the Japanese dead or by the inhabitants fallen on the field of battle were to be transmitted to suitable military authorities.

Cemeteries for the Russian dead.—The number of the Russian dead was very great, and vast cemeteries were established. After the conclusion of peace the military authorities made every effort to preserve the graves intact, but they encountered insurmountable difficulties because of the treeless, even bushless character of the country, the irregular courses of the streams, the devastating effects of the rains, and finally, the robberies of the inhabitants. From January 21, 1906, Marshal Oshima, Governor-General of Kwantung, gave permission to foreigners to enter all the districts under his jurisdiction, and to search for and carry away with the authorization of the military authorities the objects or bodies left in Manchuria. Many Russians took advantage of the opportunity offered.

Instructions to reconcile differences in the treatment of the prisoners.—The number of stations required for the prisoners of war after the taking of Port Arthur led to considerable differences in the treatment of the prisoners, especially in the matter of free promenade and living in private houses which led the minister of war on May 15, 1905, to issue instructions to the various commandants with the idea of reconciling these differences. He drew attention to the fact that while the Russian prisoners seemed to think that they had done their entire duty to their country, the Japanese regarded it a disgrace to be a prisoner, and accordingly warned the commandants against allowing this to be the occasion of provocation. Colonel Kono, chief of the station of Matsuyama, on observing that a large number of Russians could not write to their families, had advised them to take lessons in Russian. His advice was adopted and the example followed in nearly all the stations, but the minister of war warned the commandants that neither this nor instruction in physical training was to be made compulsory. He also warned against pointing the finger at prisoners or touching them with the hands, except in proper cases of discipline, and directed that officers on parole living in private houses should not be accompanied by guards. He likewise directed that the districts within which they might walk should be chosen so as to be as pleasant as possible, that they should not be forbidden to enter places where a public calling was carried on, that due respect should be shown for their wish to observe certain days as sacred, that noncommissioned officers and soldiers should be allowed more than two promenades a week as far as possible, and that except for arms and other military objects, officers on parole should be permitted to purchase objects without being required to make a previous written demand.

Repatriation of prisoners.—In accordance with the Treaty of Portsmouth and The Hague Regulations, the repatriation of the prisoners took place as rapidly as possible on the conclusion of peace. The details of the evacuation were arranged for in an agreement drawn up by the Russian special commissary, Danilow, on the one hand, and the Japanese Bureau of Information on the other. On the publication of the Treaty of Portsmouth the law for the punishment of prisoners of war was suspended and every liberty compatible with order given the prisoners while they were still allowed the privileges of free postage and freedom from duties, and transportation charges on goods destined to them.

APPENDIX II.

LAWS AND CUSTOMS OF WAR ON LAND.

A CONVENTION SIGNED BY THE DELEGATES OF THE UNITED STATES TO THE SECOND INTERNATIONAL PEACE CONFERENCE HELD AT THE HAGUE FROM JUNE 15 TO OCTOBER 8, 1907, RESPECTING THE LAWS AND CUSTOMS OF WAR ON LAND.

His Majesty, the German Emperor, King of Prussia; the President of the United States of America; the President of the Argentine Republic; His Majesty, the Emperor of Austria, King of Bohemia, etc., and Apostolic King of Hungary; His Majesty, the King of the Belgiums; the President of the Republic of Bolivia; the President of the Republic of the United States of Brazil; His Royal Highness, the Prince of Bulgaria; the President of the Republic of Chili; His Majesty, the Emperor of China; the President of the Republic of Columbia; the Provisional Governor of the Republic of Cuba; His Majesty, the King of Denmark; the President of the Dominican Republic; the President of the Republic of Ecuador; His Majesty, the King of Spain; the President of the French Republic; His Majesty, the King of the United Kingdom of Great Britain and Ireland and of the British Dominions beyond the Seas, Emperor of India; His Majesty the King of the Hellenes; the President of the Republic of Guatemala; the President of the Republic of Haiti; His Majesty, the King of Italy; His Majesty, the Emperor of Japan; His Royal Highness, the Grand Duke of Luxemburg, Duke of Nassau; the President of the United States of Mexico; His Royal Highness, the Prince of Montenegro; the President of the Republic of Nicaragua; His Majesty, the King of Norway; the President of the Republic of Panama; the President of the Republic of Paraguay; Her Majesty, the Queen of the Netherlands; the

President of the Republic of Peru; His Imperial Majesty, the Shah of Persia; His Majesty, the King of Portugal and of the Algarves, etc.; His Majesty, the King of Roumania; His Majesty, the Emperor of All the Russias; the President of the Republic of Salvador; His Majesty, the King of Servia; His Majesty, the King of Siam; His Majesty, the King of Sweden; the Swiss Federal Council; His Majesty, the Emperor of the Ottomans; the President of the Oriental Republic of Uruguay; the President of the United States of Venezuela.

Seeing that, while seeking means to preserve peace and prevent armed conflicts between nations, it is likewise necessary to bear in mind the case where the appeal to arms has been brought about by events which their care was unable to avert;

Animated by the desire to serve, even in this extreme case, the interests of humanity and the ever progressive needs of civilization;

Thinking it important, with this object, to revise the general laws and customs of war, either with a view to defining them with greater precision or to confining them within such limits as would mitigate their severity as far as possible;

Have deemed it necessary to complete and explain in certain particulars the work of the First Peace Conference, which, following on the Brussels Conference of 1874, and inspired by the ideas dictated by a wise and generous forethought, adopted provisions intended to define and govern the usages of war on land.

According to the views of the High Contracting Parties, these provisions, the wording of which has been inspired by the desire to diminish the evils of war, as far as military requirements permit, are intended to serve as a general rule of conduct for the belligerents in their mutual relations and in their relations with the inhabitants.

It has not, however, been found possible at present to concert Regulations covering all the circumstances which arise in practice;

On the other hand, the High Contracting Parties clearly do not intend that unforeseen cases should, in the absence of a written undertaking, be left to the arbitrary judgment of military commanders.

Until a more complete code of the laws of war has been issued, the High Contracting Parties deem it expedient to declare that in cases not included in the Regulations adopted by them, the inhabitants and the belligerents remain under the protection and the rule of the principles of the law of nations, as they result from the usages established among civilized peoples, from the laws of humanity, and the dictates of the public conscience.

They declare that it is in this sense especially that Articles I and II of the Regulations adopted must be understood.

The High Contracting Parties, wishing to conclude a fresh Convention to this effect, have appointed the following as their Plenipotentiaries:

[For names of Plenipotentiaries, see Final Act.]

Who, after having deposited their full powers, found in good and due form, have agreed upon the following:

Article I.

The Contracting Powers shall issue instructions to their armed land forces which shall be in conformity with the Regulations respecting the Laws and Customs of War on Land, annexed to the present Convention.

Article II.

The provisions contained in the Regulations referred to in Article I, as well as in the present Convention, do not apply except between Contracting Powers, and then only if all the belligerents are parties to the Convention.

Article III.

A belligerent party which violates the provisions of the said Regulations shall, if the case demands, be liable to pay compensation. It shall be responsible for all acts committed by persons forming part of its armed forces.

Article IV.

The present Convention, duly ratified, shall as between the Contracting Powers, be substituted for the Convention of the 29th July, 1899, respecting the Laws and Customs of War on Land.

The Convention of 1899 remains in force as between the Powers which signed it, and which do not also ratify the present Convention.

Article V.

The present Convention shall be ratified as soon as possible.

The ratifications shall be deposited at The Hague.

The first deposit of ratification shall be recorded in a *procès-verbal* signed by the Representatives of the Powers which take part therein and by the Netherland Minister for Foreign Affairs.

The subsequent deposits of ratifications shall be made by means of a written notification, addressed to the Netherland Government and accompanied by the instrument of ratification.

A duly certified copy of the *procès-verbal* relative to the first deposit of ratification, of the notifications mentioned in the preceding paragraph, as well as of the instruments of ratification, shall be immediately sent by the Netherland Government, through the diplomatic channel, to the Powers invited to the Second Peace Conference, as well as to the other Powers which have adhered to the Convention. In the cases contemplated in the preceding paragraph the said Government shall at the same time inform them of the date on which it received the notification.

Article VI.

Nonsignatory Powers may adhere to the present Convention.

The Power which desires to adhere notifies in writing its intention to the Netherland Government, forwarding to it the act of adhesion, which shall be deposited in the archives of the said Government.

This Government shall at once transmit to all the other Powers a duly certified copy of the notification as well as of the act of adhesion, mentioning the date on which it received the notification.

Article VII.

The present convention shall come in force, in the case of the Powers which were a party to the first deposit of ratification sixty days after the date of the *procès-verbal* of this deposit, and in the case of the Powers which ratify subsequently or which adhere, sixty days after the notification of their ratification or of their adhesion has been received by the Netherland Government.

Article VIII.

In the event of one of the Contracting Powers wishing to denounce the present Convention, the denunciation shall be notified in writing to the Netherland Government, which shall at once communicate a duly certified copy of the notification to all the other Powers, informing them of the date on which it was received.

The denunciation shall only have effect in regard to the notifying Power, and one year after the notification has reached the Netherland Government.

Article IX.

A register kept by the Netherland Ministry for Foreign Affairs shall give the date of the deposit of ratification made in virtue of Article V, paragraphs 3 and 4, as well as the date on which the notifications of adhesion (Article VI, paragraph 2) or of denunciation (Article VIII, paragraph 1) were received.

Each Contracting Power is entitled to have access to this register and to be supplied with duly certified extracts.

In faith whereof the Plenipotentiaries have appended their signatures to the present Convention.

Done at The Hague, the 18th October, 1907, in a single copy, which shall remain deposited in the archives of the Netherland Government, and duly certified copies of which shall be sent, through the diplomatic channel, to the Powers which have been invited to the Second Peace Conference.

ANNEX TO THE CONVENTION.

Regulations respecting the Laws and Customs of War on Land.

[For the Articles of the Regulations, see the body of this work.]

APPENDIX III.

DISCHARGING PROJECTILES FROM BALLOONS.

A DECLARATION SIGNED BY THE DELEGATES OF THE UNITED STATES TO THE SECOND INTERNATIONAL PEACE CONFERENCE HELD AT THE HAGUE FROM JUNE 15 TO OCTOBER 18, 1907, PROHIBITING THE DISCHARGE OF PROJECTILES AND EXPLOSIVES FROM BALLOONS.

The Undersigned, Plenipotentiaries of the Powers invited to the Second International Peace Conference at The Hague, duly authorized to that effect by their Governments, inspired by the sentiments which found expression in the Declaration of St. Petersburg of the 29th November (11th December), 1868, and being desirous of renewing the declaration of The Hague of the 29th July, 1899, which has now expired,

Declare:

The Contracting Powers agree to prohibit, for a period extending to the close of the Third Peace Conference, the discharge of projectiles and explosives from balloons or by other new methods of a similar nature.

The present Declaration is only binding on the Contracting Powers in case of war between two or more of them.

It shall cease to be binding from the time when, in a war between the Contracting Powers, one of the belligerents is joined by a Noncontracting Power.

The present Declaration shall be ratified as soon as possible.

The ratifications shall be deposited at The Hague.

A *procès-verbal* shall be drawn up recording the receipt of the ratifications, of which a duly certified copy shall be sent, through the diplomatic channel, to all the Contracting Powers.

Nonsignatory Powers may adhere to the present Declaration. To do so, they must make known their adhesion to the Contracting Powers by means of a written notification, addressed to the Netherland Government, and communicated by it to all the other Contracting Powers.

In the event of one of the High Contracting Parties denouncing the present Declaration, such denunciation shall not take effect until a year after the notification made in writing to the Netherland Government, and forthwith communicated by it to all the other Contracting Powers.

This denunciation shall only have effect in regard to the notifying Power.

In faith whereof the Plenipotentiaries have appended their signatures to the present Declaration.

Done at The Hague, the 18th October, 1907, in a single copy, which shall remain deposited in the archives of the Netherland Government, and duly certified copies of which shall be sent, through the diplomatic channel, to the Contracting Powers.

INDEX.

INDEX.

References are to pages.

References are to pages.

References are to pages.

References are to pages.

References are to pages.

References are to pages.

References are to pages.

References are to pages.

References are to pages.

References are to pages.

References are to pages.

References are to pages.

References are to pages.

References are to pages.

References are to pages.

References are to pages.

References are to pages.

References are to pages.

References are to pages.

References are to pages.